GETTIN' IT ON

A DOWN-HOME TREASURY BY

LEWIS GRIZZARD

GETTIN' IT ON

A DOWN-HOME TREASURY BY

LEWIS GRIZZARD

KATHY SUE LOUDERMILK
 I LOVE YOU

WON'T YOU COME HOME BILLY BOB BAILEY?

DON'T SIT UNDER THE GRITS TREE WITH ANYONE ELSE BUT ME

GALAHAD BOOKS

NEW YORK

Published in 1989 by

Galahad Books
A division of LDAP, Inc.
166 Fifth Avenue
New York, NY 10010

Published by arrangement with Peachtree Publishers, Ltd.

Library of Congress Catalog Card Number: 89-84001
ISBN: 0-88365-742-2

Printed in the United States of America.

CONTENTS

Part I
Kathy Sue Loudermilk, I Love You

To
Christine and H. B.

FOREWORD

Lewis Grizzard asked me to write the foreword to this book. I'm flattered, because Lewis is one of my favorite people.

Also, he saved my marriage, perhaps even the roof over my head. I will explain. I will begin at the beginning, when I personally discovered Lewis Grizzard.

It was 1968, when I was executive sport editor of the *Atlanta Journal.* We needed to hire a beginning sports writer, and I went about finding one in my usual scientific way.

I went to a certain coach, whom I knew to be paranoid, ill-tempered and, on occasion, inclined to lie. "Coach," I said, "who is the worst young sports writer you know?"

"Lewis Grizzard," he replied, "that jerk who works for the *Athens Daily News.*"

I hired Lewis that very afternoon.

He was an instant hit in the sports department. Being from Moreland, Georgia, he talked like people are supposed to and he understood the importance of getting the Friday night wrestling results into the Saturday paper.

He was twenty-one years old, had a pretty blonde wife, a wornout Volkswagen, and he did everything I told him to do.

Lewis was on his way to becoming the best wrestling writer in Atlanta when our sports slot man quit.

In every sports department there is an individual called the "man who does the slot." It's just a sexy term for the one who does all the work while the rest of us cover the World Series and the Sugar Bowl.

The slot man comes to work at four in the morning and sometimes works until two the next morning. But he doesn't have to worry about filling out an overtime slip because he qualifies as a supervisor.

1

That's the job I had fallen into shortly after Grizzard came aboard. My wife had not seen me fully awake in three months and my children actually thought I was deceased.

My wife called the office one midnight and made it fairly clear: "Get somebody to do the slot or get a lawyer," she said.

"Lewis," I said. "How would you like to do the slot?"

"Remember," I said, "you get a $5 raise and Saturday off."

I didn't explain that I meant every third Saturday in July. Grizzard took the job. Three months later his wife divorced him.

One day I took Lewis out for a beer. "Kid," I said, "you've got a great future in this business. What do you really want to do with your life?"

"Someday, I want to have my own barbecue place," he answered. "With sliced pork pig sandwiches and cold beer in longneck bottles. With a jar of pickled pigs feet next to the cash register and an ol' hound dog next to me. Most afternoons I would close up and go fishing, and some afternoons I would even put bait on the hook."

I knew Lewis was a comer. When I somehow became managing editor of the *Atlanta Constitution*, Lewis got my old job as executive sports editor at the *Journal*, the youngest ever. He moved on to become associate city editor at the *Journal*, and special assignments editor at the *Constitution*.

Later (I forget the details) he wound up sports editor of the *Chicago Sun-Times*.

I went up there to visit him once. He took me out to lunch, and the wind was so strong they had a *rope* you had to hold onto walking from the newspaper to the restaurant. We had to write out our order because the waitress couldn't understand us. Stray dogs in Moreland might not have eaten what they served us.

After about two years in Chicago, Lewis started calling me every night. Collect.

"I'm looking out my window," he'd say, "watching a guy mug a little old lady."

Or, "Thirty-third day in a row below zero."

Or, "Just had another bowl of boiled Polish cabbage."

He was down to 124 pounds and having fainting spells.

One night I casually mentioned I was trying to hire a columnist for the *Constitution*.

"Hire me!" Grizzard screamed.

Nevermind that he'd never written a newspaper column.

Nevermind that he's already quit the Atlanta papers about six times.

If they can't take a joke, to hell with 'em, I decided.

Besides, the long-distance charges were getting impossible to explain.

So Grizzard came back to Atlanta to write a column for the *Constitution.*

He's up to 189 pounds, and if you think you'll ever catch him in the office you're kidding yourself.

He's the hottest thing on Southern newsprint.

Everywhere I go people ask me if I know Lewis Grizzard.

"Do you ever get to talk to him?" they ask.

"No," I reply. "But one day on the elevator he nodded to me."

And one day he did.

Jim Minter
Managing Editor
The *Atlanta Journal*

CONTENTS

4

1

COMING HOME IS
A ONE-WAY TRIP

I lived in Chicago for two years before returning to Atlanta to begin writing a daily column for the Atlanta Constitution. Chicago's not a bad town. But the weather didn't suit me, and the food didn't suit me, and people talked funny.

When I lived in Chicago, I used to think of the line from the country song that went, "If I ever get back to Georgia, I'm gonna nail my feet to the ground." What the following columns about home and where my heart is should say is, I finally got back to Georgia and I'll be dipped in hot buttered grits before I'll leave again.

CHICAGO—What this neighborhood must have been fifty years ago! Eight blocks north on Lincoln Avenue is the Biograph Theatre where they shot John Dillinger down. The Biograph lives on with nostalgia flicks. Bogart and Davis in *Petrified Forest* for $1.50. Four blocks north on Clark Street is the site of the Saint Valentine's day Massacre, now the site of a home for old people who don't have homes. Capone, I am told, operated south. This was Bugs Moran's territory.

Today, it is ethnic and Democratic, congested and overpriced. It is alternately charming and frustrating. An automobile is an albatross. There is no place to park it. But this has been home for two years, and these are the very last moments.

The dwarfish old man who delivers for the liquor store on the corner has already made two runs on my street, and it's barely ten o'clock. Bloody Mary mix mostly. Bloody Marys are big anywhere on Sunday mornings. On the near north side of Chicago, they are a way of life.

The line is already forming for brunch at R. J. Grunts. For $3.50—fork in one hand, plate in the other—you can shovel through a cornucopia somebody grossly underestimated and called a salad bar. Hash browns are extra with the eggs. Hash browns are a bad joke Chicago restaurants play on breakfast.

7

The Loop is only ten minutes away. The most poignant memory will be the bleak, snowy afternoon a fire department ambulance, followed by four black limousines and a cadre of policemen on motorcycles, drove solemnly up Michigan Avenue, past the Wrigley Building and across the river, while all the power and force that is Chicago commerce came to a reverent halt. Inside the ambulance rode the corpse of Richard J. Daley.

Lake Michigan and the endless high rises on Lakeshore Drive's gold coast are just across Lincoln Park where, on days that weather permits, thousands flock to walk on something that is not asphalt or concrete. It is warm this morning, and thank God for that. Chicago has two seasons, they like to say: Winter and the Fourth of July.

Songs and poems are written about saying goodbye because it is one of those things in life that is usually impossible to do gracefully if it is worth doing at all. I got mine out of the way a day early. "If you're ever in Atlanta. . . ."

Slowly, a final order does come to the mess that is necessary for the moving of all one's earthly belongings. My plane is at noon. There is one last run through the back bedrooms, and the movers left a box. Anybody need a dart board, a rickety lawn chair, and forty-five slightly-used tennis balls?

The cab pulls out on North Cleveland, left to Fullerton, and on to the Kennedy Expressway where it's every man for himself to O'Hare. Some of it I have liked a great deal. Some of it I may have even loved. There were parts I hated. Regardless. It's over.

****

Living in a city other than Atlanta was something I had never considered. I am not native, but close. And Atlanta—even when the Dinkler Plaza was the big stop and Terminal Station was busy at midnight—was a mecca for those of us in the Coweta County hinterlands. "Atlaner" they called it where I lived, and a lot of people went there on Friday nights. Those who didn't stop at the Farmer's Market drove on to the city auditorium for the wrestling matches. No, the *rasslin'* matches.

Predictably, my first job out of school was in Atlanta. The changes were already at hand. Up jumped the Stadium and in came the Braves, the Falcons, the Hawks, and the Flames. Underground flourished and the *New York Times* did front page stories. Boddy Dodd retired, Lester Maddox faded, and Hartsfield went international. And everybody from Keokuk and Three Rivers showed up in his leisure suit for the hardware convention at the Marriot or the Regency. The Nitery? One block up and two over.

I left Atlanta two years ago for Chicago, figuring what the hell, horizons are for stretching. I was homesick at the first stop light in Cartersville. Horizons without a red clay motif are somebody else's horizons.

I did keep up while I was gone. Jimmy Carter, a Georgian, became president, and that helped. Suddenly, it was fashionable at Hotspurs and Arnie's in Chicago to be able to explain the difference between poke salet and pot likker. A man stood on the corner of Rush and State and called another a "sumbitch." I swear.

Time Magazine even devoted a special issue to explaining the South. I noted with no small measure of pride that it no longer considered H. L. Mencken's dismissal of the cultural South as the "intellectual Gobi or Lapland" to be operative.

Ted Turner was front page in Chicago. "Is he a little goofy?" I was asked more than once. Midwesterners can't really distinguish between Georgia Tech and just plain Georgia, but when Pepper upset Notre Dame last fall the question did come up. *Playboy* said the women were great in Atlanta. *Sports Illustrated* said the sports teams were lousy. Could be worse, I said. What if it were the other way around?

I am sure a lot has changed. The new hotels are supposed to be incredible. One allegedly has a lake in the lobby. It is rumored liquor may be purchased on Sunday. Parts of the city, I understand, have disappeared altogether in the wake of MARTA bulldozers. And Mr. Young has gone to New York and Mr. Fowler has gone to Washington in his place.

But folks still talk nice to you, don't they? And Harold's Barbecue hasn't closed? Northside Drive from the expressway to West Paces has not gone commercial? And late on summer afternoons what of that stillness, that cooling, that sundown in the Deep South that makes whatever happened during the day worth it and whatever may transpire that night even better? Has the Fox been saved?

I hope so. The commitment is made.

The Delta lady on the other end of the phone was talking. "There is space available on the noon flight to Atlanta," she said a few days ago. "Will this be round trip?"

I just let it hang there, savoring the moment.

"No, m'am," I answered. "One way."

No Spot Is So Dear . . .

On a cold day last week, I stood outside the church in my hometown of Moreland, Georgia, that is so dear to my childhood and tried to remember how long it had been since I was inside. Ten years? At least that long. But if there weren't still roots here, would I come back so often in my mind?

Church was about all we had. Sunday school was at ten, but preaching was only twice a month. We shared sermons and the preacher with another flock down the road.

What did they call it on Sunday night? MYF? We had a couple of rowdy brothers in town who broke into a store. They were juvenile first offenders. Their punishment was to attend Methodist Youth Fellowship for six months. First night they were there, they beat up two fifth-graders and threw a Cokesbury hymnal at the lady who met with us and always brought cookies.

She ducked in time and then looked them squarely in their devilish eyes. Soft as the angel she was, she said, "I don't approve of what you boys did here tonight, and neither does Jesus. But if He can forgive you, I guess I'll have to."

She handed them a plate of cookies, and last I heard, both are daddies with steady jobs and rarely miss a Sunday. That was the first miracle I ever saw.

Revivals at the church were the highlight of the summer. I remember a young visiting preacher talking about the night he was converted.

"I was drunk in an Atlanta bar," he said, "and I was lost. But Jesus walked in and sat down beside me. Praise His name, because that's the reason I'm with you here tonight."

That frightened me. If Jesus could find that fellow in an Atlanta bar, he certainly wouldn't have any trouble walking up on me smoking behind the pump house in Moreland. I always took an extra look around before lighting up after that.

Workers were smoking one day in the attic of our church. They left a cigarette. It took less than an hour for flames to destroy that old building. I didn't cry, but grown men did.

We built it back—of brick this time. Country folks will dig deep in the name of the Lord.

The best fried chicken I ever ate, the best iced tea I ever drank were the fried chicken and the iced tea on Homecoming Day at the church. Dinner on the grounds, we called it. The chickens had been walking in someone's backyard earlier in the morning. The tea went into a galvanized washtub. A piece of block ice kept it cold.

The day Red Murphy died, they announced it in the church. The congregation wept as one. Everyone loved Red Murphy. He ran the little post office and took children on pony rides.

Maxine Estes taught my Sunday school class. In rural Georgia in the fifties, she was big on being kind to your neighbor no matter the color of his skin. I learned to sing Hymn No. 153, "Love, Mercy and Grace," in that church. And "What a Friend We Have in Jesus." And the one I still break into occasionally today, "Precious Memories." They do linger.

My mother married my stepfather inside that church. And one hot Saturday afternoon a long time ago, a pretty nineteen-year-old girl married me at the same altar. I told her I would never forget her, and I haven't.

It's easy to fall away from the church, no matter the closeness to it in times past. I have done it. So have you. Grown people can do as they please. The 10:30 Sunday morning movie is even an excuse I use. So are Saturday nights that should have ended a lot earlier.

I never could bring myself to walk inside my old church last week. But some Sunday morning soon, maybe I will. And maybe I'll put a ten in the collection plate, and maybe they'll have chicken and iced tea, and maybe afterward I'll make a habit of it.

There is a new country song out. An old man is singing to a group of fellow derelicts. "Lean on Jesus," goes the chorus, "before He leans on you."

I'm not one to panic, but it's something to think about.

Country Store

There is no sign, but the lady inside at Bailey's General Store assured me this was, in fact, Jones Crossroads.

"The Joneses don't own the land anymore," she said, "but they still call it 'Jones Crossroads.'" Who's being picky?

Jones Crossroads is one country store and a house or two and some nice trees at the intersection of Georgia highways 18 and 219 half the distance between West Point and Pine Mountain. The population depends on how many people needed to go to the store that day.

I have a thing about country stores, a love affair that goes back to my youth and a wonderful place called Cureton and Cole's. I could never quite understand why Cureton and Cole's was owned by Lee Evans and J. W. Thompson, but again, who's being picky?

You name it, they sold it at Cureton and Cole's in downtown Moreland, as long as it was coal, sacks of guano, corn meal, Sugar Daddy all day suckers, Hollywood candy bars, Zero candy bars, Zagnut candy bars, snuff, work shirts, work pants, work shoes, kerosene, soda crackers, Vienna sausage, Home Run cigarettes, po- tatoes—sweet and Irish—Blue Horse notebook paper, ice cream in cups with lids that if you licked the ice cream off the underside you would uncover the picture of a movie star like Yvonne DeCarlo, Prince Albert in a can, chicken feed, thread, seed, moon pies, and cold drinks such as R.C. Colas, Nehi oranges, Double Colas, and NuGrapes from a box filled with chunks of block ice, and other of life's necessities.

Sadly, Cureton and Cole's has been boarded shut, never to open again. At least they haven't torn it down and put up a disco. I can see it now: J. W.'s Juke Joint.

Bailey's General Store in Jones Crossroads is a lot like Cureton and Cole's. It has a front porch and two chairs for just sittin'. It has a screened front door and a thermometer so old men can look at it and greet one another with, "Hot enough for you?"

Inside, there are hardwood floors and an air-conditioning system—a floor fan. I saw some flies. A fly is never at home until it is buzzing about a country store on a hot afternoon.

The lady inside said her daddy, Mr. Bailey, ran the store before he died. Worked hard all his life, she said, until the day he found out he had cancer. He lived five more weeks.

"Daddy did a lot of business here," she said. "Mama took it over after he died. Things have sort of gone down hill since then."

I checked out the merchandise. In the back were sacks of hog pellets and scratch feed for chickens. There was a meat box with bologna, the kind you cut directly from the loaf. A yard rake was for sale.

There was a classic candy display case. Zagnut must be out of business. Behind the counter was more snuff than your grandmother could dip in a lifetime of evenings in the front porch rocking chair. There was Bruton's snuff, and Dental snuff, and Tops snuff, and I think I spotted a can of Rooster.

I couldn't resist any longer. From inside Bailey's drink box I pulled out a Nehi orange bellywasher. From the cookie and cracker rack I plucked a "Big Town" chocolate moon pie.

I walked outside and sat me down on the front porch. The marshmallow filling inside the moon pie had become runny from the heat, but the cold rush of the orange bellywasher released its hold from the roof of my mouth.

For a moment I had been ten again, with a dime burning a hole in my jeans, and with all the pleasures a child could imagine encircling me and dazzling me. For a moment, I thought I could hear Lee Evans talking to J. W. Thompson. For a moment, that moon pie was chateaubriand and my big orange was a gentle and soothing nectar of the gods.

It's Okay to Cry

Things my mother told me would come true when I was grown that I really didn't believe at the time:

The older you get, the harder it is to quit smoking.

You might turn up your nose at turnip greens now, but there will come a time you can't get them and you will want them more than T-bone steak.

Love is the greatest gift one person can give to another.

Money can't buy love.

The kind it might buy isn't worth having.

People will tell you they love you when they don't mean it.

There are no answers in the bottom of a cocktail glass.

Its easy to go into debt. Getting out is next to impossible.

Marriage is a two-way street.

You will never meet a good woman in a night club.

One lie begets another.

If you don't take care of yourself when you are young, you might not live to regret it.

Even if you don't agree with everything the preacher says, it won't hurt you to sit still for thirty minutes and listen to him.

It's okay to cry.

Never let a friend down. You will need him someday.

You don't need to talk dirty to prove you are a man.

The Lord listens to your prayers.

He doesn't answer all of them.

The best way to tell somebody you care is to show them first.

It's not written anywhere that life is supposed to be fair.

Money doesn't grow on trees.

Always wear clean underwear. You might be in a wreck.

Children and old people appreciate kindness.

So do dogs.

Be careful when you buy a used car or an insurance policy.

Pay attention when somebody older tells you something. You can learn a lot from people who have already been down the road.

Being stubborn won't get you anywhere.

Women don't like men who drink too much.

There will be times when you are very lonely. Just remember your mother loves you and always will.

People who shout to make themselves heard usually don't know what they are talking about.

When you get older, your back will hurt and it won't be that easy to get to sleep.

Someday, a man will walk on the moon. And Pepsi Colas will cost a quarter.

Pretty faces can be deceiving.

Always say "Thank you" when somebody does you a favor. You will get more favors that way.

Ball games aren't the most important thing in the world.

Income tax will eat you alive.

You will regret not keeping up your piano lessons.

A Mother Will Worry

I have always disliked hospitals. They even smell like people are sick. And everybody who works there dresses all in white. That makes me uncomfortable, too.

Every moment I am visiting in a hospital, I expect one of those people in white to attempt to puncture my body with a needle. In medical science, when in doubt, grab a needle and look for a victim.

She was lying there in her hospital bed, asleep and attached to a strange looking machine. There was a needle in her arm. It was attached to a tube which led to a bottle of solution.

The solution, a drop at a time, rolled down to the tube, into the needle, and into her body. Each time a drop fell from the bottle, the machine made a clicking sound. The Chinese, I am certain, are behind such a torture-rendering machine.

I don't know what awakened her. Perhaps it was simply my presence in the room. I hadn't made a sound.

She looked tired. I have seen her like this so many times before. Once, when I was a child, she was sick and in the hospital for a long time. That was for something else, something she eventually whipped.

I am praying for an encore this time.

My mother first fell ill to her disease fifteen years ago. She went through a long, treacherous operation the day John Kennedy was buried.

She was better for a time after that, and then worse, and then better and then worse again. One day last week she said, "I haven't felt this good in years."

But it was no time before she was back in the hospital again and I was standing over her again, trying to say something that would help and instead talking mostly about myself.

One thing I never bring up to my mother is any involvement I might be having with the opposite sex, but she always asks about it because one thing she would like to be—like most mothers, I suppose—is a grandmother, and so far, she hasn't been close.

"There's plenty of time for that," I always tell her.

"Maybe for me," she laughs, "but how about you?"

The preacher came by. He was a soft man, who literally crept into the room and introduced himself to me by saying, "Hello, I'm a Baptist preacher."

He told my mother he was praying for her, and she thanked him. He didn't stay long.

"He goes by to see just about everybody," my mother explained. Visit the sick and calm the grieving. Nobody does it better than a small-town preacher.

I was there maybe a couple of hours. I finally pulled a chair near the bed toward the end of my visit. I think my mother sensed I would be leaving soon.

I am thirty-two years old. I have a good job. A car. A nice place to live. Friends. And more health than I deserve.

My mother is sick, lying in a hospital bed with a Chinese Solution Torture Machine attached to her arm. But here is how our visit ended:

"Are you eating well, son?"

"Sure."

"Remember to eat well. Sweets are bad for your teeth."

"I'll remember that."

"Don't ever pick up a stranger when you're driving at night."

"I would never do that."

"Do you have enough cover for your bed?"

"Plenty."

"I wish you would stop smoking."

"I've tried."

"Try harder."

"I'll try harder."

"Don't bother to get me anything for Christmas. I don't need a thing."

"I want to get you *something*."

"And don't worry about me."

"I can't help that."

"Do you have enough cover for your bed?"

"Plenty, mother. Plenty."

Mother's Day

She married late in life, compared to other women of her day. When she finally found her man, he would soon leave her and go off to war.

He was a brave soldier and performed many heroic deeds, and he lived through it all. When he returned, she loved him dearly and he loved her. A boy child was born one October morning.

But came another war that took her man away again.

She got the news from a yellow telegram. The child was playing in the yard, chasing butterflies and wrestling a playful bird dog. He can still remember her scream from within the house. He can still remember her tears. He was too young to understand why she was crying, but he tried to comfort her the best he could.

Her brave soldier, said the telegram, was missing in action. An enemy force had overrun his company's position on some barren hill a million miles away in Korea.

The child wondered about this "Korea," what it was, where it was, and why his daddy was there.

On Christmas Eve, there was a telephone call, followed by more tears. The soldier was alive. He was calling from a hospital in Pearl Harbor. He would be home soon.

"Do you still love me?" he asked his son.

The child did not yet understand the telephone. He nodded a "yes."

"Of course, he does," the mother assured the father. "And so do I."

He returned in triumph. He had been captured and imprisoned by the enemy. He had been tortured. But he had escaped. For weeks, he was hidden in an underground cave and cared for by a South Korean boy who brought him rice and kept him alive until he could make his way back to his lines.

He was weak from the diet and the fear. His feet were so severely frostbitten, they would crack open and bleed each day of the rest of his life.

He was a patriot, still. He made speeches throughout the land, his wife and son at his side. He told of his experiences and he assailed those who would keep American forces out of distant lands threatened by the spread of Communism.

He would say many times, "There is no soldier like the American soldier. The rest of the world *needs* us to keep it free."

But those many years of combat had taken their toll. He had changed. When he returned, the woman thought their long periods of separation were over. She would be disappointed again.

He brooded. He awakened nights in a cold sweat, screaming. He drank only a little at first. But then he would sit up those nights, alone with a bottle.

The Army, despite his many decorations for valor and his years of service, decided him unfit for further military duty. He wandered aimlessly, at a loss for a purpose.

The mother and the child would see him whenever they could. They would visit him in other cities and she would pretend someday they would be together again.

But she knew they wouldn't. A thousand nights, thinking the child next to her was asleep, she prayed aloud for help.

Finally, she gave up on her husband. She had no other choice. He was a hopeless alcoholic, a man lost in an imagined shame that was nearly demonic in its possession of his life.

She educated herself. She struggled to work each day and to evening classes at night. Somehow, she still managed to bring her son toward manhood and she told him, "Always respect your father, no matter what."

She would eventually remarry. She would take a man steady and kind to her and to her son. She would find at least a share of the contentment and security that had avoided her for so long.

The father, the brave soldier, would die alone. The son would grow and leave her. But he would think of his mother and her plight often. On occasion, he would remember to thank her for the sacrifices she made in his behalf.

Sadly, her burdens have never ceased totally. Today, it is an illness she battles. The doctors say it is incurable. She *deserves* a miracle.

She wanted to be with her son today, and he wanted to be with her on Mother's Day. He wonders if he made the right decision to put off a visit because of business demands.

He did send roses, however. And because she means so much to him, and because she was strong on his mind, and because he wanted to remind himself of the long road she's been down, he spent an afternoon and half a night writing what you just read.

2

OFF THE WALL

People ask me, "Where do you get your ideas for columns?" I never know how to answer that question. Sometimes I look under rocks. I think that is where I got the ideas for the following pieces. At any rate, I do hate liver and I remain convinced the world would be better off without airplanes.

They Gave the Ball Without Me

For the thirty-second consecutive year, I did not receive an invitation to the annual Harvest Ball at the Piedmont Driving Club. Obviously, there has been some kind of mistake.

Every year, I anxiously await the arrival of the white envelope beckoning me to what is certainly one of Atlanta's most prestigious and gala social events.

And every year, I am disappointed. Could the problem be I have moved around too much and they don't know where to find me?

I could just drop by the club and pick it up, you know, and I promise to leave the truck on the street.

What happens at the Harvest Ball is some of the city's loveliest and tenderest and most charming young girlpersons, whose daddies also have a big stash, make their "debuts" to society.

That makes them "debutantes." I have never quite understood exactly what a debutante is, but I'm sure there are lots of good things to eat and drink at their parties.

"When a girl makes her debut," somebody who should know told me, "it means her parents are presenting her to their friends and that she is now a part of the social scene."

I think the male comparison to that—on a lower social strata—is your old man taking you for a beer at the VFW and letting you shoot pool with Scooter Haines who was once eight ball champion of all Heard County.

They held this year's Harvest Ball last week and, again, I had to be satisfied with reading about it in the paper.

19

It was a grand affair. Proud fathers, said the report, beamed as their daughters curtsied to the audience in their expensive and chic gowns.

One of the debs did express concern her escort might get too drunk to cut in on her father when it came time for the evening's waltz. That shocked me.

I can understand getting too drunk to shoot eight ball with Scooter Haines, but the Piedmont Driving Club ain't the Moose Lodge, sport.

Dinner was divine, the story went on. Everybody had tomato aspic with shrimp, breast of chicken, spinach souffle with artichokes and almond mousse and even Scooter Haines, who once went all the way to Houston for a pool tournament, never wrapped his gums around anything like that.

Sadly, the closest I have ever come to a debutante ball was the annual Fourth of July Street Dance in front of the knitting mill on the square in downtown Moreland with a live band that played "Down Yonder" over and over again because that's all the band knew except for "Alabama Jubilee" which it didn't play so well.

What always happened at the dance was farmers from as far away as Luthersville and Arno-Sargent showed up with truckloads of daughters they wanted to marry off. If any of them had teeth, they got to ride up front in the cab.

Some grand old girls got out of trucks at those street dances. The only curtseying they did, however, was over behind the depot where nobody could see them. We were a polite society, too.

There was Cordie Mae Poovey. Cordie Mae always came in her "bermudalls." That's a pair of overalls cut off just above the knee. Cordie Mae couldn't dance a lick, but don't tell her that because she weighed a good 220 and was stronger than she smelled.

And who could forget Lucille Garfield? Lucille carried her pet pig everywhere she went. The way you could tell the pig from Lucille was the pig wore a hat and was the better conversationalist of the two.

Betty Jean Turnipseed didn't miss a dance for fifteen years. Betty Jean wasn't very smart. One time somebody brought an armadillo to school for show-and-tell and she thought it was a possum on the half-shell

But Kathy Sue Loudermilk came to the street dances, too, and when she danced, even the preacher broke a sweat. Nature blessed that child beyond the limits of this timid vocabulary.

It's like my boyhood friend and idol, Weyman C. Wannamaker Jr., a great American, said of her: "That dog can hunt."

So I'll probably never make the Harvest Ball. But I would have paid to have seen Kathy Sue Loudermilk debuting at the Piedmont Driving Club.

One curtsey from ol' Kathy Sue in something tight and low cut and the whole crowd would have been knocked squarely on their tomato aspics.

Interviewing Myself

I get letters from journalism students and other assorted weirdos wanting to know how I go about putting together a column five days a week.

"I have to write a term paper for my JRL 101 class," began one recent letter, "and I have chosen you as my topic. I want to know, in at least 2,000 words, how you go about putting together a column five days a week.

"I need your response no later than two weeks from Friday. Please double-space and try to avoid typographical errors as the instructor counts off for that."

The student who wrote that letter will probably grow to be a good columnist. Getting other people to do your work is a cornerstone of this profession.

Since it is impossible for me to answer all such inquiries, I have decided today to interview myself on the subject of writing a column for the benefit of interested students and my boss.

I know my boss is interested because just the other day he asked me, "Grizzard, how can you do this to me five days a week?"

Here, then, is the interview, conducted in my office, which is located near the men's rest room and which recently got new carpet the color of river water near a chemical dump. I am using an IBM Selectric II typewriter which makes strange sounds like a semi hauling hogs through Holly Springs, Mississippi, on a hot July afternoon:

What does a semi hauling hogs through Holly Springs, Mississippi, on a hot, July afternoon sound like?"

"Grrrrrrrrrrrooooooooink!"

When your IBM Selectric II typewriter makes that sound, what do you think of?

The odor of overcrowded hogs in a steam bath and possible death by electrocution.

Has anybody ever suffered serious injury or even death in an accident involving an electric typewriter?

Yes. One day a skinny religion reporter got his tie hung in the paper roller of his electric typewriter. In a vain attempt to remove it, he rolled his head into his machine and was typed to death by a lower case 'j' and an out-of-control ampersand.

Do readers sometimes call and suggest column ideas to you?

Every day. Recently, an anonymous caller suggested I do a column on the most handsome, best-dressed sportcaster on Atlanta television.

Did you follow up on the suggestion?

Of course not. I knew it was Harmon the minute he mispronounced "Robert Hall."

As a columnist, do you have opportunities for exciting travel and adventure?

You betcha. Just in the last two months, I have been to Memphis and Birmingham. Memphis was closed after dark and under martial law, but the hotel in Birmingham had one of those neat, revolving restaurants like the Regency Hyatt in Atlanta. Unfortunately, the one in Birmingham was in the basement.

Last year, I got to go to the Indianapolis 500 automobile race. What an interesting event that was. It was the most mental illness I have seen at one time.

Approximately, what are your working hours?

I am on call twenty-four hours a day. No story is ever too big or too small for a good columnist. If the bartender forgot to tell you the office called, however, it's not your fault.

Who are the most difficult people to interview?

Those whose names recently appeared in the obituary column, anybody in Harrison's on Friday night with a wedding ring in his pocket, and Korean soccer players.

Is it a strain on your health to write five columns a week?

Absolutely not. I have migraine headaches, stomach pains, dizzy spells, nightmares, hallucinations, ingrown toenails, smoker's cough, and my back is stiff. Other than that, I am in perfect health for a sixty-five-year-old malaria victim.

Is it necessary to drink to be a good columnist?

That is a common myth, but a young person setting out on a career as a columnist should avoid drinking at all costs. It is certainly not necessary to drink to be a good columnist. It is a great help on the days you are a bad one, however.

In summary, then, what is the most difficult part of writing a daily column: (a) the research; (b) the actual writing; (c) the need for a constant flow of the creative juices; or (d) crazies threatening to break your hands?

(E) Admitting to myself I can't hold down a regular job.

Liver Is a Fraud

Eating used to be so simple. A couple of eggs with grits, bacon, toast and coffee in the morning, a quick hamburger and fries at noon, and evening was your basic meat and potatoes.

Give me something with character in the evenings. A steak. Pork chops. Fried chicken. My mother would occasionally try to slip liver into my diet.

"Eat liver, live longer," she would say.

I'm still taking my chance. Who wants a long life that includes eating liver? I don't even like to be in the same room with it.

After I left my mother's table, eating became a bit more complicated. Restaurant food can make eating more of a chore than a joy.

When I lived in Chicago, I nearly starved. Chicago is filled with ethnic restaurants that are fun once. But man can not live on a steady diet of veal marsala and things that still have their heads and eyes.

He must also have cornbread and collards and an occasional barbecue pork-pig sandwich. Otherwise, scurvy and rickets are distinct possibilities.

Today, eating has become a major problem. That is because all the things we used to think were good for us are actually bad for us. Like light bread and biscuits. Light bread and biscuits, somebody told me, are fattening, have no food value and can lead to heart attack and cancer. Say it ain't so.

The same goes for too much milk and eggs. They cause cholesterol and cholesterol causes your arteries to clog and clogged arteries are one-way tickets to the coronary wing.

You have probably heard bacon and hamburgers cause cancer. My doctor told me not to eat pork. That's a problem. A week without barbecue, and I hallucinate and get shortness of breath.

I was hoping they would find something wrong with liver. I always figured it probably caused the spread of communism if nothing else.

"Eat liver, live longer," said my doctor, the dirty pinko.

What we are supposed to be eating today are natural foods. Foods that have not been processed. Foods that have no chemical additives and preservatives. Foods that give us bulk and fibre.

All that sounds like good advice on how to keep your lawnmower engine in tune, but I decided to at least seek more information on the matter.

I have a friend who eats nothing but natural foods. Actually, he doesn't eat. He grazes. I went to him for advice.

"Breakfast," he said, "is the most important meal of the day. I eat natural cereals with low-fat milk and no sugar.

"Or, I mix natural yogurt, a banana, a teaspoon of raw honey and miller's bran together. It gives me enough food value to last me until lunch time when I eat raw vegetables and nuts.

"The dinner meal is usually a large salad, a bowl of celery or asparagus soup, a glass of natural fruit juice and maybe a piece of cheese. The cheese is optional."

Never introduce a man with a diet like that to your house plants. I know horses and goats who eat better.

My friend explained further about people in other parts of the world whose diets include nothing but natural foods. I remembered the yogurt commercials on television. Eat a lot of yogurt and grow up to be a 112-year-old Russian. Who needs it?

"Don't laugh," he said. "Cultures whose diets are totally natural have no traces of heart disease or cancer or other such diet-related diseases. If Americans would turn to natural foods, it would do wonders for the health of our nation."

That, and eat plenty of liver, I added.

"No liver," he said. "Liver stores all the residues and chemicals the animal takes in from eating his own processed foods. I wouldn't touch liver."

I knew it! Anything that tastes as bad as liver has to be the devil's own doing. Finally, I am absolved. Liver is a lying, indigestible fraud.

Praise the Lord, and pass the roots and berries.

My House and a Word or Two About Cats

I have lived in apartments most of my adult life. I have lived in apartments all over Atlanta. I have lived in two different apartments in Chicago.

My first apartment in Chicago was on the fifth floor of a five-floor building. I had space on the roof and an excellent view of the alley behind the building.

Space on the roof is important in Chicago because that is where you go for cookouts and parties with other residents the two months you wouldn't freeze to death or be blown half way to Gary, Indiana by the wind.

Cookouts and parties on a roof in Chicago are equivalent to cookouts and parties in the backyard in Atlanta. Such occasions are more of an adventure on a roof, however, because you can't get wall-eyed and fall off a backyard.

A good view of the alley is also something nice to have in a Chicago apartment because otherwise you might go days without seeing a single mugging.

My second apartment in Chicago was on the second floor. The people downstairs had cats. Cats are snooty and wouldn't fetch a stick on a bet. They also scratch. I dislike cats.

One night a cat belonging to the people downstairs came into my apartment while I was having dinner. It jumped onto the table and walked in the mashed potatoes. I attempted to drown the cat in the gravy. Never attempt to drown a cat in gravy.

The people downstairs refused to pay for the stitches.

Several years ago, I lived in an apartment on the south side of Atlanta near the airport. It had one of those fancy, English names like Hampshire on the Lake. Or Oyster on the Half-Shell. I forget which.

Regardless, the noise from airplanes landing and taking off from Hartsfield gave me migraine headaches, and the first time it rained, the apartment flooded.

Pleas to the resident manager's office for help and a pump went unheeded. Finally, I wrote her a letter. "I can no longer live in this carpeted rice paddy," is what I wrote. She finally came over to inspect my apartment and brought her cat. It drowned.

My last apartment was on the northwest side of the city, and the most interesting thing about it was the pool and the girl who sat by it wearing nothing but two strategically placed R.C. caps and a polka-dot loin cloth.

My apartment pool was also where off-duty airline stewardesses came to sunbathe. The girl with the two R.C. caps and the polka-dot loin cloth was not an airline stewardess, however.

She was an ex-biology teacher who got fired for adding new dimensions to show-and-tell time.

The purpose for all this background on my apartment living adventures is to tell you I have finally given up apartment living, not to mention another deposit.

I bought a house. One with windows and doors and a leaking faucet in the bathtub. One with trees in the yard and squirrels and birds in the trees. One with gutters to clean and grass to cut. One with taxes and insurance and a high interest rate and dogs who roam in the yard and who had a dinner party in the first batch of garbage I dumped in my very own curbside garbage container.

One my old furniture insults. I have bought automobiles for what a couch and a coffee table costs these days. One with windows to wash and carpets to clean and leaves to rake.

One with bathroom tile that needs grouting. Until I bought a house, I thought grouting was something only consenting adults should do and only with the lights off.

But one the sun shines into in the mornings. And one I hoped for and saved for and looked high and low for.

One I wouldn't mind sharing someday.

Maybe I'll buy a cat.

Don't Get Gypped When You Need a Crypt

I started not to write this column. It's about cemetery plots. This is only my third sentence, but I've already got the creeps.

When I was a kid, the old folks used to gather and talk about their cemetery plots. I would leave the room.

When I returned, they had usually progressed to the Fire on Judgment Day. I would leave the room again.

"Where is your plot, Myrtle?" one of the old folks would ask another.

"On the hill."

"Not much shade up there," the dialogue would continue.

"It's peaceful, though. And I overlook the front of the church."

"I'm under the oak tree, next to Maude Bates."

"Won't it be cold in the wintertime?"

"I'm wearing my wool suit."

"The gray one?"

"Gray with black checks."

"You'll be pretty as a picture. If you don't break out."

"Why should I break out?"

"Wool. Maude Bates wore wool, you know. She broke out something awful."

"How do you know that?"

"Her sister Ruby told me. Ruby's on the hill next to me. We're wearing cotton prints."

I can take almost anything else. Dandruff, roaches in the sink, your last proctoscope examination. But not cemetery plots. Cemetery plots are personal, like your underwear size.

And deliver me from advertisements about cemetery plots and their accompanying paraphernalia. Classified ads in the newspaper sell plots like used cars:

"WESTVIEW—4-grave. Terrace B. Shaded, Curbside. Reasonable. Leaving state. Quick sale."

What's so important about being "curbside"? You're going to catch a bus?

Another ad caught my eye the other day:

"DAWN MEMORIAL, (2) plots with vaults, markers and perpetual maintenance. Must sell. Need money!"

That's obvious. Anybody needing money bad enough to hock his own burial vault and marker is one broke hombre.

Television commercials for cemetery plots are even worse. There was the one I borrowed from to begin this column: "We started not to make this commercial," the announcer would open.

And for good reason. It stunk.

". . . But the Deep Six Burial Company wants you to plot now for what the future holds for all of us. Don't be left out in the cold *when that time comes.* You and your loved ones will be eternally grateful you acted now."

I would be eternally grateful if I never saw that commercial again.

Some things simply shouldn't be hard-sold. Cemetery plots head the list. The announcer is somber-slick. The music is sleepy-soft. The plan is "Pay now, die later."

Any day, I expect a commercial for cemetery plots with a singing jingle:

"Pay just two-ninety-five
While you're still alive
So you won't get gypped
When you need a crypt."

I admit I'm easily spooked when it comes to this matter. And I admit I'm in the same mortal boat with everybody else. I will, in fact, need a place to lay me down for the ages.

But I don't want to be reminded of that unsettling fact as I sit in my own living room.

Among other things, it is depressing and causes me to break out like Maude Bates, rest her woolly soul.

I Don't Have Any Children

We were all close once. I thought it had been six, maybe seven years. Somebody else said it had been more like twelve or thirteen.

It was a chance reunion. There was some beer, and we told a few of the old stories again. One was about the time we had Ben E. King at the spring formal at a big, downtown hotel.

A fight broke out. We couldn't remember who started it or who won, but we did recall a lot of glass breaking and being asked never to come back to that particular big, downtown hotel.

They all introduced me to their wives, none of whom seemed particularly interested in hearing a few of the old stories again. Then they pulled out their wallets and showed me pictures of their children.

That's exactly what I needed to see, pictures of their children, but I always make polite remarks at a time like that.

"She's a sweetheart."

"This is when she was an angel in the church play."

"Looks just like you."

"His teacher says he's the brightest kid in her class."

"Fine-looking young man."

"He plays fullback."

They asked if I had any children. Somebody will always ask that, and I will normally answer while staring at the floor.

"No, I don't," I will say. What am I doing? Apologizing? Why do I always feel like I need to offer an explanation?

I don't have any children because I just don't have any. We talked about it. We even tried a couple of times, but nothing ever happened.

And by that time, it was obvious that trying to have a child, under the circumstances, would be . . . stupid. I think that's exactly the word I used. "Stupid."

I have been congratulated often for my farsighted approach to the situation.

"You're better off," people have said to me.

I've also been told I was "lucky."

"You're lucky you never had any children. When you have children, it just makes things a lot worse."

I think it was one of my aunts who said, "At least there weren't any little children to get hurt."

But I like children. Maybe that's a little strong. I don't have anything against children, and from what limited knowledge I have of them, there is apparently at least some appeal to their company.

They seem to forgive easily, like dogs, and I am impressed by that. When they first awaken, they look around for somebody to hold them. I know the feeling.

Thunder frightens children. I'm still not at peaceful terms with thunder, either.

Children give you a fair shot before they decide they don't like you.

They look fresh and cute dressed up, especially when they are dressed up and walking into a church holding their mother's hand.

Children think it's a big deal when you give them a quarter.

I've always wanted to teach a little boy which end of a baseball bat to hold. You would think little boys would be born with that knowledge, but they aren't.

One of the men who was showing me pictures of his children said when you have children you hear the word, "daddy," about a thousand times a day.

That can't be all bad.

Once I took a friend's child on a carnival ride, the Octopus. In the middle of the ride, she said she had to go to the bathroom. I explained the Octopus does not stop when you have to go to the bathroom.

I am positive she did everything in her power to wait until the Octopus ride was over.

The beer gave out about midnight. We promised each other we would get together again soon. Likely, we won't.

You know how it is when you have children.

Airplanes Are Unsafe

I was having a conversation with an airline stewardess. We were not in an airplane, however. I avoid traveling by airplane. Don't get me wrong. I'm not afraid to fly. It is crashing and burning that bothers me. If God had intended man to fly, He would have never given him the rental car and unlimited mileage.

"That's silly," said the stewardess when I told her of my aversion to air travel. "Don't you know that you are safer in an airplane than in an automobile?"

I've heard that bunk before. Anything that goes five miles into the air at 500 miles per hour and they make you strap yourself inside can't be safe.

Automobiles are much safer than airplanes because they don't go as high nor as fast, and they can be pulled over and parked and abandoned, if necessary, at a moment's notice. Try pulling an airplane into the emergency lane when the engine overheats.

I only fly in airplanes in extreme emergencies. Like when the train doesn't go there, the bus company is on strike, or I go temporarily insane.

I even hate airports. First thing you see at an airport is a sign that says "terminal." Airports are noisy, crowded and usually a $15 cab ride from the hotel, plus tip.

The stewardess said she has been flying for twelve years. "I've only been in one real emergency," she said. "I was in a two-engine prop and we lost power in both engines. We were directly over Palm Beach, so we just glided in for a safe landing."

Nothing to it. But engines don't always go out over Palm Beach. Try gliding in to Brasstown Bald, for instance.

I have tried to overcome my difficulties with flying. I decided drinking before boarding would be the answer. I scheduled a flight and then went to the airport bar. A day before the flight.

There isn't enough booze on earth, I discovered, to make me relax on an airplane.

A number of bad things have happened to me on airplanes. Once, I stepped on a woman's violin case while trying to get past her to a window seat. She called me awful names for two hours and tried to hit me with what used to be a violin.

Another time, I had to sit next to a religious nut on an airplane. I had rather be hit on the head with a broken violin than to sit next to a religious nut.

"Brother," he said to me, "do you know the Lord?" I said I knew of Him.

"Are you ready to meet Him?" he continued.

I looked out the window. We were 20,000 feet and climbing.

"I thought this was the Milwaukee flight," I said.

I do have some faith in airplane pilots, however. Especially Robert Stack and John Wayne. I know pilots go through rigorous training, and I know they are checked regularly to make sure their hands are still steady on the stick.

When I fly, I like for the pilot to have gray hair and a gorgeous woman awaiting his arrival at our destination. Something to live for, in other words.

"I dated a pilot five years," said the stewardess. "I'll never forget the day we broke up. He called me from the airport, just before takeoff. We had an awful fight and I hung up on him."

"Was he mad?" I asked her.

"Was he mad? He pulled the plane away from the gate and rammed one of the wings into another plane. He always was one to pout."

A pouting pilot. I think I am going to be sick.

My Kind of Town

Chicago isn't really a city. It's a train wreck. Five or six or seven million people live there against their will. Chicago has a river that runs through the middle of town. You can walk across it in the

wintertime because it's frozen. You can walk across it in the sum-
mertime because it is thick with various forms of waste. Like floating bodies.

Chicago's political system is "vote for the Democrat, or I'll break
your arms." It is not safe to ride the city's transit system. Dial "el"
for murder.

It is not safe to drive on the city's streets. Every year, hundreds of
motorists are lost after driving into potholes which the city repairs
once a decade whether they need to or not.

Say something nice about Chicago for a change. OK. There hasn't
been a mass murder there in nearly three weeks.

The worst thing about Chicago, of course, is the weather. There is
no autumn in Chicago, and there is no spring. Summer lasts an hour
and a half. The rest of the time it is winter.

I lived in Chicago two years. It was so cold, my precinct captain
was Frosty the Snowman. A precinct captain is the one who gives
you the bottle of whiskey on election day.

The current winter in Chicago has been the worst since 1912, the
year Mayor Daley was elected. Already this month, there have been
two blizzards. I saw it snow in May once. Welcome to Ice Station
Zero.

There is some humor in all this, however. Something new called
Chicago jokes. A few were offered in a Chicago newspaper the other
day:

How many Chicagoans does it take to drive a car in winter?
Seven. One to steer, six to push.
Why do Chicago-style pizzas have such thick crusts?
What isn't eaten can be used for insulation.
How do you drive a Chicagoan crazy?
Send him or her a $5 gift certificate toward a Florida vacation.
I thought of some Chicago jokes of my own.
How do they start the baseball season in Chicago?
The mayor thaws out the first ball.
*How does a robber disguise himself while holding up a Chicago
liquor store in the wintertime?*
He takes off his ski mask.
Where had your wife rather live than in Chicago?
Wait a minute. Alaska.

I feel sorry for people who still live in Chicago. They should have
their heads examined for brain warts. I especially felt sorry for them
Thursday. Thursday was a spring day in January in Atlanta.

I even called one of my old Lincoln Avenue haunts—the Twenty-
Three Fifty Pub—to inquire about the health and well-being of some

of my old drinking buddies, the ones who used to insist Chicago is a nice place to live.

"Your mother's a polar bear," I would say to them just before the beer-throwing started.

Chuck Dee came to the phone. He runs the joint. I asked about the weather.

"Colder'n (something I can't print)," he said. "Thirty inches of snow on the ground and more falling."

"Nearly sixty degrees here," I told him.

"That's cold," he said.

"Sixty ABOVE, dummy," I said.

"Go to (somewhere it's at least warm)," he said back.

Chuck lives near the pub.

"The people on my street got together and hired two snowplows to come dig us out," he explained. "The drivers took one look and refused. I'm the only one who can get out. But I had to buy a four-wheel drive jeep to do it."

Some people never learn, which reminds me of another Chicago joke I made up Thursday.

What do you say to a smart Chicagoan?

Welcome South, brother.

3

COLD BEER AND COUNTRY MUSIC

I fell in love with country music when I was nine years old and somebody slipped a nickel into the juke box at Steve Smith's truck stop in my hometown of Moreland, Georgia, and played a hurtin' song by Hank Williams. Everybody likes beer, of course.

The Best Beer Joint in Georgia

Jim Stone led me inside the "No-Name" beer joint. "This place just ain't been the same," he said, a certain sadness and longing in his voice, "since the monkey died."

The monkey and its passing are another story I will get around to later. Before that, meet the winner of the Lucille's Memorial Best Beer Joint Search Contest, Jim Stone.

Several months ago, I asked for nominations for the best beer joint in the state of Georgia and named it for Lucille, who sold me my first beer. There were contest rules. The juke box had to be all-country, there couldn't be any mixed drinks or cheeseburgers on sale, wives or girlfriends of regulars weren't allowed, neither were smart-aleck college students, and a bottle of imported beer within thirty miles of the place would be grounds for automatic disqualification.

Jim Stone entered the "No-Name" beer joint in Willacoochee. It is called the "No-Name" because it doesn't have a name. A broken Pabst sign outside is the only evidence the one-room building is where a man can break a dry spell. Otherwise:

—— The jukebox is all-country.

—— Beer costs 55 cents. *All* beer, including gloriously cold long-necks.

—— Cans of Vienna sausage adorn the back counter.

—— There is a sign that says, "No Bumming and No Begging." ("They ain't kiddin'," said a regular.)

—— There is another sign that says, "No Gambling: Anybody caught gambling will be 'prosuted.'"

—— There are two pool tables in the back, which is the reason for the gambling sign.

—— There is no air-conditioning. The windows and doors are kept open in the summer, closed in the winter.

—— There is a new paint job on the outside toilet, despite the fact an indoor facility was installed a month ago.

—— You can still use the outdoor toilet if you want to.

—— The regulars inside do a lot of pulpwooding in the swamp, but they are friendly.

—— The bartender's name is "Hoss," and he chews tobacco.

First prize in the Lucille's Memorial Best Beer Joint Search Contest was that I come to the winner's favorite spot and we drink beer and I pick up the tab.

We started as the evening sun was going down on Willacoochee, which straddles the Seaboard Coast Line tracks and Highway 82 between Pearson and Alapaha, on the west end of Atkinson County, a hard day's ride from Atlanta in the flats and piney woods of deep south Georgia.

Jim Stone had driven in from Douglas, where he works for South Georgia College. "A lot of folks come here from Douglas," he explained. "Willacoochee is to Douglas sort of what Hyannis Port is to Boston."

"Hoss" was behind the bar, his jaw bulging. Luther, one of the regulars in overalls, had dropped by. So did Lace Futch, the mayor of Willacoochee, a man of constant good humor. Amos, the jailer, was there and so was Henry, who owns the No-Name.

Henry was proud to know his place had won the contest.

"I can use the business," he said.

"You ain't doing so bad, are you, Henry?" asked Jim Stone.

"I ain't saying for sure," replied Henry, "but I got three head of young'uns at the house, and ain't none of 'em mssing no meals."

We sat ourselves down at one of the two tables, the one nearest the jukebox, which Henry turned up because we asked him to. We proceeded with the longnecks.

The hot south Georgia sun poured in through the windows. Tired and thirsty men who sweat for a living poured in through the doors in search of relief for dusty and parched throats. The jukebox blared.

She stood outside the door, not daring to come in. She wore bermudas. She was barefoot in the sand. She held an infant at her hip.

"Your old lady's out there," Henry said to a young man as he pulled on a tall bottle. The young man finished his beer. But slowly.

Only then did he walk outside and disappear with his family west on Highway 82.

A slow Seaboard freight passed on the tracks outside. Somebody said Mayor Futch ws ready to take on the entire Seaboard Coast Line.

"They got boxcars parked right in the middle of town, and they won't move 'em," the mayor said.

"How long have they been there?" I asked.

"Eight years," he answered.

Jim Stone finally got around to the monkey story. It is fairly complicated.

A few years back, there was a girl in town who was an excellent basketball player. Her family gave her a pet monkey for high school graduation. But the monkey was messy. Her parents told the girl to give the monkey away.

"She brought it here," said Jim Stone. "It was some kind of smart monkey. They trained it to take the change off the table anytime anybody passed out. Everybody's got to earn his keep."

I had to ask how the monkey died.

"Bad diet," Jim Stone explained. "You can't live that long on just beer and peanuts."

"That ain't nothing," interrupted Mayor Futch. "They used to have a coon in here, too. People would come in and the coon would crawl up on their table. They'd fill the ashtrays full of beer and the coon would drink it all."

We were pondering that when the mayor spoke up again.

"I'll tell you something else," he said, "about half drunk, that was one mean coon."

The tab for the entire afternoon was less than $30, and that even included a round of Vienna sausages and Conway Twitty's "We're Not Exactly Strangers" five times on the juke box.

Somebody said it was the only thing the monkey and the coon ever agreed on. It was their favorite song.

Zell and Fuzz

NASHVILLE—The distinguished lieutenant governor of Georgia, Zell Miller, is a big man in Nashville. He knows practically all the country music stars, and they know him.

Zell Miller was instrumental, a lovely choice of words, in helping Don Williams acquire a new drummer for his band from England recently.

For the uninformed, Don Williams was named male vocalist of the year Monday night at the spiffy Country Music Association awards program here.

Zell is also big buddies with Bill Anderson. Ronnie Milsap, who has reached superstar status, was a student of his at Young Harris College. Zell Miller is a country music expert, a country music superfan, and if he is ever elected governor, I would not be surprised if he didn't start work on moving the Grand Ole Opry to Marietta. Make that "May-retta."

Monday afternoon in Nashville, the lieutenant governor went down to old Music Row to The Alamo, Nashville's top shop for rhinestone suits, boots and cowboy hats.

He tried on hats. He priced a $350 pair of boots. But all he bought was a jar of boot polish and a pair of gray socks.

"This is the same way I feel state government should be run," he said, counting out the $3.50 total to the cashier. "You look around at everything you would like to have, but in the end, you buy only the necessities and make do."

A wonderful thing happened to Zell Miller in Nashville this week at the CMA awards show.

Zell met country comedian Jerry Clower, who is from Yazoo City, Mississippi, and who tells funny stories in person and on records for a living. He used to be a fertilizer salesman.

"I've been wanting to meet you, Lieutenant Governor Miller," Jerry Clower said, "'cause I have done used one of your stories on my latest album, and I give you credit for it. I say, 'This story comes from the lieutenant governor of the great state of Georgia.'"

News that George Busbee had just abdicted the governorship couldn't have made Zell Miller happier.

Later, I asked him to tell me the story. There was a reason for that. He's our lieutenant governor, the story happens in Georgia, and we deserve to hear it before the rest of the world.

Ladies and gentleman, Jerry Clower's budding ghostwriter, Zell Miller:

"This is a true story. It happened up in my hometown of Young Harris. Young Harris is a very small town. We didn't even have a fire department. Not even a volunteer fire department.

"One day, a house caught fire. The whole town gathered around to watch it. We were helpless to put it out. About that time, we saw a pickup truck come over the ridge. It was a local character named Fuzz Chastain. He had his wife with him, all their kids, a cousin or two, and some aunts and uncles.

"Fuzz drove right down to where we were all standing, but he didn't stop. He drove that pickup right into the middle of the fire. He jumped out and so did everybody else. They started beating the fire with anything they could find—even their clothes.

"It took 'em thirty minutes, but danged if they didn't put out the fire. The mayor of Young Harris was there. He said, 'This is the most courageous thing I have ever seen in Young Harris. Let's pass the hat for Fuzz Chastain.'

"They raised $17. The mayor presented the mony to Fuzz. 'Fuzz,' he said, 'the people of Young Harris appreciate this heroic act of yours.' Fuzz's hair was singed. His clothes were burned and torn.

"'But Fuzz, there is one thing I'd like to know,' the mayor went on, 'What are you going to do with this money?'

"Fuzz thought a minute and then said, 'Well, Mr. Mayor, I guess the first thing I ought to do is get the brakes fixed on that pickup.'"

If Zell Miller's new "career" takes off, don't worry if he can mix show business with politics. Lest we forget, in many respects, they're the same.

Dreaming at the Twilite

It was Ladies Night at the Twilite Club down on Stewart Avenue, but it was too cold for a crowd. Nights like this are for covering up early, even if the bedroom is a lonely place. There is always the cat.

The band was allegedly country. Mostly, it was loud and did too many Elvis numbers. The singer's shirt was unbuttoned nearly all the way down. That's not country.

"Y'all got any requests?" he asked the sparse audience.

"Yeah," said an old girl sitting at the table next to mine. She was drinking salty dogs. "Turn that thang down."

Big Jim Cook had an easy night. He's the bouncer. The Twilite Club isn't a rough place, by any means, but like the lady who runs it said, "We're getting a little more riff-raff since the Nugget Club burned down."

Jim Cook is twenty-seven and big as a Haggard hit single. He's 6-4 and 240 and he still goes home to Milner, which is near Griffin, on the weekends to see his mother. "I ain't nothing," he says, "but an old country boy from the woods."

He probably could have been more than that, and may yet be. That is his story. Jim Cook was a good enough high school basketball player that Georgia Tech offered a scholarship. He turned it down. "I

just didn't know what I wanted to do," is his explanation. That's not
the best reason in the world to pass up a free college education, but
like the man said, ten years later it will have to do.

The band *was* loud, but we talked between ear-splitting choruses,
and I found out what Jim Cook wants to be more than anything else
is a famous professional wrestler. Granny says *rassler.*

He used to be skinny, he said, but he wandered into one of those
health spas one day and now he could walk around with a Datsun on
his back.

"Some of the wrestlers come in here," he said. "They got me
interested. You can make a lot of money."

You can. You can also get thrown on the floor and crab-locked and
full-Nelsoned until you are a walking bruise. And you can spend a
great deal of your time jumping around in your underwear in front of
screaming crowds packed into tank town high school gymnasiums.
Wrestling has its bush leagues, too. Verne Gagne and Lou Thetz
stayed at the Ritz and drank call brands. Jim Cook is doing Carroll-
ton and Porterdale.

He was married, but that ended in divorce and one child. He was a
yardman at an auto transport company in Atlanta. That ended when
he was laid off. A wrestler now retired, one Rocket Monroe, helped
him learn the basics, and Jim Cook took off for California and
Canada to seek his wrestling fortune.

He didn't find it. Vancouver can be rotten lonely and rainy. He
worked his way back South, back through Kansas City and Oklahoma. A man in Oklahoma told him to go home and find somebody to
teach him to wrestle.

"That's the problem," the big man said. "Most of the guys I know
have to wrestle every night. They don't have the time to train me."

He insists wrestling isn't fake. "You can get hurt if you don't know
what you're doing," he said. No matter where he wrestles, the place
is packed. Watching wrestling is like eating collards. If you're
hooked, you're hooked.

He's gone against some of the biggies in the area: The Anderson
Brothers, Stan Hansen, Dick Slater, a Korean guy whose name he
can't spell, Bill White, and a masked fellow who calls himself The
Executioner. Mostly, he loses. "But I'm a good guy," he explained.
"The people always cheer me on."

Jim Cook stayed around until the Twilite Club went dark for a few
restful hours. "The only time we really have trouble," he had said, "is
when somebody comes in from another part of town and doesn't
know what kind of place this is. Usually, by the time anybody is
ready to do more than talk, he's too drunk to fight."

When he finally went home, it was to a room at the Alamo Plaza Motel, a southside relic. There would hopefully be the chance to work out the following day. And maybe there will also be the chance someday to get off the bottom of the cards, to get out of the preliminaries and into the main events. To make a name. To make a buck. To be there in the City Auditorium on Friday nights when the masses come and the lights are shining brightly.

A country boy from Milner has a dream.

The Den Mother of Country Music

NASHVILLE—They put Tootsie Bess to rest on a snowy hillside in Nashville Tuesday afternoon. When she died of cancer at sixty-four the other day, they should have lowered every flag in the city to half-mast. She was somebody. She was the den mother of country music.

Without her, there might not have been the stardom and the music of people like Tom T. Hall. Or Kris Kristofferson. Or Roger Miller. Or Johnny Rodrigues. Or Hank Williams, or any number of pickers and singers who have made what otherwise would have been nothing more than Chattanooga North into a multi-million dollar recording Mecca called Music City U.S.A.

Without her, many who stayed and finally caught their dreams might have long since caught the next bus back home. Like a man said at Tootsie's funeral Tuesday, "You can find rhinestones and applause in Nashville, but before you do, it can be the loneliest place in the world."

Hattie Louise "Tootsie" Bess ran a beer joint in Nashville at Fifth and Broadway called Tootsie's Orchid Lounge. There was a back door. It led to an alley that led to the stage entrance of the old Ryman Auditorium, for years the home of the Grand Ole Opry.

Grant Turner, the Opry announcer, said, "You could leave Tootsie's at 7:58 and still be on stage at the Opry at 8 o'clock." So many did just that.

When Tom T. Hall first came to Nashville, he nearly starved. Tootsie fed him. Tootsie encouraged him. Tootsie gave him pocket money. Today, Tom T. Hall sells millions of records and trucks on television.

Kris Kristofferson worked construction and swept floors in Nashville while trying to peddle his music. He was one of Tootsie's pets. She kept him going until another star was born.

Roger Miller was a Nashville bellhop. He would write one of his biggest hits, "Dang Me," in a booth at Tootsie's.

"She ran a beer joint," said Tom T. Hall, "but to young songwriters and musicians, she was a small finance company, a booking agent, and a counsellor."

Maybe Ernest Tubb put it even better. "Tootsie," he said, "was the softest touch in town."

I was in her place only once. But I remember the beer being cold and the atmosphere being warm and Tootsie saying as my party left, "Y'all come back when you can stay longer."

Her juke box had million sellers. It also had non-sellers. When nobody else would play a youngster's record, Tootsie would put it next to "Hello Walls," and give the kid the best chance she could.

She kept order with a hatpin. Get rowdy and out you went at the point of her hatpin. Come back tomorrow and apologize, and all was forgiven.

There were five inches of fresh snow on the ground in Nashville Tuesday. Still, the funeral home was packed with people and flowers.

The registry was a country music who's who. Mel Tillis sent flowers. There was a wreath from Ben Smathers and his mountain cloggers. Ernest Tubb and his son Justin sent a heart-shaped arrangement. There was a break in the middle of the heart. It was pierced with a hatpin.

Roy Acuff sat down front for the services. One of the Wilburn Brothers was close to him. Included in the grieving family was Tootsie's son-in-law, who is an Opry drummer. Tom T. Hall was one of the pallbearers. Grant Turner got up and said a few words. And Connie Smith stood behind Tootsie's lavender casket and sang "In the Sweet By and By," "Amazing Grace," and "How Great Thou Art." She has never sounded better.

Tootsie had friends who weren't stars. "She was just as happy to see a ditch digger walk in as the biggest name in town," said a friend. Sitting next to a millionaire singer at the funeral was a man in a service station outfit. He hadn't had time to wash the grease off his hands.

The preacher read a telegram from Tennessee Sen. Howard Baker. He talked about the necessity of loving one another and said Mrs. Bess, as he called her, performed that task exactly as the Good Book intended.

It could be the Good Lord likes the company of a bighearted saloonkeeper, too.

Willie at the White House

WASHINGTON—People wearing bags over their heads and carrying signs that screamed about "massacres" in their native Iran paraded in front of the White House Wednesday evening.

To the north of the city at Camp David, three powerful leaders of three powerful nations struggled to find a way to bring peace to another troubled land.

The papers were filled with stories of death and destruction in Nicaragua, and half the world is on strike.

But the night was clear, and cool and the moon was full and bright in Washington Wednesday. And out on the south lawn of the White House, a million miles from everything else, a bearded man wearing a red bandana took a long pull from a wine bottle and commenced to sing.

He sang "Whiskey River" first; then he sang "Crazy" and "Amazing Grace" and "Georgia" and something called "Blue Eyes Crying in the Rain." As he sang "Blue Eyes Crying in the Rain" I had a thought, probably an outrageous one, but at least worth a moment of consideration:

Jimmy Carter didn't make his own party Wednesday night, the one he threw to honor stockcar drivers. His wife announced to the crowd that "only something the magnitude of the summit talks would have kept him away."

He made a mistake by not coming. And he made a mistake by not bringing Egypt's Sadat and Israel's Begin with him.

Sit the two of them down together in front of Willie Nelson, I thought. Bring the people with the bags over their heads inside, too. Give them all a cold beer and let them listen to Willie Nelson. After "Blue Eyes Crying in the Rain," who would still want to fight?

Wednesday night was Jimmy Carter fulfilling a promise. When he was governor of Georgia, he made it an annual practice to host stockcar drivers and even sportwriters at the mansion on West Paces Ferry.

You know about the stockcar racing. Stockcar racing isn't Watkins Glen or spiffy gentlemen in sleek Porsches and Ferraris. It is Talledega and Daytona and Atlanta International Raceway and beer and fried chicken and a punch in the nose because you said a Chevrolet can whip a Dodge or, worse, you insulted the glorious memory of Fireball Roberts.

"Jimmy told us if he ever got to be president," explained driver David Pearson, "we would share in some of the glory. Here we are."

And there they were. Pearson, Petty, Waldrip, Yarborough, and Bill France, the head kabolla of stockcar racing. And even some sportswriters and even Billy Carter, and especially Willie Nelson, who sang with Amy and Rosalynn and Billy's wife, Sybil.

The night was heavy with doubleknit and denim.

The Washington papers the next day didn't quite know what to make of the affair. They said it did prove we are under the reign of a populist president. They went into great detail concerning the Carters' love for stockcar racing and explained stockcar racing grew in the South from an earlier preoccupation with running moonshine.

"I ain't never run moonshine," Richard Petty told a reporter, "but I don't know about the rest of my family."

I go back to those parties at the governor's mansion. The first one was a flop because Rosalynn had charge of the food and entertainment. She offered an exotic menu that included fish-like things that still had their eyes. The entertainment was an operatic trio.

I can still see A. J. Foyt shifting uncomfortably from one cowboy boot to another and Jabe Thomas driving to the front of the mansion in his mechanic's truck. I can still hear somebody saying, "This would make Curtis Turner roll over in his grave." Rosalynn Carter stepped onto the bandshell behind the White House Wednesday night and apologized for all that. She had learned her lesson. The fare this evening was beer and wine and roast beef and ham and corn bread. The program announced, "Selections by Willie Nelson."

I could probably dabble around in all this for some hidden political meaning. But the heck with that.

What happened Wednesday night at the home of the president of the United States was a large group of mostly Southern people got together in the backyard for a picnic and to listen to one of their own sing his red bandana off. Andy Jackson used to give the same kind of parties here, and he wound up on the $20 bill.

In the middle of that singing, when people had squared off to clog on the lawn, a fellow I know from Georgia came to my table and whispered in my ear:

"My great-grandfather was wounded at the Battle of Sharpsburg. He was captured at Gettysburg. He had to limp all the way home to Georgia. If he could see this tonight, he'd think we won after all."

Sweet Innocence

That was her daddy, the girl said, playing with the country band that performed, sort of, in one corner of the room. They played the old songs—hungry songs and cheatin' songs—and they made them sound even older.

Her mama was in and out, too. She was a stout, tightfaced woman and she gave the appearance of running things. A would-be rowdy was rendered nearly peepless after mama suggested his conduct was reaching the bouncing stage.

It doesn't matter the name of the town or the name of the joint, because there are maybe a million towns and million joints just like them.

Picture a two-lane highway running through what seems like nowhere on a warm Georgia spring night. Suddenly, up ahead, the glare of neon is blinking and beckoning. Park some trucks around. Behold, the local fast crowd in its natural habitat.

The girl worked feverishly behind the bar while daddy played and mama patrolled. She was pretty. Dark hair and dark eyes. Plump, a little, but pleasingly so. She wore pink chiffon. Tight pants and a blouse that exposed little, but enough to gather the eyes of the gentleman customers seated around on the bar stools.

I judged her innocent somehow, and trained to perform. At her obviously tender age, could she know what her audience was thinking as she moved gracefully back and forth behind the bar? Likely not.

They ordered beer, of course, and from some unseen cache she produced it in cold, longneck bottles. They were emptied nearly as fast as she could bring more.

There was booze, too. That was surprising, this far into the hinterlands. I wondered to a man next to me how long the county had had liquor.

"Long as there's been anybody around to drink it, I guess," he said. Then, he corrected himself. "You mean how long's it been legal? Four or five years, I guess."

And the Baptists and the bootleggers are still fighting it, somebody added.

I watched the girl. She had been trained well. Her performance was splendid. I waited for a slip, something that would unveil that innocence that seemed unfit for midnight in a smoky, backroads saloon. It never came.

A youngster sat alone at the end of the bar, nursing a beer.

"One more?" the girl asked.

The youngster nearly blushed from her attention. He held the bottle against a light. It was nearly empty.

"Believe I've had enough," he said.

"Just one more?" the girl persisted. "For me?"

"One more," the youngster said. He seemed pleased he had pleased her.

She even sang. Daddy played while she sang. The place was hers all over again.

"Sounds just like Linda Ronstadt, don't she?" the man with the liquor information said to me.

I agreed. It's smart, I figured, for a stranger to agree.

The band took a break, and the girl asked nobody in particular for money to play the jukebox. To a man, her subjects reached into their pockets for change.

The chosen one marched to the jukebox and obediently pushed the buttons as the girl called out the numbers of her favorite songs.

The crowd began to thin later. There were no more calls for drinks. The girl walked to where I was sitting and propped herself on the bar. She asked where I was from. I told her.

"I was in Atlanta once," she said. She named the hotel. "I didn't like it. That place is too big for me."

There it was. Simple girl, simple tastes. Maybe one day she can leave this, I thought. Find some nice fellow with a good job and raise a family.

"Daddy gone?" the girl asked a waitress, who nodded yes.

"Mama, too?" she asked next. Mama was gone, too.

"Damn, it's about time," said the girl, reaching for a bottle of vodka on the shelf. She filled a glass and heaved down its contents in one hard gulp.

4

THOSE WERE THE DAYS

The first column in this section is about my fifteenth year high school reunion that turned out to be a tremendous success. One of my ex-wives came. She looked terrific. Dudley Stamps, who was a good friend in school, also came to the reunion.

He said to me, "I see your damn picture in the newspaper sometimes, but I don't read any of that garbage." When we had some beer later, I hugged his neck anyway.

The last column in this section is about Bill Johnson, who was a classmate in college. He died. I wish I could hug his neck one more time.

The Class of '64

The fellow who was president of my high school senior class called the other day to ask a favor. He wants me to write something witty and clever to be used as an invitation to our fifteenth year class reunion next summer.

We never had a tenth year reunion, which was just as well with me. The principal's office statute of limitations probably doesn't run out in ten years. They might still have had something on me.

Like there was the book I never got around to returning to the school library. The posse didn't come back until the early seventies. Our librarian was also the principal's wife, and she ran the library with an iron hand. Nuclear power plants are maintained with less regimentation.

I was remembering some of the library rules at my high school:

—— Thou shalt not touch a book unless your hands have been scrubbed clean and thoroughly inspected by the head librarian. ("A smudge on a book is an insult to literature.")

—— Thou shalt not wear wristwatches or bracelets into the library because a wristwatch or a bracelet could make a scratch on one of the library tables, God forbid.

(I am convinced anybody caught scratching a library table at my high school would have been draggd out behind the auditorium and shot, not to mention having his or her library privileges taken away.)

—— Thou shalt not talk while in the library, nor giggle nor grunt nor pull a chair from under a table so as to make the noise a chair being pulled from under a table will inevitably make.

(Once a fat girl, who was stronger than I, punched me in the belly in the library because I wouldn't give her the sports section of the newspaper. I grunted from the punch and attempted to flee for fear of further blows.

(In my haste, I pulled my chair from under the table and it made a noise. I had to stay after school every day for a week and my stomach hurt for a month. The fat girl's nickname was "Mean Mama," incidentally.)

Irregardless—which isn't a word but was used a hundred times a day by one of the coaches—I still look back on my high school years with favor.

I was on the baseball team and the basketball team, and I was in the Key Club and I had a steady girlfriend, which is another reason I wasn't particularly disturbed when we had no tenth year reunion.

The last time I saw my steady girlfriend, who later became much more than that, she was loading our living room furniture, my stereo, the bed, and the washer and dryer into the back of a truck.

Who knows what she might still have been in the market for?

Frankly, I am puzzled as to what to write witty and clever for the invitation.

I can say we'll all drink a few beers, likely, and we won't have to hide behind Robert's and Alf's drive-in to do it.

We'll take a look at one another and say things like, "You haven't changed a bit" when what we really mean is, "I wouldn't have known you in a million years because the last time I saw you, you had hair."

We'll see who is fat now who didn't used to be, and who lost weight and who is still obnoxious and who got rich and who wouldn't kiss you goodnight for love nor money in school but has been pregnant practically every day since graduation. And who has retained all his hair and his slim, boyish figure. Like me.

We'll listen to the old songs and tell a lie or two.

And maybe for old times' sake, I'll even have a dance with my steady girlfriend who later became much more than that while somebody sings, "In the Still of the Night."

Come to think of it, fifteen years later is a perfect time to have a high school reunion. It's a short enough period for the good memories to be fresh and for the ravages of age to have taken only a soft toll.

And long enough to have forgiven an overdue library book, a punch in the belly, and even the night I walked into an empty house and found out for the first time adulthood isn't all it was cracked up to be.

They Were Playing Our Songs

The three of us were children of the forties, but we had left the campus when the trouble began. We were born of men back from the war and the women who waited for them to come home.

We barely remember Korea. My daddy was gone two years, and I really never knew why. The name Harry Truman rings a vague bell. The thing I remember most about Ike was how the people down home cursed him for spending too much time playing golf at Augusta.

Kennedy was ours, but we lost him in high school. Vietnam was festering during our college days, but on a sleepy Deep South campus, it would take longer for the explosion of dissent to finally come.

After school, one of us—ordered to do so—went to the fight. The other two, lucky as hell, stayed home and learned about making a living.

We made the same fraternal pledge fifteen years ago. That tie still binds us somehow. One of us is losing his hair. Another has put on a few pounds. I get down in my back occasionally and I don't sleep as well as I used to.

Monday night was a reunion of sorts. It is rare we can be together as a threesome for an evening out anymore.

But this was special. They were playing our songs at a club called the Harlequin. We wouldn't have missed it.

First, you must get this picture: The year is 1964. The band is black and loud. Beer cans are illegal on campus. There was such a thing in those days, however, as "Humdinger" milkshake cups. They would hold two full cans until they became soggy and fell apart. A date must be selected carefully. She must not mind beer on her skirt. There were a lot of good women like that in 1964.

And the band would play until midnight, time to beat the curfew back to the girls' dorms. The frolic before was always grand and glorious because, as that campus anthem went, we came to college not for knowledge, but to raise hell while we're here.

Our music was a soulful strut. Maurice Williams and the Zodiacs, "Stay;" The Isley Brothers, "Twist and Shout;" The Temptations, "My Girl;" The Drifters, "Save the Last Dance for Me;" Marvin Gaye and the classic, "Stubborn Kind of Fellow."

And two more groups, hallowed be their names: The Atlanta Tams. The Showmen.

We were on the edge of our seats Monday night. And then, there they were. Four black men from Norfolk, Virginia. Four black men who can dance and sing and take you back where, the Lord knows, you never wanted to leave in the first place.

Four black men called The Showmen who put "39-21-46" on a record years ago.

"We're gonna take the roof off this place," they said, and they did.

The Tams were next. "Atlanta's own Atlanta Tams," announced the announcer. They have aged, the Tams. But their voices still blend in perfect, deep harmony, and when they sang "What Kind of Fool?" everybody in the house was nineteen years old again.

As is the custom, we went down front to the stage before the night was over. We sang and we danced along. Our parents did the same to Big Band swing. A group of teenyboppers went crazy over a child named Shaun Cassidy at the Omni the other night. Who knows what sound will attract our children?

But does it really matter? Music, any kind of music, is memories and sometimes hope for the future. Music can soothe, music can hurt. Music can be lost loves and old friends. Music can give advice worth heeding.

"Listen to that," said one of us to the other two Monday night. "They're right, you know."

The Tams were singing. It was one of their old songs. You have missed something if you have never heard it. Three fellows bound for middle-age gathered in every word:

"Be Young.

"Be Foolish.

"Be Happy."

When the Smoke Had Cleared

Dorsey Hill still laughs about the night I came through fraternity rush at the Sigma Pi house in Athens.

"Damn'dest sight I ever saw," he says. "You were wearing white socks and black, pointed-toe shoes, and your head was skinned. I mean *skinned*. I said, 'Where on earth did THAT come from?'"

But they took in the skinhead anyway at the house on Milledge Avenue, the one with the white columns, and there were some high times the next four years.

I forget exactly who went to put the Chi Omega owl to the torch. The Chi Omega soroity house was across the street from ours, and they were an uppity bunch. One year they built a paper owl, a huge thing, for rush.

We were sitting on our front porch in those marvelous rocking chairs, and somebody thought it would be a good idea to burn the owl.

Every firetruck in Athens showed up to put it out. So did Dean Tate, dean of University of Georgia men. When the smoke had cleared, we were on something called "social probation."

That meant we couldn't have another party until every member had graduated from school, had fulfilled his military obligation, and had fathered at least two legitimate children.

In retrospect, it was worth it. Fifty silly sorority girls, outraged and bewildered, watching their precious paper owl go up in a glorious blaze. Strike another one for dear old Sigma Pi.

I could do this all day. There was the basement we called the "Boom-Boom Room." Beware, young coed, to enter there. It was in the "Boom-Boom Room" where we administered a water-drinking torture called "Cardinal Puff" during initiation. A pledge almost died after "Cardinal Puff" one night.

Maybe that is what started it. Sigma Pi once thrived. We had the captain of the football team, the captain of the basektball team. But hard times came along.

I heard they had to sell that beautiful old house to pay their way out of debt. I heard the membership had fallen off to almost nothing. I heard the university had even taken away the charter and that Sigma Pi had died a quiet, slow death on the campus.

I shed a quick tear, but nothing more. It's been a long time.

But there was a telephone call last week. It was from a Georgia coed. She had a sense of urgency in her voice.

"You've got to help," she said.

"Help who?" I answered.

"Sigma Pi at Georgia," she went on. "I'm dating this guy who's a member. They're trying to make a comeback, but they're about to go bankrupt. They lost a couple of pledges who were supposed to move into the house. They needed their money for rent. One of them joined the Navy."

I called the Sigma Pi house in Athens. The president answered the telephone. We used to have eighty members. "We've got eleven," he said. We sent more than that to burn the Chi Omega owl.

The new house is being rented from a university faculty member, the young man said. The current members are trying to hold on to the house until more members can be pledged. More members, more money.

"We even keep the heat turned off," he said, "to save money." There are no parties, the president told me, because there is no money for parties. There are no meals at the house because who can afford cooks? What Sigma Pi in Athens needs and wants is some help from the alumni. A donation, maybe, at least a visit to help with rush.

"Just some encouragement," said the president.

That's not much to ask. I'll try to get up a group and come over, I said. We'll have a few cold ones and talk about it. And afterwards maybe we'll all go over to Chi Omega and apologize.

In a pig's eye, we will.

Sweetheart of Sigma Chi

How I got invited to a University of Georgia fraternity party at my age isn't the story here. The story is what I saw when I went there.

It was the Sigma Chi's annual gathering to select a chapter sweetheart. Sigma Chis the nation over take selecting a chapter sweetheart seriously because somebody once immortalized young ladies so chosen with a popular song entitled, appropriately enough, "Sweetheart of Sigma Chi."

A banquet preceded the party. I don't know what I expected. I had seen *Animal House*. I knew that it was only a short time ago the college campus was a social battleground. Sometimes, it was just a battleground.

But what, I asked myself, are the prevailing moods and customs of the campus on this, the eve of the 1980s?

I knew about the early sixties. It was button-down, slick-it-back, eat, drink and chase Mary in the tight skirt and monogrammed sweater. The late sixties and early seventies were angry and hip and taking things that made you crazy and wearing clothes to look the part.

The Sigma Chis on this night came dressed as a GQ ad. They were three-pieced and button-downed and blown-dried almost to a man. Their dates were clones from the Phi Mu house fifteen years ago.

The chapter president, whose hair was shorter than mine, opened with a moving invocation. Gentlemen rose from their seats when ladies excused themselves from the tables. The dinner lasted well over an hour. Nobody threw a single morsel of food.

When the new sweetheart was introduced, the chapter stood as one and sang her their delicate, obviously inspired rendition of the sweetheart song while she cried. Donna Reed would have played her part. John Belushi would have been asked to leave.

There was some loosening up when the party began, but the frolic that followed wouldn't have qualified as even a mild public disturbance.

The band played Marvin Gaye's "Stubborn Kind of Fellow," "Sixty Minute Man," and the Temptations' "My Girl." I know all the words to all three songs. A young man asked for something by Jackie Wilson, and the band gave him "Lonely Teardrops." Who turned back the time machine?

The booze was mostly beer. Somebody had a half-gallon of Jim Beam bourbon and was pouring it into Coca-Cola. The smokers I saw were pulling on Marlboros.

Later in the evening, a small ice fight broke out—it always did—and everybody danced the "Gator." I know grown people who still dance the "Gator," which involves lying on the floor and acting like a half-crazed reptile with a bad case of the shakes.

The University of Georgia was never a leader in the radical league and the war is over now and things are quieter everywhere, but it did occur to me after the Sigma Chi party that perhaps life on the campus has returned to normal, sis-boom-bah.

—— Fraternities and sororities, spurned by many students just a few years ago, are making a big comeback at Georgia. "We are nearly overrun during rush," a Sigma Chi told me.

—— Pot smoking is still prevalent among some students, I was told, but "drinking is back stronger than ever." Sigma Chi fines members caught smoking pot in the fraternity house.

—— Political activism is down on the Georgia campus. SDS is dead and gone. The student body president ran with a bag over his head, the "Unknown Candidate" with no platform. He won in a walk.

The strongest and most active group on campus, believe it or not, is the Young Americans for Freedom, a conservative, pro-Reagan outfit.

"They don't want to stop a war," said an editor at the student newspaper, "they want to start one."

Wonders never cease, and spring quarter approaches. Let's go get a six-pack and have a panty raid.

One for Bill Johnson

ATHENS—Winter quarter was a sinus headache that seemed to linger on and on. The glory of the fall and football had passed. Springtime on the University of Georgia campus was always brightness and color and cold beer in tall cups and young things from Fitzgerald and Dalton whose mommas would have fainted had they known their babies were parading around in public dressed like that. And would it all ever return again and save us from January's gloom?

There was only a trickle of people about the campus Monday. Joggers ran up Lumpkin Street. Will this generation's legacy be a pair of worn running shoes and a green sweatshirt? The Campus Crusade for Christ is presenting *Master of Illusion* this week. One of the sorority houses has a banner hanging outside congratulating a sister for being accepted to the Harvard Law School. Girls used to go to college to find a husband.

But things change. There is even a sign now at the entrance to the athletic department training room in the Georgia Coliseum that reads, "Women are in the training room. Remember to wear your shorts." I was thinking of some names like Rissmiller and Swinford and Ridlehuber as I read that sign. Would they have stood for such encroachment? Women in the training room, indeed.

Who can come back here—even in the depths of the winter doldrums—and not launch himself into a sentimental journey? Boys become men here. Gangly, chirping girls become sophisticated women. How many of us had that first, heady taste of sin on these grounds? I recall being anxious to leave. I was out of my mind.

Bill Johnson loved Georgia. He loved everything about it. We were in the same, overloaded boat. We both had school, and we both—by choice—had work as well. Bill Johnson was employed by an Athens radio station. I worked for an Athens newspaper.

How do friendships begin? He was "the voice" of Athens High School sports. I was second on a two-man sports department totem pole. The boss covered the Bulldogs. I had Athens High. My friend Bill Johnson and I were together in a thousand rickety, crowded press boxes in places like Gainesville and Augusta and Hartwell and Elberton.

He was good at what he did. Bill Johnson was barely past twenty, but there could be no question as to his promise as a sportscaster. His voice was smooth, yet strong. There were those nights after games we would drive back to Athens together and fantasize about our futures.

"Do you think," he would ask, "we'll ever get to the big time?"

I reckoned that we would. We promised if one of us made it and the other did not, the friendship would last. I have never made a more sincere promise.

There is something about those days of dreaming. There are no limits in an ambitious mind. Bill Johnson would be as good and as important as Ed Thilenius someday. And I would be paid to write a story about a ball game for an Atlanta newspaper.

The last time I saw Bill Johnson was the day he graduated from Georgia. We had a few last beers together and said how much we would miss each other. He also had to leave a young wife in Athens for a short military obligation. But then he would be back and look out, Lindsey Nelson.

That was March 1966. Spring quarter was beautiful that year. We wrote back and forth. He was stationed somewhere in Texas.

Came the autumn and a wonderful Georgia football team. You remember. Kirby Moore. Kent Lawrence. George Patton. Bill Stanfill.

There was the second half comeback at Auburn that gave Vince Dooley his first Southeastern Conference title. Undefeated Georgia Tech fell the next week in Stanford Stadium. And Georgia would go on to the Cotton Bowl and belittle Southern Methodist.

Somewhere tucked away I have Bill Johnson's last letter. He was ill, he said. It was the first I knew about it. Some crazy blood infection. But he said don't worry. He said the doctors were thinking of letting him go to Dallas to see Georgia in the Cotton Bowl.

A week later, on December 7, Bill Johnson died. He was twenty-three.

The church up in Summerville, his hometown, was packed. When we carried him through town to the cemetery, the old men stopped on the streets and covered their hearts with their hats. The young widow cried hard.

Monday, as I walked across the campus, I remembered another promise. I told Bill Johnson I would mention him one day in a column if I ever got a job with a big city newspaper.

This is that mention. It's for a friend, a long time gone.

5

THE VIEW FROM LEFT FIELD

I knew it was time for me to get out of sportswriting when I covered the 1978 Super Bowl game between Dallas and Denver and enjoyed the halftime show that featured dogs catching frisbees more than I did the football game.

I will still fall into a sports column now and then, however. It's comfortable there, like an old pair of sneakers.

At the Ball Game With My Dad

I would have taken my father out to the ball game Tuesday night. I would have taken him to the Atlanta Stadium to see Pete Rose try to break Wee Willie Keeler's hitting streak record.

His birthday is Saturday. He would have been sixty-six. A trip to the ball game would have been a nice present from a son to his father.

He was an athlete himself, my dad. And he was a strapping man with alleged blinding speed in his youth. He was taller than Pete Rose, but similar in stocky frame. One time he picked up the back of a 1949 Hudson. I saw him do it.

My father would have loved Tuesday night at the ball park. Nice summer evening. Big, noisy crowd. My father always enjoyed singing the national anthem at baseball games.

He had a big voice, a booming voice that could cut you down at one hundred yards when it broke into "He Leadeth Me" or our national anthem, his two favorite songs. He always sang along when they played the national anthem, no matter where or what event. One time I said to him, "I wish you wouldn't sing so loud. It's embarrassing."

He said to me, "Son, it's embarrassing when you don't sing along with me."

55

Tuesday night, just before Pete Rose stepped up to bat, going for forty-five straight, my father and I would have stood shoulder-to-shoulder and sung the national anthem together.

Pete Rose is my father's kind of man, I was thinking when Rose approached the plate in the first inning. Just before the game began, he had his picture made with a crippled boy and put his hat on the crippled boy's head.

"Look at the way that man moves," my father would have said of Rose. "He doesn't waste a motion. He has speed. He has strength. He has determination. That's the kind of man you want in a foxhole with you."

My father was a soldier. A damn good one.

His only objection to Pete Rose might have been Rose's hair. I noticed it precariously near his shoulders. His ears disappeared weeks ago. My father wore a crew cut. He thought everybody else should.

"I'll never get used to long hair on a ballplayer or a soldier," he might have said as Larry McWilliams of the Braves threw the first pitch of the ball game—a curve—"It's not what the Lord intended."

The curve to Rose is low for ball one. And then a foul deep to right that misses being a double by five feet. A fast ball outside, a curve catches the inside corner, the count goes full, two more fouls, then ball four. The streak holds at forty-four.

I never saw a major league baseball game with my father. We saw plenty of service ball together. He once coached the Fort Benning team. Coached in a Hawaiian shirt and a straw hat.

Later, we bummed around South Georgia one summer. My father had fallen on hard times, but he kept a ten-year-old fed and cared for during three of the best months of my life.

That summer, we spent night after hot South Georgia night fighting gnats and eating peanuts in broken-down Class D parks in Waycross and Moultrie and Tifton where something called the Georgia-Florida League still had life.

There is something special about a man with his son at a baseball game. A man and his son sat next to me Monday night when Pete Rose extended his batting streak to forty-four. As Pete strode to the plate for the first time, the boy asked his dad if he would take him to the rest room.

"Not now, son," said the father. "Not now. Pete Rose is batting."

The boy held on, uncomfortably, but appearing to understand the necessity of the effort.

When a man takes his son to a baseball game, I think, it establishes a link, one that won't easily be broken even in the face of a subsequent premature parting that might leave other scars.

I know that to be a fact.

Rose came up for a second time. "Let's go, Pete," my father would have screamed, loud enough to be heard in LaGrange. What the heck. Let him have his fun.

First pitch, Rose swings. A shot up the middle. Young McWilliams' gloved hand appears from nowhere and spears the drive. Rose drops his bat and gives the youngster a hand. Mostly, my father would have enjoyed the game Tuesday night because it was a vivid American scene. It was an act of patriotism, somehow, to have been there.

He would have looked at his fellow Americans eating hot dogs and drinking beer, he would have heard their cheers for the home runs by Horner and Murphy, and he would have said something like, "This is why your daddy went to war, son. This is what we fought to keep."

Rose is up again. The inning is the fifth. The game is tied, 3-3. A fake bunt, ball one. Another ball. Then a ground out to short. The tension builds.

Now, it is the seventh. The brutal Gene Garber is pitching for the Braves. A runner is on. One out. A fast ball strike on the outside corner. Two straight balls. A foul tip, the count is even. Then, another shot by Rose, toward left, the opposite field. But Horner is there for the out and a double play.

A final chance, and only that, remains. The ninth. The game has turned to slaughter. The Reds, for once, are the victims, 16-4. Atlanta has twenty-one hits. Even Garber has one. Pete Rose, whose name even sounds like a line drive, has none.

Two outs. Rose at the bat. "Pete! Pete! Pete!" the stadium is begging.

The first pitch from Garber. An attempted drag bunt to third goes foul. Two straight balls. A foul tip.

The ball leaves Garber's hand. A split second later, we will know.

Strike three. Swinging. It is over.

What Pete Rose did—hit safely in forty-four straight games— wasn't a man on the moon, I reminded myself as the stadium lights dimmed. It wasn't a lonely flight across the Atlantic or the first heart transplant.

But it was a good and honorable thing, a fierce man with a bat in his hand, playing a boy's game as it was meant to be played.

And I am thankful I had the chance to witness part of it, even the bitter end.

Tuesday night at the ball game, me and my dad had a helluva good time.

A Case of the Bleeps

I missed Pete Rose's post-game television interview Tuesday night after he had failed to extend his batting streak.

I was busy typing in the press box. I never promised the news editor a Rose column, but it seemed the thing to do what with the excitement the hitting streak had generated.

I understand it was an interesting interview. Ted Turner's nation-wide network carried it, and little old ladies coast-to-coast were swallowing their snuff.

Pete Rose, American Hero, said some dirty words. There were cameras all around him. He didn't know one was live. Ah, the magic of television.

I know some of the words Pete Rose said. Randy Donaldson of the Braves staff told me. Obviously, I can't print any of them here, but one has four letters and the other two have seven.

One of the other two may be hyphhenated, come to think of it. Spelling dirty words can be a tricky business, because most of them aren't in the dictionary. It's anybody's guess.

What we use in the newspaper for dirty words people say is "bleep." Using "bleep" shows how the influence of the electronic media is even slipping into real journalism.

When Johnny Carson says a dirty word on television, you don't hear the dirty word, you hear an electronic sound that goes "Bleep." Ah, the magic of television.

Wednesday, I was reading one of the local sportswriters' stories from the Rose interview. He quoted Pete as saying to Atlanta pitcher, Larry McWilliams, who robbed him of a base hit with a grand catch. "Why the hell did you catch that bleep-bleep ball?"

"Hell" is now OK in the newspaper. It is finally off the bleep list, in other words. Calling it a "bleep-bleep" ball also seems to indicate my earlier suspicions were correct. "Bleep-bleep" must be a hyphenated dirty word.

The sportswriter also quoted Rose as saying to all the sportswrit-ers Tuesday night, "I'm going to miss you bleeps."

That bleep is no mystery to me at all. I know what ballplayers call sportswriters. Once, a ballplayer said to me, "You bleeping bleep, get your bleeping bleep away from my locker, or I'm going to knock the bleep out of you, and you can print that in your bleeping news-paper, and I don't give a bleep if you bleeping do."

I ran for the door. To save my bleep.

I am sure there were viewers Tuesday night offended by Rose's language. I just hope nobody was surprised that a big league baseball player curses. Cursing is a part of the game. Like spitting tobacco juice, scratching and adjusting, and becoming a free agent.

The first curse word I ever heard was at a baseball game. We chose up sides in the second grade and my team's first baseman, a fat boy named Roy who should have been in the fifth-grade game, chased a foul ball. He stumbled into a gully where there were many briars.

"Bleep!" he said as he picked the briars from his bleep, which was sore for a week.

The only thing Pete Rose said Tuesday night that surprised me was his expression of displeasure that the Braves' Gene Garber would pitch to him in the ninth inning "like it was the seventh game of the World Series."

What did Rose expect from a professional like Garber? Gene Garber pitches like Pete Rose bats. With the intensity of a runaway locomotive. Would Rose have eased up had it been Garber going for some sort of pitching record?

I know a word worse than any Pete Rose used on television Tuesday night. As much as I admire the man, I insist it must be applied to his remarks concerning Garber.

I has four letters, too.

B-U-S-H.

Scooter T. Washington: Blue Chipper

It was all over the Sunday paper about the recruiting of young athletes to play football at large universities in the region. It's that season. Children are snatched away from their mothers' arms back home in Twobit County and the next thing you know, the Head Coach is saying, "Ol' Dram Bowie from down in Twobit County is the finest prospect since Jiggy Smaha." Which brings up that musical question, has anybody seen Jiggy Smaha lately?

Recruiting is important. "You gotta have the horses," a coach once told me, "before you can pull the wagon." Coaches talk like that. Translated, it means if he doesn't get off his tail and sign some talent, he'll be selling tires at K-Mart the next time toe meets leather.

What I hear is that Tennessee is making a big move into Georgia this year in search of recruits to rebuild the once-mighty Volunteer program. You don't sign to go to Knoxville. You are sentenced there. Clemson is also usually heavy into seeking Georgia material. A Clemson raid especially makes Georgia Tech people mad.

"You know that tractorcade this weekend?" one asked me.

"They weren't farmers," he said. "They were Clemson fans on their way to Sears to buy clothes for the Gator Bowl."

From the various sources around the Southeast, I have come into possession of the list of the most-wanted high school athletes in the state. None have been signed yet. They are known as "blue-chippers" to the alumni. Coaches call them "job-savers." Here's the list.

ARDELL GROVER—Linebacker from Atlanta. Missed half his senior season with terminal acne. "He'll hit you," say the recruiters. Especially if you call him "Zit head," which a tenth-grader did shortly before Ardell rendered him unconscious during fifth-period study hall.

MARVIN PALAFOX—Marvin is a tight end. He's from Macon. Wears No. 82. Scored same number on his college boards. "Great hands," say the coaches. So do the cheerleaders.

SCOOTER T. WASHINGTON—Half-back from Savannah. Olympic speed. Expensive tastes. Wants two Cadillacs and a mink coat like Reggie Jackson's to sign. Answers the telephone, "You need the loot to get the Scoot." Contact through his agent Sam the Fly at the Wise Owl Pool and Recreation Hall, Savannah.

BILLY BOB WALTON—Offensive tackle from Moultrie. Extremely offensive. Friends call him "Dump Truck" because that's how big he is and he could eat all the pork chops and mashed potatoes out of the back of one. Made *Tifton Gazette* All-Area team. Makes Junior Samples look like David Niven. Loves buttermilk, but can't spell it.

LAVONNE (The Rolling Stone) LARUE—Led Columbus school in interceptions. Also led burglary ring to back entrance of Harry's One-Stop Stereo Shop. Got one-to-five, but sentence suspended when entire student body turned out as character witnesses after suggestion they do so by several of The Stone's "acquaintances."

"Can start for any college team in the country," says his coach, who didn't start him once and still carries the scars.

IRVING BOATRIGHT III—Quarterback for a fashionable northside Atlanta private school. Father prominent Atlanta attorney with homes on Hilton Head and Sea Island. Can't play a lick, but the head coach gets free legal advice and either house three weeks each summer. Started every game during high school career. Bedwetter.

BARTHANATOMAY RIMJOB—Place-kicker. Son of Pakistani professor of Eastern philosophy at Clayton Junior College. Kicks soccer style. Made 110 straight extra points during prep career. Does not speak English and goes through fifteen-minute ancient ritual

before every kick. Weighs ninety pounds soaking wet. Once scored
winning touchdown on fake field goal by hiding ball in his turban.
   ALBERT WARTZ JR.—From South Georgia. 6-4, 250. Plays quarterback. Questionable student. Thinks Henry Cabot Lodge is a motel
in Bainbridge. Filled out recruiting questionnaire. By "sex," wrote:
"Not since Mavis Wilson moved out of Hahira."
   "This kid," says his high school coach, "doesn't know the meaning
of 'quit.'" Doesn't know the meaning of third-grade arithmetic either.
Leaning toward Alabama.

Super Girls

   NEW ORLEANS—Actually, the Dallas Cowboys cheerleaders wear a
lot of clothes, comparatively speaking. Seen *Sports Illustrated*'s
annual porno issue this week? The cover is a lovely Brazilian child
named Maria Joao, who is on the beach in Bahia. She is not naked,
but you have to look closely to see that she isn't.
   Inside the magazine, which is usually reserved for pictures of huge
men perspiring in the name of sport, are more pictures of Maria and
other Brazilian girls, all of whom would make a good man leave home
for south of the border. I was especially impressed by a photograph of
the same Maria Joao posing in much less than what underpants used
to be in a fruit stand in Itapoa. Yes, she has some bananas.
   Sports gets sexy occasionally. *High Society*, which makes Larry
Flynt's *Hustler* look like *National Geographic*, is out with a picture
spread (a bad choice of words) of girls cavorting in hockey uniforms.
We recently went through the annual girl-in-the-dorm story with
Arkansas. Jim Bouton's *Ball Four* was a study in major league voy-
eurism and the latest rumor is San Francisco leads all leagues in
homosexual athletes. What more do you expect from the gay bay?
   It is the Cowboys cheerleaders in their white hot pants and short
halters, however, who currently rank first in sporting sensuality.
Who cares if Roger Staubach will occasionally run out of the pocket?
He doesn't even shave his legs. If he played in San Francisco he
might, but that is beside the point.
   There are thirty-two of them. The *Dallas Cowboys Weekly*, a
publication sponsored by the team that will play the Denver Broncos
here Sunday in Super Bowl XII, calls them "luscious lovelies." I'll hit
some highlights:
   There is Cheri Jo Adams. Have mercy. There is Monica Muehl-
hause. There ought to be a law. There is Debbie and Charyl and
Connie and Lisa and Janice Garner, I think I love you.

Some of the other National Football League teams have tried to start their own cheerleading corps. Chicago has the Honey Bears. It's too cold in Chicago to show your navel after Labor Day. Curt Mosher, who was instrumental in founding the Cowboy cheerers, started the Atlanta Falconettes this past season. Get the hook. Denver has the Bronco Belles. They will compete sideline-to-sideline with the Cowboy cheerleaders here Sunday. I'm giving the Cowboy cheerleaders and three wiggles.

Steve Perkins is editor of *Dallas Cowboys Weekly* which has over 40,000 circulation. Each week of the season, the paper features a centerfold of one of the Cowboy cheerleaders. That is the main reason circulation is over 40,000.

"There were times," a Dallas man was saying, "when the pictures really got risque. Perkins didn't want to run them, but Tex Schramm (Cowboys president) said go ahead."

Perkins is here for the Super Bowl. The cheerleaders will be in Sunday. Perkins gives Schramm the credit for the cheerleaders' success and popularity. Watch a Dallas game and see the cheerleaders in action between almost every play. Television cameramen are no dummies.

"What Tex wants," says Perkins, "Tex gets. He demands the best in everything. He gets the right girls. He doesn't take any chances on them if he thinks they might cause a scandal."

So far, so good. Many of the cheerleaders are students. There are also legal secretaries, even a check-out girl at a supermarket. Some are married. There has been only one near-miss in the problem department.

A well-endowed young lady walked into a Corpus Christi topless bar recently and told the owner she was a Cowboy cheerleader and she was available for duty. The owner broke his neck getting an advertisement into the local newspaper. Schramm got wind of the hoax and informed the owner his new talent was no cheerleader. The show was cancelled.

Nearly 700 girls showed up for tryouts in Dallas last year. Those chosen are paid $15 per game. They are choreographed by a lady named, appropriately enough, Texi Waterman. The big bucks come later for personal appearances.

"It's a very lucrative situation for them," Perkins explained. "They might get $200 to go to San Antonio for the opening of an auto dealership. Five went to Little Rock the other day to open a store. They come from all over to try out. If a girl from Houston, say, makes the squad, she'll just move to Dallas.

The hottest-selling poster in the country pictures the Cowboy girls. The same photograph adorns T-shirts. They are on sale throughout the New Orleans French Quarter. Farrah in her wet suit is now a distant second. The first twenty days the posters were on the market, sales reached 20,000.

A number of questions remain concerning the Dallas darlings:

Do any of the players date cheerleaders?

Randy White rolled out of bounds late in a Dallas rout and asked one of the girls to dinner. She accepted.

Do any of the cheerleaders also have brains? Vanessa Baker, a six-year veteran, was recently awarded her master's degree in education from Texas Woman's University. She made all A's.

How can I get a Dallas Cowboy cheerleader of my very own?

A man from Hollywood called one of the cheerleaders last year and told her he had seen her on television and she was beautiful and he wanted to give her a screen test.

She went to see him. Not once, but twice, and then a third time. The last time, the man was no longer with the studio. He was fired for flying a Dallas Cowboy cheerleader to California three times when there were no jobs available at the studio.

Lest We Forget

For the past two weekends, the Falcons, Flames, Hawks, Techs, and Georgias have all been winners, and Losersville is surely dead they say. What miracles next? Wyman C. Lowe winning an election? MARTA making a friend?

In New York, they celebrate winning the World Series. Dallas holds the Super Bowl trophy. Even tiny Green Bay rejoices. It leads the league again. Here, we celebrate winning weekends. Atlanta is a sports cancer patient that just got the word its head cold is clearing up.

But forgive us our headiness over what others might consider routine. Little things mean a lot when the suffering has been long and constant.

Georgia Tech people are talking about a bowl game. Georgia's football team—and we can claim it as being at least "local"—was supposed to embarrass the basketball squad. Now, it has a chance to win the Southeastern Conference title.

A Falcon placekicker actually attempted a field goal in the waning moments of a game and made it for victory. The basketball Hawks defeated powerful Denver. And the Flames defeated Montreal in hockey. That's impossible. Montreal invented ice.

Sound the trumpets for the lame and downtrodden. A Polish boy has grown up to be pope, and Atlanta may be slowly rising from the ashes of athletic ruin.

(The only words of caution I might offer are not to forget that the Braves open spring training in just five months, and you remember what happened to the last pope.)

But before the seedy and checkered past of Atlanta sports is dumped into history's garbage pile, I would like to recall briefly a few of the dumpees. We simply cannot say goodbye to Losersville that quickly.

Now without at least a mention of some of our classic losers and the moments they gave us:

—— In the final game of the 1972 season, Falcon running-back Dave Hampton became the first player in the team's history to gain over 2,000 yards in a season. Play was stopped, and he was awarded the game ball. On the next snap, Hampton was thrown for a big loss and time ran out before he could regain the lost 1,000th.

—— In his first major league game, Braves' rookie shortstop Leo Foster booted the first ground ball hit to him. In his first major league at-bat, he hit into a triple play.

—— How did Losersville maintain itself year after year? Here are some of the names of Number One draft choices of Atlanta professional teams:

Skip Harlika, Gerald Tinker, Ron Broaddus, Tom Workman, John Small, Greg Marx, John Valleley, Joe Profit, Gene Hobart, George Trapp and Leo Carroll.

Of that group, Leo Carroll is the most notable. Drafted by the Falcons to improve their offensive line, he disappeared one night from training camp.

All he left was his Tiny Tim "Tiptoe Through the Tulips" record.

—— Early in their history, the Flames launched an ad campaign warning fans all season tickets would soon be gone, the demand being so great. A few years later, management was begging city leaders for donations to help meet the team payroll.

—— The closest the Falcons ever came to making the playoffs was in 1973. They won seven straight, but then collapsed and lost back-to-back to Buffalo and St. Louis to be eliminated from post-season play.

The head coach, Norman Van Brocklin, blamed it all on "Peachtree Street whores and bartenders."

—— In the middle of a thirteen-game losing streak, the Braves' team bus got lost in the middle of a swamp between the airport and downtown in Philadelphia.

—— Great Trades Number One: The Falcons gave Minnesota their top quarterback, Bob Berry, and their top draft choice for the coming year in return for the Vikings' number two linebacker, Lonnie Warwick, and number two quarterback, Bob Lee. The Vikings later used the draft choice to obtain a player named Chuck Foreman.

—— Great Trades Number Two: The Hawks gave Pete Maravich to the New Orleans Jazz.

—— For opening game 1977 the Braves asked Bert Lance to throw out the first ball. He was stuck in a stadium elevator for thirty minutes and finished the season lower than the pitiable team he had launched.

—— Falcons' quarterback Randy Johnson, sacked several times this given Sunday, led his team out of the huddle and lined up behind a guard.

—— That's nothing. Falcon fullback Art Malone and tight end Jim Mitchell went into an Atlanta huddle and got into a fistfight before the next play could be called.

—— Georgia Tech's 1971 football team was invited to the Peach Bowl, but voted not to go, much to the relief of head coach Bud Carson. Athletic officials demanded that another vote be taken, however, and the pressured players this time voted "yes."

Tech lost the game 41-18 in the mud and Carson got fired.

—— The first Falcons game ever was an exhibition at the Stadium against Philadelphia in 1966. The Falcons were to kick off to launch themselves into the National Football League.

The whistle blew and kicker Wade Traynam approached the ball. He whiffed it.

Third Down and Praise the Lord

A few years ago, I talked to a wonderful preacher named William Holmes Borders, pastor of the Wheat Street Baptist Church, about the political problems Atlanta was having at the time.

The conversation was background work for a series the *Atlanta Constitution* produced called "City in Crisis." A lot of people didn't like what "City in Crisis" said. It said Atlanta had polarized politically, our leaders were more interested in bickering than progressing, and the City Too Busy To Hate was growing ornery.

What I remember most about that conversation was William Holmes Borders saying, "What we need in this city more than anything else is for our sports teams to get off their behinds and give us something to cheer. The Lord willing, maybe someday they will."

"The Lord willing . . ." is the key phrase here. I will be the first to admit the recent rise to prominence of our local sporting heroes is nothing short of miraculous, but never have I heard so much credit given to Providence for athletic success.

Take the Falcons. The Falcons have seven victories and only four losses, and Sunday in New Orleans, the tipped-pass-for-a-touchdown that defeated the Saints in the final seconds was hailed by one reporter as the "Immaculate Reception."

The phraseology is superb. The man who threw the ball, oft-injured and maligned Steve Bartkowski, makes Lazarus look like an amateur. He has risen time and again from the quarterbacking graveyard, and he has also announced he has been "born again."

Another writer wondered, "Now that he has found the Lord, will he be able to find his secondary receivers?"

Here is what Steve Bartkowski said Sunday after his prayerful pass was answered:

"I just said, 'Praise the Lord.' He was with us. I was praying real hard."

You would think if anybody was going to get help from Above, it would have been the Saints, who are named for those with, I would imagine, heavy influence when it comes to heavenly decisions.

I don't know how much the Flames figure God has had to do with their resurrection. It wasn't that long ago there was talk of the franchise going broke, but now the Great Goalie in the Sky is certainly smiling down on Omni center ice.

Last time I looked, the Hawks were only a game behind in their division. Holy turnover! Sadly, the only team yet to be saved from the fiery depths of the league cellar is the Braves. Let's all stand and sing the first and last verses of "Just As I Am."

Even our collegiate athletes are in the spirit. Just about the time I had decided Vince Dooley had sold out to the devil for his Georgia team's incredible 8-1 season, I find out the Bulldog quarterback, Jeff Pyburn, has linked up with the Almighty.

And recall what happened a few weeks back when Georgia played Kentucky. Kentucky led 16-0 in the third quarter. But with seconds to play, there stood kicker Rex Robinson with a field-goal attempt to win the game.

"I just put my faith in the Lord," Robinson said after the kick was good, "and He blessed me."

Eddie Lee Ivery, the Georgia Tech running back who set an NCAA single-game rushing record against Air Force Saturday? He's deeply religious and occasionally offers a locker-room sermon.

And to think Atlanta used to have athletes like Alex Hawkins, the former Falcons receiver, who, admittedly, once made the Fellowship of Christian Athletes' all-opponent team.

I certainly don't want to cast aspersions on other people's faith— athletes included—but I do sort of wonder what with the Middle East (which is sort of God's home town), starvation, crime, and discos, does He really have time to bless a field goal or a touchdown pass?

Since I couldn't get a direct interview, I can only speculate the answer would probably be: Only when it is absolutely necessary. Like when Notre Dame is playing for the national championship.

The best religion-in-sports story I know is an old one, but one I would suggest every athlete and fan who thinks God gives an angel's feather about third-and-long should hear again.

A spectator at a boxing match was sitting next to a priest. When the bell rang, one of the fighters crossed himself before heading to the middle of the ring.

"Will that help him, Father?" asked the spectator.

"Not if he can't fight," said the priest.

Dwayne Sanders

DURHAM, N.C.—On September 19, 1978—a sweltering, late summer Saturday—Duke and Georgia Tech played a game of college football in a tattered, half-empty stadium named after an old coach.

Georgia Tech will remember the occasion as a nightmare, its second, thanks to Duke, in less than a year.

The Tech sidelines, as the end drew near, was an outdoor death row. Men and boys, condemned to bitter and solid defeat, cursed themselves, cursed the officials, and cursed the heat. Mostly, they cursed the heat.

A giant Tech lineman, his body bloody and drenched in sweat, looked toward the sky and spat at the sun.

Football, when you are losing, is a game of reassurance. We are surrounded by a million Indians, but any minute now the Cavalry will appear and the day will be saved. Sure, it will.

"We'll win it," said a Tech assistant at halftime, the score 10-3 in favor of Duke. "I can feel it."

"The second half," added a player, "belongs to us."

There was agreement all about. But help never came. The bugles never blew. And the heat—damn the heat—grew worse, completing the agony.

September 9, 1978: Duke 28, Georgia Tech 10.

Remember the day, if you favor the White and Gold, as an ungodly day of frustration.

Then, forget it. And put your mind to the misfortune of a young man who had a stinking Saturday, too.

His loss was worse than any silly football game ever played. As Duke was kicking Georgia Tech Saturday afternoon, he was in the Duke University Hospital fighting for the use of the bottom two-thirds of his body.

It happened shortly before the game began. Dwayne Sanders, who is eighteen, was warming up with his fellow Georgia Tech cheerleaders.

It was to be his first game as a cheerleader. He's a sophomore at Tech. "About the hardest worker we got," said one of his partners.

Dwayne Sanders, from Atlanta's Henderson High School, did a few flips on the trampoline in front of the Tech supporters.

Then, he did one more. The kickoff was near. The bands were playing, balloons filled the air. Duke was worrying about the running of Eddie Lee Ivery. Tech was worrying about the passing of Stanley Driskell.

"He made the flip okay," a Tech cheerleader explained it, "but when he did his roll coming out, that's when he got hurt."

It took the ambulance a half hour to arrive. Dwayne Sanders lay on the grass, unable to move the bottom portion of his body.

His neck was broken. His removal from the field was barely noticed. The remaining Tech cheerleaders gave him a good-luck cheer.

At this writing, Dwayne Sanders was in intensive care at the Duke Hospital. He was to undergo diagnostic surgery. A doctor explained:

"It's too early to know what the outcome will be. Depending on the swelling and the pressure, he could regain his movement. It was a freak thing. The only thing you can do is hope."

The doctor crossed both his fingers.

Another doctor said, "Had the injury been higher, it could have been fatal."

So scream if you will about Georgia Tech's football ineptness Saturday. Granted, the defense leaked. And the offense proved why Pepper Rodgers doesn't like the forward pass. And there were questionable calls by the officials at times. "Welcome to the Atlantic Coast Conference," somebody said.

And, of course, focus the blame for it all squarely upon the shoulders of the head coach, for that is the American way of losing.

But do it quickly and then get along to concern for Dwayne Sanders. There will be other Saturdays and other chances for Tech's football team. Believe it or not at this point, there will even be times to praise it.

On such occasions, may Dwayne Sanders, the Lord willing, be there to lead the cheers.

(*Dwayne Sanders did not recover. He remains confined to a wheelchair.*)

Baseball's Spittin' Image

Watching baseball on television offers a rare opportunity to see the players up close. The Big Eye can put you nose-to-nose with your favorite stars, most of whom apparently do not shave on a regular basis.

Thurman Munson of the Yankees, for instance, looks like Pancho Villa after a two-week binge. Davy Lopes of the Dodgers looks like the guy who waters his horse.

The reason television has so much time to show closeup shots of the players during a game is there is a lot of standing around in baseball. Baseball is the only sport where three-fourths of the game is a time out.

Here comes the batter towards the plate. Watch him take a few practice swings, knock the dirt out of his spikes, fondle the tar rag, and scratch and adjust. (When a game is on national television, players should be reminded to cut down on the scratching and adjusting.)

There stands the pitcher on the mound. Watch him tug at his cap, pound the ball in the glove, pick up the resin bag, throw it down again, lean over for the sign, shake it off, nod agreement to the next one, and then throw over to first.

The batter steps out and here we go again, more practice swinging, dirt-knocking, and, if you must know, more scratching and adjusting.

Television even goes into the dugouts now. Dugouts used to be off-limits to civilians. A player could scratch and adjust and yawn and figure tax shelters until the last man was out, and who would know?

"Now," a ballplayer told me, "you have to act interested in the game for nine full innings."

Seeing the players close up on television during this year's Yankees-Dodgers World Series has also brought to my attention another interesting thing about men who play baseball for a living.

They spit more than anybody else. I don't suppose they spit on each other that much, but they spit on everything else. Home plate. The bases. The on-deck circle. Their hands. They used to spit on the ball, but that was outlawed. Leo Durocher once spit on an umpire.

Many baseball players chew tobacco. They all look like they have cheek tumors, but at least you expect them to spit. God help them if they didn't.

But watching the World Series games, I've noticed even baseball players who chew nothing at all also spit a lot.

Take Reggie Jackson of the Yankees. He spits constantly, even when he is figuring tax shelters in the dugout. He spits walking to the plate. He spits while he is there. He spits on balls. He spits on strikes.

Reggie Jackson spits with style. He has two distinct spits. There is the straight "ptui!" spit where he simply applies cheek and lip pressure.

His deluxe, superstar spit—typically flamboyant—is his through-the-teeth-line-drive-spit, however. He can fire away five to ten quick streams through the gap in his two front teeth faster than a Ron Guidry fastball.

One of the advantages to playing major-league baseball, I suppose, is it is one of the few professions that allows you to spit on national television and not be considered uncouth.

Other professional athletes don't have that luxury. Imagine Jack Nicklaus walking away from a putt on the scenic sixteenth green at Augusta and spitting. Basketball players wouldn't spit on a shiny hardwood floor. Hockey players might spit on the ice if they had more teeth. Jockeys don't spit during horse races out of concern for their fellow riders to the rear.

A private citizen certainly can't spit in public. It is considered nasty, and it could spread disease. It's like a New Yorker mentioned to me recently.

"Strange thing about the subways in New York," he said. "You spit and they fine you $25, but you can throw up for nothing."

I really don't have anything against baseball players spitting. Maybe what bothers me is television insists upon showing them doing it close up.

Then, again, perhaps I should count my blessings. Television has gone face-to-face with the players and into their dugouts today. Tomorrow, the showers?

Georgia 28, Georgia Tech 28

ATHENS—I was totally biased about the Georgia-Georgia Tech football game they played here Saturday. I admit it. Openly, and without shame. None of that I'm-just-here-to-report-the-facts nonsense for me.

I wanted a tie, dammit. When Georgia scored a touchdown in the waning moments to make the score 28-27 in favor of Georgia Tech, I hoped Bulldog Coach Vince Dooley would momentarily lose hold of his faculties and go on for a one-point conversion.

It's happened to him before. Just two weeks ago in Auburn.

Why should anybody have to lose a game like this? A tie at Auburn cost Georgia the Southeastern Conference title and the Sugar Bowl trip.

A tie Saturday, and neither Tech nor Georgia would have suffered the slightest pain. The Yellow Jackets would still have had their Peach Bowl bid, and the Bulldogs would have kept their date in Houston's Bluebonnet, and ABC would still have had the hit of their collegiate telecast season.

Tech-Georgia 1978 was more than a game. It was a spectacle. A classic. One team, Georgia Tech, builds an early lead. Twenty-to-nothing. But the other team, Georgia, fights back and with the stadium falling in, scores to lead 21-20.

But Georgia Tech won't hold, either. Drew Hill runs the kickoff back 102 yards for a touchdown, and the score is 28-21. ABC should double its payment to both schools for the right to show the rest of the nation such a show.

It isn't over. Here come the Bulldogs behind a boy-child quarterback named Buck Belue. And Georgia scores. Twenty-eight-to-twenty seven. Two minutes, twenty-four seconds remaining.

Of course, Vince Dooley went for the two points and the victory. And his people in red were successful in the attempt, and despite what I thought, somebody did have to lose Saturday—Georgia Tech.

Twenty-nine to twenty-eight.

"It was the best Tech-Georgia game I have ever seen," said Georgia publicist and historian, Dan Magill.

Georgia celebrated into the dusk. There is something Bulldog fans say at a time like this. They say, "How bout them Dawgs?", a grammatical insult, but it gets the point across.

There is something Georgia Tech people say at a time like this too, and player after player was saying it in the Tech dressing quarters after the game. That's as far as I will go. Use your imagination.

I had rather be a brain surgeon than a big-time college football coach. There's less pressure. Lose in brain surgery, and you can say you did your best, and you still get paid.

"What are they doing over on the winner's side?" asked Pepper Rodgers, a big-time college football coach who wished he had chosen another line of work after the heartbreak of Saturday.

The Tech players were stunned. They sat there, staring at nothing, slowly pulling off equipment and tossing it into a heap of tape and bloodied jerseys on the floor.

I've been to funerals more lively. And speaking of funerals, Rodgers did: "This is like a death in the family," he said.

"I want it to hurt! I want it to hurt!" a Georgia fan, flowing in the spirit, said to the Tech team as it filed off the field. He got his wish.

Georgia was brilliant in its comeback. And credit the Bulldog faithful. At 20-0, Tech, they were still on their feet, beseeching their team to recover from enough early mistakes to lose five games. The crowd was worth at least a touchdown.

And Georgia Tech was so close. Had Eddie Lee Ivery, the best player on the field, not been injured in the second half, the Jackets would have likely been able to hold their lead that vanished at the eleventh hour.

"It was like losing a tennis match when the last shot hits the tape," said Rodgers.

There is something both sides should remember after the events of Saturday. It's something a Georgia man said to me once.

It was a dozen years ago, and I was talking to Bulldog lineman John Kasay, now a Dooley assistant. Georgia had won a big game. The Bulldog dressing room was New Year's Eve.

But John Kasay looked around him and put the moment in its proper perspective.

"Why is it," he asked, "the highs are never as high as the lows are low?"

There is another way to put it. Losing hurts worse than winning feels good.

A tie, dammit. Georgia 28. Georgia Tech 28. Everybody shake hands and go home happy.

Larry Munson: Better Than Being There

Sometime in the wee hours of Sunday morning, my telephone rang. Even the ring sounded drunk. Among a number of other bad things, alcohol in large quantities dulls the ability of the user to tell time.

I muttered a groggy, hesitant, "Hello?"

"Gooooooo Daaaawgs!" was the reply from the other end. Deliver me from Billy Bulldog when it's the middle of the night, Georgia won, and the whiskey hasn't run out.

"That you, Dorsey?" I asked. It had to be. It had to be Dorsey Hill, the world's biggest Bulldog fan. Dorsey Hill thinks when you die you go to Vince Dooley's house. He can't wait.

Last year, when Georgia lost to Kentucky, 33-0, Dorsey claimed it didn't count because Kentucky was on probation for recruiting violations and had too many players from New Jersey.

"Best team money could buy," is how he described the victorious Wildcats, who went on to tie for the Southeastern Conference title. Dorsey dies hard.

I was awake enough by now to realize why the telephone call. Only hours before, Georgia had avenged last season's loss to Kentucky with a thrilling 17-16 victory in Lexington. The Bulldogs had trailed 16-0 in the third quarter.

"I never gave up," Dorsey said. "After the miracle at Grant Field Saturday, I knew the Lord would give us one, too."

He was referring to Georgia Tech's equally thrilling 17-13 defeat of Florida Saturday afternoon. Dorsey doesn't like Georgia Tech or anybody who does.

"I like it when we sweep a double-header," he explains. "That's when Georgia wins and Tech loses."

I have never quite understood that thinking, but there are those among the Georgia Tech followers who feel the same about the Bulldogs.

"I wouldn't pull for Georgia," a Tech man once told me, "with one engine out on the team plane."

I thought Saturday was one of the grandest days in Georgia collegiate football history. Tech wins its sixth straight and Grant Field hasn't been that full of life in years. That old house on North Avenue literally trembled with delight when Eddie Lee Ivery scored the Yellow Jackets' winning touchdown.

And Georgia's drive to the Rex Robinson field goal in the final moments was a classic profile in sporting courage. Georgia is only two victories—Florida and Auburn—away from another SEC championship and a trip to the Sugar Bowl. That is astounding when you consider that in the pre-season, the Bulldogs bore a strong resemblance to Vanderbilt.

I am almost frightened to consider the ramifications of a Falcons' victory over the Rams Monday night at the Stadium. If the clinkers win, close the schools and banks and I demand a parade.

There was one other hero Saturday besides the Eddie Lee Iverys, the Willie McClendons and the Rex Robinsons. He is a fiftyish fellow from Minnesota.

He worked in Wyoming for a time, and then spent years and years in Nashville. He moved to Atlanta only a few months ago, but he is one of us now.

"The traffic here," he says, "is murder."

Larry Munson has been broadcasting Georgia football games for thirteen years. Saturday night was his finest hour. His description of the closing moments of the Georgia-Kentucky game, said a man listening with me, "is Bobby Thomson's home run against the Dodgers all over again."

It was so good, the Sunday paper reprinted Munson's call of the winning Georgia field goal word-for-word.

"It's set down, it looks good—watch it! YEAH! YEAH! YEAH! YEAH! Three seconds left! Rex Robinson put 'em ahead, 17-16"

It was so good, Dorsey Hill said, "listening to Larry Munson was better than being there."

Frame that one, Larry. There is no higher praise.

Two Little Girls

Two little girls went out to play in the sun one day. One wore a pretty yellow dress. She was tall, and she wore her hair in a pigtail.

The other little girl wore blue shorts. She was shorter, and her hair was red. She had many freckles.

It was very hot this day.

"What should we play?" asked the little girl with the pigtail.

"How about tennis?" said the little girl with red hair.

"That sounds like fun," said her friend. "I'll serve."

The two little girls played tennis for a long, long time.

The little girl with the pigtail won the first five games. Her friend won the sixth game, but soon the first set was over. The score was 6-1.

The little girl with red hair played much better the second set and won by the same score. Six games to one.

"Let's play one more," she said.

"I'll serve," said her friend.

The two little girls played on and on. The redheaded girl led 2-0. Then, she lost three straight games. The score became 5-5. Golly, what a neato match. Back and forth and back and forth went the tennis balls. There were crosscourt backhands and down-the-line forehands. There were deep lobs and excellent gets and much top-spin.

One time, the little girl with red hair had a match point against her. She hit a drop-shot winner. Jimmy Conners wouldn't try a drop-shot winner facing a match point.

The little girl with the red hair was not old enough to know better.

It was very exciting, but suddenly the two little girls weren't having as much fun as they thought they would. So tense was the little girl with the pigtail, she began to cry after missing an easy shot.

She cried and cried, and she stomped her foot and she contorted her face into an awful shape.

The little girl with red hair did not cry, but when she missed a shot, it hurt her very badly. Once, she hit herself on the head with her racquet because she missed a shot.

"Dummy," she muttered to herself.

By this time, the little girls were covered in perspiration and their cute play outfits were soaking wet.

The sun beat down on them ferociously during the final game. The little girl with red hair was leading 6-5, serving for the match.

She had three match points, but each time the little girl with the pigtail sent the game back to duece. The little girl with the pigtail cried between almost every point.

"I wish we had decided to play something else," she thought to herself.

Suddenly, it was over. The little girl with the pigtail hit a back-hand over the baseline. She said, "Nice match" to her friend and then she cried some more.

Many people had gathered to watch the two little girls play tennis because they played so well. "There is probably a quarter of a million dollars worth of lessons between them," said a man.

Other men made wagers on the outcome of the tennis match between the two little girls who will probably grow up to be million-airesses.

The two little girls each received a silver dish for playing so well. The little girl with the red hair got a bigger dish because she won the match.

Her name was Margaret Hopkins, and she lives in Illinois. Her friend was Cari Hagey. She lives in California. They played at the Bitsy Grant Tennis Center in Atlanta.

Margaret Hopkins, because she beat Cari Hagey, is now the top-ranked twelve-year-old girl tennis player in all of the nation. When the match was over, she smiled and showed her braces.

It was the first time either of the two little girls had smiled in over two hours.

Wow. Tennis is such fun.

Eighty-Pound Lawsuit

I have always been a bit skeptical about organized athletics for children not old enough to have all their permanent teeth.

What is it about a society that will put a bat in the hand of a six-year-old, dress him in a baseball uniform, and ask him to perform on a diamond with real bases and everything, including umpires, coaches, and shouting spectators?

There is something called the "T-League." That's for kids who have just graduated from potty training. How can a child who hasn't learned his ABCs yet be expected to know to hit the cutoff man?

In the T-League, there is no pitcher. The ball is placed on a tee at the plate and the batter takes his cuts. Once I saw a T-League game where there was a close play at the plate. The runner was called out.

The runner's coach disputed the call. A grown man who would argue with an umpire at a baseball game involving toddlers is a sick person.

As the rhubarb continued, the opposing team's centerfielder became bored with the proceedings. He took off his glove, sat down in the outfield and began playing in the sand next to the fence.

Now, the other coach came storming out of his dugout. "Johnny!" he screamed to the youngster. "Do you want to play baseball, son?"

The child, still engrossed in the sand, studied his coach's inquiry for a moment, and then answered him by shaking his head, "No." Sand is marvelous when you are six, but it's lonely in centerfield.

I read an incredible story in the newspaper the other day about children playing organized athletics. It happened in Cobb County. Two midget football teams, nine-to-eleven year olds, play a game Saturday that ended in an 8-8 tie.

The winner would have gone on to the league playoffs that lead to an eventual "Super Bowl" championship. I am convinced adults organize children's athletic teams for their own enjoyment and glorification. Otherwise, who would care which team of nine-to-eleven year olds would emerge as champions over other teams of nine-to-eleven year olds?

Since the game ended in a tie, neither team qualified for more play. Wait until next year, and let's all go home and play with the dog.

But, first, let's file a lawsuit.

Adults involved with the Mableton team claimed the other team, South Cobb, had hired its own officials for the game and had not gone by rules stating officials should be named by something called the Cobb County Midget Football Conference.

They wanted the game played over. They filed a protest to the conference. Protest denied. They hired an attorney. He asked a Superior Court judge to stop the playoffs until the matter could be settled.

"When you set up an organization, you say you are going to go by the rules," attorney for the plaintiff, Laurie Davis, told me. "But when there is a clear violation and nobody will listen to you, where do you go?

"Do you have a fistfight to settle it? No, you try to find somebody who will listen and make a fair decision."

That is Laurie Davis' explanation of why an issue involving eighty-pound football players was taken to court.

Good for Judge Luther Hames. Why he even agreed to hear the case is a puzzle, but at least he denied the request to stop the league playoffs and found there was no reason whatsoever for the court to get involved further.

Why not let children be children while they have the chance? Whatever happened to games where you chose sides and played in the yard and made up your own rules and never invited the overgrown kid across the street because he could hit the ball too far?

Whatever happened to damming creeks and climbing trees and playing in mud and marbles?

And what do you tell your ten-year-old son, the quarterback, when he asks, "Hey, dad, what's a lawsuit?"

Gatewood Dooper at the Masters

AUGUSTA—The press corps that covers the Masters at Augusta National ranks just above the guys with the pointed sticks who go around the course picking up paper "the best gallery in golf" strews from Flowering Paranoia to Blooming Threeputtomia.

I was lucky enough this year not to qualify for a Genuine, Official, Keep-It-Pinned-on-Your-Person-at-All-Times press badge.

So I have set up shop in a tree overlooking the beautiful par-three twelfth. I have disguised myself as Tom Weiskopf having a nervous breakdown.

Tom Weiskopf is one of my favorite golfers. Last year, he shot a bad round in the Masters and stormed out of the locker room with a number of reporters in hot pursuit. He slammed the screen door that leads to the clubhouse grill with such force it knocked the frown off a Pinkerton man.

"Tommy takes a bad round hard," somebody said. They should take away his shoelaces and hide all sharp objects while Weiskopf is on the grounds.

The toughest thing about being a member of the press corps for the Masters tournament is the players' interviews. Contending players sit on a platform in the press barn while grown men from Tokyo to Tuscaloosa write down everything the golfers say concerning their day's rounds.

The fun part is when a golfer "goes over his round." Going over one's round is describing in full detail every blow struck for eighteen holes. . . .

"On number 1, I hit a driver 267 yards just to the right, hit an eight-iron twenty-three feet, six inches from the pin, etc., etc."

It is not as boring as watching wheelchair needlepoint, but it is close. I have this recurring fantasy about listening to a golfer go over his round. I know what Nicklaus did. He hit a drive down the middle 4,000 yards, hit a wedge to the stick and tapped it in with his middle finger. On 16, he walked across the water to the green after holing his tee shot. That's everyday stuff.

I want them to bring in Gatewood Dooper from the Clubfoot Links in Oshkosh who got into the tournament by some strange quirk of Masters eligibility fate and then played like a goat with muscular distrophy.

Let me hear *him* go over his round with the world's press assembled. Here is Gatewood Dooper describing his 107, worst round in Masters history.

"On the first tee, I wet my pants. That's a two-stroke penalty and very embarrassing. I was hitting three on my opening drive. It landed in a trap. I wound up with a nine. My wife went back to the car.

"On 2, I went into the trap again. The one behind number 3 green. I managed to save double bogey. My sponsor made an obscene gesture and went looking for my wife.

"On 3, 4 and 5, I had bogeys. My caddy agreed to stay for one more hole. I triple-bogeyed 6 and he went back to my car, too. To slice my tires.

"At 7, I hit a spectator. I had to. He came at me with a rock.

"I made the turn at seventeen-over. Before I teed off on 10, the tournament committee asked me to withdraw, my wife came back to the course and asked me for a divorce, and my sponsor stripped his company's name off my bag and hat.

"I fell into the lake on 12. One of the marshals pushed me. My drive went into the crowd lining the fairway at 13. I had to take another penalty. They hid my ball.

"Number 14 and number 15 were both disasters. At 16, they threw beer at me. At 17, I twisted my ankle. My playing partner tripped me. At 18, they sang 'Turkey in the Straw' while I tried to hit out of the rough.

"After I finally putted out, they put my card in the paper shredder and I had to hightail it to the locker room. The tournament committee had ordered sniper fire from the roof of Ike and Mamie's cottage."

Tough luck, Gatewood, but hang in there. From the nearest magnolia. Incidentally, Tommy Weiskopf usually brings extra rope.

I Am the Wind

I have received a lot of nasty mail from joggers lately. All I said was joggers make lousy conversationalists and their feet smell bad.

Even Gayle Barron, the famous runner, agreed with me in part. "The last thing I want to talk about at a party," she told me, "is how far everybody ran that week."

Gayle Barron is the prettiest jogger I know. It's OK if her feet smell bad.

I am not against physical fitness. I am against talking about it night and day. There are too many other topics that interest me more. Like famous left-handed Chinese yacht racers.

A man from Sandy Springs finally got to me. "The reason you don't like joggers," he wrote, "is you are jealous. I'd like to see you run the Peachtree Road Race. You wouldn't make the first one hundred yards."

I can't believe he said that. I took it as a dare. Never let it be said I am the kind of man who would back down from a challenge. My boyhood friend and idol Weyman C. Wannamaker Jr., a great American, once dared me to put a dead frog down the front of Kathy Sue Loudermilk's dress in biology class.

I would have done it, too, but there was a problem. There wasn't room for anything else down the front of Kathy Sue's dress, that lovely child.

I won't run in the Peachtree race Tuesday with the 12,000 official entrants. It is a matter of principle.

Let Hal Gulliver, our editor, carry the *Constitution's* banners. Hal

Gulliver, incidentally, is the perfect example of what can happen to a person who jogs. Before he started jogging, he looked like Tarzan. There was a picture of him in his running clothes in the paper. Now he looks like Jane.

I didn't want to mention it, but the smart-aleck letters have forced me to reveal I have already run the Peachtree Road Race 6.2-mile course.

I did it over the weekend. Alone. Just me, my swim suit, and a pair of slightly used jogging shoes I borrowed from my neighbor who recently gave up running.

"I had to," he explained. "My wife wouldn't run, and I didn't think we could survive a mixed marriage."

I made my run under the cloak of darkness. I wanted no publicity, no spectators, no big-name hoofers to run behind.

I departed Lenox Square from what will be Tuesday's starting line at 3 A.M. I crushed out a final cigarette, took a deep breath of the humid air and jogged away into the night.

Lonely is the nocturnal runner. The only sound was the rhythmic beat of the soles of my neighbor's jogging shoes. *Clop! Clop! Clop!* The first mile fell to its knees behind me.

Like an eagle swept through the air by some unseen current, I reached the International House of Pancakes, which was closed, still in a smooth, graceful glide.

Only an occasional passing motorist and an empty MARTA bus broke my solitude. That and a wino asleep in the entrance to an adult movie house in Buckhead and two fellows strolling on the sidewalk near West Wesley. I think they were more than pals.

I imagined myself upon a gallant steed, loping toward the dawn and the liquor store, which was also closed, at the top of the next hill.

On past Brookwood station and past Spring street. I reach Colony Square, slowing down, but still in forceful stride.

I am the wind.

I turned left on Twelfth Street, crossed Piedmont, and swept into the park. I rounded the lake and headed toward what will be Tuesday's finish line. My strength was fading, but my courage was not. Frank Shorter was on my heels. I left him in my wake.

Finally, it was over. The eagle had landed. My time is not important, for I ran not for glory. I ran simply to prove to a clod in Sandy Springs with jock itch on the brain I could conquer his silly 6.2 miles of asphalt.

Mission accomplished.

The Grief Passes Slowly

Billy Henderson has one of the last crew cuts in captivity. When he talks, he talks about how much he enjoys doing a job that involves young people, and there is no doubting his sincerity. Saturday is an important day in his life. In the evening, the football team he coaches, Clarke Central High School, will play Valdosta High for the state AAA championship. The game will be played in Athens.

Billy has been the full twenty yards during his career. Once he played before 73,000 people in the Sugar Bowl. Wally Butts was his coach. Georgia was his school. And he has seen the view from the other side, too. Before he moved to Clarke Central, he coached at tiny Mt. de Sales, a private school near Macon. When he went to Athens to interview, the nuns at Mt. de Sales held a mass and beseeched Providence to keep him in their fold. It was Clarke Central's prayers that were answered.

Billy took his team to Jekyll Island for its preseason training camp back in August.

Four months and thirteen games later, it is still undefeated. And it still remembers what happened on Jekyll the day it broke camp. These things are always so sudden. But the shock lingers. And the grief passes so slowly.

It was August 19, at 1:20 P.M. to be precise. Barry Malcom was sixteen. Billy Henderson, who cared for him deeply, recalls every detail.

"We were having our final lunch before heading back to Athens. Some of the players' families always come down for a few days at the beach together.

"We were about to eat when Mr. Malcom, Barry's dad, came up to me and asked if Barry could join the family. I invited him to stay for lunch. He said he'd come back later.

"After we ate, Barry left with his dad for their motel. We left for Athens. I was listening to the radio later that afternoon. The news came on. A youngster had been struck by lightning and killed on Jekyll. I froze. I was speechless. It was Barry."

Barry Malcom was a guard on the Clarke Central team. He weighed only 150 pounds. "But he would tackle a giant," said Billy Henderson. "He was a shining example."

Barry was standing outside, fifty yards from the front door of the Jekyll motel, when the bolt struck. Every effort was made to revive him. His father put him in his car and drove him into the hospital in Brunswick. At four o'clock that afternoon, he was pronounced dead.

"We drove on into Athens," the coach said. "There was the tendency to turn around and go back, but we knew there was nothing we could do. When we pulled into the parking lot at the high school, cars were lined up for blocks. They didn't know if we had heard the news."

What still hurts Billy Henderson is to talk about the Malcom family's drive back to Athens that night. "I don't know how they did it," he said. "They came all that way, with that burden, in the rain."

Life goes on. The season would open soon, against rival Cedar Shoals. "The team wanted to do something," Billy said. "They wanted to do something that was a tribute to Barry."

Barry Malcom would have worn number '65'. That number is on the top of every Clarke Central player's jersey. The mothers did the sewing.

Barry Malcom's parents have seen every game this season. They will be at the field behind Clarke Central High School Saturday night for the game of the year.

"They are wonderful people," said Billy Henderson. "It's not a wealthy family, but they have stuck by us. They are a part of us."

As we talked, Billy had to choke some of the words out. Death took a favorite player. It is obvious, his coach is still taking it hard.

Thirteen years ago, he had gone through the same thing. Billy Henderson was coaching football at Willingham High in Macon. His team opened with a 21-0 victory over Warner Robins.

Monday was Labor Day. One of his players was parked at a stop sign in Macon with his girl. Somebody ran the stop sign and crashed into them. Both the player and the girl were killed.

The player was Billy Henderson's quarterback. He was also sixteen. His name was Brad. Brad Henderson, Billy's eldest son.

Boston

BOSTON—As I sit on my rump smoking cigarettes and typing this, I can still see runners coming in from the suburb of Hopkinton, 26 miles and 385 yards from the Boston Marathon finish line at the downtown Prudential Center.

It will be hours before the last of the 7,800 official entrants, and maybe a couple of thousand more who ran anyway, finally come to the end of their exhausting journey.

The big names arrived to the cheering throngs what is now nearly two hours ago. Bill Rodgers was first. Actually, a cop on a motorcycle was first, but Bill Rodgers was right behind him with a record time of two hours, nine minutes, and twenty-seven seconds. It was his second straight Boston Marathon victory.

Appropriately, Bill Rodgers is from Boston and he sells sneakers. For accomplishing his feat, Bill Rodgers had a laurel wreath placed upon his head, and a medallion was hung around his neck by the governor of Massachusetts, Edward King. The crowd booed Edward King on Patriots Day in Boston.

What else the winner of the Boston Marathon gets is a bowl of beef stew. I hope they never change that. What occurred here Monday in cold and drizzling rain was a sporting event—a human event—that is still relatively pure and unspoiled by promoters and agents and television, not to mention candybar and beer companies that want to get their names in the newspapers.

Bill Rodgers crossing the finish line at the Boston Marathon Monday was as thrilling a moment as I have seen in sport. My goosepimples from the cold doubled in size.

But what is even more thrilling is watching now, watching the stragglers, the "nobodies"—the teachers, the housewives, the doctors, maybe even a cop or two, or Joe Futz the insurance salesman from Pottsdown—push their tired and worn bodies to limits they probably never believed possible when they ended a two-pack-a-day habit and decided to become athletes.

Grown men are hugging each other at the finish line. Many are finishing in tears. A medical center is located in a nearby garage. Freezing, cramping runners are wrapped in cellophane sheets and placed on cots. Doctors move from cot to cot treating frightful blisters. It's the rescue center after an earthquake.

I asked a man who looked like he was dying was it worth it.

"I ran the sonuvabitch," he said, "and I beat it." On his soaked T-shirt were the words, "Human Power."

As I looked at him, I thought about Bob Horner of the Braves and Pete Rose and what's-his-name Parker with the Pirates and Reggie Jackson of the Yankees, as well as Jim Rice of the Red Sox, who at that moment was only a few blocks away at Fenway Park, lolling around in left field for something like $50,000 a game.

Columnist Leigh Montville of the *Boston Globe* was apparently thinking of the same sports millionaires' club when he so aptly advanced the Boston Marathon Monday morning.

"There are no agents involved today," he wrote. "There are no options being played out, no deals being made, no fleets of Mercedes being pulled into any special parking lot.

"The athlete of the day is an athlete, period, not some modern

Clark Gable figure, some *Photoplay* sports god, cast in bubblegum and set atop some big rock-candy mountain.

"He is one of us again. As he runs the grand promenade from Hopkinton to the Prudential Center, he beckons us to come along, to sweat and enjoy. . . .

"The runner in the eighty-third Boston Marathon returns fun and games to fun and games. Somehow, he makes the rest of the sports page seem silly on this day."

You sense the trend vividly here, the fitness trend that has 20 million Americans running, the trend that has the rest of us at least thinking every time we light up a cigarette or spend another wasted, stinking afternoon watching overpaid balloonheads perform on that wretched talking box in our living rooms.

Grandmothers and grandfathers ran in the Boston Marathon Monday. A woman was telling her dinner companions in Boston Sunday night about announcing to her husband two years ago she was going to run in this race. His reply can't be printed here. But Monday, she showed him. There was a wheelchair brigade in the race. There were no fat people. A husband and wife, wearing matching outfits, finished together in an embrace.

Human Power. May the first promoter with the idea to turn this event into $100,000 Colgate Foot Race of Champions and move it to Las Vegas be shot at the next available sunrise, and may Howard Cosell never get close to it.

For the record, the Boston Marathon champion, Bill Rodgers, made a salary of $7,000 last year selling shoes. He drives a dented, 1963 Volkswagen. He lives with his wife, and they pay $165 a month in apartment rent.

Somebody once asked him what he thought of golf as a sport.

"You get about the same exercise in a hand of canasta," he said.

In the same interview, he was asked if he thought Joe Namath was a great athlete because he could throw a football straight.

"I'll be running over his grave," was Bill Rodgers' answer.

Farewell to Sports

I saw my first major league baseball game in Clark Griffith Stadium in Washington, D.C., in July of 1959. You don't forget your first major league baseball game.

The White Sox were visiting the Senators. Billy Pierce pitched for Chicago. Camilo Pascual pitched for Washington. It was a warm night.

There was no score until the top of the seventh. Nellie Fox, who is dead now, singled home two runs for the Sox. Jim Landis brought Fox home with a sacrifice fly. Chicago led, 3-0.

Pierce had a no-hitter into the eighth. Ron Samford broke it up with a double to left field that scored a runner who had walked. The final score was 3-1.

Harmon Killebrew struck out three times. Luis Aparicio made two great plays at shortstop. I drank three Cokes and ate two boxes of popcorn and one bag of peanuts. At one point during the game, I looked around at the stadium and spotted an enclosed seating area behind home plate. There were men inside.

"Who are those people?" I asked my adult companion.

"Sportswriters," he said.

"Do they see all the games?" I went on.

"It's their job," he said. "They don't even have to pay to get in."

That settled it. I was twelve. Anybody, I figured, could become a doctor or a lawyer or a car dealer. Nineteen years later, I don't own a boat, but I've seen a lot of ball games free. And once I went to Callaway Gardens for four days to cover a water-ski tournament and the newspaper paid for it. I made the right choice of professions.

A week from Sunday, I am moving my typewriter to another part of the building. My boss and I went through lengthy negotiations concerning the switch.

"Grizzard," he said, "your column is moving out of sports."

"Okay," I said.

Both the *Constitution* and the *Journal* are taking on new graphic faces, and I am to be relocated in a new section that will concern itself with news of city and state. I am told I can still write about sports but that when I choose not to, I won't have to feel guilty about it anymore.

I'm not very good at goodbyes, but before I go, there's a few more things I wanted to say:

—— I will never get used to Al Ciraldo not broadcasting Georgia Tech basketball games and Whack Hyder not coaching the team.

—— The best place to watch a baseball game is Wrigley Field in Chicago. The worst place is Yankee Stadium because crazy people go there.

—— My favorite sportswriter is Dan Jenkins. My favorite sports book is *Semi-Tough*, which he wrote. My favorite sports movie is not *Semi-Tough*. It is *Bless the Beasts and Children*, a movie about shooting buffalo.

—— Soccer and hockey are boring. Horse racing is exciting only if you have money on the race. The Indianapolis 500 should be against the law. Wrestling is fake. Organized sports are harmful to children under twelve. Tennessee has the most obnoxious fans in college football. Alabama is second. I'll be glad when Woody Hayes retires.

—— Jesse Outlar wrote the best line I ever read about the National Basketball Association's long-winded playoff system: "If the NBA had been in charge of World War II, Japan and Germany would still be in the running."

—— I still miss Harry Mehre.

—— The sixteenth hole at Augusta National on a Sunday in April is the prettiest place in the world.

—— There will never be another pitcher like Sandy Koufax, another college quarterback like Joe Namath, another stockcar driver like Fireball Roberts, another stockcar writer like Bill Robinson, another golfer like Arnold Palmer, and I wish Rod Laver were twenty years old.

—— I loved it when Dan Jenkins wrote, "The only thing worse than track is field."

—— Al McGuire is beautiful. Once he said, "The only time winning is important is in surgery and war."

—— The second best line I ever read about the NBA's long-winded playoff system came from a guy in Philadelphia who said, "The only uncomfortable thing that lasts longer than an NBA season is pregnancy."

—— Of all the people I have met in sports, Dan Magill, the Georgia tennis coach, is the most unforgettable. "Can I help you?" asks the waitress. "A Heineken's, honeykins," replies Magill, "and a sliced, barbecue, pork-pig sandwich."

—— If Alex Hawkins says that pot was planted in his car, I believe him.

6

FERGIT, HELL!

I make no apologies for anything that appears in this chapter. I was born in the South and I love the South and once my grandmother told me we had a relative who fought with Stonewall Jackson. That would be Uncle Beauregard Grizzard who died in 1882, singing "Dixie" and hating Yankees.

Homer Southwell, Author

Occasionally, Ludlow Porch of WRNG radio calls me on the telephone. That is because I knew him before he was a star. I knew him when he was a mild-mannered insurance claims adjuster with a secretary and a messy desk in Decatur. Ludlow wasn't as much fun in those days, but he caused less trouble.

What Ludlow Porch does for a living now is host two hours of madness on Atlanta's all-talk WRNG. Five days a week, he is set loose on the air to say anything he wants to. Listeners call in and the result is the city's most popular radio show.

You may recall Ludlow's revealing the "Montana Myth." There is no Montana, he said. Or the Great Parsley Debate. Ludlow claimed parsley causes several rare blood diseases and shortness of breath.

Recently, he set about to prove smoking is the cause of homosexuality. He also interviewed an official from HEW who announced all marriage licenses issued in the seven Southern states—"and parts of Florida"—since 1958 were void because they were issued outside HEW guidelines.

"The only exceptions," Ludlow explained, "are marriages conducted on navigable waterways or in a Winnebago."

Ludlow called last week to tell me about Homer Southwell.

Homer Southwell, it turns out, has been a frequent guest on the Porch program. He is the alleged author of books assailing the constant flow of Northerners southward.

"First he wrote, *Yankee Go Home,*" Ludlow said, "and then followed it with a sequel, *And Stay There*. He is terribly disturbed about Yankees who come South because of our warm weather and good food."

Homer Southwell has stirred the masses. Calls come by the thousands when he is a Porch guest. Irate transplanted Northernpersons want him lynched. Southerners who share his feelings concerning Yankee emigration want his statue erected on the grounds of the state capitol. A Porch sponsor canceled.

I caught up with Homer Southwell Thursday as he worked away in his East Cobb County home.

"I'm starting my first novel," he said. "It's called *Return to Marietta* or *East of the Big Chicken.*"

The hero of his latest literary endeavor, Homer said, will be a fellow named Jimmy James Cheetwood.

"Jimmy James is a real person I knew growing up in Cobb County," Homer explained. "He was the meanest man I have ever seen. He was so mean, he was *born* with a tattoo. They think he inherited it from his mama."

I probed deeply into Homer Southwell's disdain for Northern infiltration into the South. After all, I pointed out, the war has been over 113 years.

"So what?" Homer asked. "They're flocking down here by the millions. What will happen to our wonderful Southern way of life if we let every fast-talking Yankee who wants to live on our precious soil?"

Homer immediately launched into a tirade. I hurriedly copied down all the remarks I could follow:

—"I wouldn't go North for a three-week orgy with 'Charlie's Angels.'"

—"I encourage ripping-off of Yankee tourists on the interstates. You don't even need a mechanic to do it. You just tell 'em you're going to change their shocks and then don't."

—"The greatest form of birth control known to man is a Bronx accent."

—"God lives somewhere in the Alpharetta area."

—"I once made the mistake of dating a woman from Des Moines. She had hairy legs. All Yankee women have hairy legs."

Frankly, I had suspicions Homer Southwell might be a fraud, a figment of Ludlow Porch's weirdo imagination.

Then I asked him what he did for fun and relaxation when there is a break from the rigors of writing and Yankee-hating.

"I have a hobby I have enjoyed for years," Homer said. "Reading the *New York Times* obituary page."

Fergit, hell.

The Cyclorama: A Disgrace

The strains of "Dixie" come up softly at first and then grow louder and louder. Recorded musket fire bristles in the background. There is a vague human cry from somewhere in the background. There is a vague human cry from somewhere in the distance. Perhaps it is a Rebel yell, or perhaps it is some mother's child catching a bullet 114 years ago.

"Ladies and gentlemen," booms a familiar voice, "this is Victor Jory."

I remember Victor Jory. Last time I saw him, he had a whip in his hand.

There are a couple of things that have always bothered me about the Battle of Atlanta production in Atlanta's Cyclorama:

The painting is from Milwaukee, and the man who does the narration, Victor Jory, played the part of a most hateful carpetbagger in *Gone with the Wind*. I don't forgive easily.

Today is Confederate Memorial Day. All state offices will be closed. The United Daughters will celebrate. I prepared by spending a morning revisiting the Cyclorama. It had been a few years.

The guns are still blazing out of Hurt House. Sherman still watches the "inferno" from his mounted perch. The Wisconsin farmer's eagle still soars above the battle. And there remains the classic portrait of brother meeting brother in the midst of hell.

One is dying. The other, his enemy, gives him water to ease the pain. "This," roars Victor Jory, "is not a memorial to the decay of brotherhood, but a memorial to the birth of freedom. . . ."

For a time Tuesday morning, I was alone with the *Battle of Atlanta*. Tourists weren't exactly tearing through the turnstiles.

I paid my two dollars. A young black woman took my ticket. She was polite and urged me to hurry. "The next presentation," she said, "is about to begin."

I noticed posters on the walls, posters asking donations for the Cyclorama. I walked up the winding staircase that leads to history in the round.

It took 8,000 pounds of paint to put the *Battle of Atlanta* on canvas. It has faded now. There are visible cracks.

Red is the dominant color around me. Victor Jory announces the earthen floor of the painting's three-dimensional foreground is "actual Georgia red clay." What did he expect?

Red covers the faces and chests of the dying and wounded figures that seem as real now as they did the first time a child looked upon them in amazement. ". . . Die they do by the thousands," says Victor

Jory of a Confederate charge that was, perhaps, the South's last charge, on that day, July 22, 1864.

Once there was talk of moving the Cyclorama to another site. The building is old. It leaks. There was a fight for restoration funds, and somebody said, "If we don't do something soon, it will be too late."

It appears the Cyclorama will be restored now. Improvement can't come too soon.

Four ladies from someplace like Akron finally joined me and broke my solitude Tuesday morning. When the presentation was over, we walked outside. I heard one of the ladies say to the others, "From the looks of this place, the South has finally forgotten the war."

This shrine is, frankly, a disgrace. The years of neglect are taking their toll. And we really don't have "Dixie" to play anymore. "Dixie" is considered offensive.

One of the papers had to remind Atlanta readers that today is Confederate Memorial Day. Most of them wouldn't have known, otherwise. I heard a woman on a radio show the other day say, "We celebrate Confederate Memorial Day up North. We call it a tribute to Yankee marksmanship." That got a big laugh from a group of southerners.

I don't want to rally around the Rebel flag again. I don't have a picture of Stonewall Jackson over my fireplace.

I do know, however, Robert E. Lee once said of the men we are supposed to be honoring today, "They were asked to give more than should have been expected of them," and I know that they gave it.

That's good enough for me.

The Truth About General Lee

Dr. Emory Thomas came on the line from Athens where he is a professor of history at the University of Georgia.

My question was quick and to the point:

"Is it true," I asked, "what they are saying about Gen. Robert E. Lee?"

No true sons or daughters of the Confederacy have had a decent night's sleep since President Carter, of all people, visited Gettysburg the other day and said His Majesty General Lee made a "big mistake" in the key battle of the Civil War.

Heresy. Pure and simple.

To make matters worse, there is a new book concerning Lee, *The Marble Man*, in which a Nashville military historian named Thomas Connelley fires further salvos at Our Hero and Leader.

Lee, says Connelley, was a man obsessed with failure, who suffered from "repressed vibrance." ("He would have been a hell-raiser if he had had the opportunity" is Dr. Thomas' translation of that phrase.)

Connelley also says Lee was depressive because of an unhappy marriage to a woman prematurely arthritic and that he used religion as a crutch.

Dr. Thomas recently reviewed *The Marble Man* for *Virginia Magazine*.

"The reference to religion," he explained, "is basically that if Lee met anything he couldn't deal with or didn't want to deal with, he would simply put it off on Almighty Providence."

But that didn't answer my original question. Did, I asked Dr. Thomas—a Civil War authority and a native of Richmond, by-God Virginia—Robert E. Lee blow Gettysburg?

"Lee, himself, said it was all his fault," Dr. Thomas began, "and it was."

Allow the shock to wear off, and then we will continue. Recall that Lee had invaded the North in hopes of a major confrontation with the enemy. Although there was no clear-cut victor at Gettysburg, the loss of manpower and supplies Lee's Army of Northern Virginia suffered was the knockout blow of the war to the South.

I pressed for more details from Dr. Thomas as a tear rolled down my cheek.

"My interpretation," he went on, "is that Lee got up there, figured he had come all that way, and had gone to all that trouble and that it was maybe his last chance to do it big and do it right.

"He wanted a showdown battle. He had tried to turn the left and he had tried to turn the right. Finally, he said to hell with it, and went right up the middle.

"It was suicide."

Dr. Thomas does take some of the blame away from Lee. Ewell, he explained, didn't occupy Cemetery Ridge the first day he arrived, allowing the Yankees to take that strategic position.

Lee wanted Longstreet to take Little Roundtop. Longstreet could have, had he moved earlier.

"One of the problems," said Dr. Thomas, "was that the Army of Northern Virginia was basically a command of gentlemen. Lee didn't give his commanders specific orders. He just suggested what they *might* do."

Lee ordered a charge, said the professor, "at the geographic center of the entire Yankee army."

Get the picture: Flags are flying, bugles blowing, bands playing. And men dying. Fifteen thousand Confederate soldiers tried to take

Cemetery Ridge from the Yankees. Maybe 300 made it to the top. They were easily repulsed.

"They were doomed," said Dr. Thomas, "before they started."

We talked more. About Pickett's tears after the battle. About his dislike for Lee after the war. About Lee making the same mistake in the Seven Days Battle. About Lee's words, "It is good that war is so terrible, else men would grow too fond of it."

My heart breaking, an idol from my first history class crushed to mortal dust, I had to ask one more question:

Would the South have been better off with somebody else in charge of its military besides Lee?

"The best answer for that," Dr. Thomas said, "is certainly it would. Then, it would have lost the war about two years earlier."

7

ON THE ROAD

My favorite place to be is home. I know all the bartenders and where to get great barbecue. But a man can have an occasional high time in Memphis, the music is good in Dallas, Washington isn't such a bad place if you don't have to work there, and they like to hear me talk in New York.

And once an angel cooked my breakfast in Tellico Plains, Tennessee. . . .

"Honk If You Love Elvis"

MEMPHIS—I don't know what I expected Wednesday at Graceland on the first anniversary of the death of Elvis Presley. Graceland is the walled mansion in Memphis where Elvis, the late King, lived and died and is buried behind the swimming pool, next to his mother.

I didn't expect dignity because neither Elvis' life nor his death was dignified. He lived in a world of glitter and rhinestones and $50,000 automobiles, and he died in his pajamas on his bathroom floor.

One doctor said death was from "acute blood pressure changes," caused by straining for a bowel movement.

But I expected at least a certain reverence. A certain respect for Elvis' memory. A man born to near-poverty rose to fame and the millions that went with it. And I have read so much about the love of his fans.

A sign on a car in downtown Memphis this week read, "Elvis—We Will Love You Forever." Another said, "Honk If You Love Elvis."

I expected respect and reverence at least. I found a circus. Worse, I found a carnival of money-changers.

It was hell-hot Wednesday morning, and the line in front of the wall at Graceland was long and barely moving. Thousands waited hours for a chance to file past the gravesite.

Across the street from the mansion were rows of Elvis souvenir shops. Hawkers were at every corner, and they worked the ready-to-buy crowd with the intensity of a worrisome fly. They had to be shooed away.

For sale: Elvis T-shirts, Elvis posters, Elvis plates, Elvis clocks, Elvis portraits, pictures of Elvis riding horses, pictures of Elvis riding motorcycles.

For sale: Elvis belt buckles, Elvis hats, Elvis bumper stickers, Elvis black armbands, and a game called "King of Rock 'n Roll," a sort of Elvis Presley monopoly board with play money, lots of it.

For sale: copies of Elvis' driver's license, copies of Elvis' birth certificate, copies of Elvis' high school report card (F's in English), copies of Elvis' marriage license, and for $5, get your picture taken sitting in Elvis' first Cadillac, a 1956 purple El Dorado.

For sale: Elvis Frisbees.

Flowers and a picture of a hound dog covered the Graceland lawn. Flowers covered the gravesite. A pink teddybear had been placed nearby. "I love you, Elvis," read a card around its neck. It was signed "Your teddybear, Columbus, Ohio."

Back at the gate, national guardsmen, in the city because of the police and firemen's strike, had stopped allowing people inside the gates.

"The family wants a little time to itself," said a burly sergeant.

In came Vester Presley, Elvis' uncle, blowing the horn of his Cadillac. His books are on sale at the gate. In came Ginger Alden, Presley's girlfriend who was with him at the time of his death. She rode in the back of a car with two men in the front.

Later she would be driven out again. She would be in the back seat, crying. Twenty people would rush to the window of the car to snap pictures of her. Look for those pictures on sale here next year.

A Memphis garbage truck pulled out of the Graceland driveway Wednesday after its daily pickup.

A man standing in the line said to his wife, "Grab a sack of that garbage, honey. No telling what it would sell for."

Texas Chic

DALLAS—There are a lot of things I like about Texas, but let me start at the top: in Texas, they sell barbecue downtown.

Take the lovely city of Dallas, for instance. A person can step right out of his hotel onto bustling Commerce Street, walk into Neiman-Marcus for a little shopping, and then lunch at Gus's or the Copper Cow or the Golden Steer and feast upon sliced barbecue sandwiches in a modern, urban setting of glass and steel and taxi and bus exhaust fumes.

You can't do that in most other cities.

There are good barbecue places accessible *from* Atlanta—like Harold's at the federal pen—but in mid-city, the closest thing to barbecue is a truckload of hogs in a traffic jam on the downtown connector.

Regardless of where barbecue is eaten, its flavor and enjoyment are always enhanced by something cold to drink—preferably beer.

In Texas, you can have Coors beer with your downtown barbecue. Coors, the Colorado light nectar, is the favorite beer of Americans who can't get it. Coors isn't sold in Atlanta. It is smuggled into the city by airline stewardesses who fly out West.

I was in Dallas over the weekend for the Texas-Oklahoma football game, a good excuse for three-fourths of the population of both states to get drunk for three days.

Before the game, I stepped out of my motel room onto bustling Commerce Street, walked into Nieman-Marcus for a little shopping, and then had lunch at the Golden Steer in a modern urban setting of glass and steel and taxi and bus exhaust fumes.

I ordered two sliced barbecue sandwiches and a Coors and settled into thinking about why Texas has suddenly become so popular and chic. Do you realize New York City has even discovered Texas?

One of the hottest spots in town is a country music bar where they serve the Texas state beer, Lone Star, in longneck bottles, and the clientele wears cowboy hats and boots and is attempting to learn the correct pronunciation of "sumbitch."

I asked a Texas native about the phenomenon.

"Texas just *feels* good," he said, and "it encompasses about everything. We're out West, but we're also down South. And look what we've done for the culture of this country."

The list of Texas' cultural donations is staggering. Texas gave us chicken-fried steak and Walter Cronkite. It gave us Dan Jenkins and his marvelous book, *Semi-Tough*.

Don Meredith is from Texas. So is Phyllis George, and I would imagine most of the Dallas Cowboys cheerleaders. Which brings up the musical question: Whatever happened to the Kilgore Junior College dancing rangerettes?

And you know who else is from Texas. Willie Nelson. His buddy, Waylon Jennings, says everybody in Austin thinks when they die, they go to Willie's house.

Dallas is my favorite big city in Texas.

"It's nothing more than a big Mineola," said another native. "Dallas is made up of all the people who left the farm and learned to count."

But the people are friendly in Dallas. A hotel clerk didn't ask me for a major credit card and actually said when I checked in, "Nice to have you with us."

And Dallas is the home of the annual State Fair of Texas, perhaps the last of the great expositions of its kind in America. It opened Saturday and it will run two weeks and attract over 3 million visitors.

There will be horse shows and a rodeo, and livestock exhibits and gospel and country singing. The carnival midway is massive. See the world's smallest woman for a quarter. She's only four inches tall. See Emmett, the Alligator Boy. Billy Earl and his wife, Clovis, come every year all the way from Lubbock.

"This is where we spent our honeymoon," Clovis smiled proudly. Billy Earl looked embarrassed and disappeared to look at the tons of prime meat on the hoof down at the cattle barn.

Texans are a proud and courageous lot. Remember the Alamo. The University of Texas football team, incidentally, had about the same chance against Oklahoma Saturday at Dallas' Cotton Bowl. But they are a little crazy when it comes to football in Oklahoma, where the school president once said, "We want a university the football team can be proud of."

Texans simply know themselves, what they like, and what they expect of each other. I heard it put this way from across the bar after a few more Coors at the Golden Steer Saturday: "If you don't like Willie Nelson, longneck beers, long-legged women, rodeos, football, barbecue, the state fair, and an occasional fist fight, then you ain't no Texan. You just live here."

Cash Only

WASHINGTON—Here I sit in a big hotel room.

What fun.

When I was a kid, I liked hotel rooms because I could jump on the beds. Now, I like them because I can throw towels on the floor and somebody else will pick them up.

Washington is full of big hotels, because this is an important city and a lot of people from other places come here to work and to visit and to be politicians.

I suppose that the reason they always give you a booklet on security when you check into a Washington hotel is that there are lots of politicians here.

My booklet says, "Do not leave money, jewelry or other valuables in your room."

It also says, "Please bolt your door. This will shut out all keys. Also, insure that the security chain is engaged and that the connecting room door is locked."

Some rooms in Washington come with their own German shepherds. They are the ones nearest the Capitol.

This is a classy hotel I'm in. I knew it was classy when I saw the room service menu. The only thing cheaper than the $4.95 cheeseburger is a cup of coffee, which is $1.50.

One morning, I saw a fight between two taxicab drivers in the parking lot of my hotel. They were arguing about whose turn it was to pick up a fare. One driver bopped the other driver in the face, thus settling the argument. The other driver threw a rock at his colleague's cab as it sped away with the fare. Like I said, this is a classy hotel.

Hotel front desks are usually manned and womanned by young people who are very clean, wear expensive clothes and have a habit of acting snooty. Whatever happened to the friendly night clerk in his undershirt reading tomorrow's race entries?

Even the bellmen have come up in the world in today's hotels. The bellmen here wear red uniforms like the one Omar Sharif wore when he danced with Julie Christie at the Leningrad ball.

There is one staggering problem in hotels today, however. Hotels do not like to deal in cash. They abhor cash, as a matter of fact, along with anybody who would deface their front desk with it.

I deal in cash. Credit cards are financial heroin.

"May I see a credit card?" the snooty young woman at the front desk asked me when I arrived at my Washington hotel.

"Don't carry them," I said.

She called over the assistant manager.

"He doesn't carry credit cards," she said to him.

A lady behind me gasped in horror.

The assistant manager called over the manager.

"He doesn't carry credit cards," the manager was told.

I rattled my change as loudly as possible.

"If you don't have a credit card, sir" the manager asked me, his hands squarely on the hips of his designer trousers, "then how do you propose to pay your bill?"

Now, he had me.

"Cash," I said. "American," I quickly added, hoping to regain at least some face.

They wanted to see it.

A half hour passed before a decision was made. Finally, after I paid in advance, I was allowed to proceed to my room. They gave me a little card to read on the way up, however.

It said, "Because you have made a cash payment and did not present a major credit card at the time of your arrival, our operational procedure is to request that you make all futher payments in restaurants, bars, and the gift shop at the time the bills are presented."

How can you trust a man who carries cash?

The only time cash is accepted cheerfully in a hotel is when you give it to a bellman in the form of a tip.

After the experience of checking in, I followed a squatty version of Omar Sharif at the Leningrad ball up to my room.

He put up my bags, switched on the lights and the air-conditioner, and then waited impatiently by the door for his tip.

"Got change for a hundred?" I asked.

"No," he answered, "but I can get it from the front desk. I heard some yahoo just checked in using cash."

We both got a big laugh over that.

Disco Zoo

NEW YORK—The hottest spot in town is Studio 54, a disco on West 54th Street, appropriately enough. Not just anybody can get into Studio 54.

Here is how it works: every evening at midnight, a throng gathers outside and waits to be chosen for entrance. The lucky ones are then allowed to pay $20 per couple for admission. Once inside, there is a huge dance floor, flashing lights, and music to give birth to a buffalo by.

The dancing and the music and the lights go nonstop until dawn, when many of the customers must scurry back to the sewers. These are the beautiful people? A regular had mentioned to me earlier, "Go stand by the men's room. You might see Andy Warhol."

I'm not certain by what criteria entrants are selected. Judging from some of the clientele I saw, it would appear to be in your favor to come from another planet. Besides the men's and ladies' rooms, there is one marked "it."

I was given some advice on getting inside: "Make sure you dress in something unusual, or grease the doorman with a fifty."

I needed the fifty for breakfast the next morning. I wore my college rush outfit—a navy blazer, gray slacks, yellow Polo tie and Weejuns.

I was inside in a New York second.

"Funky outfit," said the doorman. To him, a wetsuit tux and snow shoes are normal.

"Disco" is our nation's latest nervous breakdown. Studio 54 is the home office. Truman Capote might drop by with Norman Mailer. For that matter, Godzilla might shake his booty with Yasser Arafat while Leon Spinks plays the flute. This is a strange place.

There was a movie made about disco, *Saturday Night Fever*. In the movie, they danced the hustle, and the moves were graceful and with style.

In Studio 54, they dance something that resembles a monkey halfway there on an LSD trip. Say it ain't so, John Revolta.

I paid my admission and went directly to the men's room to interview Andy Warhol. He wasn't there. Fan Man was. Fan Man wore a ribbon in his hair, lipstick, a long skirt and peered out from behind a fan.

"Funky outfit," he said as I walked past him.

There was more. Golden Boy strolled through. He was a stunning blond. For the evening, he had chosen a sleeveless blouse, open to the navel. He carried a gold purse and wore a gold lamé skirt and gold bedroom slippers from the Aladdin collection.

Later, he danced with Peter Punk. Peter Punk came in his father's old bowling shirt, which he wore outside his mother's jodphurs. He had a black ring painted around his left eye.

There was a girl in fatigues carrying a hula hoop. There was another girl in a wraparound evening dress she had fashioned from a bedsheet. She had washed her hair in Thousand Island dressing and blown it dry with an acetylene torch. Fan Man was looking better all the time.

My companion and I eventually braved the dance floor. We immediately provoked stares. My companion was a girl person in a chiffon, ankle-length dress, appropriate for dinner at "21."

"Funky outfit," said the girl in the bedsheet dancing with Hoola-Hoop Hattie next to us.

Studio 54 is loud and kinky and, on this night at least, predominantly gay. Teenage boys wait tables in silver underpants, tennis shoes and nothing else. After they clean your table, they dance on it.

Two models show up in running shorts, pull off their blouses and dance barebreasted. Shirtless men dance with other shirtless men. I puffed a Marlboro. Most of the crowd rolled their own.

In the wee hours, it was time to leave. There was still the mob scene outside. As I walked through the crowd, a breathless girl grabbed my arm.

"How did you get in?" she asked, in full swoon.

With an air of self-assurance, I replied, "My funky outfit," and disappeared down the street into a fog of reality.

"Chicken" and the "Worm"

PLAINS—A regular walked into Billy Carter's Service Station one hot afternoon last week and greeted Leon, the man who takes up money for gas and beer.

"Last time I saw you," he said, "we were both drunk."

"Believe we were," agreed Leon.

"We go in them bad places, don't we?" the man continued.

"Them dives," said Leon.

"Them places we go in," the man went on, "are so bad they got blood on the ceiling. Place with blood on the floor don't worry me. Place with blood on the ceiling, that's a tough place."

He noticed a jar on the side of the bar. The jar had money inside it.

"What's that for?" he asked Leon.

"For 'Chicken'," Leon replied. "We're gonna get him in the state senate. You gonna help us?"

"Damn right," said the man. "I'd do anything to get rid of that damn Hugh Carter."

Some introductions are probably necessary. The Hugh Carter here is Cousin Hugh Carter Sr., antique dealer, state senator, worm grower and author of the book *Cousin Beedie and Cousin Hot*, in which he wrote all sorts of things about First Cousin Jimmy and First Cousin Billy and anybody else who came to mind.

Hugh Carter Sr. lives in Plains, and he is running for re-election as state senator from the Fourteenth District. The primary approaches on August 8th.

"Chicken" is another story. He is Malcolm "Chicken" Wishard, a local farmer with no political experience to speak of. He's the man the regulars at Billy Carter's Service Station want to see whip the pants off Hugh Carter in the election.

That includes Billy himself.

"Miss Lillian's with us, too," said Leon. "She said she would spend every dime she had to see Chicken whip that damn Hugh Carter. Billy's done give his dime."

It took some talking and a six-pack, but I finally got to the bottom of this split in the Carter political camp. For one thing, Hugh's book didn't set well with the family. And for another, said a woman at

Billy's, "there never has been no love lost between Billy and Hugh, and Miss Lillian and Billy are just alike."

Chicken Wishard's campaign was cranking up full blast at Billy's this afternoon. Leon passed out cards that read, "Help Chicken Take the Worm."

The "Worm" reference is to Hugh Carter, of course, the self-styled "Nation's Worm King." Even Mrs. Chicken dropped by for a visit.

"Why do they call Chicken 'Chicken'?" she was asked.

"When he was a little boy," she answered, "He was the first one in the family to get chickenpox."

Leon calls him "One-Eyed Chicken."

"That's because he ain't got but one good eye," said Leon. Leon also had a stack of campaign posters with Chicken's smiling face. Somebody put an empty beer can on the stack of posters.

"Get that off of there," Leon screamed. "You might get beer in Chicken's good eye."

I pressed for more details on campaign issues.

"Only issue I know," said Leon, "is we can't stand Hugh Carter and we finally got somebody to run against him. You can talk to Chicken. He's loud and if he walked in here right now, you'd think he was half a fool. But he ain't. He's a good man."

Billy Carter would eventually drop by the station. He was sipping something clear over ice. The tourists flocked around him. He signed autographs, posed for pictures, and sold six-packs of Billy Beer for $2.60. The local line is, "Jimmy's making $200,000 a year running the country, and Billy's already made $500,000 running his mouth."

And Billy would do his best for Chicken too.

"We need two things from you to help Chicken," he said to a farmer who came in for refreshment.

"What's that?" asked the farmer.

"Your vote and your money," said Billy.

I had to ask Billy Carter how he could go against his own flesh and blood. "Isn't this man your cousin?" I said.

"He ain't my cousin" Billy answers. "I gave him away."

Riding the High Lonesome

ON A GEORGIA BACKROAD—There are only two sounds out here. Four tires are humming as they hug the taxpayers' asphalt on Georgia 15. And the radio—God bless an automobile radio—has me in touch with you wouldn't believe the faraway places.

I am constantly turning the dial. Voices with no faces fade in and voices with no faces fade out. But at least there are voices, and without them the loneliness would creep even closer.

I have just departed from Sandersville, northbound through the deep-hole blackness the night brings to middle-eastern Georgia. There was a shooting in Louisville, clear-channel WHAS reports, but invading static keeps me from the details.

Dallas comes in loud and clear. It will be nice in Dallas tomorrow, with highs in the mid-seventies. I even pick up Cleveland.

You know they tried to recall the mayor in Cleveland. Now, the city council has been charged with accepting kickbacks. Things are tough all over.

Chicago's country WMAQ, an old friend, is beaming to thirty-eight states and Canada. A man sings a song that includes the line, "Plant them 'taters, and pull up another tomorrow."

It is difficult to avoid a hockey game, turning the dial on latenight radio. Hockey is enough of a problem for me in person. On the radio, it might as well be the noon news from Mars.

"Ro-jay brings the puck to center ice! Marcham-bo checks him there. Jablare intercepts, and there is a whistle for icing the puck!"

I am on the fringes of Hancock County, Georgia, listening to a man from Fort Wayne, Indiana, describe the actions of twelve foreigners on ice skates, chasing a rubber disc.

I turn back to Cleveland.

My headlights tunnel through the darkness. The tall pines frame the road, and two beady pearls of light suddenly appear in the distance.

This is the Halloween season, but a stray dog crossing the road has simply turned its head toward the lights of the car, and its eyes have reflected back.

Give me a dime for every stray dog on every Georgia back road, and my creditors can relax. I'll take a quarter for every dead possum.

I am trying to make Atlanta and home before sleep takes me over. Interstate 20 is somewhere ahead, just out of a place called Siloam in Greene County. The interstate is an auto jet-stream after crawling over two-lane. There is no other traffic because of the late hour and because country people have been in bed for hours. They get up early out here, you know. Don't let the sun catch you a-restin'.

There are tiny frame houses here and there, but not a sign of life to go with them. I grew up in a frame house that went dark at an early hour. The peace and comfort it held until morning has been difficult to relocate.

Downtown Sparta approaches. There are street lights, but no people. The old tavern in the middle of town, a historic landmark, looks haunted. It probably is.

Sparta lasts thirty seconds. The village of White Plains will be next. I cross Copeland Creek and Whitter Creek. There is a newscast coming in from WCAU, Philadelphia. Damn, I'm a long ways from Philadelphia.

What I am thinking is maybe everybody ought to do this occasionally. I am at least free with my thoughts here. Out like this, a man can talk to himself and it seems perfectly natural. You can ask yourself a question on a Georgia back road and get an honest answer.

Finally, Siloam. Siloam won't awaken for hours yet. The interstate approaches, laden with eighteen-wheeled monsters with big eyes and loaded backs bound for the city.

Parting with Georgia 15 is more difficult than I figured it would be. I will be home in just over an hour, but I realize that out on that primitive stretch I had maybe stumbled upon one of the modern urbanite's last escapes. I had ridden about all that remains of the High Lonesome on a pony with automatic transmission.

Cleveland has faded off the radio. I turn the dial again and a preacher is chasing the devil out of Tulsa. "Be saved or be damned!" is his warning.

Rolling along the interstate, I search for another hockey game.

Covering the Arrival of Spring

HILTON HEAD ISLAND, S.C.—Soft rain is falling, the wind is blowing, and the skies are cloudy. But the temperature is pleasantly mild, and for three days previous to this one, late winter's coastal sun has shown brilliantly. I will be leaving here soon, and that thought saddens me.

I will miss my duck. There has never been such a duck. I don't know much about ducks, but this one lives in a lagoon outside my bedroom window and makes a sould like, "Braaaack! Braaaack!"

He works the night shift. His job is keeping the alligators awake. Ditto for any other creature within the sound of his quack.

He begins precisely at sundown. He doesn't hush until the dawn. I have nicknamed him "Hosea."

News from the outside world filters in slowly to a place like this. A big story here is that a cosmetic surgeon is moving to the island from Florida to take the wrinkles out for the summer parties at the Sea Pines Club.

That announcement brought an interesting remark in a local paper from a man identified as an "island punster."

"Instead of having your face lifted," he asked, "why not have your body lowered?"

So the Reggie Eaves controversy rages on back in Atlanta, does it? Here, they are more concerned about the bleak outlook for shrimp. No white shrimp have been seen in coastal waters for five weeks. The cost of appetizers goes up and up.

Coal strike? What coal strike? Bless my Lincoln Continental, the cost of a membership to the Sea Pines Club will go up from $3,000 to $5,000 come April 1.

There has been some interest, however, in the story out of Arkansas where the preacher put his deceased eighty-year-old mother in a freezer locker and then tried to raise her from the dead. The older retirees here are keeping a close eye on his progress.

I came here to cover the arrival of spring. It comes two weeks earlier to coastal paradise.

I lived without any spring at all for a couple of years. There are only two seasons in Chicago. Winter and the Fourth of July. A year ago today, I was in snow navel-high to a tall Yankee.

Missing springtime is like missing a woman. You never really noticed her and then she was gone, and all that she was returns and makes the separation even more painful.

I think I read this somewhere. "Springtime is the land awakening. The March winds are the morning yawn."

People are already on bicycle jaunts around the island here. Sunbathers were on the beach at Turtle Cove over the weekend. Two couldn't wait and hit the surf in mid-seventies temperatures.

Squirrels cavort everywhere, I saw a bluebird and a starling. Four deer crossed a road in the Sea Pines Plantation and loped casually through front yards of island residents.

Soon will come another sign of the season. I usually gauge the appearance of spring by the arrival south of the professional golf tournaments. Hilton Head's annual Heritage Classic, a prelude to Augusta National's Masters, is only a week away.

"The boats are already coming in," said a man in Harbor Town Tuesday. "The Heritage and spring brings them south."

Let It Be is docked from Ithaca. Taranak is here from Plymouth, Maine. Ravissant came down from Wilmington, Delaware. I see them and think of the old line about nobody ever retiring north.

The rain has stopped. There is a mist hanging over the marsh behind the Harbor Town Links' sixteenth green. The wind has ceased, and the stillness that has followed offers an added comfort.

Let them fight it out at City Hall, and where on earth is South Molucca, anyway? Spring is rushing in, and me and my duck wish you were here.

New York Subways

NEW YORK—I had planned to ride a lot of commuter trains around New York to practice for when Atlanta's new rapid rail system opens. That will be just as soon as the excavation is completed and the city is put back together again.

Presently, Atlanta looks like what Sherman would have left if he had been carrying bulldozers and jackhammers.

Also, I figured the subway would be the best means of transportation around New York, following the big snowstorm last week. After the snow came warmer temperatures and rain. The snow melted and the streets flooded.

The crud that normally just sits on the streets of New York started floating. Egg shells, potato peelings, and salami sandwich parts I stepped over on 52nd Street passed by me again as I tried to cross 63rd.

I decided, however, to brave the flooded streets and to look for nonexistent empty taxicabs rather than attempt to take subway trains. That is because the snow and flooding were causing problems underneath New York, too.

One train on its way to New Jersey quit running in what they call a PATH tube somewhere underneath the Hudson River, speaking of floating crud. The people inside the train were three hours getting out.

"Everybody stayed calm," said one of the passengers. "We sang songs to pass the time."

If I were on a stranded commuter train on the way to New Jersey in a tube somewhere underneath the Hudson River, I would not stay calm, nor would I sing songs. That is because I can't panic and sing at the same time.

I heard some other horror stories about subway trains from native New Yorkers who ride them all the time.

"We were going along one morning," a young woman told me, "and it became quite obvious the train was going faster than it should have been. Everybody got a little nervous.

"Suddenly, the motorman walked out of his little compartment and threw up. He was drunk. At the next stop, they came and took him away."

Another commuter topped that.

"You never know what you'll see," he said. "I was on my way to Queens. A guy and his wife or girlfriend got on the train having a big argument.

"They argue for four or five stops. They get louder and louder. Finally, the guy takes all he can stand and starts choking the woman. He chokes her until she's blue.

"Another man nearby grabs him and pulls him away from the woman and belts him one to settle him down. Soon as that happens, the woman cranks up and bops the poor guy who saved her life on the head with her pocketbook. He's out cold.

"At the next stop, the couple gets off and walks away arm-in-arm."

You simply have to know certain rules about riding commuter trains. Here are some I picked up in New York for Atlantans to remember in the future:

—— If somebody decides to choke his lover on a commuter train, don't interfere unless you want your head bashed in.

—— No matter how crowded a car looks, it will always hold one more.

—— Let sleeping drunks lie. Unless one happens to be driving your train. In that case, launch an immediate search of the cars for a priest.

—— In case of an emergency, like having to walk out of a tunnel, avoid the third rail. Ignore this rule and that sizzling sound is you, Bacon Face.

—— Discourage pickpockets and thieves. Swallow your wallet before entering the train.

—— If several young men in black leather jackets appear and ask for your wallet, do not tell them you swallowed it. Notice the fellow passenger who did is now minus one wallet and bleeding to death.

—— Never shove a friend off a platform in front of a speeding commuter train as a practical joke. Unless he gave you a hot foot when you were packed in like sardines during rush hour the day before. Then it's OK. You owe him one.

—— If you are now frightened about riding Atlanta's new commuter trains after reading all of the above, don't be. Remember none of that could ever happen in our city.

Saltines and Solzhenitsyn

TELLICO PLAINS, TENN.—I had been days without newspaper, locked away in a careless world of mountains, rivers, dirt roads, and a supply of Vienna sausage and sardines and a gift for which we can never offer enough gratitude: the saltine cracker.

God bless the saltine cracker, for it is constantly loyal in its service to enhance the flavor of even the barest edible. You could eat dirt with a packet of saltine crackers on the side.

I can't go many days without a newspaper because I can't go many days without certain information necessary to my peace of mind.

I need to make sure the world hasn't been blown away, and I need to keep up with the Dodgers. In this rustic village, which is located at the foot of some mountains near the Tennessee-North Carolina border, I purchased a newspaper and found the world still in one piece, which is more than I could say for the Dodgers.

Interest in the Dodgers is a carryover from my youth, but must a man have to explain every quirk of his character? The Dodgers, I read, have sunk to a lowly third. And the Giants, whom I hate, are still holding to first place. So help me Junior Gilliam, my favorite all-time Dodger, that can't last.

My companion and I needed a hot breakfast, if for no other reason than to take a brief leave from the joys of saltines. We walked into a place in Tellico Plains that was a combination beer joint and restaurant, mostly beer joint. The regulars were already at their stations. A card game of some variety was in progress, and an old man in a hat played the game with a boy-child on his knee.

"You have grits?" I asked the lady.

"Not grits," she said. She was missing some teeth. "I could fix you potatoes."

Where does it say an angel must have teeth?

Over eggs and country ham and fried potatoes—the kind that are round and thin—I read the rest of the newspaper. Carter this. Carter that. All hail Proposition 13. And a bearded man had made a speech in the Harvard Yard and had said some nasty things about our country. He made the speech in his native tongue, Russian.

The man, who has never been to Tellico Plains, Tennessee, said we ought to eat dirt for awhile because we have become fat and too interested in material goods, like nice places to live and motorboats. He said we are suffering from a "moral poverty."

He said if he could change his country, which would put him in jail if he went back to it, he wouldn't use our country as a model.

I finished my breakfast and the newspaper, left a nice tip for the lady and walked out on the streets of Tellico Plains.

It was a gorgeous late spring day. Just beyond the fruited plain that surrounds the village was a mountain majesty more green than purple, but stunning nevertheless.

Passing by me were simple folk, dedicated to the day's work and the simple pleasures. Most of them, I am sure, had never heard of the Harvard Yard, much less of the bearded, exiled Russian author who spoke there.

A pickup truck passed through town, its rear bumper bearing a message I don't entirely agree with, but one I needed at the moment. The Dodgers were going badly and what the Russian had said upset me.

"America," read the sticker, "love it or leave it."

But where would you go, Mr. Solzhenitsyn? Where would you go?

8

RAILROAD BLUES

One day there won't be anymore trains to ride, and a part of me will die. The part that enjoys good conversation in the club car, morning coffee crossing the Potomac into Washington in the dining car, and little boys and old men who, as long as there are passenger trains, will stand beside the tracks and wave at them.

She Goes Bump in the Night

ABOARD THE FLORIDIAN—She used to have a more romantic name. She was The South Wind, and Johnny Cash mentioned her in a song: "She left me on The South Wind. . . ." When she was younger, she dazzled them with her speed and grace for over 2,000 miles of railed opulence.

Now, she is a tattered, financial mess that is unloved and unwanted. By way of introduction she is Amtrak's Chicago-to-Miami Floridian. She is old, she is slow, and she goes bump in the night.

The Floridian, nine cars and a brightly painted engine with a red snub-nose, left Miami just after dawn the morning before. The feminine personification is hardly applicable anymore. "It" passed through Fort Lauderdale and Orlando and rolled into Jacksonville nearly eight hours later.

Then, there was a westward swing through the flatlands of south Georgia, through Waycross, Valdosta and Thomasville, before a turn north into Alabama and Dothan, Montgomery and Birmingham.

The Floridian is notorious for running behind schedule. It is supposed to make the 2,576-mile journey between Chicago and Miami in just over thirty-seven hours, two full days and one night.

It is due in Birmingham's old Louisville and Nashville railroad station—located in the middle of downtown—at 1:48 A.M. The rest of Birmingham sleeps unaware in a soft rain.

A station agent, a baggage clerk and four passengers await the train on a platform outside the station. Precisely at its expected time of arrival, the Floridian's headlight peers around a corner south of the station. "'Train comin'," says the station agent. Train comin' right on time, for a change.

I have made this trip before—Birmingham to Chicago, Chicago to Birmingham—aboard The Floridian. Nashville and Louisville are two of the stops in between. Rail travel remains a personal adventure, despite the hardships it often entails. Although Amtrak, the government-subsidized authority that runs most of the nation's remaining passenger trains, has managed to upgrade some of its service, much of it remains a frayed relic of the past. The Floridian falls into that category.

This train is one of Amtrak's biggest losers. This train, to borrow from songwriter Steve Goodman, "got them disappearin' railroad blues." This train is bound for a permanent siding if a providential solution isn't found that would increase its ridership and cut down its annual losses. The yearly deficit runs into millions.

One problem is its patronage is seasonal. "We are packed in the summer," the dining car steward will tell me during the trip. "We'll get two or three hundred people—most of them on vacation to Florida—every day. After school starts back, that changes."

When the Floridian arrives in Louisville the next day at noon, there will be twenty-one passengers on board.

A route change was one of the possible solutions Amtrak was looking into before its management recommended complete scrapping of the train. One proposal would have sent the Floridian south out of Nashville into Atlanta, then to Macon and Savannah—or to Macon, Albany, and Jacksonville. Public hearings were held in Atlanta and in cities on the Floridian's route.

If Amtrak's board of directors goes along with management, Atlanta will remain the nation's largest city not receiving Amtrak service. Southern Railway, which is not an Amtrak member, operates its own passenger train, the Southern Crescent, daily between Atlanta and Washington, D.C., and three times a week between Atlanta, Birmingham, and New Orleans.

It is 713 rail miles between Birmingham and Chicago. Arrival in Chicago is scheduled at 9:02 P.M., nineteen hours after the Birmingham departure.

I am asleep thirty minutes out of Birmingham, despite a ride reminiscent of the tilt-a-whirl from county fairs past. For $71.50, I have purchased a first-class, one-way ticket that entitles me to a roomette accommodation—a private room with a bed that folds out of the wall. There is also a tiny toilet, a tiny lavatory, and a tiny closet inside.

A regular ticket—you sleep in a reclining seat in one of the day coaches—costs $35.00. Amtrak offers a number of special fares on the Floridian, including a Florida package that provides free use of a rental car for a week.

I can sleep on a train. Most people can't. I talked with a companion from the sleeper the next morning at breakfast.

"Sleep well?" I asked.

"No," he replied. "There are only three ways to go to sleep on this train. Be dead tired, dead drunk, or just plain dead."

The equipment was old when Harry and Bess were in the White House. It is vintage thirties and forties. It includes a baggage car, one Pullman, four day coaches, a diner, a rounded-end observation lounge car and a mail car tagging along at the end.

One of the coaches has a domed top with huge windows for sightseeing. It is located behind the diner. The greasy smoke from the diner's kitchen exhaust has opaqued the windows in the sightseeing dome car. The view from the back of the rounded-end observation lounge car is the front of the mail car. Nobody has ever accused Amtrak of planning ahead.

Two middle-aged women boarded the train in Louisville. They will go to Chicago, spend the night, and board another train the following evening for California. They will arrive almost three days later.

"The train is the only way to fly," one tells me.

"It's the ONLY way I'll fly," laughs her companion.

They are sitting in the lounge car, drinking beer. They have at least six beers each between Louisville and Chicago. When we reach Chicago, they are flying higher than anybody else on the train.

Out of Birmingham, the Floridian crosses Sand Mountain. There are two tunnels. It gradually rolls down into the Tennessee Valley and into Decatur, Alabama, where it crosses huge Wheeler Lake, a TVA reservoir. Dawn catches up just outside Nashville.

The terrain is hilly, the scenery is autumn-in-the-country. We are in Nashville's crumbling Union Station at 7 A.M. We cross the Cumberland River and travel on into the Kentucky morning. There is a quick stop in Bowling Green and then another river, the Barren. A brochure describing the Floridian's route says that near the Barren River is Lost River Cave, once the reputed hideout of the James Gang. The James Gang used to rob a lot of trains.

Out of Louisville, we cross the Ohio river after a forty-five minute wait for our turn on the bridge. "This is what kills us," says the dining car steward. "If it's between a freight and us, we always have to wait for the freight to pass first."

Across the river is Indiana. Indiana, I notice, is mostly small towns, with miles of pig farms, cow farms and horse farms and acres of dying corn stalks in between.

I also notice it is difficult for most people not to wave at a train when it passes by them. As long as there are passenger trains, there will be old men and little boys to wave at them.

At Bedford, Indiana, we stop for the southbound Floridian to pass. It is nearly empty, too.

My sleeping car porter is classic in the railroad sense. He is black, with a full crop of gray hair. He is smart in his black trousers and starched white frock. He is polite, patient and helpful. We talked about this train.

"I told 'em they ought to put this train through Atlanta five years ago," he says. "They ought to run it like the old Dixie Flyer that went to Atlanta and Albany and Jacksonville out of Chicago.

"That was some kind of a train. It left Jacksonville at night and got to Atlanta the next morning. The businessmen used to ride it. A lot of people down there might ride it up to Atlanta now if Atlanta had any ball teams that were any good. But I don't believe Atlanta will ever have any ball teams that are any good. Do you?"

I said we would probably see pigs fly first.

The young man introduced himself as a songwriter from Nashville. He said the work was indoors and there was no heavy lifting, but he was having a hard time feeding himself.

"All day," he began, "I've been sitting here trying to write a good song about trains. 'City of New Orleans' really ran trains down. I just can't think of anything good to say."

The Floridian has been called the "dirtiest and smelliest" train on the Amtrak fleet. It isn't dirty. The smell is from another coat of fresh paint. The train is simply worn out and tired from overuse.

The cars were taken from the pool of equipment donated by the nation's freight-minded railroads when Amtrak was established in 1971. Some of the shorter runs are now using modern equipment built for Amtrak. The Floridian gets mostly scraps.

The Amtrak color scheme inside is a horrid scarlet and purple. The lounge car decoration is something from topless-a-go-go. It is kept spotless, however, by a pleasant bartender. Drinks are $1.50. Beer is 80 cents. The sterling of years past is gone from the dining car, but on each table sits a pair of fresh carnations.

The rest rooms are usable. In each are two signs. One is the familiar, "Kindly flush after each use EXCEPT when train is standing in the station." The other is, "It is impossible to clean rest rooms after every use. Please consider the next passenger."

It has been my experience that people who do not consider the next passenger—or people who can't read—are usually responsible for dirty rest rooms on trains.

The Floridian has had a number of accidents, although none has resulted in a passenger fatality. Once I was on this train and the bartender, a woman, passed around color photographs of a recent wreck. It was an unsettling experience.

A couple of months ago near Plant City, Florida, the Floridian hit a camper as the camper attempted to cross the tracks. Ten people in the camper died.

Some of the waiters were talking about train wrecks at lunch.

"My wife told me to get off this train," says one. "She say it's always trying to jump off into the woods."

"It's better than being on one of those big planes when it goes down," interrupts another. Everybody agrees to that.

One of the waiters was on the train when it hit the camper. He gives all the details. It is a gruesome description.

"Everybody is always wantin' to beat the train across the tracks," he says. "All they got to do is be patient for a couple of minutes and then go on about their business. Those people in the camper got plenty of time now," he goes on. "All the time they need."

Food is not included in the price of a ticket. A breakfast example is juice, two eggs, bacon or sausage, and coffee for $2.75. Lunch is a cheesburger and potato chips for $2.35. Or an Amtrak Chef's Salad Bowl for $3.

Dinner might be a ten-ounce sirloin for $7.50. Or red snapper filet for $4.25. Or broiled chicken for $4.25. Wine is $2 per half-bottle.

The food is only fair. But the service is excellent. A conductor told me about the food on the old South Wind.

"The railroad raised its own pork," he said. "And everybody knew it had the best country ham anywhere. Everything was cooked right on the train. First thing the cooks would do is start baking. They baked all their own pies.

"Breakfast was something. Country ham, red-eye gravy on the grits, and hot biscuits. People would ride that train just to have the breakfast."

Grits aren't listed on the Floridian's menu. You have to ask for them. They are instant grits.

Smoking is not permitted in any of the coaches or in the dining car. You can smoke in the rest rooms, in private rooms, or in the lounge car. If you do not smoke, you will appreciate all that on a long train ride. If you do, it will drive you slightly crazy.

We arrive in Bloomington, Indiana, 200 miles out of Chicago, on time. Same for Lafayette, where the train station is the Lahr Hotel in the middle of town. There are two hours to go. The route has straightened. It is smoother than before, which is saying very little. At times, we have crept along. After Lafayette, the train picks up speeds that reach eighty miles per hour. Just before sundown, I looked out the window near Cloverdale, Indiana, and saw three deer huddled together in a clearing in the woods.

Chicago comes at us suddenly. The lights of the Hancock Building and the Sears Tower are visible for miles over what is now flat terrain. At seven minutes until nine—nine minutes early—we are standing in Chicago's massive Union Station. A miracle has occurred.

I can't recommend the ride, but I can't curse it, either. There were no telephone calls. There was time to read, and time to think. A man who made the entire trip from Miami said he felt "defloovicated." I suppose that meant drained from the experience.

There was another conductor on the trip. His name was McWhirter. He had been on this run for twenty-five years. Promotion, he felt, would have been the Floridian's saviour.

"There is nothing wrong with this train some advertising couldn't change," he began. "I pick up the paper everyday and see these big advertisements on airplanes. I never see anything on Amtrak.

"Why don't they spend a million dollars advertising this train? It would get 'em 5 million back. Nobody knows about us."

As he talked, I remembered a conversation with a Birmingham bartender long before Amtrak's management decided the Floridian should be scuttled. I asked him if people in Birmingham were concerned they might lose their train to Atlanta.

"What train?" he asked back.

Jimmy Harmon

It wasn't that long ago all little boys loved trains. Most of them grew out of it. Some of us didn't.

Jimmy Harmon, who was thirty-one, didn't. He knew the joy of dinner in the diner and watching America go by at eye level.

He knew about the lights of Washington passing behind the Southern Crescent as it pulls away from Union Station on its daily run to Atlanta. He knew about crossing the Potomac and catching pitch darkness in the woodlands of northern Virginia, rolling gently on Southern rails.

And morning on the Southern Crescent, he knew about that. Breakfast at sunrise in the mountains near Toccoa. Then, Gainesville, and finally Atlanta.

Atlanta is bustling and traffic-snarled as the train arrives here shortly before 9 o'clock. And Atlanta in her morning greenery from the window of a train can be a magnificent way to welcome another day.

Just a few days ago, Jimmy Harmon experienced all that again. He rode the train from Atlanta to Washington and from Washington back through Atlanta and on to New Orleans—the Southern Crescent from start to finish.

It was his idea—he was a news film photographer for Channel 11—to put together a thirty-minute documentary on the Southern Crescent for his television station. The train's future is in doubt. Southern Railway wants to orphan it to Amtrak.

Jimmy Harmon went to work with John Pruitt, the new man at Channel 11 who was lured away from Channel 2. They took the long ride up and down the Southern line together.

John Pruitt was telling me Wednesday, "I didn't know anything about trains, but Jimmy did. He was a train freak. He could tell me what kind of diesels were pulling the train. I didn't even know that train Arlo Guthrie sings about, the 'City of New Orleans,' was a real train. Jimmy told me it was, an Illinois Central train."

The documentary will be aired as planned on Channel 11 sometime in September. It will be dedicated to Jimmy Harmon—news photographer, husband, father—who died Wednesday trying to make the product just a little better.

From a number of sources, here is what likely happened to him:

The filming of the documentary was actually completed. But he had been out each morning this week, trying for even more footage of the train's arrival in Atlanta.

Wednesday morning, there was fog in Atlanta. Jimmy Harmon may have envisioned a shot of the Southern Crescent rolling out of that fog.

He set up two cameras on a relatively new trestle that crosses North Druid Hills Road near Peachtree Road in DeKalb County.

One camera, a sound camera, was rolling at one side of the tracks where the train would soon pass. A silent camera, small enough to be embedded in the gravel between the tracks, would perhaps pick up a dramatic shot of the train roaring directly over it.

There are two buttons to be pushed to activate the silent camera. One button starts the camera. The other locks it into the "on" position.

Jimmy Harmon apparently tried to wait until the last moment before the train's arrival from around a curve to activate his camera.

He moved too slowly. The engineer of the train said he was directly in front of the huge diesel when he was swept underneath the train and dragged 600 feet.

"I've just come to work here," John Pruitt was saying, "and I hadn't really known Jimmy that long. But we worked closely together on the documentary. I feel like I've lost my best friend."

They called Jimmy Harmon a "damn good photographer" at 11. They talked about the grief of his wife, Donna, his son, Cary, twelve, and his daughter, Shana, six. They were working at the station to produce for the evening news broadcasts a sensitive goodby to one of their own.

A little boy never lost his love for trains. Wednesday, in the line of duty, it killed him.

The Smiling Chef

Yeah, I knew Lewis Price. I have eaten his cooking, and I have shaken his hand. And what comes back now is the recollection of the morning I poked my sleepy head into his office—the kitchen of the Southern Crescent passenger train dining car—and inquired as to the state of his general health and well-being.

We were northbound, a few hours out of Washington. He had been up for hours and busy every minute. He made his own bran muffins for breakfast, a South Crescent speciality.

He replied to my inquiry, smiling. "Everything is beautiful, Cap'n. Everything is beautiful." The man used all his face when he smiled.

He went to work as a chef on the Southern in 1941, and for thirty-seven years to come, he would practice his arts midst the grease and smoke and crowded dining-car kitchen facilities.

Company executives, the story goes, often tried to lure him away from the passengers to their private cars. And once he left the rails altogether to become chef at the Alabama governor's mansion. He could cook, understand.

But he was back on the trains shortly. "Too many female bosses" is why Lewis Price said he departed Montgomery.

He died Sunday morning. Lewis Price, sixty-four and a native of Athens and a resident of Atlanta, was one of six people killed when the Southern Crescent left the tracks in Virginia shortly before dawn on its daily Atlanta-to-Washington run.

The smiling chef—wearing his starched white frock—was preparing breakfast when the crash occurred.

The photographs of the wreck were horrible. Twisted cars strewn about the tracks. I make a habit of riding the Southern Crescent. I might have been in the dining car talking to Lewis Price.

He leaves a widow. He leaves five children—the youngest a daughter enrolled at Georgia State—and five grandchildren.

Larry Price is one of his sons. He is twenty-nine and a real estate developer. He was at his father's Burbank Drive home Monday, awaiting news of when his father's body would be returned from Virginia.

"We waited all day Sunday to hear the inevitable," he said. "Finally, at about six o'clock in the evening, we heard the news."

I asked him to talk about his father. He complied without further persuasion.

"He had an eighth-grade education," Larry Price began. "And what he wanted most was for his children to have the education, the independence, the chances he never had.

"When he went to work for the railroad, black people didn't have that many choices. But he liked the railroad, and he worked hard at his job because he wanted to provide for his family.

"And he did provide. We never lived in Sandy Springs or anything like that, but we never wanted for much, either. We were never hungry. We were never cold. And we never went barefooted.

"I never heard him talk about it, but I suppose he thought something like this could happen. There is always that chance.

"All his children were close to him. He taught us to have pride in ourselves. He instilled that in us. And he made us happy."

The Southern Crescent's future is in doubt, of course. Southern Railway wants to discontinue the train because of heavy operating losses.

"That bothered my father," Larry Price said. "He was thinking about retiring early because of it. I think he would have retired next year if the train had been stopped."

I will remember Lewis Price mostly for his smile and his food and the fact he was a vanishing breed. Passenger trains and the people who made them the Grand Conveyance of another time are running thirty years behind schedule and losing ground.

"All my father would want," the son said, "is to be remembered as loyal to the Southern Crescent. It was his life."

Engine Ride

ABOARD THE SOUTHERN CRESCENT—This weirdo little kid I know who loves passenger trains and wouldn't give you a dime for what the Wright Brothers thought was such a big deal got to ride in the head engine of the Southern Crescent twice this week.

North to Greenville, South Carolina, in the evening, and south back to Atlanta early the next morning.

I went along as a sort of chaperon.

It was the kid's last opportunity to experience such an adventure. Wednesday night, Southern Railway got out of the passenger train business, 149 years after it began, when the last Southern Crescent pulled out of Atlanta's Peachtree Station bound for Washington, D.C.

As of Thursday, Amtrak controls Atlanta's only passenger train. It is now called, simply, "The Crescent," and even its future may be limited.

This kid should have his head examined. Once he paid $50 for a conductor's hat. He wears it when he listens to his record of train sounds. He has pictures of trains on his walls, and once he even spent a honeymoon night on a train.

He's a mature kid.

He climbed up the side of the green and gold Southern engine Number 6914 shortly before 7:30 P.M. at Peachtree Station, and he heard the conductor from the back of the train, "Train Number Two, the blue flag is down! Let's leave here!"

He remembered to go to the bathroom before his trip began. That is important for a little kid because riding in the engine of a passenger train is very exciting.

He got to sit next to the engineer and watch him pull back the throttle and turn on the air brakes and blow the whistle of the ancient, snorting diesel when school buses approached crossings.

There are fifty-two crossings between Atlanta and the train's first stop, Gainesville. The whistle must be blown before reaching each one. Two long blows. One short. Another long.

That is 208 pulls on the train whistle the first hour of the trip.

"I love my job," said the engineer, "But people at crossings will drive you crazy. I fear school buses and tank trucks. In that order."

Occasionally, people attempt to beat trains across road crossings. Occasionally, they don't make it and get themselves wiped out.

The engineer's name was M.D. Hester, a man steady-handed, clear-eyed, and steel-jawed. He wore a green baseball cap and said he has been at his job for thirty-nine years, the last six of which have been spent driving the Southern Crescent between Atlanta and Greenville.

He will continue to drive the train for Amtrak "until I get disgusted." You know how working for the government can be.

A passenger train engineer stays busy. He reads signals that tell him which track to take because there is a freight train on the other one. He reads orders to tell him now how fast to run the train.

His maximum speed on curves is sixty miles per hour. His maximum speed on straight track is seventy-nine. In December, the Southern Crescent ran off the track in Virginia because the train was going too fast for a curve. Six people died.

A foreman in the engine explained how that happened. The engineer had sent the fireman, his co-pilot, back into the engine because of a power malfunction.

Alone in the cab, the engineer was busy with controls at his back and did not notice he had reached the curve at a speed of eighty miles an hour. Once he realized his mistake, he attempted to brake the train. When he applied the emergency braking system, the second engine came off the tracks and all hell broke loose.

Human error, they call it.

M.D. Hester was driving the Southern Crescent into Atlanta one morning and hit a local television cameraman filming his train. The cameraman was killed.

It wasn't Mr. Hester's fault, but he doesn't want to talk about it, other than to say he still has trouble sleeping at night.

He did say, however, the person driving the train is often in danger, too.

"We're sitting ducks up here," he explained. "People throw things off overpasses and hang things off overpasses for us to hit. Once I hit a concrete block hanging from a rope off an overpass."

Why aren't people who would do things like that in institutions?

"You never know what you will see," the engineer went on. "One morning I was coming in and a man appeared at the side of the train. He wore a hat he had made out of honeysuckles, a pair of clodhoppers and nothing else.

"He ran along the side of the train, flapping his arms trying to fly." Probably somebody late for work at the state capitol.

We were thirty-four minutes behind schedule leaving Atlanta for Greenville. You cross Piedmont Road, then Interstate 285, on and on out through Duluth and Buford and Flowery Branch.

We whisked past Bill Miner's Crossing, named for the last person to hold up a Southern Railway passenger train. That was 1907. He got $18,000 in gold but was captured a few days later, passed out drunk in a Dahlonega hotel room.

There is a downhill glide into Toccoa, taken at a smooth sixty, and there is a tall trestle to cross over the river into South Carolina.

Clemson is a flagstop. More than the normal number of passengers boarded the train at the old station in Greenville, northbound for such places as Charlotte, Greensboro, Danville, Lynchburg, and finally, Washington, at shortly past eight the next morning.

The sun rises on the southbound Southern Crescent in the still-icy hills of Banks, Habersham and Hall. Greeting morning in the engine of a passenger train, with three other engines behind you making the noise of the devils of 10,000 hells, is something Freud should have experienced and interpreted.

The little kid loved every minute of it. When we had left the engine back at Peachtree Station, I asked him what he thought of Brock Adams, Jimmy Carter's secretary of transportation, who is trying to do away with 10,000 miles of the Amtrak system, including the route of the Crescent.

"Why doesn't he go to lunch with a highway construction lobbyist and leave the rest of us alone?" the little kid asked back.

I didn't have an answer for him.

Besides, his eyes were still wide and his heart was still pounding from what the engineer had allowed him to do as the train had approached the station moments before.

He let the little kid blow the whistle, on the Southern Crescent. And his life was complete.

Saying Goodby

ABOARD THE SOUTHERN CRESCENT—I don't know exactly where we were. Between Spartanburg and Charlotte perhaps. Midnight approached. Four hours earlier, the Southern Crescent had pulled out of Atlanta's Peachtree Station bound for Washington with three green-and-gold engines, thirteen cars and a pack of riders come to attend the funeral-on-wheels of America's last privately owned overnight luxury passenger train.

"I just wanted to say goodby in person," said a man who had boarded in Gainesville for a half hour ride to Toccoa.

There were three of them. The big one had a full beard, and he wore a cowboy hat. Somebody said his daddy was a big wheel with Southern Railway. You could have fooled me.

From somewhere in the back of the train they had each pulled out a guitar, and the music they were making had hushed what moments before had been a noisy, close-to-rowdy crowd that had gathered in the lounge car to drink its final respects to the Southern Crescent.

A black man and a black woman, wearing white starched coats in the South tradition, poured.

Train songs. Naturally we wanted train songs. The guitar trio obliged. The big one with the hat and beard had a voice on him.

They began with "The Glendale Train." Somebody robbed it. They played "City of New Orleans," of course, and everybody sang along.

People took pictures. Channel 5 rolled its film. A girl got drunk and suggested we all greet the waiting passengers in Charlotte with a group "moon." The vote was close against her. A passenger ordered more beer for the singers, and I was in the middle of thanking the Lord for letting me be there when in walked Graham Claytor.

Graham Claytor is secretary of the Navy. Before Jimmy Carter gave him that job, he was president of Southern Railway and a fine friend to people who like to ride in passenger trains.

It was Graham Claytor who had insisted that the Southern Crescent continue running—and continue its excellence of service—when all others around him wanted it stopped. He was a paying passenger this night, however. He had his own goodbys to say.

The big one cut down on "Wreck of Old '97," a damn fine train song, and Mr. Secretary of the Navy Claytor soloed to the top of his voice.

It was a poignant moment in the storied history of railroading.

He lingered with the passengers after his song. He even signed autographs, and he assured those who asked that Amtrak, which assumed control of the Southern Crescent Thursday, would continue the train's branch of service.

"This isn't the end of anything," Graham Claytor said.

But the Department of Transportation Secretary Brock Adams has proposed doing away with even the Amtrak version of the train.

"I don't think that will happen," said Claytor. "The political reality is this train will continue."

Another round for the singers, please.

Southern's plush office car number 11, fit for the company brass it carried, brought up the rear of the train Wednesday night. Atlantan Jack Martin, a power in the National Association of Railroad Passengers—the group that would like to hang Brock Adams—was on board. And somebody said they spotted Marvin Hamlisch. Marvin Hamlisch, among other things, wrote the music for *A Chorus Line*.

There were reporters and photographers and television people. And a group from the Atlanta that would ride northbound to Salisbury, North Carolina, and then return on the final southbound Southern Crescent at 2:30 in the morning.

One Atlanta man had ridden the train from Atlanta to New Orleans Tuesday then boarded again Wednesday morning for the full trip back to Washington.

"It's my birthday present to myself," he said.

Southern also had extra security on the train. That was to keep souvenir-seeking passengers from stripping it. Extra security didn't help that much. Menus disappeared by the dozens from tables in the dining car.

So did napkins and coasters, and a sleeping-car porter was missing his platform stool.

"My God," said a conductor, "I'm glad the toilets are bolted down."

There was one ugly incident. A young woman who had driven from Jacksonville to Atlanta to ride the train had her purse stolen. Security men finally located the culprit in a dark coach. They retrieved the purse and put the thief off the train in the cold and dark of Greensboro, North Carolina, at 3 in the morning, which is exactly what he deserved.

The Southern Crescent had been ten minutes late in arriving in Atlanta from New Orleans. With maybe a couple of hundred standing in the cold night to watch. The train finally poked its nose around the corner, gave a blast of its horn, and there was scattered applause.

"It's a sad day," said a man taking pictures.

Over the Peachtree Station loudspeaker came the Southern Crescent's final call. The caller sang it out: "Here comes the Southern Crescent, all the way from New Orleeeens!"

He added, "Thank you for riding Southern all these years." A touch of class.

All these years were 149 of them. Southern Railway opened regularly scheduled passenger service in the United States in 1830. The Southern Crescent was born the Washington and Southwestern Vestibuled Limited in January of 1893. Timetables advertised trips to Atlanta, the "Queen City of the New South."

Gainesville was the first stop Wednesday night. Then Toccoa, Clemson, Greenville, Spartanburg, Gastonia, Charlotte, Salisbury, High Point, Greensboro, Danville, Lynchburg, Charlottesville, Culpeper, Alexandria and finally across the Potomac River into cold and windy Washington and Union Station. Twenty minutes later than the advertised 8:50 A.M.

There were no bands, no speeches. The train pulled in. The train stopped. The people got out. An era passed.

I own a book called *A Portrait of the Rails*. A man named David Morgan wrote the introduction. As I left the Southern Crescent for the last time Thursday morning, I thought about a line from that introduction.

The unmatched adventure of rail and steel is nearly over. I admit that. So does David Morgan. But at least he sounded hopeful when he wrote, "Oh, Lord, but it will take some doing for America to get that adventure out of her soul."

9

AIN'T LOVE GRAND?

Somewhere in this chapter is a column that expresses my feelings about homemade biscuits and their relationship to love and marriage. You would think a column like that would not make anybody mad.

You would think wrong. They came at me with hatpins. One militant women's rights group wanted to chase me down Peachtree Street with large sticks.

I have always considered myself an expert on women's liberation. In the last fifteen years, I have given two their freedom myself.

Valentine's Day Massacre

This may be an inappropriate time to break such news. Then, again, today is Valentine's, and this is a love story, or what's left of it.

It began when I was in the third grade. So was my boyhood friend and idol, Weyman C. Wannamaker Jr., a great American.

The summer break had passed, and it was the first day of the new school year. We were standing, Weyman and I, by the playground swing set where Weyman ran a thriving porno business.

Weyman's older brother was in the Navy. He came home on leave and brought Weyman a deck of playing cards with pictures you didn't see that often in those timid times.

For a dime, you got a blind draw out of Weyman's deck, and you didn't have to give the card back until lunch period. Weyman sold out almost every morning, and by the time the cards and pictures were too worn for further rentals, he had a downpayment on a movie projector, which is another story.

"There's a new girl in our class," Arnold Bates walked up and told us. Arnold, who was one of Weyman's best customers, got all the inside information at school because his mother taught sixth grade.

125

Arnold also wore thick glasses and got extra dessert in the lunchroom. "Arnold ain't worth killing" is what Weyman thought of him.

This time, however, Weyman was keenly interested in what Arnold had to say. I knew that because when Arnold wouldn't tell him the new girl's name unless Weyman rented him his favorite card for free, Weyman belted him one.

"Kathy Sue Loudermilk," said Arnold, picking himself up off the playground dirt. You didn't make deals with the third grade godfather.

It was love at first sight. Weyman already had a stable of gradeschool lovelies that even included a fifth-grader, Margie Roundtree, who wore lipstick and was talked about in faculty meetings.

"She's headed for nothing but trouble," is what Arnold Bates said his mother heard the principal say about her. Weyman simply wanted to be there when she arrived.

But there was something special about Kathy Sue Loudermilk. Even at eight, she made a tight sweater seem much more than a woolen garment.

I had never seen Weyman act as he did over the new girl in class. He brought her candy. He walked her home from school every day. He tried to break Arnold Bates' arm for talking to her during morning recess. He even offered her one of his playing cards for half price. Weyman was *delirious* with love.

As the years passed, nothing changed. When Weyman was sixteen, he bought his first car, a 1953 Ford. He covered the backseat with a chenille bedspread, put shag carpets on the floorboard, and hung a pair of foam rubber dice from the rearview mirror.

It was in this romantic setting that they spent evening after evening parked in the pecan grove behind the Line Creek Fundamental Back-to-the-Bible Church.

One night the preacher dropped by the church to prepare his Sunday sermon. He caught Weyman and Kathy Sue as they were about to drive away. The lint on her skirt was a dead giveaway.

"My children," asked the preacher, "have you sinned?"

"I don't know about her," said Weyman, "but I did all I could."

Nobody knows the real reason they never married. Weyman bought a truck and went into the produce business. Kathy Sue had already filled out her ambitions by the time she was out of high school. They retired her sweater when she graduated.

Weyman called the other day. I could tell something was wrong.

"Hear about Kathy Sue?" he asked.

I hadn't.

"Ran off and got married," Weyman said.

"I'm sorry," is all I could think to say. "Anybody I know?"

"Arnold Bates," Weyman answered, choking back the tears. He was sacking a load of onions at the time.

He will eventually get over the hurt, of course. Not Weyman. Arnold. Weyman went on to mention he had given the happy groom a wedding present. They'll take the cast off in six weeks.

Charlie and Julia

I called the Atlanta federal pen to inquire about Charlie Hines, Number 31579-120. Charlie, who is sixty-four, robbed a bank down in Florida a couple of years ago. After his conviction, he was shipped off to the "Big A."

"Yep," said a most unpleasant voice on the other end of the phone, "we still got 'im."

And probably will have for some time to come.

Charlie sent me something in the mail once. It was a copy of an article by a *Florida Times-Union* reporter named Ken Cruickshank. The article explained how Charlie became a bank robber.

I'll take the story from Cruickshank's article. He said he didn't mind.

Charlie got married in 1968 to a lady named Julia. Cruickshank told me, "They were a very devoted couple."

But hard times soon followed the marriage. Charlie had trouble with his feet. He was a diabetic. He had managed an amusement park in Tampa, but his health forced him to quit.

He bought some property in Tampa and opened a tavern and restaurant.

But Charlie Hines was in and out of the hospital and was eventually declared disabled by the Social Security Administration. He and his wife were trying to live on $156 a month.

In 1973 their problems worsened. Julia had to have an operation for cancer.

Charlie tried to go back to work to pay for her medicine. He tried a paper route of 125 miles for eleven months. Because of his health, he lost money on the route and was forced to quit again.

The bank took the tavern and restaurant away. Charlie turned sixty-two. His disability payments stopped. Social Security payments started. Now, Charlie and Julia Hines were trying to live on $137.10 a month.

Julia was in terrible pain, the story continues. Her medicine was expensive. Liquor was cheap. She began drinking heavily.

"I would mix her a drink to ease her," Charlie told Ken Cruick-shank. "That's how it started."

Charlie's condition hadn't improved, either. He was having dizzy spells and periodic blackouts. A doctor ordered a brain scan.

"I couldn't do it, though," Charlie explained. "I didn't have that kind of money."

It was May 1977 and Charlie Hines was desperate. He borrowed a .22 pistol and took five times his normal amount of painkillers—"so I could walk"—and went out to look for a bank to rob.

He found one in Inverness, Florida. Charlie doesn't know exactly how much money he took. He never got a chance to count it. He was captured an hour later, fifteen miles away. He tried to plead insanity, but the jury wouldn't listen.

"I thought I was dying anyway," he said. "We had no food, no money and no prospect of getting any. So I went in and robbed that bank."

Last I heard, Charlie hadn't seen his wife since his interview with Ken Cruickshank. She can't come for visits.

Julia Hines, who accompanied her husband everywhere, was outside in the car that day while Charlie was inside robbing the bank.

Her number, incidentally, is 01129-179, Women's Unit, Lexington, Kentucky. She got fifteen months.

What made me think of Charlie and Julia was the exciting news that heiress Patty Hearst, who was also convicted of robbing a bank, had been freed from prison in time for her upcoming wedding to her former bodyguard.

It may be "the biggest wedding California has ever seen," said one news story, or just a "simple, private ceremony."

Whatever, they can afford it.

Let's all wish the happy couple well.

Lovin' in the Oven

Jerry Clower, the funniest man alive, does a routine on one of his records about biscuits. Jerry says the absence of homemade biscuits at the American breakfast table is one reason the divorce rate is going up.

"Saddest sound in this world," Jerry once told me, "is the sound of them little canned biscuits being popped open early evah mawnin' in evah house in the neighborhood."

Jerry goes, "Whop! Whop! Whop!" as an illustration. It's enough to make a grown man cry.

I agree with Jerry Clower. Give a man homemade biscuits in the morning, and he'll come home to you at night. The Pillsbury Doughboy, with his dratted canned biscuits, is a lousy home-wrecker.

There was a time, especially in the South, when the woman arose early enough in the morning to prepare homemade biscuits for her husband and family. It was a simpler time. Before mixed doubles replaced sex.

Women in those days served plates of piping hot biscuits. Big, fluffy biscuits. Cut one open. Slap a portion of butter between the halves and then cover that with your choice of jam or jelly.

"A breakfast without biscuits," went a famous saying, "is like a day without sunshine."

But what, if anything, endures? The last homemade biscuit I saw was in a museum behind a glass case.

It is time, women of America, to come to your senses. Halt the alarming increase in the divorce rate! Bring the homemade biscuit back to your breakfast table! We can all work together! You make 'em, we'll eat 'em. What could be more fair?

I must insist on taking a hard line on this matter. Any woman within the range of this column who subsequently serves her family canned biscuits for breakfast in anything but an extreme emergency is a brazen hussy who smokes filterless cigarettes, drinks beer from a can and doesn't shave her legs.

I called the editor of a famous cookbook, A Taste of Georgia, for help. She lives in Newnan and later this month, she is taking her book to the White House to present a copy to Rosalynn Carter.

A Taste of Georgia is in homes all over the country, including Alaska, where the Eskimos are now eating grits with their whale blubber. The book contains thousands of Deep South recipes, including some for biscuits.

The editor of A Taste of Georgia is Mrs. White. Mrs. John N. White. Martha White. I swear.

"It's not that hard to make biscuits in the morning," said Martha White. "It's just that it takes a lot of time. Most women these days simply don't want to spend that much time in the kitchen in the morning when there are so many other options open to them."

Like watching "Donahue"? Like playing in the Wednesday Morning Serve and Chat Doubles? Like running for political office? Like marching on a nuclear plant?

I accept no excuses, and there is nothing uglier than a hairy-legged girl. I asked Martha White if she cooked biscuits in the mornings for her family.

"Not on weekdays," she said. "Besides, my husband doesn't like a big breakfast."

Mr. White could not be reached for comment.

I looked in *A Taste of Georgia* for a biscuit recipe. One is for "Angel Biscuits."

You need flour, baking soda, salt, baking powder, sugar, shortening, yeast and buttermilk. Cook for twelve minutes. Sounds divine.

And one more thing, an ingredient most important. The last woman to cook biscuits for me in the mornings was a lady I lived with for seventeen years. I can remember asking her, "What makes these biscuits so good?"

"Love, son," she would say. "I put in lots of love."

Homemade biscuits for breakfast, ladies? At least once? And soon?

He'll taste the love. I promise.

Making Up

I remain convinced love conquers all, even in this day and time of rampant divorces and the breakdown of the family.

Take the recent example of the lovely Oregon couple, John and Greta Rideout. Greta called the cops on her husband one day and claimed he had raped her.

John said everybody knows you can't rape your own wife. That would be like stealing your own car.

A messy and much-publicized trial resulted. Besides raping her, Greta said, another thing she didn't like about her husband was he didn't keep his fingernails trimmed and clean. John countered and said Greta had these weirdo sexual fantasies thet didn't include him.

Luckily for husbands everywhere, the jury said, "Not guilty."

But that was not the end of the story. Almost before the jury could get out of its box, Greta and John announced they had resolved their differences and were returning home to live as husband and wife.

If John and Greta Rideout can patch things up again, anybody can. Including the Marietta couple that was divorced last week.

I couldn't believe my eyes as I read news reports of what finally put their marriage asunder. It happened last October. On Halloween night.

There stood the wife, who was separated from her husband at the time, minding her own business in her kitchen. Into the room walked the muscular figure of the man she married.

He's an avid weightlifter, so the story goes. Apparently, that's not all of his problem.

He was dressed in the costume of the television character, the "Incredible Hulk," all green and scary looking. On television, the "Incredible Hulk" is a quiet, unassuming, puny physicist who has this chemical imbalance in his body.

When riled, the physicist swells to several times his normal size, and his face changes into something that would scare a dog off a meat wagon.

Frightening his wife right out of her apron wasn't enough for the Cobb Clonker, by day a pharmacist.

According to the news story, he also pounded his wife one to the head, rendering her unconscious as they say at police headquarters.

He denied belting her and said he had simply dropped by her kitchen on his way to a Halloween party where he later won "best costume" after eating the glass punch bowl.

The divorce was granted last week. I called authorities in Cobb County for further details. I was told the man is presently free on a $3,000 peace bond following another assault on his wife.

I also found out policemen hate dealing with this sort of situation because it can be extremely dangerous duty.

"What drives us crazy," a Cobb officer said, "is when you go into one of these things where the man has beaten up his old lady and she wants him thrown in jail, sometimes she'll turn on you if you have to take him out by force.

"These officers went into a house one night. The woman was all bloody and bruised. Two or three young'uns were crying, and the man was drunk. They tried to take him to jail, and he put up a fight.

"Before you knew it, the woman and the young'uns were breaking things over the officers' heads. They knocked the brim clean off one officer's Stetson."

That's what I was saying. When the going gets tough, love can still overcome the greatest obstacles. I think there is definite hope for the ex-couple from Marietta.

He wants to be the "Incredible Hulk." Fine. She could dress up like "Wonder Woman." Give and take. That's the answer.

Just like the Rideouts. John is going to get a manicure, and Greta, sweet thing, has promised to try to work him into at least two fantasies a week.

My Little Cupcake

Dear "Sweetie-Poo,"

Bet you thought you'd never hear me call you that again. Cupcake, we may be living apart now, but there are some things I will never forget about the six weeks we had together.

Just the other day, I was remembering how I started calling you that name, "Sweetie Poo." Do you remember, Dovey? I used to leave little notes on my pillow before I left for work so you would find them when you awakened later.

I would write, "Roses are red, violets are blue, and I love my Sweetie-Poo." I know you enjoyed them because you would always call me the minute you turned over and found them.

I'm sorry I was hardly ever in the office when you called, but the boss insisted we knock off for lunch at one o'clock on the dot.

Darling, I've been doing a lot of thinking about what happened to our Little Blue Heaven. I have never had a shock like the one you gave me when you said you believed we should separate and I should move out because marriage was stifling your career.

Honey, I still believe you could be married and teach bridge at the club, too, but I suppose it's too late to turn back now. I guess you know your lawyer has talked to mine and we'll be going to court soon to get the divorce.

Maybe you didn't know. I ran into your best friend Gladys, and she said you've been traveling a lot. Aspen, huh? I'll bet you turned a few heads on the slopes with those new ski outfits you bought for the trip.

Didn't think I knew about that, did you, Pumpkin? The bill you had the department store send me came this morning. We've worked something out so I can pay a little at the time. It probably helped that your old man owns the joint.

Incidentally, if Gladys mentions anything about my saying I hoped you broke your leg in five places, I was only kidding, ma chérie.

Drove by the house the other night to pick up the broom and dustpan set you gave me as a wedding present, but I was afraid to come in. It looked like you might be having a party.

The band sounded tremendous. I know you are going to think I'm crazy, but for a moment, I thought I could see you and your lawyer dancing without any clothes on by the pool. Silly me. Just my imagination, I'm sure, or the lighting from the Japanese lanterns.

By the way, was that a new car I saw parked in the driveway? Gladys also said something about your Dad giving you a new Jag to help you get over the grief of our sudden breakup.

Love that color! You always did look good in red. Besides, the burnt orange Porsche he gave you for your birthday last month simply wasn't you, Cutes.

Sorry I got so upset last month when you said you had run out of money again and I'd have to make the house payment. I had some fool notion you could put what I send you together with the allowance from your old man and have plenty for the mortgage and some left over.

But you're right. I had no idea the price of tennis outfits had gone up so much, and I didn't know your father had cut you to a grand a week because of the way his stocks have fallen off.

I managed to scrape by. The watch my grandfather gave me on his deathbed was worth a pretty penny at the pawn shop, and I sold a few pints of blood to get the rest.

I'm doing just fine in my new place, Gumdrop. The landlord said he couldn't do anything about the rats for a while, but I'm getting used to them. It's nice to have some pleasant company for a change. (Ha! Ha! Still kidding, my little Sweet Potato.)

Better close for now, Puddin'. Know you're busy. Me, too. Working two jobs can sure keep a fellow hopping. One more thing, I really laughed when Gladys made that crack that you and your lawyer planning to "take me to the cleaners" in divorce court. You're a regular riot, Loveykins.

All for now. Write soon.

Always,
Your "Precious Lamb"

P.S.: My lawyer just called and told me the Supreme Court has ruled that women with a lot of money may now have to pay alimony to their husbands.

P.P.S. See you in court, Snorkel-Face.

Hope

ELLIJAY—The day has grown old gracefully in Ellijay, where the mountains are about to begin, and as is the custom in such settings, men with nothing better to do have gathered around the courthouse. In this case, it is the Gilmer County courthouse. There is a tree in front. And benches.

I still love a courthouse because it was on the steps of one I learned to play checkers and dominoes, and I learned about the Book of Revelation, which is what the old men would talk about after they tired of checkers and dominoes.

"Gon' be an awful day That Day," one old man would say at the courthouse.

"Gon' be a lot of folks caught short That Day," another would reply.

I even tried to read Revelation once. I stopped. It spooked me.

Standing with the men under the tree in front of the Gilmer County courthouse, I noticed the heat again—it remained stifling despite the approaching dusk—and perhaps that is what brought back Revelation's fiery warnings so vividly.

I am in Ellijay to watch the campaign tactics of Mary Beth Busbee, wife of the governor who is the first man in our state's modern history to seek a second consecutive term to that post.

I watch her closely and decide she loves her husband deeply or she wouldn't be working with such fervor. That feels good to me. He is campaigning south. She is campaigning north. Mary Beth Busbee says to people, "I'm Mary Beth Busbee, and I hope you will vote for my husband."

As I watch her, I think about marriage and how it has failed me— or how I have failed it—and I wonder if there is hope for those of us who have seen only marriage's bad side.

Earlier, Mary Beth Busbee had walked into a book and magazine store on the Ellijay courthouse square. "I'm Mary Beth Busbee," she said to the woman working there, "and I hope you will vote for my husband."

The woman spoke up quickly, "I lost my husband, you know. A year ago. He had a massive heart attack."

Mrs. Busbee listened. The woman's voice cracked with emotion. A year later, her voice still cracked with emotion.

The governor's wife introduced herself to the group standing at the courthouse.

A man in a T-shirt said, "If I was runnin' for office, the last person I'd want out tryin' to get me votes is my wife."

Mrs. Busbee wanted to know why.

"'Cause," the man went on, "she ain't never said nothin' good about me at home, and I know she ain't gonna say nothin' good about me out in public."

That brought a laugh all around. A good marriage needs a little levity, I was thinking.

Grady was there, and he met Mrs. Busbee, too. Grady is wearing overalls. His hat is twice my age. Remnants of the day's snuff encircle his mouth. For every courthouse, there is a Grady.

"Grady's ninety-three," somebody said.

"He still gets up and preaches over at the Holiness Church," somebody else said.

"That's my wife over there," Grady said to me. I looked and saw a little lady in a print dress, sitting on one of the benches alone. She drank water from a tall soft-drink bottle. There was evidence she dips now and then, too.

"How long you been married?" I asked Grady.

"Twelve years," he answered. "She's a good woman."

As I drove from Ellijay, I looked back once at the courthouse. Grady and his bride were walking away. It may have been my imagination, but I think I saw him take her hand.

Only one thing spooks me more than Revelation. Marriage. But Mary Beth loves George, a woman in a store grieves a year later, a husband makes a loving joke, and a ninety-three-year-old newlywed still feels the spark.

There is hope. There is hope.

10

A STINKING
PLACE TO DIE

A good father. A good cop. A good friend. And a porno hustler who saw the light. Death and near-death from Guyana to Lawrenceville, Georgia.

Don Harris

Ray Tapley is a man I have known for a long time. He has a good job with an insurance company in Atlanta, but he continues to insist upon working for the newspaper on Saturday nights.

Ray Tapley writes headlines and edits stories that appear in the Sunday sports section.

Saturday night, he said he only glanced at the front page when the final Sunday edition came up to the newsroom for a final read-down.

"I saw the headlines about Congressman Ryan possibly being killed in Guyana," Ray said, "but I didn't look at the story any closer. Only after I got home and read the entire report did I know about Don Harris.

"And it took me a minute to recall 'Don Harris' was Darwin Humphrey's television name."

Don Harris—or Darwin Humphrey—was the NBC reporter from Los Angeles who was murdered along with Rep. Leo J. Ryan, two other newsmen and a member of the suicidal People's Temple settlement in the Saturday ambush at Port Kaituma, Guyana.

I am still not certain where Guyana is, or even *what* it is, but I do know it is a million miles from Vidalia, Georgia, and one stinking place to die.

Darwin Humphrey was from Vidalia, down Route 297 off Interstate 16, in the heart of tobacco country. Vidalia is 11-12,000 people. Ray Tapley says it is the largest town between Dublin and Savannah. He also says it is the largest town in Georgia—outside a metro area—that is not a county seat. Lyons keeps the courthouse in Toombs County.

Ray is also from Vidalia. He and Darwin Humphrey used to ride the school bus together thirty years ago.

"Both our families lived in the country," Ray Tapley was saying Tuesday. He would be leaving his office soon to return home to Vidalia for Thanksgiving. And for Darwin Humphrey's funeral Wednesday morning.

"His mother always came out on the front porch to see Darwin when he got on the bus in the morning and when he got off in the afternoon."

Later, Ray Tapley's family and Darwin Humphrey's family—there were two younger brothers—both moved into Vidalia, country folks come to town. They settled around the corner from each other. "I saw Darwin grow up," Ray said. "He was only fifteen when he started announcing for our radio station. They were a middle-class family, good people. His father worked behind the vegetable counter at the supermarket."

Darwin Humphrey left Vidalia for Statesboro and Georgia Southern. He had a radio job while in school. Then, it was Charleston and a stop here and a stop there and a name change to a more flattering-for-television "Don Harris," and on to Los Angeles and NBC.

And finally to that airstrip in Guyana where a shotgun blast ended his life. He was forty-two, the father of three.

There is more about Darwin Humphrey. His speech teacher at the high school in Vidalia says that in twenty-five years, he was her most gifted student. Another is a New York actress.

Both his younger brothers followed him into radio careers. A daughter—Claire, sixteen—has lived in Los Angeles for five years. She says, "Vidalia is my home."

I talked to Claire Humphrey Tuesday afternoon at her grandmother's house in Vidalia. She says she is proud of her daddy.

"He was always leaving, we were used to that," she explained. Her voice was strong. "We knew what he was going to do was dangerous, but he did other dangerous things. We expected him back in a week.

"He was a very brave man. We are proud of him."

I don't know if Darwin Humphrey was aware of it before he died, but his daughter told me something Tuesday that would have made him proud.

"My brother is seventeen," she said. Her brother's name is Jeff. And he has already decided upon his future.

"He wants to be a television reporter," said Claire. "Like his father was."

Jesse Frank Frosch

Jesse Frank Frosch of Speedway, Indiana, was twenty-seven when he died. We had both struggled together on a struggling daily newspaper in Athens, and I looked up to him because he was a genius.

Frank Frosch was a brilliant writer. Once he wrote a story about what it's like in his hometown the night before the Indianapolis 500 automobile race.

That story remains the best sports story I have ever read.

Besides teaching English at the University of Georgia, Frank also led the band at a rural high school near Athens. He was well qualified to do that because he played something like thirty musical instruments.

Frank raised dogs, too. Basset hounds. When they sent Frank off to Vietnam in 1968, he asked me to keep one of his dogs while he was away. The dog's name was "Plato" and his pedigree reached for miles. Frank had paid $500 for the dog.

When he came back from Vietnam, the dog and I had become very close. I was prepared to pay Frank any amount of money to keep "Plato."

That wasn't necessary. Frank gave me to the dog. That's a friend.

Frank Frosch was an Army intelligence officer in Vietnam. He knew all about what had happened at My Lai, and after leaving the Army, he detailed his knowledge in a masterful piece in *Playboy*.

He later went to work for United Press International in the Atlanta bureau. That job bored him. He wanted to go back to Southeast Asia, this time as a reporter.

He got his chance. They would eventually make young Frank Frosch the UPI bureau manager in Phnom Penh, Cambodia. Like I said, he was a genius.

I took "Plato" over to Frank's house in Atlanta a couple of days before he left on his new mission. We sat on his front porch and took turns patting the dog, and I recall asking Frank if it ever occurred to him he could get killed.

"If I do," he laughed, "at least it won't be because a beer truck ran over me on my way to cover a stupid county commission meeting."

There were all sorts of stories about what actually happened to Frank Frosch. There were even rumors maybe Frank knew too much about My Lai and political motives were at the dark bottom of his death.

Nine years later, the details are still sketchy.

Frank was working in his office in Phnom Penh. A report came in of fighting on the outskirts of the city.

Frank grabbed a photographer. They jumped into a Volkswagen and drove out in search of the reported action.

When they didn't return for several hours, other reporters went searching for them.

They found both Frank Frosch and the photographer dead in an open field near their car. They had been shot several times by automatic rifle fire.

There was blood in the car. They had apparently been ambushed.

UPI now gives an annual Frank Frosch award for meritorious service to journalism. And his dog lived a long, full live. One hot day when he was fourteen, "Plato" curled up in a cool creek and died in his sleep.

Why I'm discussing Frank Frosch should be obvious. Another American newsman trying to get a story in a foreign country was murdered Wednesday.

The television film of the cold-blooded execution of ABC's Bill Stewart in Managua was sickening. He was unarmed. He was helpless. And some animal kicked him and then blew his head off at point-blank range.

The list of American correspondents killed in stinking places like Cambodia, Guyana and Nicaragua grows while the rest of us in this business wrap up our days with tax relief, gasoline shortages and a four-column headline on the Astros' winning streak.

Frank Frosch of UPI. Ron Harris of NBC. Bill Stewart of ABC. And all the others, rest their brave souls.

At least they didn't die because a beer truck ran over them on the way to cover a stupid county commission meeting.

Mournful Silence for Steve Vann

On a cloudy day, spring's first rain approaching, they came by the hundreds to mourn the death of Steve Vann. One of the preachers got up and said, "This is the Christian act of mourning. That is why we are here."

The chapel was packed with people who had known him, who had loved him. Who still did. Perhaps now more than ever. The hallways outside the chapel were also crowded. Those who couldn't find standing room inside waited in silence outside. Grief is rarely loud.

He was seventeen. He was a senior at Lakeside High School in DeKalb County. He was a quarterback on the football team. He lived in an upper middle-class neighborhood. He had a lot of friends. He had parents who gave him their time and their attention and, of course, their love.

Saturday morning, somebody found him dead in a creek.

"There were all sorts of rumors going around," said a classmate at the funeral. "Somebody at first said he had been stabbed. I knew that wasn't true. If Steve had an enemy, I never heard about it."

The county coroner was on television trying to explain it. Steve Vann died of exposure to cold. He was found in creek water that had been below freezing the night before. The temperatures the night before were also below freezing.

Evidence of drugs were found in Steve Vann's body. There was no overdose, but there were drugs.

I talked to more classmates at the funeral.

"I don't guess anybody will really ever know what happened," said one. "He went to a party Friday night, but Steve just wasn't the type to take anything. He might have smoked some grass, most everybody else does; but I can't see him drinking and taking pills."

"Somebody could have slipped him something," added another. "I knew him as well as anybody in school, and he knew better."

The death has been ruled an accident. The most popular conjecture is Steve Vann, because of drugs, became disoriented, wandered into the creek and remained there—unconscious—until the cold killed him.

Something like this shouldn't happen here, I was telling myself at the funeral. Look around you, I said. This isn't the ghetto. This is suburbia, good life America.

Steve Vann was no mindless punk.

He was an athlete. He was the second-string quarterback, but Lakeside is a state power with a huge student body from which to draw its talent.

"He had the best arm on the team," somebody said. "It hurt him that he wasn't a starter, but he threw a touchdown pass in one of the last games. He must have thrown the ball sixty yards."

But it happened. Steve Vann's death was drug-related. There is no way to hide it.

A young man standing outside the chapel said, between puffs on a cigarette, "If this don't make you think nothing will."

I could make this a sermon. Parents tell your children. Teachers shout it. Drugs kill. What I had rather do is take you back to the funeral. There can be no more drastic lesson.

There were flowers, always there are flowers, and their scent inside a funeral home is a sickening sweet.

The casket was a metallic blue. There were flowers on top of it. The mother cried hard. The father appeared stunned. Old people hung their heads. Young people stared in disbelief.

An organ played softly. A man sang, "Will the Circle Be Unbroken?" and "I Come to the Garden Alone" and "The Lord's Prayer."

One preacher said, "We are all in shock."

Another said, "This is a great tragedy."

A third said, "He esteemed his elders, he respected his leaders, he was growing into a man of worth."

And at the end, the father walked to the podium and spoke from his breaking heart.

"If any of you are ever in trouble," he told his son's friends, "if any of you need any help, or need to talk, then come to me. This," he went on, looking at the casket before him, "is enough."

God bless him for saying that.

One Year Later: A Father's Pain

The longer I sat and talked with Ed Vann last week, the more I realized what had happened to him since the last time I saw him.

That was at a DeKalb County funeral chapel. He was standing behind a flower-draped casket telling the young people who had gathered there not to take drugs.

Inside the casket was the body of his seventeen-year-old son who had been found dead in a shallow creek one year ago today.

Steve Vann's death shocked the community in which he had lived. He had been an athlete, quarterback at Lakeside High, an upper middle-class suburban school that is an annual football power.

He had scores of friends. The teary young eyes at the funeral home said that. And he was certainly no foggy-brained junkie. He had no prior record of ever having taken drugs.

But evidence of drugs was found in his body. What on earth could have happened?

Conjecture at the time—still undisputed—was Steve Vann had possibly taken some pills at a party he attended the night before his body was found.

Later, because of the effect of the pills, he had become disoriented and he had wandered into the tiny creek. Unconscious, he died there from exposure to the wet and cold of the March night.

Ed Vann still isn't satisfied with the investigation of his son's death by police. "Somebody gave my son bad pills," he said last week.

And he will never be satisfied with his performance as a father.

"Maybe Steve needed something to pick him up, maybe he was tired and was being pushed too hard to excel," Ed Vann said. "I did a lot of talking to him, but that was the problem. What I didn't do was listen. Everybody wants to talk to kids. But nobody ever listens to them."

What has happened to Ed Vann is he is haunted by guilt. Unnecessarily so, probably, but the agony that has lingered this long runs deep within him. "Living hell" is what they call this.

He and Steve's mother are no longer living together. He said she has had her own problems, coping with their son's death.

Ed Vann has taken a small apartment, one he had already leased to give to his son after his high school graduation.

He writes poems about his son. He carries them with him at all times.

He grasps at every straw. He asked a family friend along when we met last week. The friend claimed to have seen a vision at Steve's funeral.

"I was standing in the back of the chapel," the man said, "and suddenly everything in the chapel disappeared and in its place came another picture.

"I saw a spring day and a green hill. I saw Steve walking up the hill with Christ. When they reached the top of the hill, Steve turned and waved goodbye. Then, they both disappeared over the hill."

Others have seen similar visions, Ed Vann told me. Another friend, he said, claims to have seen his son twice in the past year.

He even attaches significance to the fact his hair, solid gray a year ago, is now getting darker.

"Who ever heard of that?" he asked. "I don't know what is happening here, but all these experiences must mean something."

Ed Vann's emotional plea to his son's friends at the funeral received a great deal of publicity. That bothers him, too. "Ed Vann Joins Fight Against Drugs" is one of the headlines he can recall.

"I don't want that," he said. "My son was a wonderful human being. You wouldn't believe the things his friends have told me he did for them. I'm not the one who should be praised for anything. The good one, my son, is gone."

I didn't have any answers for Ed Vann last week. I don't know what it is to lose a son. But I do know if a person doesn't eventually accept death, no matter how difficult that might be, he will eventually go straight up a wall.

All I can offer is a couple of suggestions. First, let go, Ed. Forget the visions. Forget your guilt and bitterness. They will destroy you.

And what you might do to help purge those feelings is whenever you see a man with his children still by his side, simply remind him to enjoy and cherish every minute of it.

You would probably be surprised how many fathers need that reminder.

Frank Schlatt: Don't Forget

The story didn't make the front page the other day, and I doubt the television stations even bothered with it. It was filled with a lot of legal-beagle mumbo-jumbo, and it didn't have anything to do with the price of oil, cracks in big airliners, or who's running—or not running—for the U.S. Senate.

"Slaton Appeals Ruling," whispered the uninspired headline.

So what? So this:

The story told about Fulton County District Attorney Lewis Slaton's efforts to convince the Georgia Supreme Court to reconsider a ruling it made May 31.

On May 31, the Georgia Supreme Court cited a technicality and overturned the murder conviction and life sentence of somebody named David Burney, Jr.

The court said that when David Burney, Jr. was tried, the trial judge had erroneously disallowed his request to act as his own co-counsel.

The legalese in the story was taxing, but from what I could gather, the trial judge had decided that since David Burney, Jr. already had two defense lawyers, granting him the right to act as his own co-counsel would have led to "undue disruption" of the trial.

District Attorney Slaton said a trial judge has the inherent authority to make decisions like that.

I don't know one end of a gavel from the other, and I would certainly hate to see David Burney, Jr.'s right to a fair trial violated, so I'm not about to take a stand for or against the Georgia Supreme Court's ruling.

After reading the story, however, I did want to bring up three other persons who have a fair stake in all this. They are the ones usually lost in the shuffle in such high-level maneuverings by men carrying law books. They come under the heading of "victims."

They shouldn't be forgotten.

There was Frank R. Schlatt, who was thirty-one. He was an Atlanta policeman. One day he answered a robbery call in a local furniture store.

David Burney, Jr. and three other goons were at the store. One of them blew off Officer Schlatt's head.

I went to his funeral. It was a pretty day and lots of people came. The chapel was packed. Fellow officers wearing white gloves stood at each side of Officer Schlatt's casket.

Somebody blew "Taps." Lester Maddox sat down front. High commissioners and police department czars arrived in limousines.

The preacher talked about what a good life Officer Schlatt had lived. I remember him trying to explain, then, how the Lord could allow such a good man to die. I forget his explanation.

At the graveside later, a policeman said to me, "We'll find the animals who did this, no matter how long it takes."

Then there was Officer Schlatt's widow. She was young and pretty. For a time, she held together well, but then the reality of the moment hit her again, and she cried hard and long.

God, there is nothing that tears at the heart like the sight of a young widow crying.

By her side under the funeral tent that day was Officer Schlatt's little girl.

What a brave little girl, everybody said. She was nine, I think. She fought off her own grief and tried to console her sobbing mother.

There was an American flag on Officer Schlatt's casket. Atop the flag lay a single flower. The little girl had placed it there for her daddy.

For as long as I live, I will never forget the moment an honor guard solemnly folded the flower into the flag and handed it to the grieving widow and daughter.

I don't really have an ending for this. I just wanted to make sure Officer Frank Schlatt and his family were at least mentioned while our judicial system contemplates how it can best serve David Burney, Jr.

Death of a Stripper

People are killing other people in droves in this city. So far in 1979, there have been 109 murders in Atlanta. In 1978, there had been "only" seventy-three murders by this date.

One hundred-and-nine citizens shot, stabbed, and strangled by other citizens.

Sometimes it happens in the nice neighborhoods, and it's page one. But mostly it happens where the sun doesn't shine. The victims wind up no more than statistics in the roundup of brutal crimes in the next morning's newspaper.

Young Hui Griffin, for instance. They called her "Young." She was thirty-two and petite and pretty. She was a native of South Korea. She married an American serviceman, and he brought her to this country.

The couple had a child, a daughter. Later, they divorced. Young Hui Griffin had to go to work to support herself and her child.

She took a daytime job, but that didn't bring in enough money. So she took a nighttime job, too.

She was a dancer at a place called the Purple Onion on Stewart Avenue. I don't need to tell you what kind of dancer.

She danced without her clothes.

Young Hui Griffin needed money. Young sent her daughter to live with the child's grandmother during the school year. Grandmother lives in the country.

"She didn't want the kid growing up in the city," a friend of Young's explained. "She had to live in a bad neighborhood. She was afraid to leave the kid in her apartment while she worked. She was saving to buy a house so the two of them could be together all the time."

There were also Young's relatives back in South Korea. She was sending as much as $500 a month home so that two brothers and a sister could receive the education she never had.

Young Hui Griffin made the papers this week, inside section, in a roundup story headed, "Four Slayings Boost City's Total to 109."

Police had received a report of her screams. Evidence, said the story, indicated she had staggered into her living room after being stabbed in a bedroom.

So far, there are no suspects.

The man at the Purple Onion this week said he would be glad to talk about Young Hui Griffin.

"She was a damn good person," said Mike Acker, the manager. "You know about how she was trying to help her kid and her relatives, don't you?"

I said I did.

"She was like that. She worked here off and on for three years. She was a good worker. She had a reputation as always being respectful to management.

"She was never late, and if she was going to miss work or something, she would always let you know about it in advance."

I asked Mike Acker about his place, the Purple Onion.

"It used to be a little rough," he said, "but we moved, and we get just about all kinds in here now. We get the men who fly the airplanes, and we get the ones who load 'em. We get construction foremen, and we get construction workers.

"Young danced topless. She would do Oriental dances, like with fans, to basic rock 'n' roll music. A lot of customers really got off on that. She would dance two numbers, and then wait tables.

"Know what else she would do? She was some kind of cook. She was always bringing in things like egg rolls for the other employees to eat. We'll miss that."

There had been some talk around, Mike Acker said, some talk that maybe Young had taken some crazy home with her and that's how she got killed.

"I don't pay any attention to that, though," he said. "What she did after she left this place was none of my business. And we'd probably all be surprised how many working girls leave their regular jobs and turn tricks for money or kicks or whatever."

I'll tell you what else would probably surprise us. To find out those 109 Atlanta murder victims were real people, not faceless, nameless statistics. Real people with hopes and dreams and crosses to bear like the rest of us.

Real people like Young Hui Griffin, a topless dancer who got her throat cut. But she was also mother to a daughter, and a sister who cared to a family who loved her and needed her and, no doubt, hates like hell that she's gone.

A Right to Private Grief

This is when it is hell working for a newspaper.

A young woman is driving home from a party in Cobb County nearly a year ago. She is twenty-five and single, her best years still ahead of her.

She has friends and loving parents. She has a boyfriend.

She never makes it home that night. She disappears with no traces whatsoever. Police can turn up no clues.

And the months and months of grief begin for those close to Nancy Carol Campbell.

The rain was pelting down all over the metro area Wednesday. Most of the talk in the newsroom of the *Constitution* concerned Tuesday's election.

Then, the call came. A car had been found submerged in water alongside the route Nancy Campbell was believed to have taken the night of her disappearance.

Slowly, the details came in. It was Nancy Campbell's car, and she was inside it. Early reports said her death appeared to have been accidental. It's a lousy job, but it has to be done. The softies say, "Leave her family and friends alone. They have enough to bear."

But this is a big city, and this is big city journalism and somebody has to make those calls.

I tried the parents' home first. What would their reaction be? Relief? What were those months and months of no answers like? Another reporter, who had worked on the Nancy Campbell story from the beginning, was with me.

"I don't believe I could do it," she said. "I don't believe I could talk to the parents after what they've been through."

The phone rang at the Campbell home. A woman answered. I identified myself. My hands were shaking.

"I'm sorry," said the woman, "but the Campbells aren't taking any calls. You must understand."

I understood. Frankly, I was relieved.

There were other calls by other reporters. To Colorado, the last known address of John Kurtz, Nancy Campbell's boyfriend. There were calls to an Atlanta friend who has since moved to California. No luck.

I tried a former sorority sister of Nancy Campbell's. She answered. I told her what had happened.

"Oh, my God," said Peggy Reese. "I'm in shock."

We talked maybe fifteen minutes. Peggy Reese, who teaches school, said she had been "very close" to Nancy Campbell, that she had always felt something "bizarre" had happened to her friend.

I asked how they became so close.

"We were at Georgia together," she said, "and I had been in a car accident. My leg was all bandaged up, and I was telling Nancy how bored I was because I wasn't getting to go out.

"Nancy got me a date. We wound up dating these two guys who were friends, and we saw a lot of each other after that."

After Georgia, Peggy Reese and Nancy Campbell stayed in touch. They talked on the telephone, about their lives, about their futures. "I really believe Nancy was a happy person," Peggy Reese said. "She like her job. She was doing some photography which she enjoyed.

"She and John had been dating a long time, but I don't think she was ready to get married. We are in that age group where we are looking for a lot of things in life."

We talked about Nancy's parents.

"I just went to see them several times," Peggy said. "It was awful. They were so down, so depressed. I was convinced they would never breathe another happy breath.

"What happened today will be rough on them right now, but maybe in the long run, it will be better they know."

Later, I thought about trying to call Nancy Campbell's parents again.

I decided not to. To hell with big city journalism on a dreary Wednesday afternoon. People have a right to grieve in private.

Religion and Larry Flynt

It was the prettiest day of late winter. Larry Flynt was somewhere between life and death on an operating table in Button Gwinnett Hospital. Lawrenceville radio station WLAW was on the air with its daily gospel hour.

The first record, the announcer said, was the number one gospel tune in the country, "I'm A Believer Since Jesus Showed Me The Way."

Some nut gunned down Larry Flynt and one of his lawyers on a Lawrenceville street Monday. "Nothing like this has ever happened here before," said an old man at the hospital. Larry Flynt was on trial here for peddling dirty books. Larry Flynt said recently he is a believer since Jesus showed him the way.

Many people don't believe that.

One woman was talking to another woman outside the hospital emergency room.

"I bet the Mafia done it," she said. "He made too much money for the Mafia not to be in on this."

The other woman agreed.

Somebody else said it was probably "some religious fanatic." Larry Flynt gave his views on religion at the trial last week. Some didn't hold to the strictest of Christian doctrine. I remember one of the things he said: "The Bible is a tool to live by, but it shouldn't be an obstacle course."

Flowers were already pouring in for Flynt. There were roses from somebody named Stan Coakley in Killbruck, Ohio. The card read, "Hang in there."

Another arrangement came in from a Bob Flamm. There was no address. The card read, "You showed me how fear can shake a mountain and how faith could move it. Keep the faith. I'm pulling for you all the way."

One of the flower-bearers at the hospital said, "You haven't seen anything. We're making one up from the PTL Club that's gonna be six-foot tall."

PTL stands for "Praise The Lord." The PTL Club is a Christian television program that is shown all over America, Canada and Latin America. Atlantans see it on Channel 36. Its headquarters are in Charlotte. A man named Jim Bakker founded it, runs it and is the television program host.

He sent the flowers.

I couldn't reach Jim Bakker Monday. I talked to his assistant, Robert Manzano, by telephone. Here is what he told me about Larry Flynt and religion:

"Some of our members met Larry Flynt in New York and invited him to Charlotte to talk with Jim Bakker on the PTL Club.

"He came but he was not put on the show. He and Jim Bakker went into another room and talked about religion off the record. Jim was concerned about Mr. Flynt's sincerity concerning his recent conversion.

"The interview was taped, and when it ended, Jim Bakker said he really believed Mr. Flynt was a born-again Christian and that he was honest and sincere.

"He said he was a brandnew Christian and confused and not clear in his philosophy. We caught a lot of flak from religious groups for having anything to do with Larry Flynt at all.

"But Jim Bakker said because he was a new Christian and confused, we needed to love him and help him rather than reject him. He said, 'It is the job of a Christian to love and not to judge.'"

I asked the man to repeat that for me. I wanted to make sure I had it straight.

"It is the job of a Christian," he said, "to love and not to judge."

The woman with the Mafia idea was talking to her friend again.

"You reckon he REALLY got religion?" she asked.

"If he didn't before," her friend said, looking into the emergency room, "I bet he's got it now."

11

SOME OLD PEOPLE

Come to think of it, the one burning ambition in my life is to live long enough to become an old man. . . .

Smokey Bailey

The past few months had been good ones for Ottis "Smokey" Bailey, a friend of mine. Smokey Bailey is the man who collects Bibles and then gives them away to people he thinks "need a good talkin' from the Lord."

I first met him in the cool of a springtime evening as he sat in his favorite chair under some trees behind the big apartment buildings at 2450 Peachtree. Smokey worked there as the building custodian. He lived in the basement.

"I come out here in the evenings," he told me, "to study the Book. Every answer to every question ever been is in the Book."

I wrote a couple of columns about Smokey, and you responded with hundreds of Bibles for him. He beamed each time I brought over a new load.

Later, I would see him on street corners from Buckhead to Brookwood, preaching to anybody who would listen—preaching to anybody.

There was the sweltering day in Buckhead. Smokey, long sleeves and a hat, stood in the park across from the old Capri Theater, Bible held high in one hand, the other hand waving toward the heavens.

He was glad to see me.

"Done give every one of them Bibles away," he said. "Lot of folks out there got the Word wouldn't have had it if you hadn't brought me them Bibles."

I passed along the credit to those who had taken the time, who had gone to the expense to load Smokey's Biblical arsenal.

Smokey Bailey is nearly sixty. He's a color-blind black man without family, without a purpose other than to do what he thinks the Lord has insisted he do.

For his custodial work at the apartment buildings, he was paid $200 a month. Most of that went for new Bibles. He had layaway accounts at Buckhead book stores. Smokey was always busted, and Wednesday his world caved in.

There are several versions to the story. Aycock, the management company that runs Smokey's building, said Smokey was evicted Wednesday because the building owner, Mrs. Dorothy Johnson, instructed that it be done.

"He wasn't doing his job," said Garvin Aycock. "All I could do was what the law directs me to do."

Mrs. Johnson has refused comment.

A resident who asked that her name not be used ("or I'd be evicted, too") said, "A lot of it was racial. One of the men residents here complained that Smokey put his hand on some of the women's shoulders. He put his hand on my shoulder. And then he'd say, 'God bless you.'

"There wasn't that much work for Smokey to do in the first place. Mrs. Johnson didn't like him preaching either. Whatever else Smokey was, he was harmless. What happened today broke my heart."

Smokey was fired from his job and kicked out on the street. A half-dozen sheriff's deputies came and moved his meager belongings from his basement apartment out to the sidewalk on Peachtree.

Smokey *had* been warned. His checks had been stopped. "I didn't know where else to go," Smokey told me later. "I didn't know they would do me that way. That ain't no way to do anybody."

People from Atlanta's Housing Support Service came to help Smokey. They hired a truck to move away his belongings. Bibles were scattered up and down the sidewalk. A chair wouldn't fit in the truck. A passerby stopped and purchased it for seven dollars. The movers gave the money to Smokey.

He was eventually taken to the Salvation Army, which has agreed to house him for ten days. Somebody paid to have his few possessions stored.

I can't place any blame here. Maybe Smokey should have spent more time on his custodial duties before heading for his streetside pulpit. And he did have notice that the eviction was coming.

But an old man with a big heart and a message of love is homeless today, and that makes me sick to my stomach.

I do remember something Smokey said to me once, however. It had to do with not being overly concerned with personal gains and security while running in the human race.

"Money ain't never worried me," he said, "'cause my wages are comin' later. The Lord's been holdin' 'em for me."

Pauline Jones

Pauline Jones had enough troubles as it was. She is crippled and in a wheelchair. Arthritis. She was married once, but that was a long time ago. There were no children.

She has two sisters in Atlanta, but they have health problems of their own. They can't help. Pauline is sixty-eight. And she is alone in the city.

What keeps her going is her stubbornness. You need that, and a good measure of it, when you fight The Big Red Tape Machine.

Two months ago, she entered a hospital for surgery on her legs. Doctors say there is a possibility she may even walk again. Pauline is still in the hospital going through a period of rehabilitation.

But it has been slow. Slower than normal because she doesn't know if she will have a place to live when the hospital releases her.

It all began months ago when the Atlanta Housing Authority ordered her to leave her apartment at the AHA high-rise at 2240 Peachtree.

The other tenants were complaining. Mrs. Jones drinks too much, they said. She gets frightened in the middle of the night and calls the fire department, they said. And she keeps cats in her apartment. There is a rule against pets in AHA apartments.

Pauline wouldn't budge. "Somebody's poisoned one of my cats," she says. "I had two kittens left in my apartment. They are all I have."

The AHA took her to court. Tenants from her apartment came by bus to testify. The jury ruled she must leave. Her attorney managed to hold off any further action by appealing to a higher court. Recently, the higher court ruled against Pauline Jones again.

She got that bad news in the hospital the other day from her own law firm, which decided to inform her in a rather matter-of-fact letter that also mentioned she might be evicted within ten days. Pauline didn't need that. "Physically, she is coming along fine," said a doctor at her bedside. "But psychologically, all this hasn't helped a bit."

I talked with two lawyers and one housing authority spokesperson about Pauline Jones this week. "We had no choice," they said. "We had the other tenants to think about. We even offered her another apartment, but she wouldn't take it." Graciously, the AHA says it will not evict Pauline from her apartment until the higher court sends down its final order to the lower court. "Then," said the spokeperson, "we will proceed."

The AHA's suggestion for Pauline Jones is a private nursing home.

I looked to finger a heavy here, but I don't know exactly who it is.

The housing authority is legally within its rights to evict resident Pauline Jones. The other tenants, just as needy, were howling. Fire trucks in the middle of the night aren't exactly what elderly people living in a high-rise apartment building need to see.

And the AHA had offered Pauline another place to live. It had warned her of the consequences if she didn't vacate.

And she is stubborn, and she is eccentric, but at sixty-eight, she has every right to be.

She doesn't understand how bureaucracies work, and she doesn't understand legalese. And the thought of moving frightened her.

And when it gets lonely in the night, who can begrudge her a drink and a couple of cats to keep her company?

And when she asked me last week, "Where will I go when I leave the hospital? How can I afford a nursing home on $188.40 a month?" I didn't have an answer for her.

It's a big-city dilemma. An urban-living standoff. Nobody to blame. Nobody to go to for help. And a little old lady nobody seems to want is caught squarely in the middle of it all.

The Man With No Socks

He was an old man out of a picture book, and I am a sucker for old men. We would get along famously, I was certain. I would ask questions about the mysteries of life and living and he would provide answers based on the truths experience had taught him.

I watched him totter across the street toward the bus stop in downtown. He wore a tattered baseball cap. If I live long enough to be an old man, I will wear a tattered baseball cap.

His shirt was wrinkled. His pants were baggy. There were no strings in his shoes and he wore no socks. Why, on such a fine spring morning, should a man have to lace his shoes and wear socks if he chooses not to?

He carried a newspaper under his arm. He shaved sometime last week. If I live long enough to be an old man, I will browse over the newspaper at my leisure in the morning and shave only when I damn well please.

He peered at the first bus that came by and chose not to board it. He asked the obnoxious dude standing next to him had such-and-such bus been by. He got no reply. The young tough ignored the old man. The young tough also wore an ear ornament. Never trust or strike up conversations with men who decorate their ears.

It was my chance to talk to the old man.

"Need any help?" I asked.

"Help?" He asked back. "I don't need any help. I need a bus. I ain't stayin' down here all day."

I apologized. Old men can be stubborn and independent. If I live long enough to be an old man, I will be stubborn and independent and defy anybody to treat me like an old man.

"I came down here to get my check," he went on. "The government gives me enough to live on. I don't need much. I don't smoke. I don't drink. I used to drink, but I don't drink anymore. And I don't fool with no women. That's what costs money, foolin' with women."

I was pressing my luck, I knew, but I wanted to keep the conversation going.

I asked if he had any family.

"I had a wife," he said. "She's been dead thirty-five years."

And children?

"A houseful. That's why I never did marry again. You get that many young'uns to raise, you ain't got no time to be out chasin' around for another wife."

A bus came by. He squinted through the morning sun and tried to see the sign above the front window. It wasn't his bus. I was glad. I wanted to hear more.

"You believe I'm eighty-one years old?" he asked me.

He looked every day of it, but I lied. I told him I couldn't believe he was eighty-one.

"Well, I'm not," he laughed. "I'm just eighty. But if the Lord lets me live another month, I'll be eighty-one."

He was rolling now, the old man. He talked about his children. Some were successful. One son had a house with eight rooms in it. Some were not so successful. He had a daughter who had been in a wreck.

"Drinkin' caused it," he said. "She had $35,000 worth of doctor bills. I told her to quit the bottle. She wouldn't listen to me. I knew something bad was going to happen to her, and it did."

He had another daughter bad, too, he said. The old man said he went to her house last week and gave her $37 and some food stamps and then went back later and found her and her husband at the kitchen table drinking beer.

"I'm through with 'em now," he said. "I tried one time to get 'em to come live with me, but they won't. You know why?"

I didn't have the slightest.

"'Cause every morning I get me some good preachin' and some good gospel singin' on the radio, and they don't want to listen to that," he said. "I guess they're afraid it might do 'em some good."

His bus finally arrived. We shook hands and he was gone in a cloud of MARTA fumes. If I live long enough to be an old man, I'll play my preachin' and singin' as long and as loud as I please and the devil with any of my ungrateful children who don't have the good sense to listen to it.

Invitation

The speeding Metroliner from Washington to New York last week had already passed through Baltimore and its railside ghetto that seems to stretch into an endless prairie of shacks from the window of the train.

Wilmington would be next. Then Philadelphia, and on to Trenton, through the ruins of Newark, and into the tunnel that leads to Pennsylvania Station.

I had seen all this before. I know every junkyard by heart. This is one train ride where the scenery is a liability to those who would espouse the benefits of downtown-to-downtown rail travel.

I do not want to be accused of provincial prejudice. I sat next to a man from New Jersey on this same trip once. I'll let him describe the view traveling by train up the eastern seaboard:

"One big dump," is how he put it.

You look for diversions on a trip like this. A newspaper will last you barely past Capital Beltway, the first stop out of Washington. I like to pass the time talking to people who will talk back.

Like the old man who sat down bside me out of Baltimore and ordered up a cup of coffee, cream and sugar. One gulp into his refreshment and he was gushing with conversation.

A lot of people won't listen to old men. A lot of people are stupid.

His clothes were wrinkled and tired, but he had at least bothered to wear what was left of his tie. There was a dignity about him.

When he talked, his blue eyes danced about. His hair was solid in post-gray white. He was a little man, but not stooped.

"Goin' to New York, sir?" he asked me. I said I was. He said he was, too. The traveler's ice was broken. Imagine, I thought to myself, this old man addressing me as "sir."

"I'm seeing the ball game today at Yankee Stadium," he continued. "I live in Baltimore, but I go to see the Yankees. The Orioles have no team, no team at all. Now, the Yankees, there is a team."

I used to talk a lot of baseball with my grandfather. He barely got out of Heard County, Georgia, in his seventy-three years, but he knew some baseball.

"Do you know, sir," the old man went on, "I saw Mr. George Herman Ruth hit his first home run in Yankee Stadium? That was fifty-six years ago. Nineteen-and-twenty-three.

"They talk about ball players today. There are no ball players today like we used to have ball players. Ever hear of Mr. Ty Cobb, sir?"

I said I had heard of him.

"Hit three-sixty-something lifetime. LIFETIME! Can you imagine somebody hittin' three-sixty-something lifetime today?"

He took another gulp of coffee.

"Did you know, sir, Mr. George Herman Ruth was also a pitcher? He was also one fine pitcher. Held some records for shutout innings in the World Series. He was the greatest ball player of all time. I saw him hit his first home run in Yankee Stadium in Nineteen-and-twenty-three."

If I had seen something like that, I would repeat myself, too.

"I know all about the Yankees," the old man said. We were coming into Wilmington. "I could name you the starting lineup of the 1923 Yankees, sir, do you believe I could do that?"

I didn't have time to answer. He was already off and naming. Few of the names meant anything to me, but his feat was impressive, nevertheless. I can name the starting lineup of the 1959 Dodgers and White Sox. It didn't seem worth bringing up, however.

Philadelphia was next. When they finally close Thirtieth Street Station in Philadelphia, they can use it for a dungeon. Trenton. Then, Newark. I would hate to live in Newark.

Five minutes into the tunnel that leads to New York, the conductor announced Pennsylvania Station. The old man was still talking. Among other things, he predicted the Yankees would win the World Series again because Tommy John keeps his pitches low.

"You're a busy man?" he asked me. Very, I said.

Later, after he had tottered away, and I had departed the station for a task that wasn't all that important in retrospect, I concluded the old man had probably considered asking me if I wanted to go to the ball game at Yankee Stadium with him. But I was too busy, I had said. A lot of people are stupid.

Barney

Barney Wisdom is dead. It happened Monday. Everybody has a right to an obituary, I was thinking. Even old winos. This is Barney's. It's the least I can do.

It won't be that complete, however, because nobody knew much about Barney—and he could barely talk—except he was a pitiful sight hobbling around the Howell Mill-Collier Road area in Northwest Atlanta looking for his next drink.

"I'm not that sad Barney died," a lady from the neighborhood told me. "It's probably a blessing. It just breaks my heart he had to live the way he did."

Barney was sixty-nine. A policeman found that out. Somebody said he was a native of Alabama and used to work in a sawmill. Somebody else said he had a son in Florence. There was talk he might have a sister in Summerville in north Georgia, and I even heard once he had a brother over in Lawrenceville.

A man at the coroner's office told me Wednesday he had tried to contact a relative to claim Barney's body from the Grady morgue.

"So far," he said, "nothing."

Barney was the *quintessential* wino. He worked at it all his waking hours. His favorite drinking perch was atop a bench on the side of Springlake Pharmacy at the corner of Howell Mill and Collier.

Barney never bothered anybody that I knew of. Give him a buck and he would return a toothless smile that was certainly not without charm. Barney was the subject of another column of mine a few months back.

Two rascal children were throwing rocks at him as he sat beside the drugstore one Saturday afternoon. I wrote about the incident in the newspaper. I heard the two children moved out of town. Good riddance.

Barney slept in the woods off Howell Mill. Or in the basement of a neighborhood laundromat. Or, when the weather became unbearable, down at Atlanta's Union Mission, thanks to rides by caring Atlanta policemen.

That's where he died. A passing motorist found him nearly comatose on the sidewalk Monday afternoon. Barney had been fading fast lately. A few months back, there was even a rumor he had died, but Barney showed up again, thirsty as ever.

The motorist took him to the Union Mission. One of the spokesmen there told me what happened:

"Barney was in bad shape," he said. "The first thing we do is give them a shower and then find some clean clothes. We gave him the shower, and then he just fell over dead."

He was taken to the Grady morgue. Police investigated and did find Barney had a small bank account.

"I believe he has enough to bury him," explained a teller at the bank. "I hope so. He didn't have a very good life. I would at least like to see him put away nicely."

The alternative, of course, is a pauper's funeral at county expense.

I live in the Howell-Collier area, and I always marveled at the special—and surprising—interest the neighborhood had in Barney, the old boozer who was as much a local landmark as Springlake Pharmacy, home of the world's finest limeade coolers.

I made a speech to the local Garden Club last week. After the speech, I asked for questions:

"How's Barney?" was the first response from a little, gray lady.

Capital City Liquor store is across the street from Springlake Pharmacy. Needless to say, Barney spent a great deal of time there.

"We cashed his social security checks," said one of the men there. "Barney didn't beg when he was out of money. He'd just stand there and look at you.

"He could wear you down psychologically. I wish I had a nickel for every fifty cents he got from me."

I hope some of Barney's relatives—if there are any—read this, and I hope they show enough interest to make sure one of his own is standing by when shovels of dirt cover his last remains.

Everybody has a right to blood kin at his funeral, I was thinking. Even old winos.

Part II
Won't You Come Home, Billy Bob Bailey?

To Kathy,
Who loves me anyway

CONTENTS

1

TAKE MY
ADVICE . . .
PLEASE!

Grits Billy Bob

There are probably some things more important than learning how to cook good grits—or, learning how to cook grits good—but I can't think of any off the top of my head, so that is why this book begins with the following piece, written by my good friend, Billy Bob Bailey of Fort Deposit, Alabama.

Billy Bob writes my newspaper column for me occasionally, like when I have to get a haircut, and he has become quite popular with my readers, except those who are from the North. They are quite offended by Billy Bob.

Of course, they don't like grits, either, which is how all the following got started in the first place.

My name is Billy Bob Bailey, and I live down in Fort Deposit, Alabama, which ain't close to nothing but the ground. Plumbing maintenance is my game—you name it and I can unstop it—but on the side I write a newspaper column for the local weekly.

It's called "The Straight Flush with Billy Bob." My dog Rooster's the one who thought up that name.

Me and Lewis Grizzard go way back. We knew each other before Studebaker went broke. He's a good ol' boy, Lewis, but he's bad to get into what I call one of his sorry spells. Too sorry to work, and too sorry to care if he don't.

If his hind end ever gets any weight on it, they ought to hang the lazy scoundrel.

167

So here I am bailin' him out again while he takes another day off. I bet his time card's got more empty spaces on it than the doctors saw when they examined the Penn State football team for brain damage after it was run slap over by the University of Aladamnbama in the Sugar Bowl.

We're still celebrating knocking Four-Eyed Joe Paterno out of the national championship. It's true we got us an Auburn man sittin' in the governor's chair in Montgomery now, but it's Mr. Paul Bryant who's still the king, roll Tide.

Football ain't what's on my mind today, though, but I've got something to talk about that's just about as important.

Grits.

You heard me right. G—for "good"—r-i-t-s, grits. This all started a week ago when me and Rooster went down to the diner to have breakfast.

Sittin' in the diner were these two Yankee tourists who got lost trying to find Florida, which ain't exactly hard to locate like Rhode Island or Kansas. You just drive that big black Buick until everybody you see is two years older than Lydia E. Pinkham's hat.

Clovis, the waitress, asked the two Yankees if they wanted grits with their eggs, and they turned up their noses and said they'd rather eat mud first.

Clovis blanched, and it was all I could do to keep Rooster still. I don't know why it is people from up North who come South want to make fun of the way we eat and talk.

Before I got down in my back, I used to have a special way of dealing with riff-raff like that. After they got out of the hospital, they couldn't wait to get back to New Jersey where it smells like what it took me half a day to unclog at the bus station last week.

But Billy Bob ain't as young as he used to be, and I'm learning to be a little more tolerant about ignorance. This is a free country, and if somebody ain't got the good sense God gave a sweet potato, it ain't up to me to move his nose over to the side a little.

The reason Yankees don't like grits is nobody ever told 'em how to eat 'em. If you don't doctor up grits a little, I'll be the first to admit they taste like something I wouldn't even say.

Grits need a little help, and what I'm going to do today is give out my famous recipe for Grits Billy Bob, and if you have anything to do with any Yankees, you might pass it along.

Grits Billy Bob:

First, don't fool with no instant grits. The idiot who invented instant grits also thought of frozen fried chicken, and they ought to lock him up before he tries to freeze-dry collards.

Get yourself some Aunt Jeminas or some Jim Dandys. Cook 'em slow and stir every chance you get. Otherwise, you'll have lumps, and you don't want lumps.

Salt and pepper and stir in enough butter to choke a goat. Fry some bacon and sausage on the side and crumble that in, and then come right on top of that with all the cheese the law will allow.

Grits Billy Bob ought not to *run* out of the pot. They ought to *crawl.* Serve hot. Cold Grits Billy Bob are harder than a steel-belted radial.

Speaking of tires, it was a shame the bad luck those two Yankees had before they could get out of town. All four of their tires blew out right in front of Clovis's brother's service station. His name is Harvey.

Harvey made 'em a good deal on a new set, though. Said he never had seen tires punctured that way. Said they looked like something with real sharp teeth had gnawed right through 'em.

Rooster said he figured they ran over a possum.

On Living Alone

This was written before I got married—again—which will all be explained at the end of the book. But for those of you who are still living alone, or who are planning to give it a try, there should be some excellent advice for you here. Like the part about underwear. Clean underwear doesn't grow on trees, you know.

I'm not certain who digs up such information, or who pays for the digging, but there was an item on the evening news about more and more Americans living alone these days.

I can think of at least three reasons for that:

1. People are waiting around longer before they get married.

2. Those who didn't wait around to get married are getting divorced in droves.

3. Maybe there are more nurdy-type people who can't find anybody who will live with them.

I am sort of an expert on all this becaue I live alone. I could go into details as to why, but that isn't really necessary. Just check somewhere between aforementioned reasons-for-living-alone "2" and "3."

A lot of people actually enjoy living alone. There are certain advantages:

1. People who live alone can leave their underwear lying around all over the floor.

2. There are never any arguments over what to watch on television. If you live alone, you can even watch "The Dating Game," and who will know?

3. The phone is always for you.

4. You never have to hear, "Honey, there's something I've been meaning to talk to you about," when Dallas is fourth-and-one on the Washington two-yard line.

5. If you find a hair in your soup, you know for certain whose it is.

I could go on, but those are the highlights. Perhaps what I am trying to say is, if you are sharing a dwelling and think you would like to kick the bum or old bag out, think twice.

The item on the evening news went on to say people who live alone tend to die younger than others.

I think I know why. I can only speak for the male of the species, but there are certain shocks that will come the minute she's gone, fellows.

Let's go back to the underwear for a second. You probably think your underwear walks to the washing machine, dives in, and after washing itself, marches back to your dresser, gets inside, and folds itself.

Soon after I was cast adrift, I wore all my underwear once, and then looked in the dresser for another fresh pair. My underwear was where I had left it—lying around all over the floor.

A man of my standing and upbringing certainly wasn't going to wash his own underwear, so I did a second-time-around on the dirties. After that I had no choice. I went to K-Mart where they were having a special and bought a six-month supply of undershorts.

When they were dirty, I did what any other just-divorced American male would do. I threw them away and bought another six-month supply.

There are other similar problems. Toilet paper and fresh towels don't grow in the bathroom. Strange green things do if you don't clean it, however.

Light bulbs. Light bulbs will drive you crazy. They are always burning out. You have to take the time from your busy schedule to go out and BUY more light bulbs and then bring them home and screw them in. That alone can take years off your life.

Food. You live alone, you try cooking for yourself. You cook for yourself, you can get poisoned, and then there are the dishes. You don't cook, you eat a lot of heat-and-serve Mexican dinners, which annually kill thousands of men who live alone.

Beer cans. Who is going to throw his own beer cans in the garbage? Let me tell you something about beer cans. You leave a couple of empty beer cans around, and the next time you look there will be four beer cans, and then eight, and pretty soon, you are up to your eyeballs in empty beer cans.

If you are about to strike out alone, big boy, I don't mean to frighten you with this, so to soften the blow, maybe I should offer one more advantage to living by yourself:

If you do happen to die young, maybe the end will come before you finally have to break down and change your sheets.

The Truth About Dentists

Nearly every society has had its element of cruel and sadistic monsters, preying on the helpless and innocent. We call ours "dentists."

Get ready for this, because I don't want you to be caught off guard. The American Dental Association has launched a new propaganda scheme aimed at people who will do anything to stay out of the dentist's office—people like me.

We are not small group. According to its own figures, the ADA says only half the population goes to the dentist each year.

The purpose of its scheme is to get the other 50 percent strapped into that chair so the dentist can scrape and pull and drill and make the poor suckers hurt and bleed and then charge them for his trouble.

The scheme includes sending out ADA "ambassadors" all over the country to tell you incredible lies, such as, it doesn't hurt to go to the dentist anymore.

One of those "ambassadors" is a lady dentist named Dr. Sheva Rapoport, of Allentown, Pennsylvania. I read a newspaper account of some of the baloney she is peddling.

Get a load of this song and dance. According to Dr. Rapoport:
• Dentists' offices now offer a more pleasant environment than before.
• Dentists are now more aware of their patients' feelings.
• Dental equipment has been improved.
• If you ask for one, a dentist will provide a cost estimate before he starts excavating in your mouth.

Big deal. So dentists have put in Muzak and hung a few pictures, and now you can find out about their outrageous prices ahead of time.

What the ADA wants to do is double root-canal sales, and I, for one, will not be fooled by its would-be clever trick.

Do not listen to the ADA, America. Listen to your Uncle Lewis, who knows all there is to know about dentists, because he was held prisoner by one until he was old enough to escape without parental consent.

The *truth* about dentists—clip and save:

• Of course, it still hurts to go to the dentist, because dentists WANT it to hurt. They like to watch you squirm, they like to hear your muffled cries of agony, they like to fill your mouth with cotton and then ask you, So who do you like Monday night? The Cowboys or the Steelers?

• Dental equipment will be improved only when the heinous drill is totally silent, has a rubber tip, and tickles, rather than feels like someone has taken to your mouth with the first cousin to a jackhammer.

• When a dentist says, "This may sting a little," he really means, "How high can you jump?"

• Oral Roberts University is not a school of dentistry.

• Beware any dentist whose nickname is "Mad Dog" or "Nick the Grinder."

• Beware any dentist with a nervous twitch.

• Beware any dentist who is missing one or more fingers.

• Beware any dentist who is wearing an inordinate amount of leather and whose chair has straps.

• Beware dating dental assistants. They kiss with their teeth, and floss in public.

• Despite what the American Dental Association says, there are worse things than having all your teeth rot out.

• I would gladly list a couple, but it's late and I have to go gum dinner.

Learning to Mix With the Idle Rich

I am the only person in my family ever to have spent a weekend at The Cloister on Sea Island, or anywhere like it. However, my Uncle Gaylord once spent a weekend in Tulsa, where he finished second in a pool tournament and met his fourth wife, who was performing on the tables in the motel lounge. Uncle Gaylord always knew how to live.

Sea Island, Ga.

Soon, I wll be checking out of The Cloister, a famous resort hotel for rich people. Soon, I will be penniless again.

A weekend here costs four houses and a mortgage on Marvin Gardens. Harley Devonshire Billups III, the big butter and egg man from Shreveport, might have that kind of stash, but I was hoping somebody would put me on scholarship before settle-up time came at the cashier's window in the lobby.

This place is so spiffy, you have to wear a tuxedo for tennis. The Cloister, people always say, is full of "old world charm." That means that if you don't own at least one small European country, you'll choke when you see your bill.

The bigs come here. Corporation presidents, heads of state, politicians who haven't been caught yet, and wealthy baseball players like Pete Rose, would come, if they had any class.

All weekend, I have felt like a leisure suit at the club's spring formal.What if the other guests, I kept asking myself, discover a charlatan has slipped into their midst?

I took extra precautions, like wearing dark socks and parking the truck off the island, but rich people can usually sniff out a taxpayer. We fold our wallets inside out.

One fellow almost caught me over drinks in one of the club rooms. He was from New York and several other places. I think he owned Canada or something.

"What's your game, old chap?" he asked me.

"Newspapers," I said.

"Buying or selling?" he persisted.

I took a long sip from my drink, a Rednecker. That's an amaretto straight-up with a long-neck Bud chaser.

"Buying," I said, which isn't a total lie. When I can't rip off my daily copy from the boss's office, I have to pop for a quarter and go to the rack like everyone else.

There is a lot to do at The Cloister, located on the opulent Golden Isles of Georgia and a million miles from the back room of Harold's Barbecue in Atlanta, one of my other favorite vaction spots.

You can go for a walk on the beach, or play tennis, golf, croquet, lawn bowls, shuffleboard, and bridge. You can shoot skeet at the gun club, go horseback riding, take dancing lessons, or drink afternoon tea with the older folk.

It is true that a lot of older people do visit here. In fact, the line on The Cloister goes, it's the spot for "newlyweds and nearly-deads." Often, young couples honeymoon here who fit both categories after a week of bundling in their ocean-front bungalows.

One of the older people I met here was a delightful man they call "The Colonel." The Colonel is a West Pointer, class of '15. Eisenhower was one of his classmates. He is looking forward to his next reunion.

"Only nineteen of us left now," said the Colonel as he gunned down a final prune juice and left for his dancing lesson.

The reason I did this—took a room at The Cloister for the week-end—is I deserved it. The rigors of work have been piling up, the heap I drive blew a gasket, the moths ate another hole in my sports-coat, and I left my favorite Willie Nelson album on a window ledge the other morning and the sun warped it, which is why Willie sounds like Kate Smith with a bucket over her head.

So I came here to get away from it all. I had patio breakfasts overlooking the gray Atlantic. One morning I even ordered Kadota figs fresh from South Kadota. I dined in graceful elegance, played tennis, rubbed and bent elbows with the landed gentry, and dozed in the sunshine with the Colonel.

It's like they say in those beer commercials, "You only go around once . . ." so grab all the cucumber aspic you can.

Besides, next week I can eat the soap I stole off the maid's cleaning cart.

How to Survive an Airplane Crash

A lot of people aren't really serious about their fear of flying. I am. I once rode a bus from Atlanta to El Paso and back to avoid flying. Don't knock it. The bus station in Shreveport, where you stop for dinner, has terrific meat loaf, which is impossible to find on any airline in the country.

A reader who obviously knows of my problems with air travel has passed along a clipping of an article about how to survive if you happen to be in one of those winged monsters and worst comes to absolute worst.

The article is entitled, appropriately enough, "How to Survive a Plane Crash," by former flight attendant Sarah Uzzel-Rindlaub, who has miraculously survived two.

I read the article with great interest. There ARE things that frighten me more than flying—nuclear war, losing my travelers' checks in Tehran—but not very many.

One, I don't understand flying. I don't understand how anything that big goes that high and stays up there that long and is able to come down softly.

Two, I have this thing about being burned to a crisp or getting separated from myself, both of which can happen in an airplane crash.

Sarah Uzzel-Rindlaub survived a crash at Kennedy airport and, six weeks later, another during a landing in Istanbul.

A normal person would take a bus next time. Not Sarah. She is now emergency procedures instructor for United Airlines.

In a couple of words, she says you will have a better shot at living through a plane crash if you "don't panic."

Somehow, I knew she was going to say that. Every time I tell somebody how much it frightens me to ride in an airplane and how afraid I am it will fall out of the sky and I will die, they say, "Don't panic."

I panic dialing the airlines for reservations.

I panic getting a shoeshine before my flight.

In flight, it is Terror City at 30,000 feet.

I dare not eat anything. In order to eat, I would have to loosen my grip on the seat.

I dare not have a conversation with a fellow passenger. I must remain completely quiet in order to listen for changes in engine tone.

I dare not go to the restroom when I fly, either, because once I did. The plan hit turbulence and a light came on in the restroom that said, "Return to your seat immediately."

When you are in the restroom on an airplane, it is not always possible to return to your seat immediately. What did I do? I panicked, of course, but I will spare you the details.

I gave up flying once for six years. I rode a bus through Alabama, took a cross-country train trip or two, and one night I was driving through a lonely stretch of Arkansas and had a blowout, and my jack was bent.

Along came a semi hauling hogs. I hitched a ride to the next town, seventy-five miles away. The stench was awful. Hogs have poor personal hygiene.

"Sorry about that smell," said the driver.

"No problem, good buddy," I replied, "at least I'm not flying."

But it is next to impossible to live in today's fast-paced world without occasionally having to board an airplane.

My first flight after my absence from the skies was leaving at two o'clock in the afternoon. By ten in the morning, I had already broken out in some hideous rash and had checked and rechecked my will.

I decided to call a friend, an ex-Air Force pilot, for encouragement. Perhaps he could calm me.

"I've flown thousands of hours," he began. "If anything happens to the plane, or there is any sign of trouble, just do the following:

"Bend down as far as you can behind the seat in front of you. Grab each ankle securely. Bend your head between your legs, and. . . . "

"I know," I interrupted him, "'don't panic.'"

"No," he said, "kiss your bohunkus goodbye."

I know the reader who sent me Sarah what's-her-name's article was just trying to help. Next time, don't bother; I'm beyond it.

Fun and Games at Home

It could happen, you know. No gasoline, and there you are, stuck at home. Make the best of it with my Treasure Chest of Homespun fun.

According to an article in the *Wall Street Journal*, Americans are staying home these days in droves because of the gasoline shortage.

(For the record, I have never purchased a copy of the *Wall Street Journal*, but a junior executive friend of mine buys one every day to wear to work. He passes his copies to me, along with an occasional pair of dark over-the-calf-socks.)

The *Journal* article said resort areas can expect to start taking financial beatings because people are beginning to find all sorts of ways to entertain themselves in their very own homes.

The article mentioned sitting by your pool, watching cable television and videotape machines, and riding bicycles.

Since the average price of a house is closing in on six figures, it does make a great deal of sense to spend a little more time where you get your mail.

Our is the only country in the world where we pay $150,000 for a house and then leave it for two weeks every summer to go sleep in a tent.

The obvious problem here, however, is not all of us can afford swimming pools, cable television and videotape machines, and riding bicycles is hard work.

I have no swimming pool, no cable television, no videotape machine; and the last time I rode a bicycle I was twelve and obviously mentally retarded, or I would have known to take a taxi.

But as an experiment in lifestyle-changing, I stayed home a couple of days and entertained myself. I discovered a person doesn't have to go bowling to have a good time.

Right in the comfort of your own home, no matter how modest it might be, you can have loads of fun and tell the Arab oil peddlers to go eat some sand.

What follows is Grizzard's Treasure Chest of Homespun Fun. Planning a trip to Disney World? Who needs it?

Stay home, America, and:

• PLAY WITH THE KIDS: You remember your kids. Skeeter is eleven. Barney is eight. After you have played with your kids for a while, lock the little boogers in a closet and have a couple of belts.

But remember to let them out in time for tomorrow's roof climb and picnic.

• EAT: Fun for the entire family. Instead of three meals a day, eat twelve. If you take an hour for each meal, and an hour in between, that's an entire day and it's time to eat again.

Soon, the opportunity will arise for other fun home games. Like trying to find Mom's original chin. Hide-and-go-seek in Dad's trousers. And pin the tail on the "Whale," baby sister's new nickname.

• TAKE BATHS: Rub-a-dub-dub, just relaxing in the tub. Invite your neighbors. If things go well, you may never want to leave home again.

• CLEAN OUT YOUR ATTIC OR BASEMENT: Who knows what you might find there? Remember your Uncle Fred, who's been missing since 1958? Dust him off and you've got another entry for the houseplant-swallowing tournament.

• STOMPING ANTS: There are always a lot of ants around the house. How many ants can you stomp?

• COUNTING STOMPED ANTS: Tedious as heck, but a great way to relax after stomping a few hundred thousand ants.

• SETTING THE GARAGE ON FIRE: Wow! See the bright red fire engines! Hear the shrill of their sirens! See the brave firemen battle the blaze! See the friendly insurance man deliver the check!

• MEMORIZE THE PHONE BOOK: "Aaron" to "Zzbowski," hours of good, clean fun. Unless, of course, you live in Yellville, Arkansas, where it will take you approximately nine minutes.

• MONOPOLY: Four can play, but Monopoly may have changed a bit since you played it last. "Free Parking" is now a condominium complex, and when you pass "GO" you have to PAY $200.

Also, you can't take a ride on the Reading anymore. With the gasoline shortage, trains are booked solid.

The Pass-the-Maalox Diet

More advice for singles: If you don't cook, follow this simple diet and you'll be dead in a year, which is better than having to face breakfast at McDonald's indefinitely.

There are all sorts of diets to choose from today. Diets for people who are overweight, diets for people who want to live a long time. Scarsdale diets. Pritikin diets.

There is no diet, however, for the segment of our population that is always being left out—the American Single Person Who Lives Alone and Would Probably Starve to Death Were It Not for Chinese Take-Out Restaurants.

I am one of those persons. I am not married, I live alone, and if I eat one more cardboard box full of fried rice and chicken almondine, I may start quacking like a Peking duck.

I do not cook. I cannot cook. I refuse to cook. Cooking takes a lot of time and causes greasy pots. Weird things that are green grow on greasy pots when they are not washed in several weeks.

But I survive, and I still have my slim, boyish figure. Unfortunately, I also still have sunken eyes, protruding ribs, and a daily bout with acid indigestion that would gag Mother Tums.

A lot of people are making a lot of money writing books about their diets. I do not have time to write a book, because I have to finish this in a hurry so I can meet somebody at Long John Silver's for lunch.

Therefore, I will make it quick and simple: The Grizzard Diet for Single Non-Cookers Who Are in a Hurry.

Eat, drink, and be merry, for tomorrow you may get lockjaw and your troubles will be over:

MONDAY

BREAKFAST—Who can eat breakfast on a Monday? Swallow some toothpaste while you are brushing your teeth.

LUNCH—Send your secretary out for six "gutbombers," those little hamburgers that used to cost a dime and now cost thirty-five cents. Also, order French fries, a bowl of chili, a soft drink, and have your secretary stop on the way back for a bottle of Maalox, family size.

AFTERNOON SNACK—Finish off the bottle of Maalox.

DINNER—Six-pack of beer and Kentucky Fried Chicken three-piece dinner. Don't eat the cole slaw.

TUESDAY

BREAKFAST—Eat the cole slaw.

LUNCH—Go to the office vending area and put ninety-five cents into the machine and close your eyes and push a button. Whatever comes out, swallow it whole. Chewing that garbage increases the inevitable nausea.

DINNER—Four tacos and a pitcher of sangria at El Flasho's.

WEDNESDAY

BREAKFAST—"Jaws" couldn't eat breakfast after a night at El Flasho's.

LUNCH—Rolaids and a Pepsi.

DINNER—Drop in at a married friend's house and beg for table scraps.

THURSDAY

BREAKFAST—Order out for pizza.

LUNCH—Your secretary is out sick. Check Monday's "gut-bomber" sack for leftovers.

DINNER—Go to a bar and drink yourself silly. When you get hungry, ask the bartender for olives.

FRIDAY

BREAKFAST—Eggs, sausage, and an English muffin at McDonald's. Eat the Styrofoam plate and leave the food. It tastes better and it's better for you.

LUNCH—Skip lunch, Fridays are murder.

DINNER—Steak, well-done, baked potato, and order the asparagus, but don't eat it. Nobody really likes asparagus.

SATURDAY

BREAKFAST—Sleep through it.
LUNCH—Ditto.
DINNER—Steak, well-done, baked potato, and order the Brussels sprouts, but don't eat them. Take them home and plant them in a hanging basket.

SUNDAY

BREAKFAST—Three Bloody Marys and half a Twinkie cake.
LUNCH—Eat lunch, waste a good buzz. Don't eat lunch.
DINNER—Chicken noodle soup. Call your mom, and ask her about renting your old room.

2

FAMOUS PEOPLE YOU HAVE NEVER HEARD OF

Mama Willie

Soon after dying, "Mama Willie" went to the heaven it talked about in her Bible, and she is presently very happy there. For some reason, I am absolutely certain of that.

Moreland, Ga.

Willie Smith Word died last week, and they took her down to the little cemetery on the south end of town and put her next to the only man in her life, Charles Bunyon Word, who will have been gone twenty years come April.

Willie Word lived to be almost eighty-nine. She was the mother of five children. I can't begin to count the grandchildren, great-grandchildren, and even great-great-grandchildren.

The funeral was what Willie Word—we called her "Mama Willie"—would have wanted, two hard-shell Baptist preachers shaking the rafters in the tiny church and duet renditions of her favorite hymns, "Amazing Grace" and "Precious Memories."

"I've known this good woman all of my life," one of the preachers · said. "She was solid as a rock."

She was. I knew Willie Word all of my life, too. I think you would have liked her.

She laughed a lot. I will always remember that. And she enjoyed a little dip of snuff before bed, and she knew a number of important things she passed along to those fortunate enough to find a place under her wing.

Important things. Like thunder won't hurt you, but running with a pointed object can. Like if you don't take a nap after lunch, you could get polio; and Jesus said the red words in the Bible.

She could cook. The woman never failed at a pie or a cake, and she must have fried 10,000 chickens in her lifetime. I hope I remembered to thank her for the portion that wound up on my plate.

She was born dirt poor in another century. Think of the changes she saw in her eighty-eight-plus years:

Two world wars, the Great Depression, running water, the automobile, the airplane, radio, television, William McKinley to Jimmy Carter, horses and buggies to moon shots.

This was the same woman who never missed a rasslin' match on television and dared anyone to suggest the punches might be pulled.

She saw some troubles. A son died young. Her man went suddenly. And her last years were filled with pain.

She was taken from her little frame house a couple of years ago and hospitalized, never to come home again. There was no hope. But she lingered on and on, barely conscious of her surroundings.

"How she must have suffered," a daughter was saying at the funeral.

The modern technology that can send a man to the moon and can even stall death may be thanked.

Willie Word lingered with only the support of drugs and devices, and perhaps she did suffer; and she died in somebody else's bed, and I think she deserved better.

Who's to blame? We all are, because those prolonging drugs and devices say we still haven't accepted the fact that when a life ceases to be precious, it is an affront to that life not to allow its natural—and dignified—leave.

My family—and other families in similar situations—might not have wanted to be reminded of that, but I think Willie Smith Word, my grandmother, would have wanted me to say it anyway.

The Lady at the Diner

I've heard a lot of highly-educated women say that what's wrong with most men is we go around looking for somebody to mother us all the time. They're right, you know. We do.

She sits there behind the cash register every day with her bad leg, and she takes the money from the people who have been through the line and filled their plates with the wonders of Southern cooking.

They ruin us early in the South. Our mothers do it. Heaping plates of country-fried steak, smothered in gravy, and the like. And when they cook vegetables, they cook them in conjunction with something known as "fatback," which is something left over from a pig, and the resulting taste defies description.

And we are taught not to leave a morsel. There was a fellow I knew from Alabama who tried to explain his 400-pound frame.

"I grew up during the war," he said. "Every night, my mother would fill my plate and say, 'Don't leave anything, son. Every time you leave something on your plate, you're wasting food and feeding Hitler.'

"Hell, I tried to starve the entire German army."

We never quite get over that. We leave our mothers' tables and then we roam endlessly in search of a reasonable facsimile of her servings, and more often than not, the search is fruitless.

That is why the lady behind the cash register and her little diner down in a shaky part of town are so important to me.

The food is genuine. Monday is spare ribs. Tuesday is the country-fried steak, praise the Lord. Wednesday might be fried chicken, Thursday is ham and maybe some homemade chicken pot pie, and on Friday there's fried fish, and every day the strong beans and the squash with onions and the baby limas will take your breath.

The lady behind the register was gone for a time with the leg, and her husband, as gentle and kind as she, handled both their duties. Now she is back, but he is gone with an illness of his own.

And the neighborhood is going down as the crime rate in the city soars.

Derelicts line the sidewalks and pass around their paper sacks with the drunken dreams inside. Gangs of toughs are all about.

I stopped in the diner last week and took a corner booth.

Three urchins from the street, eight or nine or ten, had entered through a side door. Near the line of food is a counter of candies and tobaccos. The smallest of the three snatched something and then bolted for the door.

It was a nickel crime in progress. The lady behind the cash register never left her stool, but bellowed out:

"Come back here! All three of you, come here to me right now!"

There was something in her voice. Another lady I know used the same tone to me maybe a thousand times.

The trio of urchins walked to her, eyes down to the floor. The little one, the guilty one, was pushed to the front.

"I saw what you did," the lady said. "Do you know what I do to little boys who take things from me and then run away?"

The little one shook his head.

"I cut their ears off," the lady said. "You wouldn't look so good without ears, would you?"

The little one shook his head again.

And then he looked up at her—he was filled with terror—but she was smiling down at him now, and she said, "You're not going to do anything like that again, are you?"

And he shook his head another time and replied softly, meekly, "No, ma'am." He left the diner with his ears intact, and maybe he will never forget his rookie attempt at theft.

Most of us long gone from home forget too soon the magic of a mother's touch, be it at her table or when the need for a lesson to be learned is great.

God bless the lady behind the cash register for an occasional reminder.

Warren Newman

If Warren Newman had lived long enough to have had a book published, he would have mentioned me in it, I am sure. It's been months since he died. Sometimes, late at night, I still miss him hard.

Warren Newman, for a country boy from Sandersville, Georgia, was quite sophisticated. He didn't like clichés, nor anything that was "hokey." I have put quotations around that word, "hokey," because it was a word Warren used a great deal.

The man was an idealist, was what he was. That, and a perfectionist.

He disliked such things as plastic flowers and neon cowboys. What he liked were old people who sat in front of country stores, dozing and telling good stories, dogs, and Vienna sausages eaten directly from a can on a riverbank.

I suppose knowing all that about Warren Newman is what is making writing this so difficult. The last thing he would have wanted would have been—as he would have put it—"one of those God-awful sad stories about what a great guy I was."

But here I sit on a bright Sunday morning in May writing one of those God-awful sad stories about what a great guy he was.

Maybe the only thing I can do to temper this is to leave out a lot of gush about how much I loved him and how much I will miss him and just stick to the parts about how he cracked me up and how a number of us who knew him best often wondered if he were really from this planet.

Warren had a bizarre sense of humor, and his ideas and thoughts must have come from some celestial left field where the rest of us could never reach for inspiration.

There was his Lyndon Johnson impression. He did Lyndon Johnson announcing he would not seek re-election better than Lyndon Johnson. I can still hear him—Warren, not Lyndon Johnson—pronouncing, "Mah feller Amuricahns. . . ."

There was his small-town disc-jockey voice. I think somewhere in Warren's past he had been a small-town disc jockey.

The act was a riot, and I stole it from him and I use it when I make a speech.

And there was the thing he did about a fellow getting arrested for murder down in Sandersville and what he told the authorities when they came to get him, but I couldn't come close to capturing it in print, and another thing that makes me sad is now that Warren is gone, so is that story. Forever.

What else. He was an artist. He did sketches, and they were quite good. He played guitar. He was an expert on the Civil War.

He owned a famous dog, "Springfield," the last of the long-nosed Egyptian coon hounds, which is another story.

He snored with the best of them. I shared a tent with him for seven nights on a wilderness river somewhere out in Arkansas last summer, so I ought to know.

The funny thing that happened on that trip was one morning as we started to launch our canoes, we discovered a rattlesnake in Warren's. The three adults on the trip were all afraid to remove the snake, but, luckily, there was a fifteen-year-old along who wasn't old enough to be frightened of rattlesnakes. We let him handle the situation while the three of us hid behind a tree.

One other thing. Warren Newman was a talented writer. Three years ago, he was a bartender. Then, he got a job at the newspaper helping count football contest ballots. Soon after that, he moved to some boring job on the desk. Soon after that, he became the *Atlanta Constitution*'s brightest sports star. The man was moving up fast.

He would have left sports eventually, I am certain, and written of the world as he saw it. Damn, we missed something there.

Warren Newman, thirty-one, ran into a tree in his automobile Saturday morning, and he is dead. I went over to his house Saturday afternoon and petted his dog and talked to his pretty, heartbroken wife.

She told me about a short poem she had written about her husband a couple of months ago. She read it to me and said she was thinking about having it put on his gravestone. She asked me if I though it was "hokey."

Here's the poem:

> *Son of the Southland,*
> *A dreamer, kind and wise.*
> *More than most men dare imagine*
> *Shone clearly in his eyes.*

That's not "hokey." That says it. That says it all.

Dudley Stamps

Of all the people I have met in my life, Dudley is one of them, which is the one of the nicest things anybody ever said about him.

It was great to see Dudley Stamps at my fifteenth high school reunion. It was great to see everybody, but seeing Dudley was special.

Dudley and I used to hang out together and do weird things. Actually, Dudley did weird things and I would go along to see what he was going to do next.

Dudley enjoyed driving motorized vehicles as fast as they could possibly go. The fastest I have ever traveled on land was inside the 1960 Thunderbird Dudley's parents bought him for his sixteenth birthday.

Often I questioned Dudley's parents' judgment in buying him that car, because he spent his entire junior and senior years in high school attempting suicide in this 1960 Thunderbird.

One night, the highway patrol stopped Dudley and gave him a ticket for speeding. The patrol man said he had clocked Dudley at 110 miles per hour.

Dudley was incensed. He swore he had been going at least 120.

Dudley also owned a truck. We were driving around in Dudley's truck and he said to me, "I wonder if trucks will float."

An idle thought, I figured. I figured wrong. Dudley was a man of action. He immediately drove his truck into the middle of White Oak Creek.

I learned a lot of important things hanging out with Dudley Stamps. One thing I learned is trucks won't float.

Dudley also enjoyed climbing. He would climb anything that wouldn't climb him first, like forest ranger towers, water towers, statues on the town square in the middle of the night, etc.

I was in the front seat, and Dudley was driving. We passed a tall water tower. Dudley stopped his car and attacked the water tower. I remained in the car where it was safe. It was never safe around Dudley.

Soon, I began to hear large objects crashing onto the top of Dudley's car.

Dudley had filled his pockets with large rocks before he climbed the water tower. He thought it great sport to frighten me by dropping large rocks onto the top of his car.

When Dudley eventually traded his car, for a case of beer and several back issues of Guns magazine, it looked like it had been through the Third Punic War.

The best fist fight I ever saw involved Dudley Stamps. It was the heavyweight championship of the ninth grade, between Dudley and the school bully.

The school bully was a dummy. He verbally assaulted Dudley one afternoon in study hall when the teacher went out of the room.

It was a close fight; but the judges, one of the tenth grade girls and myself, gave Dudley the decision. Soon afterwards, the school bully joined the drama club.

About half the class turned out for the reunion. We had a picnic in the afternoon and a dance at the Elks Club that night. They played the old songs.

We also gave out awards. I won most divorces. One of the people who helped me win that award was there. I don't mind admitting it. She looked terrific.

A couple of my classmates are now lawyers. One is president of a company. The girls who were pretty in high school still are.

I was proud of myself because several of my classmates walked up to me and said they read what I write in the newspaper. Some even mentioned they enjoy it.

I imagined Dudley as a hired gun. Or at least a steeplejack. He's married and has a child. He farms a little and repairs Volkswagens, he said.

We had a brief conversation.

"I see your ugly picture in the newspaper sometimes," Dudley said to me.

"Oh, yeah?"

"Yeah. But I don't read the garbage," he continued.

"Oh, no?"

"No. And the only time I see your picture is when I need some paper to put under a car so it won't leak oil on my garage floor. I look down and say, 'There's that damn fool with oil all over his stupid face.'"

Thanks, Dudley. I needed that.

"Flash" Noles

Since LeRoy "Flash" Noles died, incidentally, the Atlanta Constitution *has been struggling to right itself. The jury is still out as to whether we will make it without him.*

The funeral is over now, and LeRoy "Flash" Noles, celebrated copyboy of the *Atlanta Constitution*, has been put to rest on a day hung with mist and pall, an appropriate day for a funeral, as if there can be such a thing.

Flash died Saturday. Somebody said he had a heart attack. He was sixty-three. He had worked here for forty-two years. His "office"—a supply room marked, simply, "Flash"—was next to my own.

Flash never married, but he had a good dog once. His aunt cried on the front pew of the funeral home chapel.

What the man did for an honest living was carry newspapers and good cheer throughout the building at 72 Marietta Street.

We talked a lot. Flash enjoyed fishing. Once, he showed me a picture of himself holding a mess of catfish.

"Them things are the devil to clean," he said, "but they make good eatin'."

I will remember him. Floppy hat, boots, a limp. Over lunch after the funeral, they were saying how he thought Conway Twitty hung the musical moon.

The newspaper sent Flash away in style. His obit made page one of a section front in Sunday's paper. They even ran his picture.

Columns and editorials followed.

"I think I'm going to do something on Flash for tomorrow," I was saying.

"Not much left to say," a co-worker replied.

"I'm going to do something anyway," I said.

Flash never wrote a line of copy for the *Constitution*. He never made an editorial decision, never took a picture, never wrote a headline.

But to anyone looking around at the funeral, his importance could not be doubted. The biggies were there, publisher, editor, managing editors, and their assistants. A columnist also came and wondered if he would have drawn the same heavy crowd.

And if Flash Noles' death accomplished anything, it at least brought those of us who cover a rather hectic and complicated world, and grow cynical from the effort, into contact with an element of simplicity some of us had forgotten, and many of us had likely never known. Flash had a country funeral. There is no other description, that is the only description. The last country funeral I saw was the one they gave for my grandfather in a hot Head County church twenty years ago.

The organ was playing softly, tenderly. It was playing selections from a brown Cokesbury hymnal of my youth.

"In the Sweet By and By" was one selection. "I Love to Tell the Story" was another. And then a girl wearing glasses sang "Precious Memories." How they linger. A woman across the aisle from me dabbed at her eyes with a crumpled tissue. The women always bring crumpled tissues to a country funeral.

The preacher wore his best suit, three pieces of blue that were snug. He read the twenty-third Psalm.

He preached a "warning" service. A "warning" service is where the preacher looks down at the casket and says we're all going to be in the same shape one of these days, and we'd better get ready. Or else.

It's the "or else" part that spooks me, but truth is normally frightening. At a country funeral, they figure nothing more can be done for the dead, so let the living take heed.

That's about it. If there is a deeper message, I frankly don't feel like searching for it. Just a couple of more things.

One, the only bad thing I ever knew Flash to do was occasionally cuss a slow elevator, but that is certainly a forgivable sin, so I'm not concerned about his address in the hereafter.

Two, I just figured out why I went ahead and wrote this anyway. I wanted the late, great LeRoy "Flash" Noles, forty-two years at his post, to have something to do with one more edition of the *Atlanta Constitution*.

Courage in the Pulpit

Good news. Some months after I wrote this, the preacher and his wife decided to give it another try.

It is one of those big downtown churches—a "rich folks' church," they would have called it back home.

There are a couple of assistant preachers who handle the preliminaries at the Sunday morning service, and then the head preacher delivers his message through a microphone. A radio station carries it out to the "shut-ins," a good church word you may or may not remember.

All the preachers wear long robes and have important-sounding degrees, and the choir sings difficult arrangements you can't tap a toe to, and people around you would probably look at you funny if you did.

There is carpet and there are expensive windows, and you feel like the Lord *expects* something more than a few loose coins when they come around with the collection plate.

I have been there in the congregation a few Sundays, and despite all the "luxury," for the lack of a better term, the fellow worshipers are friendly and the head preacher, when he finally takes command, is a bright and forceful man who sprinkles his sermons with humor.

I have always liked a preacher with a sense of humor. So many of them seem never to take off their funeral faces.

I don't see the need to be specific here, as far as the name of the church or the name of the head preacher, the man who can smile and fan a hell-fire at the same time.

It could happen to anybody. But when it happens to a preacher in a big church with fancy windows, tongues wag and eyebrows are lifted and you hear people saying, "What is the world coming to?"

The preacher's wife left him a few weeks ago. That happens to lawyers and doctors and insurance salesmen and ditch-diggers and newspaper columnists, but it doesn't happen to preachers because they know all the answers, and the good they do, you figure, protects them from such.

A shock wave went through the church.

"I always thought they looked so happy together," somebody said.

"You can never tell about things like that," said somebody else.

The preacher offered to resign. Could he continue to be effective with this wart on his face?

Good for the church. Sure, there was gossip, but the resignation wasn't accepted. Had it been, I would never have gone back. Not that I'm a regular or serve on committees, but I hate snootiness in any form.

It would have been *snooty* to let the man walk away. It would also have been cruel.

The preacher took some time off to put his life back in order, if that is possible, which it is not. He wrote a letter to every member of the church. Attached to his letter was a letter from his wife.

"Being a minister's wife," the gist of her explanations for the breakup went, "is very difficult. I can't handle it."

That's her business. His letter asked for understanding and prayers. Yes, there were children involved.

He came back to the pulpit last week. I caught him on the radio. Those who were there said he looked a little drained, but that he handled himself well.

That's an understatement. "Today," he said, "I have to go public with a private disaster in my own life." Few things are more difficult.

I felt for him throughout the sermon. He quoted scripture—Psalms, I think—and he asked for more understanding, and he said, "I know you have been praying for me already . . . I can feel them working."

I could sense his embarrassment, his "gnawing pain" as he put it. At the end of the sermon, he even called for others with similar problems to meet him at the altar afterwards for some safety-in-numbers reassurance.

Give him credit. Looking out on that sea of curious faces Sunday morning, he must have recalled a familiar lament that never has an answer—"Why me, Lord?"

Or maybe it does have an answer. Why you, preacher? Because you are only human.

Your flock will forget that occasionally. For your own peace of mind, don't you.

Preacher Jackson

Wayne Jackson did everything he could to keep my father from the devil in the bottle.

What made me think to look up Preacher Jackson after all these years was the news about Billy Carter that came on the heels of the news about Herman Talmadge.

Billy Carter, the president's brother, and Herman Talmadge, the millionaire United States senator from Georgia, are both now admitted alcoholics.

Talmadge was recently released from the Long Beach Naval Hospital in California, where they treat people with drinking problems. Billy Carter checked in this week.

Not just anybody can get help at Long Beach, but neither Talmadge nor Carter had any problems. The Secretary of the Navy intervened in Billy's behalf. Both men are obviously capable of paying the $266-a-day rate.

Long Beach is sort of the Hilton of rehabilitation centers. Betty Ford got help there once for a pill problem. Talmadge emerged after five weeks, went the news reports, looking "tan and fit."

Billy Carter, said the Nashville agent, will come out "a new man." Good luck. Alcoholism is a bear to whip.

Preacher Jackson knows that better than anybody. He's been at the business of trying to help people give up booze for sixteen years out in the sticks at a place called Hope Haven near Jefferson, Georgia.

"When you do what I do," he told me Wednesday, "frustration becomes a way of life."

Preacher Jackson is fifty-three. His first name is Wayne. He's a God-fearing Baptist, and he started Hope Haven in 1963. He had two bucks in his pocket.

He renovated an old school building and opened the doors to any man who would voluntarily submit to what he calls "Christian rehabilitation."

He uses no fancy drugs. He doesn't have any. There is no place to get a suntan. There are no jogging tracks.

"We don't have any carpet on the floor," he said, "because we can't afford it. We operate on faith." That means donations.

I asked him how many men come to him and leave with their drinking problem licked.

"The percentage is very, very low," he said. "I've had maybe 1,400-1,500 men come through here. If you keep a man sober for a day, you've helped him.

"But completely rehabilitated? Maybe 2 percent. The odds are just too high."

I first met Pracher Jackson—that's what everybody calls him—maybe ten or twelve years ago when I went to visit a patient of his, a man the preacher remembered well.

"How could we ever forget him?" he laughed.

"I retrieved him out of a lot of hotel rooms," he said, "and I spent a lot of time with him over the years. He'd come in with bleary eyes and needing a shave. Then, he'd hit the showers.

"He'd find a clean shirt somewhere, and get somebody to press his pants. He always wanted a crease in them. Then, he'd look for a bow tie. He always wore bow ties.

"Next thing you knew, he'd walk out looking like a million. He used to really liven this place up, too.

"We had a singing group here one time, and he joined them on the piano. I'll never forget it. He started playing 'When the Saints Go Marching In,' and about the third time around, he had everybody jumping up and down.

"We don't know exactly what made him drink. He lived in a fantasy world, I think, and he had some strong guilt about something.

"We used to get a lot of calls from him when things were going bad. He'd call and tell us how much he loved us. I used to say, 'Why don't you tell us that when you're sober?'"

I said the same thing to him a thousand times.

The man Preacher Jackson and I were remembering was one of the 98 per cent who couldn't overcome alcoholism. It finally killed him. He died a pauper. "What a waste of talent," said the preacher.

Yeah, and I wonder sometimes if it could have been salvaged in a swanky place like Long Beach.

Probably not. And what's the use of such speculation? Rich people and famous people who have drinking problems are called "alcoholics." The others are called "drunks."

I should count my blessings. A drunk I loved a great deal got the best help money couldn't buy from Wayne Jackson and Hope Haven, and I should never have waited this long to thank them for their efforts.

A Dying Man

August 12, 1979, Claxton, Georgia. The devil in the bottle, and perhaps a thousand more that inevitably hound a fallen hero, finally won the battle.

Claxton, Ga.

There are scenes that will never leave you. One such, for me, took place here ten years ago in little Claxton, where they make fruit-cakes. Ten years. I can't believe it has been that long.

It was an August morning, hot and damp outside. I stood inside a tiny hospital room where a fifty-eight-year-old man was near death.

Around me stood a few others who also cared about him, too. One was a preacher. As the end neared, the preacher asked that we all bow our heads, and he prayed.

He asked the Lord to take the soul about to depart the ravaged body on the bed. I said a prayer of my own. I asked the Lord to ignore the preacher and leave the soul where it was.

That was the only miracle I have ever prayed for. I wasn't ready to give the man up just yet, and, frankly, I thought the preacher was rushing things a bit.

I had never seen anybody die before. I envisioned death rattles and twitching and gasping and one final heave of breath, and then the last hold of air rushing out.

It was nothing like that. The man, who was unconscious, breathed, and then he wasn't breathing anymore.

So much for my miracle.

The preacher asked that we bow our heads again, and we did, and he prayed again, but I forget about what this time.

I wanted to say something dramatic when he had finished, something befitting the life we had just seen pass. I said something stupid, instead. I said, "He hated hot weather, you know."

The only comfort I could find in the moment was that the man wouldn't have to live through the oppressive Georgia heat the after-noon was certain to offer. He was a big man, a fat man, and the heat was always his dreaded enemy, I recalled. You think of the strangest things at times like those.

I had held his hand during the final minutes, and I will always be thankful for that. I have often wondered since if, somewhere in his fleeting subconscious, he had known I was there.

Probably not, but it is a fantasy worth keeping. He was alone a great deal during his life, which was the real cause of his death, and I will always hope he had some faint knowledge of the fact that there was an audience for the last act he performed.

How he happened to die here, in this outpost, is still somewhat of a mystery to me. Better, I thought then and I think now, years before on a battlefield of some historic worth.

Seven of his fifty-eight years had been devoted to combat, and he had distinguished himself and had inspired others, I have heard.

Better he had gone in the midst of some heroic adventure, even at a much younger age, than here between white hospital sheets.

He had found nothing but unhappiness since his last war, Korea, and he had wandered alone and lost. He was just passing through this, his last stop, when some vital organ stopped its function.

The nurse came in. Then the doctor, who noted the time before he pulled the sheet over the man's blue face.

Later, someone handed me his earthly belongings in a plastic bag. It was a small bag. Inside were shoes, socks, underwear, trousers, a shirt, an empty wallet, an old watch, and a cheap ring. Fifty-eight years, and they can put what is left of you in a small plastic bag.

I was just passing through here the other day myself, but there was time, as I drove away, to put the scene back together again. I owe the man that much—to ponder occasionally how his end had come.

I owe him a lot more than that. He's the one who gave me this name, for one thing. For another, he left me with a stockpile of stories, some of which are even true, that keep a roof over my head.

3

GREAT ISSUES

Sports Cars: Pro and Mostly Con

*If you are currently thinking of buying a sports car, read this.
Afterwards, if you still want to buy a sports car, you deserve one.*

Sooner or later, everybody goes through the stage of wanting to own a sports car. I think it has something to do with being deprived as a child.

I had plenty to eat as a child, and I was warm at night. But I never had the real necessities, like a trip to Europe after high school graduation or a sports car.

I have owned all sorts of cars. My first car was a red-and-white 1956 Chevrolet. Tennis racquets cost more today than I paid for my first car.

I have also owned a Volkswagen, several Pontiacs and a Vega. Of all the cars I have owned, the Vega is the one I have never forgiven.

It was brown and hard to crank. I used to park it in bad neighborhoods and leave the keys on the hood, hoping somebody would steal it.

Somebody tried once. I was hiding in a nearby alley watching with a pair of jumper cables just in case. When the Vega wouldn't crank, I appeared with the jumper cables and offered my services to the thief.

"Forget it," he said. I gave him taxi fare home for his efforts and called a tow truck.

I finally got rid of my Vega by giving it to my ex-wife. I am a bad person.

A year-and-a-half ago, I decided it was time I had my first sports car. The eagle inside me cried for the opportunity to soar.

Get the picture:

The open road lies ahead, begging to be conquered. I wind my way along it, two steady, gloved hands sure upon the wheel of my classic new sports car. The sleek lines are unmistakable. The perfectly balanced hum of the engine is a purr.

I pass through Barletta as a streaking blur. And on through Trani, Bisceglie, Molfetta, toward Monopoli, along the Italian shore, the blue waters of the Adriatic shimmering in the sun.

My road hat sits deftly upon my head, tilted at precisely the correct, cocksure angle. My scarf treads the breeze behind me. As the road straightens, I press the toe of my right Gucci against the accelerator, and the naked eye cannot still the motion I command.

The woman beside me? A long and most unbelievable story, my friend. It began only a fortnight ago as I stood on the balcony of my hotel room in Roma. . . .

Picture that in a brown Vega that won't crank and has a lot of empty beer cans in the hatchback.

The sports car I finally bought is a British import, one of those sexy little numbers with the racing stripes and plaid seat covers. The man who sold it to me is from Tupelo, Mississippi, and chews gum. His leisure suit matched the seat covers of the car.

"Sassy chassis, ain't it?" he remarked as we looked at the car. Somehow, I thought buying a sports car would be like shopping for rare art treasures. It ain't.

I am now an expert on sports cars because I have owned one for a year-and-a-half.

Here are the advantages of owning sports cars:

1. They're cute.

Here are the disadvantages of owning sports cars:

1. Sitting in a shoebox is more comfortable.

2. Try finding somebody to work on one on a hot Sunday afternoon in Cooper, Texas.

3. While riding with the top down it is impossible to talk, smoke, listen to the radio, or keep the part in your hair. Also, bugs occasionally fly into your mouth at sixty miles per hour.

4. A lot of silly teenage girls have one, too.

5. If you hit a trailer truck head-on in a sports car, they'd be lucky to find all your movable parts in a week, despite a three-county search.

What I am trying to say here is I have passed through my sports car stage, and it was a miserable experience. The latest bad thing to happen was Tuesday morning. I was backing out of my driveway, and the steering wheel broke off the column.

Luckily, the car came to a halt against a large tree. I don't know where the steering wheel finally landed.

And in order to leave this with a clear conscience, I must also admit I never drove along the Italian coast or the shimmering Adriatic.

I made all that up on the way to work today. My neighbor's cleaning woman gave me a ride in her Vega.

The High Price of Ice Cream

Some of you may not think seventy-five cents for one scoop of ice cream is outrageous. So if you're that spiffy, what are you doing reading a book like this?

I read about inflation and recession and depression and the portents of economic doom that are hanging over our heads like vultures. I read about the plight of the American consumer and his never-ending battle to make ends meet.

I imagine a nation on its collective way to the poorhouse. Hitchhiking. Who can afford gasoline?

And then I pick up a copy of *Newsweek* magazine and read about people gladly paying seventy-five cents for one scoop of ice cream.

Seventy-five cents for ONE scoop of ice cream.

Hard times is when people start adding water to the soup. NOT when they can still pay seventy-five cents for one scoop of ice cream.

Newsweek reports a boom in the sales of premium-quality, top-priced ice cream in the country. Ice cream like New York's Haagen-Dazs, which sounds Dutch, carries a Scandinavian label, and is made in New Jersey.

Haagen-Dazs costs seventy-five cents a scoop, and get this, $3.50 for a quart.

"If it's good," the magazine quotes a Haagen-Dazs freak as saying, "I'll buy it."

So buy it. Haagen-Dazs is described as rich-and-creamy and naturally flavored. But should you EAT it? It seems a wiser investment to WEAR it instead, like on your tie or on the front of your shirt to upgrade your wardrobe.

You are dealing with an ice cream expert here, a man who has consumed gobs and gobs of it, who lusts for it and dreams about it, but a man who thinks seventy-five cents for a single scoop of ice cream is outrageous.

We didn't need a top-of-the-line, state-of-the-art, better ice cream. Ice cream was fine the way it was.

The trouble actually began with all the new flavors introduced by people like Baskin-Robbins. What was wrong with your basic vanilla, chocolate, and strawberry?

I am, and always have been, a vanilla person, myself. One of those sex guides for the sensuous woman mentioned that men who eat vanilla ice cream usually make love the same way. Plain, Jane. I won't go into what the book said about a man who prefers tutti-frutti.

Now, we have ice cream flavors like butterscotch brandy, creamy caramel, rum raisin, and even ice cream that tastes like coffee, and bubble gum.

But don't get me wrong. I'm not a total straight arrow when it comes to ice cream. I have, shall we say, "experimented" with ice cream in its more exotic forms.

Ice cream sandwiches, for instance. An occasional ice cream sandwich is harmless, but the cake-like outer covering will stick to the roof of your mouth, and it takes two Big Orange bellywashers to loosen its grip.

Fudgesicles. I've done fudgesicles. Once at a party somebody had some groovy "dreamsicles," fruit-flavored ice cream on a stick. The danger there, of course, is where might it lead? Dreamsicles today. Eskimo Pies tomorrow?

The best, and safest, way to eat ice cream is out of a cup, with a spoon. Cones are messy, and they taste like wet plywood.

I would like to see the return of individual cups of ice cream like they sold for a nickel when I was a kid, the ones with pictures of movie stars on the underside of the lids.

Lick the ice cream off the underside of the lid, and there was a picture of Victor Mature, or maybe even Dorothy Malone.

My boyhood friend and idol, Weyman C. Wannamaker, Jr., a great American, had this thing about Dorothy Malone. Once, he bought fifteen individual cups of ice cream. He got one Debra Paget, two Joseph Cottens, three Debbie Reynolds, four Victor Matures, and FIVE Dorothy Malones.

All that for what one lousy scoop of Haagen-Dazs costs today. Haagen-Dazs, Haagen-Smazs.

It's like Weyman said after he ate all that ice cream and licked all those lids for five pictures of Dorothy Malone.

"It ain't worth it."

People Who Talk to God

I received a great many nasty letters after writing the following. Anytime you mention God, I have discovered, you get a lot of nasty letters.

I have just completed reading a newspaper interview with a woman named Margaret Schroeder of Murphy, North Carolina, who has written a book about the fact she talks to God.

Everybody who believes in prayer can make that claim, of course, but Mrs. Schroeder says God talks back to her. As a matter of fact, she says that in the past ten years, God has sent her 13,000 personal messages.

Her book is entitled *Love, Acts of the Apostles*, and it costs $3.95, a rare bargain. If I were getting personal messages from God, I would write a book, too, but I would charge a sight more than $3.95 to let the rest of the world in on our conversations.

Mrs. Schroeder says her messages from God have to do with such things as the importance of loving one another, sacrifice, and eternal life.

I am not going to say I think Mrs. Schroeder is trying to pull a fast one, because I don't doubt much of anything these days. Billy Carter stopped drinking, the mayor of Chicago is a womanperson, and a baseball team from a foreign country has challenged for a spot in the World Series.

But I must admit I have always been a bit skeptical of people who say they get messages from God.

There was a man in my hometown who claimed to have gotten a message from God—Uncle Jake Gaines, the laziest man in town. One Sunday morning, Uncle Jake stood up in church and described his experience.

"His words were written across the sky," be began. "They said, 'Uncle Jake—go preach the gospel.'"

You never know, so they let Uncle Jake preach the morning sermon. Billy Graham he wasn't.

After the service, my grandfather took Uncle Jake aside. "I think you may have misread the message, Jake," he whispered. "You sure God didn't say, 'Go plow your corn'?"

What else bothers me about people who say they talk to God, like Mrs. Schroeder, is they never get any specific information.

One of the messages Mrs. Schroeder says God sent was, "Body is a great sounding board; it is the mystic chord struck by the mind."

If God decided to give out information to twentieth century mortals, I frankly don't think He would beat around the bush.

I honestly do not want this to come off as overt irreverence, but after reading about Mrs. Schroeder, I couldn't help making myself a list of specific questions I would like to ask, given the opportunity for two-way conversation with the Almighty:

What REALLY happened at Chappaquiddick? It's urgent.

How long before you do something about Howard Cosell?

Is disco a sin?

Is there life after gasoline?

Has Anita Bryant become a total embarrassment?

Did Elvis go to heaven?

Can rabbits swim?

Is Oral Roberts on the level?

Does the name "Margaret Schroeder" ring a bell?

Are Cheerleaderrs Really Necessary?

Of course, cheerleaders aren't necessary, but we keep them around anyway. They're the parsley of athletic competition.

Last football season, I wrote a column in which I implied cheerleaders are a waste of everybody's time. I received a great deal of mail about the column:

"You are a jerk!" —Pipsie McQueen, Farrah Fawcett High, Kilgore, Texas.

"Go blow your nose!" —Precious Sweeney, University of Arkansas at Stuttgart.

"May Tony Dorsett run over your face." —Phyllis G. Brown, Kentucky.

I frankly didn't realize people felt that strongly about cheerleaders, so I attempted to enter this season with an open mind.

Say something nice about cheerleaders for a change, I reminded myself. OK. They don't perspire as much as the players.

But that is as far as I can go. This season, I have attended both professional and college games, and I would be untruthful if I said my stance on cheerleaders has changed.

It has not. They are still a waste of time.

One, cheerleaders don't really lead cheers, because most of the people who go to football games are either too involved in beating the point spread or too bombed to pay attention to them.

Two, cheerleaders usually have silly names. Like "Pipsie" and "Precious."

Three, cheerleaders, especially at professional games, do little more than wiggle their navels for a couple of hours.

Four, most cheers are stupid:

> *Wiggle your navel left!*
> *Wiggle your navel right!*
> *Wiggle your navel up and down!*
> *And fight! Fight! Fight!*

Pressed, I suppose I can abide a cheerleader or two at college games because sis-boom-bah is part of the appeal of the collegiate game, and there needs to be somebody around who remembers the words to the alma mater.

But I would like to put all professional cheerleaders on a permanent taxi squad. Autumn Sunday afternoons have become one big pompom shaking in the face of America. There are exceptions to everything, of course; but, basically, when you have seen one shaking pompom, you have seen them all.

I blame the Dallas Cowboys for this. There was a time when professional football teams wouldn't even think of allowing a group of women to stand around in their underpants on the sidelines and bump and grind for four quarters.

But later came National Football League expansion, and a team was placed in Dallas, where the men spend a lot of time out on the range with their cattle.

Spend enough time out on the range with your cattle, and football won't be enough to occupy your mind totally on the weekends either, Tex.

That's how the Dallas Cowboys Cheerleaders came to be. Watch the game, watch the girls, too, and get along, little dogie.

Soon, practically every team in the league had its cheerleaders, with the notable exception of the Pittsburgh Steelers, who said,

"We're here to play football. Get them broads off the sidelines." The Steelers, incidentally, are Super Bowl champions.

Before the letters start to pour in again, let me offer my assurance that this column was not written from a sexist point of view.

I don't like boy cheerleaders, either. Sometimes, you see boy cheerleaders at college games. What bothers me is, what will boy cheerleaders tell their sons when they ask, "What did you do in the Big Game, daddy?"

And they will be forced to answer, "I jumped around like an idiot and screamed my fool head off."

I am even more concerned about boy baton twirlers, but that is another story entirely.

The Old Chinchilla Game

All you've ever wanted to know about why NOT to invest in chinchillas, which have an alarming tendency to go bald.

What I knew about chinchillas, furry little animals that sometimes wind up as expensive coats, you could have put on the tip end of a chinchilla's tail, only I didn't even know if chinchillas have tails. (Later, I was to discover they most certainly do.)

What aroused my interest in chinchillas was an advertisement that ran in the newspaper last week.

"Own Your Own Business," said the advertisement. "Opportunity to Earn $30,000 Raising Chinchillas. Start in a spare room, garage, basement, outbuilding, etc."

The company that placed the advertisement was International Furriers Ltd.

I could use the thirty big ones, and I have a spare room. Also, there was a picture of a chinchilla included in the advertisement. Chinchillas are cute little boogers.

I talked to a Mr. Flowers of International Furriers Ltd. He became angry and defensive when I told him I worked for the newspaper. I don't think he believed I was serious about wanting to learn about chinchillas so I could possibly go into business raising them.

I think he thought I was trying to stir up trouble just because a few thousand people get ripped off in chinchilla-raising schemes every year.

Mr. Flowers assured me his company would never knowingly fleece a customer. He said people who go into chinchilla-raising and lose their shirts are just dummies who do not give their animals the proper care and handling.

After he settled down a bit, I was able to get even more vital information about chinchillas.

He said chinchillas were originally from South America, but now they all live in cages in spare rooms, garages, basements, outbuildings, etc.

He said they are nocturnal animals of the rodent family. They are about the size of rabbits, he went on, and it costs a penny a day to feed one chinchilla on Ralson-Purina Chinchilla Chow.

"Do they have tails?" I asked.

"They most certaily do," Mr. Flowers assured me.

He also said he would sell six chinchillas—one boy and five girls—for $3,400 and he would even throw in the cages.

I also wanted to know how much a ready-for-market chinchilla is worth and how many people are actually making $30,000, but that's where Mr. Flowers became testy again and I decided it would be best to hang up.

What I did next was call the Governor's Office of Consumer Affairs, to ask would it be smart for a person to get involved in raising chinchillas.

Not by the hair of your chinny chinchilla, said a spokesperson. Here's why:

1. Contrary to what a chinchilla salesman might tell you, chinchillas are NOT easy to raise. They are subject to a variety of diseases, traumas, and even emotional breakdowns which affect their breeding habits and the quality of their offspring. There is nothing worse than a chinchilla gone bonkers.

2. Chinchillas make a lot of noise at night. They're nocturnal, remember? Unfortunately, most of the suckers who get involved in raising them aren't.

3. Sometimes, chinchillas lose all their hair. A bald chinchilla is a worthless chinchilla.

4. Sometimes, even worse things happen. Sometimes, they gnaw their feet off.

5. Chinchilla salesmen often claim chinchillas reproduce three times a year. That's a bunch of Chinchilla Chow.

6. Spare rooms, garages, basements, outbuildings, etc., are NOT conducive to raising chinchillas. A New York chinchilla scam recently had people trying to raise chinchillas in their bedrooms. They are the same people who keep Florida swampland salesmen in business.

7. Companies that put people in the chinchilla business have a tendency to move around a lot.

8. Most chinchilla buying and selling is done through large associations. And the chinchilla market right now is lousy.

I wanted this to be a thorough investigation, so I also looked for somebody who has actually had a chinchilla-raising experience. I found somebody.

His name is Bill Paulidis and he is a furrier for S. Baum and Co., an Atlanta firm.

Mr. Paulidis once tried to raise chinchillas on Ponce de Leon Avenue. He had 180 of them. They all got sick and lost their hair. In one night, Mr. Paulidis had to put thiry-nine chinchillas out of their misery.

He lost $25,000.

"Anybody who puts money into chinchillas," said Mr. Paulidis, "is crazy."

End of investigation.

Me and My Guccis

Sometime later, someone stole the very pair of Guccis I am writing about here. I left them in the locker room of where I play tennis, and when I returned, they were gone, which made me feel very good. At least one person I hang around with at the tennis courts has some class. I never would have guessed it.

All my adult life, I have attempted to rise above my humble beginnings. Take shoes, for example. Now that I have steady work and live in the city, I like to wear nice shoes.

In the boondocks, we didn't wear shoes unless it was an absolute necessity. Like your feet would freeze if you didn't, or there was a funeral.

My boyhood friend and idol, Weyman C. Wannamaker, Jr., a great American, didn't wear shoes even on those occasions, but he did wash his feet twice a week whether they needed it or not.

The first time I saw Weyman in a pair of shoes they were forced upon him.

We were in the sixth grade, and the teacher organized a field trip to Atlanta to hear a performance by the symphony orchestra. As the bus pulled away from the school, she noticed Weyman was barefooted.

Horrified, she ordered the bus driver to stop at the nearest shoe store, where she bought Weyman a pair of shoes. He protested, but the teacher hit him in the mouth and Weyman didn't mention the shoes again.

During the performance of the symphony orchestra, however, Weyman's feet began hurting him, so he took off his shoes and hung his bare feet over the railing of the balcony. Unfortunately, he was between washes.

The entire percussion section and two flute players stopped in the middle of Chopin's Movement No. 5 to search for what had obviously passed away days earlier.

I always think of Weyman when I pull on a new pair of shoes. Lately, some of the fellows down at the lodge have been giving me the business because I now own a pair of stylish loafers by Gucci, the famous Italian leatherperson.

I prefer to think their boorish, catty remarks stem from ignorance, sprinkled with at least a tad of jealousy.

"I knew him," said one of the buzzbrains, wearing a pair of hideous lace-ups named for something you eat with fried catfish, "when he wore high-top tennis shoes and ran rabbits"

How utterly crude. And untrue. I wore low-cuts.

My new Guccis were a gift from a lady friend who brought them back from Palm Beach, where they have a Gucci store. They don't have Gucci stores except in spiffy places like Palm Beach. It's easier to move an NFL expansion franchise team into town.

My lady friend is always bringing me nice gifts when she goes on trips. Once she went to the drugstore and brought me a giant bottle of mouthwash and some extra-strength Tegrin shampoo.

I must do something nice for her. Maybe I'll take her bowling.

What makes a pair of stylish Italian loafers by Gucci so appealing is their softness, their master workmanship, and their price.

I've bought cars for less. Walk into a Gucci store, and they ask for your shoe size second. First, they want a quick glance at your Dun and Bradstreet.

Not just anybody can wear a pair of Gucci shoes, of course. Those crass dolts down at the lodge, for instance.

"You get a purse, too?" cracked one of the sorry lot, a hint of white socklet peering outside the top of his brogans.

Disgusting.

My new Guccis are an unpretentious oxblood, accented perfectly with buckles and slightly raised heels.

The cushioned inner soles wear the proud Gucci crest with the subtle, but effective announcement, "Made in Italy," as if there were any doubt.

When I am in the company of individuals with the proper breeding to appreciate such hallmarks of style, I am not hesitant to remove one of my new shoes to prove I am wearing the Real McCoy.

"Have you noticed I am wearing Guccis?" I asked the hostess at a dinner party.

"Frankly, I haven't," she said.

I took off one of my shoes and showed her the proud Gucci crest on the cushioned inner soles. I didn't want to stay at her stupid dinner party anyway.

I also called Weyman C. Wannamaker, Jr., back home and told him I am now wearing Guccis. I knew he would be proud.

"You wearing them shoes," he said, "is like putting perfume on a hog."

My Kind of Beauty Queen

. . . And whatever happened to Barbi Benton?

The wires carried an interesting interview the other day with the newly-crowned Miss Universe, an eighteen-year-old from Venezuela.

I take that back. It was not an interesting interview at all. As a matter of fact, it was a very dull interview, because it was like every other interview with beauty queens.

Beauty queens today have a thing about denying they are sex objects. That's nothing. So do girls who pose with no clothes on in magazines.

Open a magazine and pull out the centerfold, and there is the Lustlady of the Year revealing everything but her shoe size.

"I can't stand a man who wants me only for my body," she is saying in the caption. "I have a brain, too, and I can use it. I know six state capitals and once I went to a museum."

If I've read where one beauty queen was saying there is more to her than what she has managed to stuff inside her tight-fitting swimsuit, I've read where a thousand more were making the same irrelevant remarks.

If brains were all that important in a beauty contest, you could enter wearing a Hefty Bag.

The current Miss Universe is Maritza Sayalero. She is from Caracas. Her father is an engineer, which has nothing to do with anything but is the kind of incidental information they put in interviews with beauty queens to help fill up space.

Maritza was posing for tourists in New York City in her tight-fitting swimsuit in front of the statue of Prometheus at Rockefeller Center, and, sure enough, some reporter asked her if she considered herself a sex symbol.

And, sure enough, Miss Universe wiggled and giggled and said, "Even though I am beautiful, I don't consider myself a sex symbol."

Even though she is beautiful, what does she consider herself? Posing at Rockefeller Center in her tight-fitting swimsuit, one of those eye-poppers with slits down the sides, she was no sack of potatoes, por favor.

The interview also carried information concerning Miss Universe's plans for when her reign is over and she returns to Caracas.

She wants to be an architect.

"I want to design beautiful buildings," she said, "but with a purpose—for the poor."

I am sure the poor people in Caracas will appreciate that. Give them a few beautiful buildings and maybe they will quit complaining about being cold and hungry.

Give me a beauty queen who understands the rules of the game. Give me a beauty queen like Kathy Sue Loudermilk, who won the coveted Miss Collard Festival Queen title seven years running back home, breaking Cordie Mae Poovy's string of four in a row.

That's not the only string Kathy Sue broke. When the one that held up the top of her swimsuit snapped, that's how she ousted Cordie Mae in the first place.

Kathy Sue Loudermilk knew what a beauty contest was all about. Every year, she ordred a new swimsuit from the Sears catalog and every year, she was living proof that you could, in fact, stuff one hundred pounds of collards into a fifty-pound sack if you squeezed and packed and pushed long and hard enough.

Even the Baptist preacher always turned out to watch Kathy Sue in action at the pageant. Once, he even allowed himself a bellowing, "Hallelujah!" when Kathy Sue, sensing she might be in trouble with the judges for missing a question concerning the current price of hog vaccine, gave a couple of quick hip-flips to make up the lost points.

The county seat newspaper always dispatched a photographer and a reporter to cover the festival, and one year they posed Kathy Sue in her swimsuit on a tractor.

The reporter asked, "Miss Loudermilk, do you consider yourself a sex symbol?"

Kathy Sue never blinked.

"Does a duck have lips, Four-Eyes?" she replied as she cranked the John Deere, did a quick wheelie and disappeared down a dirt road.

I said it then, and I will say it now: "There goes my kind of beauty queen."

A Hero Unmasked

Do cowboys ever cry? Sure, even the Lone Ranger . . .

I spent an entire afternoon and part of an evening trying to reach the Lone Ranger on the telephone. You don't just pick up the telephone and ask information for the number of the Lone Ranger, but I finally resorted to that when all other efforts failed.

"I am trying to reach a Mr. Clayton Moore," I said to the operator in California. "He's the Lone Ranger."

"Is that a person or a business, sir?" she asked.

"A person," I said. "You've never heard of the Lone Ranger?"

"The rock singer?" she replied.

I hung up. Probably some mindless nineteen-year-old, high on a Hostess Twinkie.

Perhaps it was best I never reached him. What would I have said to "the masked rider of the plains"?

"Tough luck"?

"Hang in there"?

"How's Tonto"?

They stuck it to Clayton Moore, who portrayed the Lone Ranger from 1949 to 1956 on television, in a Southern California court the other day.

A judge ordered him to take off his mask and go ride off somewhere and drop dead. At least, that's what it sounded like to me.

I didn't understand all the legal mumbo jumbo—and I really didn't try—but the judge said Clayton Moore no longer has any claim to the role he made famous and ordered that he no longer make any public appearances wearing his mask.

They're making a new film about the legendary western hero of my youth, and the film company said Moore, who is sixty-four, is too old to play the character. They wanted him to remove his mask "to avoid confusion."

That's a lot of trail dust. Buddy Ebsen, who is certainly no tenderfoot, can still bring'em to justice as Barnaby Jones, so why put Clayton Moore in mothballs before his time?

According to the news, Clayton Moore cried when the judge handed down his decision. The dirty galoot.

I go all the way back to the early fifties with Clayton as the Lone Ranger and Jay Silverheels as Tonto, and Silver and Scout, who played themselves.

Merita Bread sponsored the show. "Come with us now to those thrilling days of yesteryear . . . etc."

I even remember a Lone Ranger joke. It was funny the first time I heard it, when I was ten or eleven, and it is even funnier now because Indians quit taking any grief a few year back.

The Lone Ranger and his trusty sidekick Tonto—who was always referred to as an "Injun" by badmen and other insensitive creeps on the show—were surrounded by ten million original Americans all dressed up in war paint and carrying bows and arrows and tomahawks and rifles they had borrowed from the local cavalry fort.

"Well, Tonto," says the Lone Ranger in Clayton Moore's deep, resonant voice, "it looks like we've finally come to the end of our trail."

Tonto, meanwhile, had other ideas. He replies:

"What's this 'we' business, white-eyes?"

Things have been tough all over for Old West television stars lately. Roy's got a bum ticker, you may have heard.

Hoppy died. Lash LaRue, the last word I had, was cracking the whip for Jesus in a tent crusade.

And now, this. A judge has taken the mask off the Lone Ranger.

Maybe if I had reached Clayton Moore on the telephone, I could have given him a message from his fans, and I know I could have spoken for all of them.

Maybe I could have said something like, "It's no big thing, *Kemo Sabe*. You're still the Lone Ranger to us, and we'll always love you."

He would have probably liked to have heard that. Especially the "we" part.

Shafting the Kids: Part I

Most of the time, the biggest trouble with young people is adults.
That is what I was trying to say in the next two pieces, which are
about alcohol and sex.

Sometimes I dislike being in the company of young adults. That is because sometimes they ask probing, thoughtful questions I cannot answer. I find what I do most when talking to young people is make apologies and excuses for their elders.

It will happen to me again. I will be with a group of young adults, and they will ask me why the would-be grown folks who make the laws of the state are trying to put the screws to them again.

But damned if I will hide from the truth this time. The Georgia General Assembly, which often resembles recess at the playschool, is considering depriving eighteen-year-olds—possibly even nineteen-year-olds and twenty-year-olds, too—of the right to purchase alcoholic beverages legally.

That is outrageous.

We lowered the legal drinking age from twenty-one to eighteen in this state during the Vietnam War. That was because we could no longer face ourselves knowing we could send a young man to die for no apparent reason in a war that made no apparent sense and still deprive him of a full citizenship.

But "times have changed," read an editorial last week that favored raising the drinking age again.

What on earth does that mean? That full citizenship is only valid when we are in the middle of an idiotic war? What if we get ourselves involved in another one? Times haven't changed enough that we wouldn't. And if there is a next time, guess who would get the call to duty and death again? That same eighteen-year-old the state legislature is trying to tell he must now relinquish his right to buy booze.

The state legislature giveth. I am all for that. But I personally get very nervous when any body of lawmakers or law enforcers starts trying to taketh away. Rights are not to be dangled in front of the citizenry as candy before a drooling baby.

There is, of course, the argument that because the drinking age has been lowered to eighteen, it is now easier for high school students to obtain alcohol. The proponents of raising the drinking age point to an increase in teenage alcoholism.

Teenagers drink because they are programmed to do so by adults who can't hold any function without a cocktail beforehand. By adults like the state legislators who had a cocktail party scheduled every night of the first week of their current session.

Television, movies, and advertising—all run by adults—picture drinking as chic, as fun, as almost necessary in order to be functional within our society. Until all that is changed, teenage drinking will continue to increase, and a tub full of ridiculous regulations won't even begin to reverse the trend.

Also, I find it terribly unfair to ask an eighteen-year-old, who can vote, pay taxes, and reproduce the species, to give up his or her right because we can't convince a sixteen-year-old to wait a couple of years.

The drinking age for me was twenty-one. I had no trouble whatsoever in a town of 300, getting my hands on enough beer to turn me green when I was fifteen.

When I was eighteen, I registered, by law, for the draft, I entered college, held down a job, paid taxes, successfully proposed marriage to another eighteen-year-old, and was told I could vote.

If there was anything I wasn't ready to do yet, it was vote. One afternoon in 1964, I got blitzed at the fraternity house and went out and cast a ballot for Lyndon Johnson.

We have put the shaft to young adults long enough. We have told them one thing and meant another. We have preached to them one thing and practiced another. We have insisted they pay support to and help defend our society, but at the same time we have tried to tell them they cannot enjoy all the privileges of it.

"Bless the Beasts and the Children." It was a song from a movie of the same name. And there was the lyric: "Bless the beasts and the children/For in this world, they have no voice/They have no choice."

If the Georgia General Assembly wants to take away somebody's right to drink, then so be it.

I would be solidly in favor of a new law making it illegal for any state legislator to get himself soused in an Atlanta bar before going out looking for hookers while he was supposed to be at the business of taking care of the welfare of the citizens he represents.

Let's see a vote on that one, boys.

Shafting the Kids: Part II

There was no such thing as sex education when I was in school. I take that back. There was plenty of sex education in my school, but classes were conducted behind the grandstand of the baseball diamond and the teacher usually had only a couple of years on his students.

We did have "health" classes in school. That is where you learned clean fingernails are important, if you don't brush your teeth regularly your teeth will fall out, and you can get all the Vitamin D you need by spending a lot of time out in the sun.

We also had biology classes where we did hear something about sex, but only if it involved a couple of frogs.

But times changed. Educators finally began to realize that perhaps the reason so many of their female students were getting pregnant—some at ridiculous ages like twelve and thirteen—was because all they knew about sex was the basics of how to perform it.

So, gradually, sex education has been introduced into many of our schools. There has been protest, of course, because some parents and school board members still think it best for children to learn about sex in other places.

Like behind the grandstand of a baseball diamond.

Take Cobb County, for instance. They are always fighting about something in the Atlanta suburb of Cobb County. This time, it is whether to introduce a unified sex education program into the sixth, seventh, and eighth grades.

Those in favor of the program argued at a recent school board meeting that it is important because an estimated 30,000 American girls under the age of fifteen will get pregnant this year.

Those against the program had a good argument, too. Cobb County school board member John McClure said students need less sex education and more teaching of "self-respect, discipline, and patriotism."

He also suggested sex education be handled in the home.

"But not everybody has a home," countered a Cobb County high school senior who came to the meeting.

"Hmmmp!" said board member McClure, who could be suffering from chalk dust on the brain.

We think nothing of teaching our children all about wars. Half of the time I was in school, I was learning about a war, the Third Punic all the way to the Great WWII.

People get maimed and killed in wars. Sex has to do with loving. Teach 'em about war, but ignore the little brats when they ask about sex.

The new sex education plan didn't pass at the Cobb school board meeting. The vote was 3-3, but the superintendent has already said he would not ask his teachers to teach the program if the board were split on such a "controversial issue."

I don't know if this will help, but it is probably worth a try. For those Cobb students who will be deprived of sex education for at least another year, here is my own sex short-course.

Clip and save:

• Having sex, even if you are only twelve, can make babies.

• Having a baby while you are still a kid is a bummer.

• If you are determined to have sex no matter what anybody tells you, there are ways to avoid making a baby. They are called "contraceptives." Ask an older friend who won't go berserk how to obtain them.

• There is nothing dirty about sex. It is a beautiful and necessary part of life.

• Many grown people would be better off if they realized that.

The Rumored Closing of Harold's Barbecue

Harold's lives on to this day. The barbecue and the crackling cornbread are still good, the posters about Jesus are still on the wall, and there's still no beer.

There is a nasty rumor going around the city that I would like to quash immediately.

Harold's Barbecue, that wonderful haven for lovers of pork down past Atlanta Stadium, is not going to close.

I repeat, is NOT going to close.

I first heard the nasty whisperings a couple of weeks ago when a friend, a fellow barbecue junkie, walked into my office, pale as a sheet.

"They can't do this!" he screamed. "I won't stand for it! I'll write Herman Talmadge!"

Better hurry, I said, if you want to write ol' Herman.

"OK," my friend went on, "I'll write Guy Sharpe! But somebody has to put a stop to this!"

Stop to what?

"You haven't heard?" my friend asked. "Harold's Barbecue is selling out to a trucking company, and there are no plans to reopen."

You could have knocked me over with a sliced sandwich, outside meat, toast the bread.

As I have mentioned before, to my taste, there are three great barbecue joints in Georgia. You could not rate Ruth, Gehrig, DiMaggio. Neither could you rate Harold's Barbecue in Atlanta, Sprayberry's in Newman, and Sweat's, Soperton branch.

They are all superior places to eat barbecue, the Holy Barbecue Triumvirate, if you will.

Harold's close? Harold's is one of the reasons I went through all the trouble to escape Chicago.

I dialed the number with shaking hands. I said a little prayer, "Lord, don't let it be true."

I talked to Harold himself. Harold is Harold Hembree. His father opened Harold's Barbecue thirty-two years ago. The son has operated the business for twenty-two years.

"Harold," I began, "are you going to close?"

"Good Lord, no!" he replied.

Marvelous, absolutely marvelous.

"That rumor gets out all the time," Harold went on. "There's a trucking company close to us, and one time we talked about selling them this property.

"But they were going to give us a new place nearby and build whatever we wanted, but that never worked out.

"I have no plans to close, now or ever. I've been at this too long to try anything else."

I could go on about the quality of the barbecue at Harold's, but that would only start an argument. People feel strongly about their barbecue.

What I do want to say about Harold Hembree's establishment is it *looks* like a good barbecue joint ought to look. It's small. It's not fancy. There is no glass, no potted plants, no wicker.

The food is simple. Barbecue sandwiches, barbecue plates, chopped or sliced. Potato chips. Pickles. Brunswick stew. Cornbread. *Crackling* cornbread.

"That was mama's idea," Harold said.

Harold's is a total family operation.

"Counting nieces, sisters, and wives," Harold said, "there are about thirteen of us working here."

I also like the way the walls are decorated. Harold's family is serious about its religion.

"God Is My Co-Pilot." "Lean on Jesus." There are a lot of religious posters around on the walls at Harold's.

There was one other rumor I wanted to check out as long as I had Harold on the line, the one that said maybe it wouldn't be long before you could get a beer along with your barbecue at Harold's.

"No truth to that, either," he said. "Mama wouldn't stand for it."

Some things, some people endure the ravages of progress. I will sleep better tonight knowing that.

Golf, or a Reasonable Facsimile Thereof

Golf is the favorite game of insurance salesmen, car thieves, and Methodist ministers. I don't know exactly what that means, but it is certainly worth pondering.

What's always been wrong with golf is, any way you slice it, golf is a dull game.

The players are dull, robots carrying sticks. They don't even spit or scratch their privates like other athletes. The spectators are dull. They applaud even when some guntz hits a good shot.

The television announcers are dull, too. If Dave Marr cracks you up, you probably think Bernard Kalb is a riot.

Take the United States Open golf tournament, played somewhere near Toledo last week. Dull. A couple of players tried to put a little life in the stodgy proceedings, but all those stuffy United States Golf Association (USGA) officials in their long-sleeved white shirts nearly had a hissy.

(All my life I have wanted to know the exact definition of the word "hissy." I think it means turning red in the face and stomping and raving around like something crazy.)

One of the players, Lon Hinkle, discovered it was closer from tee to green on a par-five hole to hit his drive into another fairway. To show you how dull golf is, that was front-page sports news for days.

The USGA would have nothing of it. They ordered a tree planted near the tee so Lon Hinkle couldn't take the scenic route.

Put the USGA in charge of sex and it would eliminate body contact.

Then there was young Bobby Clampett. Young Bobby Clampett missed the cut, but they asked him to play along the next day anyway because somebody still in the field needed a partner.

Graciously, Bobby Clampett agreed and took a busman's holiday. He also hit a few of his tee shots from his knees and joked around with the gallery.

It didn't matter Bobby Clampett's knee-shots were long and straight. It didn't matter there is nothing in the rules of golf that says you can't hit the ball from a kneeling position. And what's wrong with joking around with the gallery?

"Watch me hit this ball on my knees," said Bobby Clampett.

"Ha! Ha!" laughed the gallery.

The hilarity is killing me.

Anybody seen Bobby Clampett lately? Of course not. He was dragged away from the thirteenth hole by USGA officials and shot.

I played golf last week. I hadn't played golf in ten years. I quit because I was a lousy golfer and because I didn't like to walk around in the woods. There are spiders and snakes in there.

Also, it was making me a dull person. After a round of golf, I thought a big night out was a couple of hands of canasta with my neighbor, Mr. Forndyce. Mr. Forndyce was a nice enough fellow, but he was also eighty-three and had been declared legally dead from his eyebrows down thirty years earlier.

But I finally found a way to play golf that is fun. I played in the annual Busch Bash, formerly the Old Milwaukee Open, at the Newnan Country Club. Two grown men named Joe Lawson and Jim Mottola are in charge of it. If Joe Lawson and Jim Mottola ran the U.S. Open, Bobby Clampett could hit balls standing on his head and they wouldn't care.

The Busch Bash involves playing twenty-seven holes of golf and drinking a beer on each one. There are some terrific rules:

• If you don't want to hit the ball, you can throw it. I didn't hit the ball so well, but I made some excellent throws.

• If you don't want to hit the ball or throw it, fine. Drink another beer.

• If you hit the ball into the woods, forget it. Hit somebody's ball that didn't go into the woods.

• You can wear tennis shoes.

• Wives and girlfriends of participants are enouraged to stay away from the trailer parked behind the seventeenth green.

• The night before the tournament, there is a party from seven until nine o'clock that lasts until three in the morning.

• The night after the tournament, there is a party that still may be going.

There are always prizes at the annual Busch Bash, but tournament officials never remember to give them out. In fact, at the party after the tournament, I asked Joe Lawson who won, and he said, "Who knows?"

That's my kind of golf tournament. I only wish some officials from the USGA, the pompous old goats, could have been there. They would have had a hissy. A double.

4

FIGHTING CITY HALL

Grizzard for Mayor

My campaign never got off the ground. I was selling bumper stickers for $17.50 each to raise money. Counting the one my mother didn't buy, I didn't sell any. Also, I got some sage political advice from one of my readers who reminded me, "Grizzard, the only thing you ought to run for is the city limits."

I know you are all going to fall down laughing when you read this, but it wasn't my idea. It came from a group of dentists over at Emory University.

They wrote me a letter that began, "Atlanta is ready for, and in need of, responsible leadership in city government."

The understatement of the year. Our City Council is a monkey show, at best, and our mayor—you read it here first—was dropped on his head as a small boy, which explains some of his delirious actions like making plans to run in a statewide election against Senator Herman Talmadge.

Outside Atlanta, they think Maynard Jackson is the name of a new hog vaccine.

You also have to question the mayor's recruiting abilities. He gave the city A. Reginald Eaves, remember. And he is also responsible for Tweedle-Dum and Tweedle-Dee, Brown and Napper, over at police headquarters.

Their crack leadership of the police force has the rest of us looking for places to hide, as the crime rate soars. A friend in Des Moines called the other day and said, "I was planning to come visit you in Atlanta, but now I'm not sure. Shouldn't we plan to meet somewhere safer? Like Juarez or Newark?"

The dentists over at Emory have strongly suggested that because I am always writing as if I know it all, maybe I should run for mayor of Atlanta in the upcoming 1981 election.

Pull yourselves together. It's not that damned funny. I was treasurer of my freshman class in high school, and when I was a kid, I used to shovel out what the horses left in the barn. I know a little something about politics.

(What does shoveling out what horses leave in the barn have to do with politics? I don't think I have to answer that question.)

Dr. Thomas W. McDonald has appointed himself campaign chairman of the "Grizzard for Mayor in '81 Committee," and he lists Dr. George Ulrich and Dr. George Pryles as his associates.

Their letter drafting my candidacy further stated, "Campaign strategy and meetings are under way, and an effective bumper sticker blitz has been initiated."

I must say I'm flattered. "Mayor Lewis Grizzard." "Mr. Mayor Lewis Grizzard." "His Honor, Mayor Lewis Grizzard." They all have a certain ring.

But I would have some problems of my own as mayor. For one thing, I don't really need a car; and when someone else drives, it makes me nervous. And all those bodyguards scurrying around and opening my doors would make me feel a bit pompous.

I probably would do something dumb like fire my bodyguards; because I happen to think if anybody needs bodyguards in this town, it's not the mayor, it's the working stiff who has to brave the raging streets alone.

And then I would have all those fat-cat jobs to hand out, the ones you give to your pals, or former pals, like A. Reggie.

All my friends already have good jobs.

And I have no idea what to do about Central City Park, the downtown zoo. Yes, I do, but electric fencing is so expensive. I don't get free drinks at Billy's, and would that much of an outsider really have a fighting chance at getting elected?

I'll just stick here, fighting the daily battle to produce a column for a great, metropolitan newspaper. Besides, you'll have plenty of choices for a new mayor in 1981, without my getting in the way.

Statesmen like A. Reggie and Mike Lomax, who has a cute beard and knows some rock stars, will probably be in the battle. And if Leroy Johnson, the new head of the Stadium Authority, can pass out enough big cigars and free parking at Falcons games to the right people, who knows about him?

I am not now, nor will I ever be, a candidate. But collector's item "Grizzard for Mayor" bumper stickers are available. Send $17.50, or more if you can spare it, and my staff of volunteers will see that your sticker is in the mail promptly.

Sure, I'll make a few quick bucks for doing nothing. But I already told you I know a little something about politics.

Adventures of the Drug Fairy

City Councilman James Bond is one of my favorite Atlanta politicians. His tailor, incidentally, is the same guy who designed the Hefty Bag.

I called a detective in the auto theft division of the Atlanta Police Department Wednesday and promised him if he answered a few of my questions candidly, I wouldn't use his name. Sometimes such tactics are necessary in big-time journalism.

He agreed.

What would happen, I began, if I called the police emergency number, like any ordinary citizen would do, to report a theft of a radio and a tape system from my car?

"We would send over a uniformed officer," said the detective, "and he would make out a report."

What would happen, I went on, if I called the chief of police directly with such a complaint?

"You wouldn't do that," said the detective.

"But what if I did?"

"If you got through, I suppose he would just send over a uniformed officer, and he would make out a report."

There was one more question. What would happen if I were a city councilman and a member of the Public Safety Committee, which overlooks police department matters, and I called the chief with my complaint? Would I get special treatment? Would I, for instance, be sent a detective rather than a uniformed cop?

"I see what you mean," said the detective. "But let's face it, that kind of thing has *always* gone on, and it always will. Who do you think they would send over if Jimmy Carter called and said somebody had broken into his car?"

Good point. We take care of our own on nearly every level of government. It's an American tradition. Like Bunker Hill, remembering the *Maine*, and fixing traffic tickets.

That brings us to the recent case of Atlanta City Councilman James Bond, who just happens to be a member of the Public Safety Committee which overlooks the police department.

Somebody broke into his car and took his radio and tape system. He did not call the police emergency number. He called Chief George Napper. Who came to Bond's house to investigate? Not Charlie the Cop, but Detective R. T. Ford.

Detective Ford did a thorough job in his investigation. This wasn't Joe Doe he was dealing with, remember.

Detective Ford did too good a job. Somebody should talk to Detective Ford. Know what he found in Councilman Bond's car besides a missing radio and tape system? He found something that looked a lot like marijuana cigarettes, fellow citizens.

He found one unsmoked cigarette behind the front seat. He found nine already-smoked cigarettes in Councilman Bond's ashtray. Just to prove himself wrong of his suspicions, Detective Ford sent the substance to the Georgia Crime Lab for identification.

Holy Case Dismissed! The substance was marijuana! Marijuana is against the law! There must be an explanation!

There was. Chief Napper handled the matter himself. After all, this had been his baby from the start.

"There is no reason to believe the owner of the car had any responsibility for placing the marijuana there," said the chief, adding, "Somebody other than the owner could have placed it there."

Of course. The Drug Fairy, for one. The chief even mentioned the thief might have done it. That's logical. A thief decides to rip off Councilman Bond's car. He opens the door with a coat hanger and lies down in the seat to partake of the goodies.

While he is there, he decides to mix a little pleasure with business and smokes nine marijuana cigarettes in the minute-and-a-half it takes to dislodge Councilman Bond's radio and tape system. At least he had the courtesy to crush out all nine in the ashtray and leave one unsmoked joint behind the front seat for the next thief.

Just so nobody gets any wrong ideas, Chief Napper has assured Atlanta citizens that Councilman Bond's high position in the city government had absolutely nothing to do with his decision not to file charges against Bond.

Even the Drug Fairy wouldn't fall for that one.

A Toast to the Poor People

The hero of this story is A. Reginald Eaves, who once bought an expensive love seat for his office when he was Atlanta's public safety commissioner, and who likes big, chauffeur-driven limos and lots of bodyguards and shiny suits. Isn't it sad poor people in other parts of the country besides Atlanta don't have a guy like A. Reginald Eaves on their side?

In the past, when I read articles about the possibility of A. Reginald Eaves' becoming mayor of Atlanta, I would get down on the floor and roll around and laugh.

Stone Mountain will crumble, the Peachtree Plaza will fall before that will happen, I would say.

My attitude changed Tuesday night. I am now convinced A. Reggie, former public safety commissioner, current county commissioner, and a big man in a number of local discos, could become the next mayor of Atlanta.

How does that feel to me? How does it feel to stand around and wait for a homemade H-bomb to go off?

A. Reggie, as you probably know, was against the idea to raise the local sales tax. Maynard Jackson, the current Atlanta mayor, was for it, and so was his hand-picked successor, Michael Lomax.

The sales tax hike was soundly trounced in Tuesday's election. Said the political experts, "The sales tax defeat showed the strong base of support for A. Reginald Eaves."

A. Reggie didn't want anybody to forget that, so as soon as he could find somebody with a microphone, he started campaigning. I watched his performance on the eleven o'clock news.

"This is a great victory for the poor people," said A. Reggie. As soon as a person starts talking about great victories for the poor people, you can bet the farm he is campaigning.

A. Reggie wore a pin-striped gangster suit for the occasion and was celebrating in a hotel room with a lot of others, who may or may not have been drinking champagne out of the glasses they were holding.

I think they probably were drinking champagne, because that's what you usually drink when the poor people win one.

I will be the first to admit A. Reggie is smarter than I originally thought. I used to think he was a complete dummy. Now, I think he is only a half-dummy, which makes him one of our most intelligent local politicians.

Recall, he was fired as public safety commissioner by the mayor, the same fellow who hired him on the basis that they were old friends. It is difficult to get fired from a job where your boss is an old chum, but A. Reggie managed it.

Yet A. Reggie landed on his feet. He could have left town in disgrace. Instead, he chose to become a martyr. Martyrs have a big edge in elections, and that is how A. Reggie got elected to the county commission.

Then he started going around winning great victories for the poor people. The Falcons' playoff win over Philadelphia last season, for instance.

"Great victory for the poor people," said A. Reggie.

He gave away such jobs as personal bodyguard and chauffeur to poor people like county policemen, and when he walks into a local disco, he buys the first ten poor people to recognize him a drink.

There are a number of things that bother me about the possibility of A. Reginald Eaves' becoming mayor of Atlanta.

• He forever loused up the police department when he was chief. Imagine what he could do as mayor.

• I don't think he really cares about poor people. I think he cares more about personal bodyguards and chauffeurs.

After the sales tax vote was in Tuesday night, A. Reggie also said, "The people have more intelligence than we gave them credit for."

Let's hope so. God, let's hope so.

Frontier Mayor

It is very helpful to a newspaper columnist when the local mayor is taken to doing weird things, thus giving the newspaper columnist a topic. I would like to thank Atlanta Mayor Maynard Jackson for all his help through the years . . .

I've been sleeping much more soundly recently since I read about Mayor Maynard Jackson's one-man battle against crime in Atlanta.

We have a great deal of crime in Atlanta: murder, robbery, rape, jacking up cars on the streets.

The other day, the mayor was riding around town in his limousine. People probably said, "Look, there's Mayor Jackson riding around town in his limousine. Why isn't he back at his office trying to do something about the rising crime rate?"

That's the people for you. What the chumps don't realize is, you can't stop crime sitting behind a desk pushing a pencil.

"Frontier Mayor" Maynard Jackson wasn't just riding around town. He was on patrol.

Suddenly, he spotted a crime in progress. Not murder. Not robbery. Not rape. But *jacking cars up on the streets*. The mere sound of the words themselves is enough to make your skin crawl.

"Whoa!" shouted "Frontier Mayor" Maynard to his limo driver. Disregarding his own safety, the mayor leaped from the limo, opening his own door in the process, and marched right into J. K. Ramey's tire store on Walton Street.

Out front of J. K. Ramey's store were several cars jacked up for tire changes. In broad daylight.

"Mr. Ramey," said the mayor, "you've got to cut that out."

At least that's what the mayor said he said to Mr. Ramey. Mr. Ramey says the mayor also said, "I'm going to put your bleep out of business"—not because of the cars jacked up on the street, but because of Mr. Ramey's involvement with plans to erect a police protest sign in the city.

The mayor denies all that. "He was breaking the law," the mayor stated, "and if my own father was violating the law, and I was in charge of enforcing it, I would enforce the law."

I heard Matt Dillon say that very same thing once to Miss Kitty over a few beers at the Long Branch.

I happen to think Mayor Jackson is absolutely correct in putting his foot down to stop the heinous practice of illegal car-jacking.

"It's a negative reflection on the city," he said. "There are oil spots on the street where he (Mr. Ramey) had cars out there changing tires."

Oil spots today, leaking transmission fluid puddles tomorrow, and pretty soon, the entire city is down the drain.

Just to prove he wasn't picking on J. K. Ramey, the mayor also pointed out another "bust" he made recently against another rampant crime spree in the city. Illegally parked cars.

The mayor was patrolling in his trusty limo on Peachtree Street and spotted illegally parked cars in front of Salvatore's Restaurant.

"You better cut that out," he said to the owner of Salvatore's Restaurant. A couple of months later, the mayor made a routine check of Salvatore's again and, sure enough, he found two illegally parked cars in front of the restaurant. He called a wrecker and had them towed away.

Justice is swift at the hand of "Frontier Mayor" Maynard.

The mayor also announced he is personally involved in trying to halt the rise of a couple of other crimes in our city.

Not murder. Not robbery. Not rape. But illegal newspapers on the street, and throwing things out of car windows.

"I see a newspaper on the street," the mayor said, "and I pick it up."

"I see somebody throw something out a car window," he continued, "and I stop them and make them come back and pick it up."

Does this man's bravery know no bounds?

Those same ungrateful people who complain about the mayor riding around town in his limo are probably saying now, if he's so effective at stopping crimes like jacking up cars and throwing garbage out of windows, why doesn't he also tackle such crimes as murder, robbery, and rape?

That's simple. "Frontier Mayor" Maynard is no dummy. Drive around in that big limo on the dark Atlanta streets where people are being murdered and robbed and raped in record numbers and he could get HIS bleep put out of business, too.

Permanently.

Pink Flamingos for MARTA

Atlanta's new rapid rail transit system successfully opened in July 1979—just a few months after this column was written—WITHOUT expensive pieces of sculpture in the stations. You can't win 'em all, however. The inside of the Decatur station looks like the inside of the Holiday Inn Disco and Lounge at the airport in Oklahoma City.

Contrary to what you may have been led to believe, not everybody who has something to do with MARTA, Atlanta's public transportation company, is a dumbhead.

You take K. A. McMillon from suburban Gwinnett County. He is a member of the MARTA Development Committee. At a meeting of his committee this week, he actually stood up and said something that made good sense.

He said it was stupid to spend $145,000 on a sculpture MARTA was going to buy for one of its new rail stations.

"I think it's ridiculous we can't come to a meeting without having to listen to this garbage from the liberals who want to throw away MARTA's money," said Mr. McMillon.

He added, "I don't think we should spend any more on such as that until we've built the railroad first."

Two liberals fainted and another had to go to the bathroom when Mr. McMillon said that.

He is also against paying MARTA secretaries who don't know their ampersands from a hole in the ground at Forsyth Street $20,000 a year, but he's saving that one for later.

The sculpture issue has been around for a while. Atlanta artist Curtis Patterson designed the piece for the new Hightower Station.

I was very interested to find out what a $145,000 piece of sculpture looks like. Thursday, I called around.

"Abstract steel," was one description.

"One of them modernistic-looking things," was another.

A MARTA official who swore he would break my neck if I quoted him said it was "a hunk of iron."

I eventually had to go straight to the artist himself. Strangely, Curtis Patterson wasn't talking.

"I am afraid anything I say will be misinterpreted," he said.

"You won't even describe your work to me?" I pressed on.

"No comment," he persisted.

The best I can determine, then, is that MARTA's $145,000 hunk of iron is abstract, modernistic, and is probably bigger than a bread box.

Mr. McMillon won out in his battle against the sculpture and the garbage-headed liberals. He persuaded four other members of the committee to vote with him against three who voted to purchase the sculpture. Hooray!

Supporters of the sculpture were very angry, because they said some type of art work was needed in MARTA rail stations to make them aesthetically pleasing to transit riders.

I agree. All K. A. McMillon and I are saying is, you can dress up a rail station and not have to fork over $145,000 for one piece of bent iron.

Those pink flamingos with the long legs they sell on the side of the highway are cheap, for instance. Throw a couple of those around the lot, and if there are any trees, you could always paint the trunks white.

And here's an idea: what happens to worn MARTA bus tires? What you can do with worn tires is move them over to the rail station, paint them white, and plant flowers inside them.

Hang a bullfighter picture or two, and you've got yourself one finely appointed rail station.

Also, you can usually count on the transit riders to do some decorating themselves. In New York, for instance, they paint colorful slogans like "Mao Lives!" and "Keel the Gringos" on station walls.

I would be willing to pop for maybe one big statue at the main MARTA station, a statue saluting all the people who paid the taxes that enabled MARTA to be constructed and provided jobs for a lot of fat cats.

Just show some poor sucker standing on a street corner with his pockets turned out and his collar turned up. And make him look hungry.

That modernistic enough for you?

5

HAIL TO THE CHIEF!

The Perfect President

I think it was my boyhood friend and idol, Weyman C. Wanna-maker, Jr., a great American, who said it best. In the fifth grade, the teacher asked him, "Weyman, would you like to be president when you grow up?"

Weyman replied, "Hell, no. Only an idiot would want to be president."

Being president used to be a nice job. Make a few speeches, sign a few bills into law, declare war to rousing cheers, go throw out the first ball at a Senators' game.

Practically everybody liked you, or at least respected the fact you were doing the best you could. They played "Hail to the Chief" and old men saluted and pretty girls smiled when your train pulled into town.

But all that has changed. Being president now is like being sentenced to four years of wearing your jockey shorts too tight.

The president can't please anybody anymore. Our nation is so diverse in its special interests and its needs and desires, that the president automatically becomes the national whipping boy for everybody with a gripe.

Take Jimmy Carter. We elected him president because he wasn't a member of the Washington establishment. He was one of us, a simple peanut farmer from Georgia.

Read his reviews lately? Richard Nixon was in better shape, and he barely escaped a lynching on the White House lawn.

It seems a cinch now Jimmy Carter won't be reelected president in 1980. Why? Because he isn't a member of the Washington establishment, and what does a simple peanut farmer from Georgia know about being president?

Frankly, I don't think the Democrats can elect anybody president in 1980—not even Teddy Kennedy, who has terrific hair. Polls show Americans deserting the Democratic party in droves.

And who are the Republican choices? Howard Baker? Too slick. Robert Dole? Too slimy. John Connally? Too tricky. Ronald Reagan? Too dangerous. He's from California.

Name any potential candidate, and he has warts. Name any potential candidate, and I will name a faction that will eventually want his head on a platter.

Who we need for president is somebody who is perfect.

I've got just the guy.

We need a president who can unite us again, someone who can bring Anita Bryant together with the Gay Liberationists. Bring Joan Baez together with Jane Fonda. Bring Martin and Lewis together again for *Jumping Jacks II.*

We need a president who can get this country moving, who can give us an energy program that will fill the tank of every big, black Buick from Maine to California at thirty cents a gallon.

If anybody could pull off that miracle, you say, why not get him to raise the dead, too? Stay tuned.

Could he help the farmers? Of course he could. He could lower the price of fertilizer and raise the price of peas so fast the farmers would be dancing in their fields rather than clogging up the interstate with tractorcades.

Same for the truckers. Could he help the truckers in their fight against high diesel-fuel prices and idiotic government regulations? Does a semi hauling hogs pollute?

Taxes. Now there is a problem. The people with the least money pay the most taxes. My candidate would jump on that imbalance feet first.

He knows what it means to be poor. If you think Abe Lincoln had it tough as a kid, you should have seen where this guy was born.

Human rights? My man with the plan for 1980 swears by human rights. No, he doesn't. He doesn't swear. Or drink, or smoke, or lust.

SALT II? Who needs it? The Russians would be eating out of his hands.

Feed the starving? He could do it. It's a long story, but nobody knows more about how to make a little food go a long way.

My candidate could bridge all our gaps, solve all our problems. He could make George Meany a sweetie.

And if elected, there would be no need to change the towels in the White House. He has the same initials as the current president.

Unfortunately, he's probably too busy to run. But the poor sucker who winds up with the job in 1980 will still be expected to live up to all his standards.

It's the new fact of life for the American presidency. If you can't walk on water, you need not apply.

First Sister

You must admit, the Carter family has been one of the most colorful in the nation's history of presidential families. "Colorful" is a nice way to say it.

My first thought when I read about the president's sister Gloria being arrested for playing a harmonica in a late-night diner in Americus was, so let her play it.

That is mild compared to other things I have seen people do in late-night diners. I have seen egg-throwings, plate-breakings, cigarette-machine destroyings, domestic-quarrelings, and one night I saw a man dump his grits on the floor because they were lumpy.

And they most certainly were. When he dumped them on the floor, they didn't splatter. They rolled underneath the jukebox, causing an electrical shortage right in the middle of Conway Twitty and Loretta Lynn's duet.

The president's sister, Gloria Spann—heretofore known mostly for riding on motorcycles and in tractorcades—told her version of the incident in Tuesday's papers.

She and her husband and some friends went to the McWaffles restaurant in Americus early Sunday morning for a late snack. Gloria broke into "I'm so Lonesome I Could Cry" on her harmonica. She would have been happy to play something else, but that's the only tune she knows.

Moments later, a waitress came to her table and asked that she cut out the harmonica. The other customers were complaining they couldn't hear the jukebox.

No way. "Back me into a corner," says Gloria, "and I'll come out blowing my harmonica." That's the old Carter family spirit. Too bad Jimmy can't use it. As many corners as he's been in lately, he'd need a symphony orchestra with extra tubas to get out.

The waitress was no pushover, either. She called the law. It's not every night you get a call to a diner where the sister of the president of the United States is playing her harmonica so the other customers can't hear the jukebox.

But Americus was ready. Three police cars showed up to quell the disturbance. Gloria and her husband were arrested for refusing to leave the restaurant when three carloads of policemen asked them to.

"Good thing I didn't bring my guitar," Gloria said. "I might have gotten five years."

There are two sides to every story, of course. I called the restaurant to get the other side. The manager came to the phone. Her name is Chrystal Bailey. She said there was trouble with harmonicat Gloria and her gang the minute they walked in.

"We have a rule on the weekend you have to order from the counter after eleven o'clock," Chrystal said. "That's because we get so many in here who are wild and drinkin'. I couldn't keep help because they didn't want to go to the tables and serve people like that.

"This group wouldn't order from the counter. They wanted table service. I didn't know who she (Gloria) was, but it wouldn't have mattered. If I gave her table service, I'd have to give it to everybody else, too, and then I wouldn't have anybody still working here.

"They got loud, and they got rowdy. I'm not against anybody having a good time, but they were disturbing others, and they were asked twice to be quiet.

"I can't have that. This place used to be really bad when it was a Hasty House because of such carrying-on. We've tried to get rid of that reputation."

I asked Chrystal Baily if she thought the Spann party might possibly have been drinking before their arrival at McWaffles.

"I do," she said. "I think drinkin' is what it was."

I can't blame Gloria and her friends for that. Not everybody who goes into a late-night diner has been out boozing, but it helps. Sober, you would notice the grease hanging in the air and the tattoos on the cook's arms, and that might spoil your appetite.

Now that I have finally reached the bottom of all this, I think the entire matter has been blown out of proportion. Playing harmonica in a late-night diner is no big deal, but Chrystal Baily has her problems, too.

So what's the big fuss about? A day without one of the president's relatives getting into hot water and embarrassing the White House would be like a day without new allegations against Bert Lance.

What we should do is be thankful there was another Carter to take up the slack until Billy gets out of the hospital.

The Plain(s) Truth About Killer Rabbits

I'll bet covering Millard Fillmore was never this much fun . . .

It's not that I didn't believe President Carter when he reported being attacked by a "killer rabbit" during his recent fishing trip in Plains, but my vast knowledge of rabbits has left me with a number of questions I would like to ask him about the "attack."

I know a lot about rabbits, because I spent a great portion of my boyhood trying to trap one in a box. The idea is, prop a box on a stick and put something under the box a rabbit might like to eat.

When the rabbit goes under the box to take the bait, he knocks away the stick and the box falls down over him, and you have yourself a rabbit.

Sounds good on paper, but it doesn't work. The rabbit will take the bait every time, but he is also smart enough to avoid contact with the stick, and I wasted a lot of good lettuce and carrots and okra—rabbits like okra, believe it or not—before I realized that fact.

What else I know about rabbits is (a) they are lousy swimmers, (b) they are afraid of their own shadows, and (c) the president has been under a great deal of stress and strain lately, which had nothing to do with rabbits until one tried to attack his canoe in the middle of a South Georgia pond.

Since the White House would not even release an alleged photograph of the rabbit in question—some clever soul called it a "Banzai Bunny"—I don't suppose I will ever get the opportunity to question the president face-to-face on the matter.

I won't, however, be pushed aside that easily. When the man with his finger on the nuclear button starts seeing killer rabbits in ponds, I think it is time the American people got an explanation.

I submit the following list of questions to the president as a public service. Dare he not respond?

1. Have you, Mr. President, ever had similar experiences?

2. If so, how often?

3. Are these experiences often accompanied by headaches and/or dizzy spells?

4. Was Hamilton Jordan along on the trip?

5. Did he see the rabbit, too?

6. Your report concerning the incident said the rabbit, as it attacked your canoe, was "hissing menacingly." Did at any time the rabbit make a sound that could be called a "snort"?

7. Did Hamilton Jordan at any time make such a sound?

8. How tall was the rabbit?

9. One foot? Two feet?

10. Think deeply, Mr. President, but could the rabbit have been as tall as SIX feet?

11. When you were a little boy in Plains, Mr. President, did you have, uh, "playmates" that were not really there?

12. Were any of them rabbits?

13. Did you talk to them and play fun games with them, and when Miss Lillian prepared your lunch, did you ask her to set an extra place for them?

14. How old were you when Miss Lillian explained to you that people were beginning to talk about your, uh, "playmates"?

15. As a child, were you ever completely shut out at an Easter egg hunt and the other children threw rocks at you and called you names because your basket was empty?

16. If I say, "Here Comes Peter Cottontail, hopping down the bunny trail, hippity-hoppity, Easter's on its way," what is the first thing that comes into your mind?

17. The report of the incident said you "beat back" the rabbit with your canoe paddle. As a childish prank, Mr. President, did you ever put your cat in a dryer at the laundromat?

18. Are you absolutely certain the animal that attacked your canoe was a rabbit?

19. Could it have been a beaver? An otter with long ears?

20. Bob Dole in his bunny pajamas?

Who's Ready for Teddy?

It should become very obvious while reading this that I do not consider Teddy Kennedy to be one of the great leaders of our time. I do think he looks nice in a suit, however.

There was one big headline after another recently concerning Ted Kennedy's entry into the 1980 presidential race. Some of the news was earthshaking.

• First, Teddy's mom said it was OK for him to run.

• Second, Teddy's wife said if he got elected she would go live with him in the White House. I thought that was big of her.

• Third, Teddy allegedly thinks of President Carter as a "political cripple" and told Carter he'd be smart to go beat a rabbit in the head and leave the presidenting to him.

• Fourth, everybody involved said that was a bunch of "horse manure."

• Fifth, President Carter's mom, Miss Lillian, got into the act, too. She said if Teddy runs she hopes "nothing happens to him."

According to news reports, Miss Lillian's statement, made at a chicken barbecue in New Hampshire, sent a shock wave through the Democratic party.

Jerry Brown was there. He was shocked. State Democratic party chairman Romeo Dorval was there. He was shocked, too. So were Kennedy backers in the audience.

They were so shocked, they booed Miss Lillian (who is eighty-one). I wasn't shocked. I happen to think if you are eighty-one, you can say anything you damn well please, especially if your son is the president and you've been on "The Johnny Carson show" a couple of times.

There has always been something about Teddy Kennedy that bothered me, but I could never quite put my finger on it.

Now I know what it is. It is not Teddy who bothers me so much; it is people who think he would make a good president.

They really don't know why Teddy Kennedy would make a good president, and they boo little old eighty-one-year-old ladies.

"Why do you think he would make a good president?" I have asked a number of draft-Kennedyites recently.

"Because," begins the usual reply, "He, uh, well . . .

"He, uh, LOOKS like a president."

I have heard that, uh, brilliant line of political thinking before. That's how Henry Fonda got his part in *Fail Safe*, but, unfortunately, we aren't casting a movie here.

So what do you LOOK like when you look like a president?

I remember a calendar we had in elementary school. It had the pictures of all the presidents, up through Eisenhower, who had just been elected president.

Ike was bald and looked like he had just knocked his tee shot in the lake at the par-three twelfth at Augusta National.

Herbert Hoover looked uncomfortable, Abe Lincoln had a big nose, and although you couldn't tell it by his picture on the calendar, George Washington had bad teeth.

Teddy Kennedy has long hair, a pleasant smile, and he wears dopey glasses to make himself look more sophisticated. They said the same thing about Warren G. Harding.

I did find one Kennedy backer willing to list some other qualifications Teddy has to be president. Relax, this will only take a second:

• He has a good speaking voice.

• His mother is a courageous person.

• He probably learned a lot about running the country from his two brothers.

Brilliant, I was sitting here trying to think of a way to end this, and I just thought of it. What do you say to people when they fumble and stumble and try to tell you why they think Teddy Kennedy, just another pretty face who got a big break the day he was born, would make a good president?

You say, uh, two little words.

Horse manure.

The Official Candidate Quiz

I wrote this one cold afternoon during the 1980 New Hampshire primary. I seriously doubt I was sober at the time.

Manchester, N.H.

Now that we have completed caucuses in Iowa and Maine and primaries here in New Hampshire, with extensive news coverage of all three, it is high time the voters of America were well acquainted with the candidates who want to be their next president.

This is the beauty of a system that no longer allows its presidential nominees to be hand-picked in smoke-filled rooms. The people finally have something to do with the nomination process.

You may be asking yourself, "I think I am up-to-date on the candidates and the issues, but how can I be certain?"

Worry not. To get a reading on your knowledge of the 1980 presidential race, all you need do is take the following test which asks pertinent questions concerning the run for the White House.

The test, concocted by yours truly, who has been trapped in New Hampshire with babbling brooks and babbling political-types for what seems like months, is simple and easy to understand.

Mark your answers with a No. 2 lead pencil only, and make no unnecessary smudges or marks on the test paper. Correct answers will be printed in the classified ad section of the Fargo, North Dakota, *Fleaflicker-Herald* on Inauguration Day, 1981.

If you answer all the questions correctly, you are qualified to read a Joseph Kraft political column and then pretend you understood it. If you miss less than five, you probably remember who Tom Eagleton was. If you miss between five and ten, you probably think Dewey hung on to win, and if you miss more than that, your penalty should be a week locked in a room with a Right-to-Lifer, an opponent of gun control, Paul Harvey, and two anti-nukes who are protesting the Three-Mile Island incident by refusing to bathe.

The test follows. Take as long as necessary to complete. Ready? Begin.

1. Of the following, pick the most boring aspect of President Jimmy Carter's current administration.

A. His hemorrhoid condition. B. Walter Mondale.

2. Which of the previously held positions would Republican candidate George Bush say helped him LEAST in preparing him for the possibility of serving as president?

A. Congressman from Texas. B. Head of the CIA. C. Ambassador to China. D. Houston Roto-Rooter man.

3. Ronald Reagan was born in:

A. 1612. B. 1613. C. 1614. D. 1615. E. Poland.

4. The primary difference between Reagan and fellow Republican candidate John Anderson is:

A. Grecian Formula 9.

5. Which of the following are LEAST likely to win the 1980 Democratic nomination?

A. Hodding Carter. B. Bo Derek. C. The Fog. D. Jerry Brown.

6. True or false: Republican Philip Crane of Illinois is a figment of his imagination.

7. Who is shorter than a fire hydrant and speaks with a Southern Accent?

A. Little Jimmy Dickens. B. Amy Carter. C. A Vidalia onion. D. Howard Baker.

8. In the space provided below, list all the intelligent comments rock singer Linda Ronstadt made while campaigning in New Hampshire for boyfriend Jerry Brown.

9. Robert Dole is:

A. A senator from Kansas. B. A former vice-presidential candidate. C. A pineapple. D. Wasting his time. E. All of the above.

10. Which of the following embarrassing situations DID NOT involve Ted Kennedy?

A. Chappaquiddick. B. CBS interview with Roger Mudd. C. Harvard cheating scandal. D. Idiotic comments concerning the Shah of Iran. E. Seward's Folly.

11. President Carter has called for an American boycott of the 1980 Summer Olympics in Moscow. Challenger Kennedy's alternatives to that are:

A. Boycotting the 1980 NBA playoffs, instead.

12. One of the lesser-known candidates who ran in the New Hampshire Democratic primary is named "LaRouche." His first name is:

A. Anita. B. Boom-Boom. C. Lady Bird. D. Lash.

13. Former President Gerald Ford would like to throw his hat in the 1980 political ring, but he can't remember where he put his hat. Where would you suggest he look?

A. In his closet. B. In his golf bag. C. Under his pillow. D. On his head.

14. True or false? John Connally.

Political Pain in the "Neck"

Another problem with being president is somebody is always sticking his nose in your, uh, business.

Things have been tough for the president lately. Egypt and Israel still can't come to terms for peace, there has been no SALT agreement, angry farmers disrupted his holiday visit to Plains, and then there was the messy business of kicking Taiwan out of bed in favor of Red China.

I have a great deal of faith in the president, however, and I am certain he will eventually find a way to deal with those lingering issues.

But one other problem facing President Carter could lead to his eventual downfall. It might even become the battleground on which the Republicans decide to fight for reentry into the White House in 1980.

The president of the United States, the honorable James Earl Carter, Jr., has a bad case of hemorrhoids.

I am all for the public's right to know, but I was a bit shocked when the news of the president's condition came blasting over the radio one evening during the holidays.

How did such private information leak out? I called one of my White House sources to find out.

"We tried our best to keep it quiet," he said, "but the president sent Jody Powell out for 'Preparation H' and that was the ballgame."

"Preparation H" is the medicine most prescribed by doctors for relief of the painful condition known as hemorrhoids.

When I first heard the news, I laughed. But then I realized the painful condition known as hemorrhoids is no laughing matter, especially when it is the president of a large, powerful nation who has them.

"He's hurting and he's hurting bad," Newsweek magazine quoted a White House spokesperson as saying about President Carter's case.

It is probably not in good taste to discuss exactly what hemorrhoids are and how they affect their victims. But they make it hurt where you sit and often cause drastic changes in the sufferer's personality.

I once worked for a man who had hemorrhoids. Most of the time, he was the nicest guy you would ever want to meet. When his condition flared up, he was Attila the Hun with a hangover.

During a particularly painful bout with his ailment, he attempted suicide in the middle of the office as a means of relief. Only the actions of a quick-thinking secretary saved his life.

Two weeks later, when the pain returned, he fired her. A man suffering from hemorrhoids cannot be held responsible for his actions.

Which brings me back to the president. Suppose he had another flareup in the middle of serious negotiations with, say, Soviet President Brezhnev?

The pain having siphoned his good senses, who knows what the president might say in the midst of a testy situation?

"Leonid, you pork-faced imbecile!" is simply not good diplomatic phraseology.

I can hear the Republicans asking the question of the American people already: Can we feel secure knowing the leader of the free world, the man with his finger on the nuclear bomb, is suffering from the horrid fate and agony of you-know-what?

"It's a ticklish situation for sure," admitted my White House source.

"Ticklish?" I asked.

"Poor choice of words," he replied. "But I think the president can handle it. He's had experience with this sort of thing all his life, you know."

I didn't know. The president has had hemorrhoids all his life?

My source explained. "First, he had to grow up with a brother like Billy. Then, when he was governor, he had to deal with Lester Maddox.

"Now, he's got the farmers on him, the Taiwanese are marching, the Iranian dissidents are mad because he has supported the Shah, Ted Kennedy may run against him in '80, and Barry Goldwater has called him a coward."

But what, I asked, do they have to do with hemorrhoids?

"They're all a big pain in the . . ."

"Neck?" I interrupted.

"Have it your way," said my source.

6

IT'S BEEN ONE HASSLE AFTER ANOTHER

Looking for Mr. Goodwrench

How many days does it take me to screw in a light bulb? Four. Three to fool around with it myself, and one to round up an electrician to finish the job.

A man from the city water department came to my house last week and cut off my water. He had some absurd reason for doing that. I think he mentioned I hadn't paid my bill on time.

I attempted to explain. Maybe there were some goats in the neighborhood, and one was nosing around in my mailbox and ate my payment to the city water department.

You can't explain *anything* to a man with a wrench.

So there I was for a couple of days, with no water. It was a learning experience.

I learned it is virtually impossible to brush your teeth using orange juice.

I learned if you wet your face with milk and then try to shave, the pain will be incredible.

I learned if you don't shower for a couple of days, you won't have to put up with worrisome people like your friends and fellow employees.

I learned if you don't wash coffee cups, something green will grow inside of them.

I also learned that I still don't know anything about anything that is mechanical in nature. I couldn't change the oil in my salad.

241

Here's what happened:

I finally reached the city water department—the telephone there had been busy for forty-eight hours—and the woman who answered agreed with me that it was probably all a big mistake that my water had been cut off.

She apologized on behalf of the mayor and the city for the inconvenience and said if I would pay my bill, along with an additional six-dollar service charge, the man with the wrench would return to my house and turn the water back on.

Naturally, I accepted her apology and her kind offer to right the department's wrong.

I returned home that evening, expecting to find running water. Instead, I found a note in my door from Mr. Goodwrench.

"Dear Sir," it began, "I turned the water back on in your meter. However, I left it off in your property valve because of an indication there was a faucet open in your house.

"You can turn the water on in your property valve. It is located approximately twelve inches down in a metal pipe that is located approximately ten feet behind your water meter. Thanks."

Thank you. But I don't know anything about water meters and property valves. I can barely operate my shower curtain.

I called the water department again, and they tried to explain to me where to locate my property valve. They tried to explain it several times.

"You'd better talk to Mr. Something-or-Other," a woman said. Mr. Something-or-Other became impatient and said, "If you don't know where your property valve is, you'll just have to look in your yard until you find it."

It was raining outside. I searched for my property valve for half an hour. It occurred to me that I wouldn't know my property valve if it walked up to me and played the flute.

I called the department again. It was after five o'clock Friday afternoon. I went into Plan "B." I started crying.

Another half-hour search, and I finally located what I determined to be my water meter. It was located in some tall grass I should cut, but when I pull the starter cord on my lawn mower, nothing happens.

I walked approximately ten feet behind my water meter and, sure enough, there was a metal pipe like the note said. I reached twelve inches inside it and, sure enough, there was my property valve, along with a lot of dirt and bugs and worms.

I suffered a mild coronary, ruined a shirt and a pair of pants, but I finally turned my property valve and immediately felt a sensation of great satisfaction.

I went back inside my house, took a shower, and watered the green things growing in the coffee cups.

I Hate the Beach

I forgot to mention one other thing that will drive a person crazy at the beach. Is there a more uncomfortable feeling on this earth than pulling on a cold, wet bathing suit?

Kiawah Island, S.C.

Every six months or so I get a little crazy in the city and I say to myself, "What I need are a few days at the beach."

So here I am at Kiawah Island, near Charleston. Kiawah Island used to be inhabited by bugs, large birds, and alligators, but then some smart money from Kuwait came in and built condominiums, a golf course, tennis courts, and one of those trinket shops where a lamp made out of sea shells costs $175.

I like my room here at the Kiawah Inn. It overlooks the shimmering Atlantic, and at these prices, I will turn the thermostat down to any level I please.

Scenes from the nearby low-country marsh adorn the walls, and the soap in the bathroom is individually boxed.

At Howard Johnsons and Holiday Inns, the soap in the bathroom comes wrapped in paper. How gauche.

What I don't like about Kiawah Island, and what I don't like about all seaside resorts, is the beach itself. I never thought I would admit this, but I have been a closet beach-hater for years.

What I hate most about the beach is the sand. If beaches had outdoor carpet or Astro Turf, maybe I would feel differently. Sand is the pits.

There is no way to go to the beach without getting completely covered with sand. Sand in your topsiders, sand in your hair, sand in your bologna sandwiches, and if you are not careful, sand in your bathing trunks.

Sand in your bathing trunks makes a person crabby and uncomfortable and causes all sorts of unspeakable rashes.

Once you are covered with sand, it is impossible to wash it all off. No matter how long you shower after a day at the beach, there will always be sand in your bed.

Cracker crumbs in your bed are just as bad as sand in your bed, but I would rather sleep with a South Carolina three-eyed marsh hog than with sand or cracker crumbs.

I also hate the sun at the beach. Two minutes in the sun, and I look like I've been roasted on the devil's own spit. People with nothing better to do but lie around getting suntans DESERVE skin cancer and early wrinkling and smelling like *eau de Valvoline*.

Another thing I dislike about the beach is young, musclebound boys with deep tans who cavort in skimpy bathing suits and throw frisbees. Throwing frisbees is a mindless exercise designed for people with the IQs of jellyfish, which is another reason the beach is no place for the sane.

What's under that water? Jellyfish, stingrays, things with no eyes, things with teeth, like sharks. Once I read what to do in case you are in the water and a shark approaches.

"Do not run. Do not splash water. Do not shout. Wait until the shark swims close enough and then strike it on the head with a blunt instrument."

Fine. I'll just stand here without running or splashing water or shouting, and when the shark swims close enough, I'll pull this tire tool I keep in the pocket of my bathing trunks and belt him right between his bloodthirsty eyes.

I could go on. I could even make a tacky remark like, may a giant oil spill cover every beach in the world and see if I care.

But I won't. A lot of people enjoy the beach. Children, muscle-brains, and exhibitionists, for instance.

Let them all go bake their brains. I'll just sit here in my room in my overcoat and play with the knobs on my air conditioner.

Return of the Wethead

If every man in America would stop using his electric hair dryer for one week, we could save enough in energy costs to send a dozen kids to barber school. Think about it.

I took a long look at my electric hair dryer the other morning. It was a Christmas gift, and I cherished it once. Its sleek, modern styling hinted macho, but at the same time said its owner would be a man of sensitivity, a man in touch with the necessity for good grooming habits.

I recall how the handle felt in my hand the morning of that first dry. It fit perfectly. It was a part of me, an added appendage for countless mornings to come.

I began in warm, shifted to medium in mid-dry, and then gunned it to high for the finish. My hair fluffed as it had never fluffed before. One spark, however, and meet the human torch.

I realize there are a number of important issues that probably should be discussed in a forum such as this, but occasionally, the real issues of the day are hidden deep behind the headlines. Occasionally, one must stand and be heard on a matter that at first glance might seem trivial.

The time has come, America, to speak out on the electric hair dryer for men.

It came to me as I stood, nurd-like, holding my dryer to my head. Like all mornings, I had showered and shampooed with a shampoo the fragrance of blossoming apricots, the color of the dawning sky.

This, I thought, is ridiculous. This is insane. This is a horrid, useless waste of time I can do without.

I figure I have spent five minutes every morning for the past five years blow-drying my hair. That is six days of my life spent with Flash Gordon's ray gun pointed at my brain, which probably has windburn by now.

It all began with cosmetics commercials screaming at us on television. Our forefathers rallied behind "54-40 or Fight!" and "Remember the Alamo!" and "A Chicken in Every Pot!" For this generation, it has been, "The Wethead Is Dead!" Pour out your Wildroot Creme Oil, Charlie, it's a blow-dry kind of day.

What followed was a mad rush by America's male population to grow hair. Then dry it. Then spray it so it wouldn't budge in a hurricane. No longer did men comb their hair. They raked it. Hair wasn't "cut," it was "styled."

Ears disappeared from Maine to California, and ten million bottles of Vitalis sat lonely and gathering dust, an oily relic of the past.

Young and old alike, we all bought electric hair dryers. Even athletes and probably truck drivers.

I know not what course others may take, but as for me, I have plugged in my electric hair dryer for the last time.

I despise the effort and time wasted on it, and I despise its high-pitched hum. Put an electric hair dryer to your head and you couldn't hear the 7:05 flight to Cleveland take off in the kitchen.

Left completely alone, I have discovered, hair will dry itself in less than an hour. I will save time, conserve energy, and never be mistaken for a skinny sheepdog again.

I threw my electric hair dryer in the garbage. Along with my banana creme rinse somebody said would give my hair body. I don't want body. Along with my shampoo the fragrance of blossoming apricots. The fragrance of blossoming apricots is for girls and boys who drink whiskey sours and eat the cherries.

Join me if you dare, men. Wetheads, arise again and stand tall! If you must, even slick it down and part it on the side and look up your old barber.

You never know. He may still be in business.

The Doctor, Revisited

My doctor read this and called me in for an immediate reexamination. I was sore for a month.

It had been a long time since my last complete physical examination, and I was in no hurry to have another one.

When I was eleven, a doctor examined me from head to toe before my trip to Camp Thunder and pronounced me fit for everything from overnight hiking trips to towel fights in the shower.

I didn't want to go to Camp Thunder and secretly hoped he would find some horrible malady like bumps on my head, which would have kept me away from camp and couldn't have been as bad as the towel fights in the showers there.

A towel fight in a shower involves inflicting physical harm upon a fellow camper. My boyhood friend and idol, Weyman C. Wannamaker, Jr., a great American, was the king of the towel fighters.

He would wet one end of a large beach towel and fling that lethal end toward the uncovered hindparts of his victim, snapping it back on impact with a resounding, "Whap!"

Bend over to retrieve your soap in a shower with Weyman C. Wannamaker, Jr., and his beach towel, and you would be standing for campfire vespers the entire week.

I had no bumps on my head when I was eleven, and I went on to Camp Thunder. I solved the towel fight problem. I didn't take a shower for seven days.

I sat alone at campfire vespers. But I sat.

I don't know what came over me last week to have another physical examination. Doctors spook me. Their offices spook me. Their nurses spook me, and all their receptionists just got off the boat from Transylvania where their last jobs were in a blood bank.

"You vil take a seat, please," they begin. "It vil only be a little while."

It vil never be a little while. It vil be an eternity if you are as frightened of doctors as I am. Doctors' offices even smell like impending doom.

Last week, while I waited for my doctor, I tried to read a magazine. Why are magazines in doctors' offices always out of date?

I picked up a *Newsweek*. Roosevelt was on the cover. Teddy.

My doctor was a nice enough fellow. First, he asked me a lot of questions.

Do you smoke?

Yes.

Do you drink?

Yes.

Do you eat regular, balanced meals?

No.

Do you get plenty of rest and exercise?

No.

Do you ever get dizzy spells?

Only when I run out of cigarettes or have a drink before "The Today Show" goes off the air.

Then, he took me into a small room with only one door, which he closed, and examined me. He examined my head, my nose, my ears, my throat, my neck, my chest, my back, my stomach, my legs, my feet, and my toes.

I still don't have any bumps on my head, but one of my toes has an ingrown nail which he mashed, prompting a scream. That is how he pays his receptionist. She loves screaming.

He did other things to my person as well, but I can't mention any of them here except to say they were indignities that shouldn't happen to a rabid dog.

"It's for your own good," the doctor said.

Jack the Ripper told his patients the same thing.

Later, he turned me over to a nurse who put needles in me and gave me an X-ray. I have also wondered why, if there is nothing dangerous about X-rays, the nurse who administers them always stands behind a lead screen?

The doctor didn't put it in so many words, but I suppose I will live.

Otherwise, the receptionist—Countess Rubellina in the old country—wouldn't have asked, "Vil you be paying now, or shall ve bill you later?"

"Later, sweetheart," I said. "Later."

Deliver Me From Sausage Balls

I even know people who give cocktail parties you go to before you go to another cocktail party. Isn't being grown-up fun?

Standing around at a cocktail party the other evening, in honor of somebody getting married or getting a divorce or running for president—I forget which—the thought suddenly occurred to me, "I'm sick of standing around at cocktail parties."

I don't have an actual count, but I am certain I have been to somewhere near a million cocktail parties since I became old enough to stop cruising around in a car drinking beer, which is what you do until you become old enough to get invited to cocktail parties.

At first, I thought cocktail parties were sort of neat. The booze was free, and normally in great abundance, and before I had eaten several thousand of those little sausage balls they always serve as an *hors d'oeuvre,* I thought they were quite tasty. Now, the very mention of one makes me quite ill.

And, after a time, I found myself actually dreading cocktail parties and concocting all sorts of excuses to get out of them.

My best excuse to get out of a cocktail party is, "Thank you very much for inviting me, but I'm supposed to be involved in a serious automobile accident that evening."

Americans will give a cocktail party for nearly every occasion and for nearly everybody.

I have been to cocktail parties in honor of Canadian consuls, Japanese piano players, a man from Louisiana who makes duck calls, the birth of twins, the buying of a new house, the selling of an old one, the opening of a play, and the closing of a number of newspapers and magazines and even a used-car dealership. (The owner had liquidated with plans to go into the ministry. It's a long story.)

Regardless of the occasion, however, all cocktail parties are generally alike.

• There is never anywhere to sit down, and it is my firm belief that drinking is a sit-down sort of endeavor.

• You get drunker faster when you drink standing up and are therefore more liable to do something you will regret the next day.

• Somebody always does something he regrets the next day, like saying *Kramer vs. Kramer* stunk, or barging in on the hostess in the bathroom.

• You have to talk a lot at a cocktail party, and the conversation is always the same. Dull, unless someone knows some juicy gossip about somebody who wasn't invited.

• You can never find an ashtray.

• While you are listening to some juicy gossip and eating one of those little chicken wings, which are always near the sausage balls, the little plate where you are supposed to put your bones will be taken away, and you will have to stand there like an idiot holding one of those little chicken-wing bones.

• The solution to that problem is to find a person you don't like and drop the bone into his or her coat pocket while he or she isn't looking.

There simply must be more original ways for people to gather and bore one another.

Charades, for instance. Terrific game. You make a complete fool of yourself, just like at a cocktail party, but this way you have all the guests' undivided attention while you do it.

Croquet. Remember croquet? Everybody gathers in the back yard and knocks the little balls through the wire hoops. Nobody really likes to play croquet because it's a stupid game, but at least you don't have to talk.

I can think of all sorts of alternatives to cocktail parties. Doesn't anybody give wienie roasts anymore? What about hayrides?

Hayrides are for bumpkins, you say. Hayrides are kid stuff. That's all you know.

Once I went on a hayride with Kathy Sue Loudermilk, bless her heart. I was gone six days and woke up in Ocala, Florida, with a tattoo.

That, believe me, beats the absolute fool out of standing around half-crocked trying to talk to a Japanese piano player with a mouthful of sausage balls.

Interviewing Miss Fruit Fly

I admit it. This is one of those columns I wrote because I didn't have anything else to write about. I still don't want to interview any little girl ice skaters, however.

A lot of people call and write suggesting ideas for columns. I appreciate that. It should be obvious by now I need all the help I can get.

But not all the ideas I get are good ones. In fact, some of the ideas I get are insane.

There is a man who writes to suggest a column about him because he is Jesus. You would be surprised how many people think they are Jesus.

"I have followed your work closely," he says, "and I want you to be the first to have my story."

It's a dilly, I admit, but I've already heard it.

Out of sheer curiosity, I called the man who thinks he is Jesus. I got a recording. "This is Jesus Christ," it began. "I have stepped away for a few moments. . . ."

Another group of people who want to be written about are people who think they know who really killed John Kennedy. I think there are more of them than people who think they are Jesus.

"Can you talk?" a voice asked on the other end of the telephone.

"About what?" I replied.

"About what happened in Dallas."

A sports nut, I figured.

"I know who really killed JFK," said the voice.

"Who?" I asked, off the top of my head.

"I'll have to call you back," the voice said. "I hear the nurse coming."

Another group of nuts who want publicity are nuts who own talking animals. Talking dogs, talking cats, talking mules, talking rabbits, talking pigs, and the woman who called to say she had taught her parakeet to recite the pledge of allegiance to the flag.

The parakeet's name was Cindy.

"Cindy's so smart," said the woman, "next, I'm going to teach her to sing 'God Bless America.'"

God bless a milk cow before I'm going to interview a flag-waving parakeet that thinks it's Kate Smith.

In order to save us all a lot of trouble, I have compiled a list of other things I refuse to write columns about. I don't want to offend anyone, but if you were planning to call or write to suggest any of the following, go talk to your cat and leave me alone:

• BALLOON RACES: I am not interested in balloon races. I am not interested in balloon racers. I get all the hot air I can handle interviewing politicians.

• LITTLE GIRL ICE SKATERS: I don't have anything against little girl ice skaters, I just don't want to talk to one. After you have asked a little girl ice skater, "Do you really enjoy the skating?" and her mother has answered, "She just loooooves it," that's the ballgame.

Besides, all little girl ice skaters grow up to marry quarterbacks, which is what can happen if you spend too much time spinning your brain around.

• RATTLESNAKE HUNTS: Television stations love rattlesnake hunts because they can get film of some clod walking around with a sackful of live rattlesnakes and peddle it at eleven o'clock as news. I am interested in rattlesnake hunts only if somebody is bitten at one, preferably somebody from a television station.

I agree with philosopher Dupree Jenkins, who once pointed out, "Finding a rattlesnake when you are looking for one is not exciting. When you ain't, and you find one anyway, now there's an attention-grabber."

• BEAUTY QUEENS: Ever try to interview Miss Fruit Fly?

• MISTREATMENT OF BABY SEALS: If I knew any baby seals personally, I might feel differently. I'd rather help the rattlesnakes. People are all the time milking rattlesnakes, poking forked sticks in their faces and taking them to weirdo churches. You'd bite back, too.

• SOCCER: If we ignore soccer long enough, I am convinced it will finally go away.

• RUGBY: See "SOCCER."

• UFO SIGHTINGS: Don't tell me about UFOs, bring me one. Put it on my desk and let me talk to the driver. Otherwise, go sniff some more swamp gas.

• TROUBLES WITH THE IRS: About this time every year, I begin to hear from people complaining about how they've been screwed by the IRS. I don't want to hear your whining and petty gripes. It is the duty of every American citizen to pay his or her taxes cheerfully and respectfully.

Besides, I don't want to be reminded of what the lousy bloodsuckers are trying to do to me.

How I Stop Pedxxx Smookxing

To be quite honest, I did write the following piece without a cigarette, and I am proud to announce I finally kicked the nasty tobacco habit after fifteen years. Do I still want a cigarette occasionally? Given a chance, I would eat one.

I am going to attempt the impossible. I am going to attempt to write this entire column without smoking a cigarette. I have never written anything without relying heavily on the soul of tobacco.

The doctor was firm in his insistence I give up a fifteen-year, two-pack-a-day habit.

"And what if I don't?" I asked him.

"A number of things could happen," he answered. "All of them end in somebody collecting your life insurance a lot sooner than you expected."

I have tried to stop smoking before. A friend and I agreed to stop smoking together. We made it eight days. I called his home one evening to see how he was doing. His wife answered the phone.

"He smoked a cigarette," she said. "He was sitting in a chair watching television. Suddenly, he got out of the chair, jumped up on the coffee table, lit a cigarette, and looked to the sky and said, 'God wants me to smoke!'"

It made sense that if God wanted my friend to smoke, He would have felt the same about me.

There are a number of things I can do without having a cigarette while I am doing them. I don't need a cigarette while sleeping, swimming, taking a shower, playing with dynamite, or eating collards.

But write without a cigarette?

So far, I have made it this far, but I have begun to hallucinate, which always happens to me when I attempt to quit smoking. A penguin just walked into the office.

It would be just about here I would normally have a cigarette while writing a column. I need both hands to type, so I would stop typing, pull one out of the pack, light it, take two or three puffs and return to the typewriter.

Sometimes when I smoke while writing my column, I forget I am smoking and the cigarette burns down to a point where it falls out of the ashtray.

That is very dangerous with all the paper that is usually strewn about my desk. Last week, the April issue of *Playboy*, my desk calendar, and a press release from the annual Armadillo Confab and Exposition in Victoria, Texas, were burned to a crisp.

What helped me make the decision to attempt to quit smoking is some news I heard the other night at the baseball game.

I was sitting next to Sports Editor Jesse Outlar, who smokes, and he was telling me Henry Aaron had quit smoking.

"He smoked all those years he was playing ball every day," said Jesse, "and then when he's retired, he decides to give up smoking. If he had quit fifteen years ago, he might have hit a thousand home runs."

But it is more difficult for a writer to quit smoking than for anybody else because smoking sort of goes with writing. I would normally have another cigarette about here while pausing to figure out how to end this piece, which is now into the home stretch.

I think what I will do is type just as fast as I can because thisis a boutto driveme crayz, If I couldhave a cigaretteer ight xxx right now, I notonly would smokeit, I would eat thefil ter.

Ithas also occurred tome thatif I xxx reallyhad to have a cigarette, xxxI couldgo a head and smooooooke itand who would knowthe difference?

Inother words, I could lieabout this whole thing andwrite how I got through thiscolumn without having a cigar xxxxette, and have allthe cigarxx ettes Iwanted to becasueyou can't seeme whil Iam writing this.

Trust me.

A Case of the Cutes

I am always looking for ways to serve the public. Here, I discuss one of the average citizen's greatest problems: How to tell whose restroom is whose in a restaurant. Please read carefully.

Historians may look back to the current period of American life and call it our "cute" phase and wonder what happened to all the adults.

We are all driving cute little cars with funsie little names, "Rabbit" and "Pinto" and "Sunbird." Blow their cute little horns and hear the cute little sound: "Beep! Beep!"

We read cute little magazines like *People* and *Us*, and we watch cute little television programs starring cute little people with cute little names like "Mork" and "Mindy."

Imagine trying to carry on an intelligent, grownups' conversation with somebody named "Mork" or "Mindy." I'd rather try to talk to the air filter on a Pinto station wagon.

We also dress in cute little clothes nowadays, jeans and T-shirts and orange sneakers, and we wear them to do cute things like go roller skating.

Bleech!

We even have a "cutie" running for president. He is Jerry Brown, the governor of California. He even thinks he has a chance to win.

How cute.

Restaurants are the worst offenders, however. They have gone "cute crazy." Clowns serve hamburgers and waiters are in pirate suits, and the menu is printed on a balloon you can keep.

Restaurants also serve cute dishes. "Happy Meals" in a box. Seafood restaurants serve "Cap'n's Delight," which is crab meat with hollandaise, and the bottom of the plate has real barnacles.

Zowie, what fun!

You can also get all sorts of darling little drinks before you eat in a restaurant. Piña coladas, apricot daiquiris, rum and Dr. Pepper.

Also, there are those precious little green bottles with nothing but water inside that fuzz-brains drink.

Restaurants have even gotten cute with their restrooms. That makes me very angry. Going to the restroom is a serious matter, and it should be kept as simple as possible.

It used to be that when you went to a restroom in a restaurant, all you had to do was ask directions and then find the door marked "men" or "women" or in spiffy places, "ladies" or "gentlemen." You chose the appropriate door and then walked through it to take care of your needs.

That has all changed. Restaurant restrooms are no longer marked plainly "men" or "women" or "ladies" or "gentlemen." Go into a restaurant that serves Mexican food. The restroom doors will be marked "señors" or "señoritas." If the management is really into "cute," they may be marked, "muchachos" and "muchachas."

It's the same for other restaurants that serve ethnic foods. If you don't speak the language, you could be in trouble.

I suppose people with at least a fair amount of intelligence can usually select the correct restroom in those instances, but there are occasions when the choices are not that clear.

Watch yourself in restaurants that specialize in fried chicken. They often use "roosters" and "hens" on their restroom doors.

I happen to know the difference. I am "rooster." But I have an advantage. As a child, one of my chores was to gather the eggs from the henhouse. You pick up who's what in chickens rather quickly that way.

Others might not be so fortunate as to have that background, however, and there is nothing quite so embarrassing as strolling unannounced into the wrong roost.

I could go on, but I don't want to lose any more of my temper. It is simply time grownups started demanding grownup products and grownup services.

If for no other reason, there is too much else for an adult to worry about today to have to go through potty training again.

Don't laugh. Been in one of those western steak houses lately? Some western steak houses don't even bother with names on their restroom doors. They just have pictures of cowboys and cowgirls.

Whom do you favor more, Roy or Dale?

Careful, Tex. They both wore boots, you know.

7

VIOLENCE: FIVE VICTIMS

Officer Frank Schlatt

Frank Schlatt was a good cop who was blown away in the line of duty. His daughter must be nearly grown by now. And the man who shot him probably doesn't have that long before he is eligible for parole.

To the man who shot Frank Robert Schlatt:

You should have been there Tuesday morning. You should have been there at the funeral service they held for your victim.

Was it easy to pull that trigger? Was it easy to point that sawed-off shotgun at Frank Robert Schlatt and shoot him in the face?

What happened? Did you panic? You and your accomplices were robbing a furniture store. In walked Officer Frank Robert Schlatt of the Atlanta Police Department. You shot him. Three hours later, he was dead.

I want to tell you about the funeral, and I pray to God you read this. You should know about the pain, the heartbreak, the grief you caused.

Officer Schlatt was thirty-one. He was only thirty-one. It's like the priest said Tuesday morning. "How can we explain death when it occurs in the midst of a life with so much potential unfulfilled?" Could you have explained that Tuesday morning?

It was a beautiful spring day. The chapel out in Forest Park was packed with people. That many again waited outside.

You have probably been to a funeral before. You probably know how haunting organ music in the background can be. As the people filed into the chapel, the organ was playing "The Battle Hymn of the Republic."

257

A number of important people came. The mayor was there, along with commissioners and ex-commissioners and even an ex-governor, Lester Maddox. He sat alone to pay his respects to the man you killed.

There were flowers everywhere. There was even a police badge made of white and blue flowers.

Policemen from all over came to mourn Officer Schlatt. They came from as far away as Phenix City, Alabama. One would tell me, "When a fellow officer dies, it's like something inside you dying. It is infuriating."

You know what he said about you? He said: "I don't see how that killer can live with his conscience . . . if he has a conscience."

An honor guard brought in the casket. Three members of the honor guard had worked all-night shifts, but volunteered to be at the funeral Tuesday morning. That is how they felt about the man you killed.

The priest said something I wish you could have heard. He was talking about death not being final. Officer Schlatt, he said, "was a good man. And you cannot bury a good man."

The casket was bronze. It was draped with an American flag. The honor guard marched in. They wore white hats and white gloves. As the services continued, two members of the guard stood at strict attention on either side of the casket. One was white. One was black.

"These men fight among themselves all the time," said a man who is paid to monitor the police department, "but at a time like this, they all come together."

That should worry you. They will find you and bring you to justice. You can count on it.

I wish you could have been standing with me outside when they brought Officer Schlatt's body from the chapel.

Scripture was read. There was a prayer. The family sat under a tent in folding chairs, just a few feet from the one they loved so much.

There was Officer Schlatt's father. He gazed ahead in shock and disbelief. There was his mother, a tiny, graying lady who wept openly. Another relative fainted.

There was also the widow. She wore black, her shoulders covered in a white shawl. I watched her as she tried to say The Lord's Prayer aloud. She choked on every word. She was such a pretty woman, even in her grief. She was blonde and small. Young widows can break the coldest heart. Maybe even yours.

I wish you could have seen the honor guard fold the flag. Their leader broke down. I wish you could have seen the mayor hand the flag to Officer Schlatt's widow. I wish you could have heard the bugler blow taps.

More than anything, I wish you could have seen your victim's daughter. She is twelve. Her name is Jodie. She cried, too. She cried hard and she cried long.

There was a small flower on top of the casket. It was red and white. When the honor guard folded the flag, they folded the flower inside it.

It was Jodie's flower. She had placed it on her daddy's casket. You should have been there.

Two Good Soldiers

Islamabad, Pakistan. December, 1979. A group of screaming idiots attack and burn the United States Embassy. Brian Ellis and Steven Crowley, two American servicemen, are killed. Lest we forget.

Citizens have been complaining about the American servicemen who were released as hostages from the United States Embassy in Iran.

They are complaining because the soldiers accepted their releases.

"What kind of men do we have in our armed services today?" a reader asked in a letter to the newspaper.

"Those released from the embassy in Iran should have refused to leave and stayed on to protect the others and to show Iran the American military has the guts and fortitude to stick out any situation."

People who write letters like that have mush for brains.

One, it is rather doubtful that the young soldiers had any choice in the matter.

Two, what could they have realistically accomplished by staying, other than making a few mushbrains back home "feel proud to be Americans"?

Three, if there is so much concern about the courage and integrity of American servicemen, why doesn't somebody write something in the newspaper about the two soldiers at our embassy in Islamabad, Pakistan, who also came home recently?

In boxes.

It's been only two weeks since they died. Would one in a thousand Americans even remember their names?

Brian Ellis, an army warrant officer, died in Islamabad. He was thirty. They found his charred remains in the rubble that was the embassy after the attack.

The exact details of his death aren't known, but a Baptist minister in his hometown of Spring Lake, North Carolina, said Brian Ellis "loved his country and the army. He was committed to the defense of his country."

That is at least a hint that he died trying to protect American lives and American property.

Marine Cpl. Steven Crowley also died in Islamabad, one day after the second anniversary of his Marine Corps enlistment.

He was twenty. The posthumous Bronze Star citation he was awarded included what details the Marine Corps knows about his death.

When the attack came, Corporal Crowley took his post on the roof of the embassy. He was immediately exposed to a barrage of rocks and whatever else the attackers could find to throw, as well as small-arms fire.

He never budged. He was able to give valuable information to those on the inside, and he was able to act as a diversion to buy time for them to reach the safety of the embassy security vault.

A man at Marine headquarters in Washington told me over the telephone, "Corporal Crowley got it in the head. We don't know if he was shot or if he was hit by a flying missile. We do know, however, it was pretty bad. There was some debate about whether to open the casket at his funeral."

Steven Crowley was one of nine children. After his father died, said those who knew him, Steven Crowley helped support his mother and younger brothers and sisters, even when he was in high school.

He was a good Catholic. He was a member of his high school track team. He was on the staff of his high school newspaper. He was an expert cabinet maker. He worked to keep classmates away from drugs.

After his death, his hometown church in Port Jefferson, New York, carried an insert in the Sunday morning worship program, giving other details of Steven Crowley's life. The insert included these words: "He was a thoughtful young man who was personally concerned with the well-being of others."

The reader was worried about what kind of men we have in our armed services today.

I can't answer that, except to say that now there are two less damn good ones.

Morris Galanti

The problem with writing about murder in a big city is you could write the same thing every day. Just change the names. God help us.

The Atlanta police officers at the scene Tuesday morning, the beginning of a bright autumn day, were not in a pleasant mood. They were investigating a robbery murder that had taken place the day before.

Two men had robbed King's Food Market at 559 Boulevard N. E., a small grocery store that catered to lower income customers. Morris S. Galanti, who was fifty-seven, had been in business at that location for fifteen years.

"I thought the world of him," said a man standing outside the store. "It tore me up when I heard what happened. I did all my business with him."

What really did happen is still mostly a matter of speculation. Police think Morris Galanti may have been forced to lie face-down on the floor near one of his cash registers while the robbery was taking place. At least that is where and how they found him.

With a bullet in his back. He died later at Grady Hospital.

One officer was talking about what might be the mood of the killer now. That is apparently important in order to determine what might be his subsequent actions following the crime.

"I'll bet he thinks he's big . . . now," said the officer. "He's killed a man."

"If we could break out the rubber hoses," said another, "we might could put a stop to things like this."

"Scumbags," said a third policeman. "That's what we are dealing with here. Dirty, rotten scumbags."

These things happen all the time in a big city, you tell yourself. Neighborhood grocery stores are prime targets for robberies.

The papers report them the next day, but they are rarely page-one news, and soon another victim has been recorded. A couple of blocks down the street, much less across town, who even notices?

Sgt. H. W. McConnell of homicide was in the store Tuesday morning. He has seen his share of such waste of human life. He finally walked out of the store to the street and leaned against his car.

"Look at the wreath on the door," he said. "Isn't that something? A man works fifteen years and all that's here today to symbolize it is a damn green wreath."

He remembered a similar incident two blocks up the street six years before. An old man had been shot in his shoe store.

"I rode to Grady with him," he said. "Before he died, he could talk a little. I asked him who shot him. He said, 'Man did . . . Man did.'" I said, "I know a man shot you, but who was it?"

"We finally found out they called the one who shot him 'Man.' His dying words gave us what we needed."

There have been no such breaks in the case of Morris Galanti.

"There was a lot of animosity toward the ones who did this when we got here Monday," said Sgt. McConnell, "but it's still hard to get people to talk. They either don't want to get involved or they feel bitterness for the police, too."

How, I wanted to know, can storekeepers avoid losing their lives during a robbery attempt? Should they attempt to stop the robbery? What did Morris Galanti do wrong?

"He didn't do anything wrong. That's the hell of it," said Sgt. D. V. Lee. "But don't ever argue with a man with a gun, and don't ever resist him. Just give him everything he wants. He doesn't have that much to lose by killing you.

"And remember one thing: You can get more money, but you can't get another life."

Good advice. But the wreath, the green wreath on the door to Morris Galanti's store, had already said that.

Patti Barry

I was very angry when I wrote this column. After it was completed, I had second thoughts about running it in the newspaper. Maybe I had gone too far, I said to myself.

But then I thought of Patti Barry again. So young. So pretty. So full of life. It was her birthday, and some street goon gunned her down.

The column received more favorable reaction than anything I have ever written. The letters and calls numbered in the thousands. Not because I said anything new, but because I said what the people were thinking.

In fact, the only negative call I received came for a guy over at City Hall, the mayor's press secretary.

It is four-thirty in the afternoon as I write this. My deadline is approaching. I will never make it. Let 'em wait a couple of minutes.

What I have to say, I have to say. Not for the editors. Not even for you, the readers. But for myself.

I love this city. I left it once. I missed it harder than anything I have ever missed in my life.

I have cried like a baby twice as an adult. Once when I left Atlanta because I knew I had made a mistake, and once when I returned because I knew I had finally rectified it.

But this city is going to hell. It may already be there.

I don't care what the mayor says. The mayor is more concerned about his future political ambitions than the welfare of the citizens of this city.

I don't care what the Chamber of Commerce says. The Chamber of Commerce looks and sees dollar signs.

I don't care what the big-dog police commissioners say. They are the mayor's puppets.

This city is going to hell because you can get yourself killed walking its streets in broad daylight.

The details are elsewhere in this newspaper. Quickly, her name was Patricia Barry. She was twenty-six. She worked for a law firm.

It was her birthday. She and a friend were walking the streets of Atlanta at noon. They were walking to lunch to celebrate Patricia Barry's birthday.

At Peachtree and Forsyth—I walk there nearly every day—a goon shot Patricia Barry dead. "Just shot her," said her friend.

Then, the goon shot himself. He died, the coward.

Patricia Barry was the 185th homicide victim in Atlanta in 1979. My God, we've got two-and-one-half months to go.

What is wrong with this city is downtown is a zoo. A zoo. A month ago, I took an hour's walk from 72 Marietta Street down and around Central City Park and back to 72 Marietta Street again.

Drunks and punks were everywhere. Drunks and punks get crazy. They get mean. They rob. They steal. They kill.

Why doesn't somebody get the drunks and punks off the streets of Atlanta?

Why doesn't somebody, like the governor, order the state patrol back? Why doesn't somebody, like the governor, put a trooper on every corner in downtown until we can go an entire week without a citizen getting blown away?

Why doesn't somebody, like the governor, order the national guard in, if that is what it takes, to make this city safe again?

I am sick of Maynard Jackson. Maynard Jackson complains this newspaper overreacts to the city's increasing crime rate.

Call me, Maynard. I am overreacting to the point my hands are shaking.

I am sick of Lee Brown and George Napper. Let them tell Patricia Barry's family and friends, like they tell the rest of us, about the terrific job they are doing.

The *Atlanta Journal* carried the first story about Wednesday's downtown murder. Near the end of the article was a sentence that read, "The shooting was sure to revive controversy over the safety of downtown streets."

"Controversy"? What "controversy"? You mean there are those who would still question the fact there is a war zone down here?

That is exactly what we have on the streets of Atlanta. A war. The drunks and the punks against the rest of us.

And we're losing, goddammit. We're losing.

8

CRITIC-AT-LARGE

"Dallas": Pass the Trash

I heard from a lot of other "Dallas" fans after writing this. One even sent me a bumper sticker. It read, "Free Sue Ellen."

I stumbled into my very first episode of the television hit, "Dallas," the other evening. I really don't know what I expected.

It sounded like a western—gunfights and a lot of horses and somebody is always getting hanged—but westerns rode off into the television sunset years ago.

Maybe it was quiz show. Guess how high a Dallas cowboys cheerleader can count, and win a weekend at the Fish or Cut Bait Dude Ranch near Tyler.

Or perhaps it was another cop series. Sort of a cow-town version of "CHIPS," which, incidentally, is a cowchip version of Broderick Crawford's old "Highway Patrol," ten-four.

"Dallas" turned out to be none of the above. It is a prime-time soap opera—who's pregnant this week?—and what do you that about that, buckaroos?

Previously, only housewives and lazy scoundrels who wouldn't work could watch soap operas because soap operas were never shown after dark.

But with "Dallas" comes the opportunity for the rest of us to get in on the fun, even the kids, who can learn a lot watching the program, like the intelligence of adults is probably vastly overrated.

"Dallas" is a CBS production, the same network that gives us Walter Cronkite. It sits high atop the Nielsen ratings. It appears on Friday nights at ten o'clock, nine o'clock central. Check your local listings if you live somewhere it gets late earlier.

In case you have missed "Dallas" so far, don't worry. A soap opera is like a large plate of cold, boiled rutabagas. Even if you start in the middle, you haven't missed a thing.

I can, however, offer you considerable background after viewing just one episode.

"Dallas" involves the trials and tribulations of the Ewing family of Southfolk Ranch, which is located a short hop in the ol' Mercedes from downtown "Big D."

There is Jock Ewing, the head of the family, who got filthy rich in shady oil dealings. He is played by Jim Davis, who used to play "Railroad Detective" and whose face looks like it finished second in a pick-axe fight.

His wife is Miss Ellie, who seems like a nice person, but we will probably find out she doesn't shave her legs and spends a curious amount of time hanging out at rodeos.

There is J. R., number one son. J. R. runs the family business now. You wouldn't trust J. R. in the same room with your Doberman.

Sue Ellen is J. R.'s wife. Bobby is J. R.'s brother. Pam is his wife. Lucy is his cute, little blonde niece, who is bound to get invovled in something just awful because she's built like a brick hay barn and has that look about her.

J. R. and Sue Ellen have a lousy marriage, so J. R. is sleeping with Kristin, Sue Ellen's sister. Sue Ellen is no fool. Sue Ellen, somebody said, used to ride the range with Pam's brother, Cliff, but now she has roped a cowboy, whose name escapes me, ooh-la-la.

Bobby, meanwhile, has something going with an old childhood sweetheart, but you can't blame him for that because Pam went to Paris with her boss for the weekend.

Confused? You should be. "It would take a motelkeeper to know who was in what bed in the Ewing family, and why," said *Time* magazine of the "Dallas" plots and subplots.

Utter trash is what I say of "Dallas." Sex, sex, and more sex. The fact "Dallas" sits high atop the Nielsen ratings is further proof our television tastebuds are located south of where they were originally intended.

If "Dallas" were a movie, it would be rated "R." For "rotten."

If it were a sport, it would be love wrestling.

And if I miss tonight's episode, I'll die.

The Demise of Drive-Ins

There are still a few drive-in movies around, but they're not packed like they were in the old days. It is a shame an entire generation of Americans will grow up having never had to learn their way around the back seat of a 1957 Chevrolet.

Bang the drum slowly. An institution passes from our midst. The obituary appeared in last week's newspaper. Drive-in movie theaters were for watching movies out-of-doors. Then I went to one with Kathy Sue Loudermilk, bless her heart. She was a lovely child and a legend before her sixteenth birthday. She was twenty-one, however, before she knew an automobile had a front seat.

Dressed in something tight, Kathy Sue could have stopped traffic at the Indianapolis 500. When she graduated from high school, they retired her sweater.

The last time I was at a drive-in theater, come to think of it, it was with Kathy Sue. I forget what was playing. I remember it didn't matter in the least.

You had to be careful at our drive-in because of the theater patrolman, Hascal "The Rascal" Pitts. Hascal's favorite thing was to slip behind a seemingly abandoned car and surprise the couple inside with his flashlight, the biggest and brightest the hardware store had to offer.

"Ah, ha!" he would scream in delight at his discoveries. On a busy night, Hascal could run through an entire set of batteries before the end of the second feature.

Hascal did have a tough job, but he was paid well for his efforts. He got twenty-five dollars a week and all he could see.

Drive-ins have been going downhill steadily. That much was obvious when the motel industry boomed. Now they have motels with adult movies inside the rooms. That seems a waste. Once the door is locked and the curtains are drawn, most couples don't need an instructional film.

There are people, I suppose, who go to drive-ins simply to watch the movies, and they have gone low-budget, low-quality.

Macon County Line was a drive-in biggie. So was *Return to Macon County Line.* All seven *Walking Talls* played at drive-ins, and *Saturday Night Fever* should have if it didn't.

I checked the current drive-in features in the Atlanta area this week. Wonder why nobody goes to drive-ins anymore? Check this line-up:

• *Tintorera—Tiger Shark.* Another *Jaws* spin-off, filmed in one afternoon in the producer's bathtub. Stars Susan George, Fiona Lewis, Jennifer Ashley, Hugo Tiglitz, and Andres Garcia as a rubber duck gone berserk.

• *Eaten Alive.* Spin-off of *Tintorera—Tiger Shark.* Stars Susan George, Fiona Lewis, Jennifer Ashley, Hugo Tiglitz, and Andres Garcia, who should turn in overtime.

• *Chain Gang Women.* Wrenching story of lust in rural prison camp. Rated "S" for "stinks."

• *Buckstone County Prison.* Wrenching story of lust in rural prison camp. Rated "R" for "ripoff."

• *The Tool Box Murder.* Stars Cameron Mitchell, Pamelyn Ferdin, Wesley Eure, and Andres Garcia as the tool box. Intriguing drama on how to wipe out an entire neighborhood using only a Phillips-head screwdriver and four tacks.

• *Starship Invasion.* Cousin of *Close Encounters.* Greyhound bus stops in Moultrie, Georgia, and strange creature emerges. Turns out it's only Hickey Bates, local druggist, in his new beige leisure suit he picked up on sale in Macon.

A Zillion Light Years From Virginia City

"Battlestar Galactica" didn't turn out to be a smash hit, and the last time I saw Lorne Greene, he was back down to earth in his cowboy boots selling dog food.

This is the week for television's fall premieres. This is also the week the television industry should be made to take the first moon shuttle out of town.

The new shows don't concern me that much. I am too disappointed some of the old ones are back. "Starsky and Hutch," for instance. I can never remember which one is Starsky and which one is Hutch, but I do think they make a cute couple.

I would like to see a combination episode of some of the old programs. Say, "Starsky and Hutch" with "Laverne and Shirley." What happens is, Starsky and Hutch pistol-whip Laverne and Shirley during a Milwaukee drug bust and then are devoured themselves by a Channel 17 rerun of *The Blob.*

The new fall rage is supposed to be a space adventure called "Battlestar Galactica" that premiered for three hours on ABC Sunday night. Three hours is a long time for anything to premiere. In fact, the only uncomfortable television program I have seen last longer is a Braves game.

Space adventure is hot because of the smashing box office of the move *Star Wars*. I never saw *Star Wars*, but a friend of mine did. "Saw it twice," he said. "Once straight and once stoned."

I think he meant the second time he saw *Star Wars*, he was somewhere out in space himself.

I tried the same tactic Sunday night while watching the premiere of "Battlestar Galactica." I was high on a plate of butterbeans.

Space adventure is nothing new on television. In my youth, we had "The Adventures of Flash Gordon," starring Buster Crabbe, the famous swimmer.

Flash Gordon wore a Peter Pan outfit and battled the evil Ming, who was uglier than both Laverne and Shirley and meaner than Starsky and Hutch beating up a drunk in the park.

What Flash did mostly was save Dr. Zarkov's semi-beautiful daughter—I forget her name—from Ming's soldiers, all of whom looked like tree stumps with beards.

After viewing the opening segment of "Battlestar Galactica," I contend nothing much has changed about television space adventure.

You've seen one television spaceship, you've seen them all. Flash Gordon toured the heavens in something that looked like empty pork-and-bean cans covered in aluminum foil, and so did the cast of "Battlestar Galactica."

And the highlight of any space adventure is still a ray-gun battle. Ray guns make people disappear instead of blowing holes in them. If Starsky and Hutch had ray guns, their programs wouldn't be nearly as bloody, and kids wouldn't have to stay up so late to watch them.

I am conceding "Battlestar Galactica" had a plot, but it was difficult to follow. A group of people-people were involved in a deadly conflict with reptile-people and grasshopper-people and machine-people. The machine-people looked like what you might do with the rest of the empty pork-and-bean cans and a couple of leftover rolls of aluminum foil.

What upset me most about "Battlestar Galactica" was who played the head human. Lorne Greene. The last time I saw Lorne Greene, he was petting a puppy on a dog food commercial.

Sunday night, he stood behind the controls of the "Battlestar Galactica," a zillion light years from Virginia City.

Lorne Greene, who ran the grandest ranch in all of Nevada, who was "Pa" to Little Joe and Hoss, who fought outlaws and Indians and anything else the western wilds could throw at him, wore a black dress and a jeweled necklace.

I suppose a good actor can make any sort of transition, but it is a blessing, I was thinking, Hoss didn't live to see his daddy dressed up like a dance hall girl.

Tom Snyder, by Golly

"Prime Time Sunday" later became "Prime Time Saturday," which improved that show greatly because I'm never home to watch television on Saturday nights.

The big news in television is now there is somebody else to hate and say nasty things about besides Howard Cosell of ABC. He is NBC's Tom Snyder, who has bushy eyebrows and goes around saying, "By golly."

Frankly, Tom Snyder may have pushed Howard Cosell all the way to second place as the television personality who makes the most viewers sick to their stomachs.

Nobody does Howard Cosell impressions at parties anymore. Now, everybody is doing Tom Snyder impressions. He's much easier to do than Cosell.

You sit in a chair at one o'clock in the morning, light a cigarette, and say something stupid.

Cosell could not be reached for comment on the dramatic developments, but a representative at ABC in New York did quash the rumor that Cosell, missing since late December, was recently eaten alive by the defensive unit of the Pittsburgh Steelers at a banquet in McKeesport.

Tom Snyder has been on television hosting talk shows and giving the news for a long time in cities like Milwaukee, Savannah, Atlanta, Philadelphia, Los Angeles, and New York.

Mostly, he has been on television so late at night that small children and normal people had better sense than to stay up and watch him.

So much for small blessings. Besides his nightly "Tomorrow" appearances where he interviews himself, Tom Snyder is now available for viewing on Sunday evenings during prime time. NBC is calling the new show "Prime Time Sunday." They have some real thinkers at NBC.

"Prime Time Sunday" is NBC's answer to the ever-popular CBS program, "60 Minutes." That's like answering a Russian Backfire bomber with a Messerschmidt armed with water balloons.

NBC even had the shameless audacity to hire Mike Wallace's kid for its "PTS" show. Mike Wallace, the star of "60 Minutes," is a Doberman pinscher. Unfortunately, his son Chris has all the forceful technique of a cocker spaniel puppy.

In many ways, Tom Snyder and Howard Cosell are alike. They are both arrogant and oft putrescent, and they use too many big words.

But Tom Snyder is more dangerous than Cosell. He involves himself in serious topics like our gasoline shortage and religious nuts begging money at airports.

All Cosell ever does is ramble on about the Dallas punter's hang time.

I watched Tom Snyder perform during his first two "Prime Time Sunday" programs. I wanted to hit him in the mouth.

He also had dumb shows. He sits in front of a large screen and talks to people from somewhere in Canada and Decatur, Illinois, who are nervous and don't know exactly what to say or when to say it.

They also perspire a great deal. An NBC biography of Tom Snyder says he has "shown a remarkable ability to illuminate issues and personalities." It doesn't say anything about his remarkable ability to make some poor stiff standing in a Canadian oil field sweat like a racehorse.

There was also a "Prime Time Sunday" segment where the program unveiled the earthshaking information that Americans were planning to do a lot of camping on the Fourth of July. It was a thirty-second bit. Unfortunately, it lasted eleven minutes.

But there are usually two sides to every story. There must be something nice that can be said for Tom Snyder.

There is. I decided long ago what this country needs desperately to do is let Elvis Presley rest in peace and quit complaining about Howard Cosell.

Nobody has released a tribute-to-the-King record in months, and Tom Snyder has taken our minds off Howard Cosell.

By golly, that's the best news since Phyllis George disappeared.

". . . And Now for the Weather . . ."

If local television news were an animal, it would be a duck.
                                        —Old Journalism School Saying.

I was watching the local television news program the other evening, and a man walked onto the screen and talked for nearly five minutes about the weather. *For nearly five minutes.*

Television news has done it again, I said to myself. Gone slap overboard.

I can recall when the entire local television news program lasted only fifteen minutes. "President Eisenhower said today . . . ," and what followed was quick and concise.

No would-be clever repartee between the anchor person and his underlings. No "live-action" reports from the site of an afternoon fender-bender.

You got the news, a few ball scores, and then out came a man in a baggy suit with the weather report. He drew a few raindrops and snowflakes and happy suns on a big map and said, "Today, it will rain. Tomorrow, it won't."

That was the weather report. That was enough.

But local television news is always looking for a better way to do something that was fine in the first place. So Baggy Suit was eventually canned, and what followed him was the smiling "weathergirlperson."

"And what can I do for you, young lady?" asked the station manager.

"I want to be a smiling weathergirlperson," said the sensuous blonde, crossing her legs.

"Can you draw raindrops and snowflakes and happy suns?" the station manager probed.

"No, but I'm a fast learner," replied the blonde.

"You're hired," said the station manager.

So for years, we got our television weather reports from smiling weathergirlpersons.

"What's the weather for tomorrow, Bonnie Sue?" asked the eleven o'clock anchor man.

"A tornado will touch down at noon and wipe out half the city," answered Bonnie Sue, smiling.

But even that approach to television weather is dying. What stations, especially those in major markets, are doing today is hiring full-fledged, card-carrying meteorologists to give the weather, and their forecasts all have the stamp of approval of the American Meteorological Society, which sounds important even if it probably doesn't mean diddly.

The fellow I watched the other evening was one of the new breed of television weathermen. He had all the latest equipment.

He had color radar. He had satellite photos. He gave me the latest information on upper-atmosphere air currents.

He talked about "anomalous propagation," which sounded like something that should be performed only by consenting adults and only behind closed doors, and then he gave a long-range forecast that will last me from now to Groundhog Day.

I don't need that much. I don't want it. I don't understand it. Unless you happen to be a moose, who really cares if a high-pressure system is building over Saskatchewan?

All that Fancy-smancy weather reporting has taken away the mystery of the weather, the anticipation of it. We may as well forget the *Farmer's Almanac* and ignore the old man whose arthritis hasn't missed a rainstorm in fifty years.

Local television news has a basic problem. Because of its competitive nature and because people involved in television apparently do little thinking, it must constantly figure ways to combine show business with some occasional journalism.

That is what brought us giggling weather girls. That is what has now brought us weather reports that are too long and too complicated. That is what will eventually bring us television weather forecasts when somebody will walk out and *sing*.

The Painful Stigma of Roller Skates

This is a good story to read to your children on Christmas. It teaches a number of lessons, including humility, which is an important trait to learn or somebody might bash in your head with a roller skate.

A new movie is out called *Skatetown USA*, and people are flocking to see it because of the recent surge of interest in roller-skating.

I haven't seen the movie, but I have seen the advertisements in the newspaper which show a handsome boy skating with a pretty girl who isn't exactly dressed for cool and damp weather.

All sorts of big-time groups like Earth, Wind and Fire; The Jacksons; and Heatwave, provide the music for the movie; and I suppose what the movie does is portray dancing and skating on wheels as the latest chic activity of the beautiful people.

So maybe it is, but I do want to offer the reminder that roller-skating wasn't the recent brainchild of some Perrier-swilling promotor looking for a way to get the jet set out of their Jacuzzis.

Roller-skating, history tells us, has its roots deep in the nation's poor households, where Christmas was always a low-budget holiday.

When I was growing up, you could always tell the financial status of the community's families by what the kids got for Christmas.

Well-to-do kinds, like Alvin Bates, got bicycles, Erector sets, and air guns for Christmas. Poor kids got roller skates.

Roller-skating, I can imagine, was probably invented by some down-and-out-of-work mechanic who didn't have money for his children's Christmas, so he worked for weeks by candlelight in the dank basement of his three-room house until he had roughed out the first likeness of roller skates for Barney, Shirley, and little Joey.

Now, roller skates cost an arm and a leg, and stars like Cher are performing on them, and little Joey's old man didn't get a dime out of it.

I got roller skates for Christmas for six straight years. So did my boyhood friend and idol, Weyman C. Wannamaker, Jr., a great American.

After returning to school from Christmas holidays, the teacher would always put us through the torturous exercise in which everybody would stand and tell what he or she got for Christmas.

Alvin Bates was always first because he always sat at the front of the room.

"I got a bicycle, an Erector set, and an air gun," he would announce, smirking at the roller-skate segment of the classroom.

"And what did you get, Weyman?" the teacher would ask.

"I'll give you a hint," Weyman would answer. "What has eight wheels, two leather straps, and still costs a lousy three bucks at the hardware store?"

Those were terrible times, but there was one glorious moment I can still recall as if it were yesterday. Soon after Christmas in the seventh grade, Alvin Bates made the terribly stupid mistake of riding past Weyman's house on his new bicycle.

Weyman took it as a personal insult and donned his skates and rolled off in hot pursuit. Color Weyman gone on a pair of roller skates. He caught up in less than three blocks and took off one of his skates and beat large and painful knots on Alvin's head with it.

So let them disco the night away, on roller skates in *Skatetown USA*. Let the bright lights shine, and let the music play.

I will rest in the knowledge it was the poor people who pioneered roller-skating in this country, and it was Weyman C. Wannamaker,

Jr., a great American, who long ago struck the blow for those of us who had to bear the stigma of poverty that roller-skating once carried.

The scene remains so vivid in my mind: Alvin Bates sitting on the curb, holding his aching, bleeding head and crying, and Weyman, filled with sweet revenge, skating away into a hurrying sundown.

Who needs a roller-skating movie when you have already sat in on roller-skating history?

9

STRAY DOGS AND
SWEET MEMORIES

The "Marvelous" Le Fevres

After she read this, Eva Mae Le Fevre called me and said if I would drop by sometime she would play me an old gospel song. I've got that down as one of the things I absolutely must do before I die.

I grew up on gospel music, and Sunday mornings have never been the same since there was no more gospel music on the radio to dress for church by.

I'm talking about Hovie Lister's kind of gospel music. And Leroy Abernathy and Shorty Bradford—"The Happy Two"—and a group my daddy loved, The Le Fevres.

You put somebody at a piano, and the sound that emerges is almost rinky-tink. The tall fellow in the back sings a deep, hollow bass, and his short, cherubic friend on the end takes over the high parts.

Gospel music now, I gather, has gone big-time and rhinestone, and send $10.95 for a framed picture of *The Last Supper* that glows in the dark.

I found the obituary in the back pages of the paper last week. I suppose a two-column headline on an obit says the deceased achieved at least some notoriety during his lifetime, but to send Urias Le Fevre away without even a picture seemed an oversight.

He was sixty-nine, and he died last Wednesday of cancer. He spent fifty-four years of his life singing gospel music. And there was even more to him than that.

I talked to one of his neighbors a couple of hours before the funeral Thursday. The neighbor said, "He was a good man, a good father to his children, and a good husband to Eva Mae."

What memories I have. It is Sunday afternoon and the lunch dishes have been cleared away, and supper will be what chicken wasn't eaten and a cold biscuit, if you're lucky. It is the early days of television.

We watched westerns and we watched wrestling matches. And Sunday afternoons, we watched and listened to The Le Fevres.

Eva Mae at the piano. Urias and his brother Alphus in perfect harmony. Only the deaf could resist tapping a toe.

"Marvelous," my father would say, as only he could say it, "absolutely marvelous."

I can even remember the commercials. God bless Martha White Flour for bringing the music of The Le Fevres to my childhood.

Theirs was one of the most successful gospel-singing television shows ever. The show was live for years, but videotape later made it possible for the Le Fevres to syndicate to sixty-five other stations across the nation.

It all began for brothers Urias and Alphus before their teens, when they would sing about the Lord with their sister Maude, back home in Tennessee.

Urias Le Fevre's obituary last week said the group turned down many offers to leave gospel music and go into the more lucrative field of country-western music. The Le Fevres weren't interested; they saw their musical talents as a "Christian calling."

The senior members of the Le Fevre group, Urias, Alphus and Eva Mae, retired a couple of years ago. They had a million miles and a million songs behind them. The younger members of the family are continuing, and one son, Mylon, sings rock 'n' roll.

"I think the family's already left for the funeral," said the neighbor last week as we talked. "I took a half-day off to go myself. Everybody in this neighborhood loved Urias."

But the neighbor had a little time. So he asked, "Want to hear something pretty?"

I didn't have to answer. He already had the record in his hand, and he placed it on the turntable. It was The Le Fevres, and they were singing "He Pilots My Ship."

We listened, and when it was over, I never hesitated with my reaction:

"Marvelous," I brought back from a long time ago, "absolutely marvelous."

Country Mudhole

Journalism students sometimes ask me, "Where do you get your ideas for columns?" They wouldn't believe me if I told them. Inspiration may be found in the strangest of places, even in muddy parking lots.

Statesboro, Ga.

What I happened to be doing in Statesboro has nothing to do with what is to follow. Let's just say Statesboro is one of my favorite stops in the hinterlands, and I have a buddy here who tells good stories and enjoys staying up late telling them.

What this is really all about is mudholes. My buddy and I were going to this place in Statesboro for lunch, and we pulled into the dirt parking lot, and in the middle of the parking lot was a good country mudhole, the likes of which I hadn't seen in years.

We don't have mudholes in the city. We have potholes. There is a difference. Potholes are synthetic. They are caused by cars and trucks driving over cheap asphalt and concrete, and they are a sorry thing that causes much cursing and even damage to the cars and trucks that drive into them.

Mudholes are real. I don't know what really causes mudholes but my guess is they are caused by God's rain hitting God's good earth, and I like that.

Mudholes, like potholes, can be ornery, too. Drive into one with a new wash job on your car, and so much for your new wash job. But anybody stupid enough to drive a just-washed car onto a dirt road where there are likely to be mudholes deserves what he gets.

But mudholes can also offer good times and much recreation. There was a big mudhole in the schoolyard of my youth. When it rained, it was days before the mudhole dried up.

During recess, it was great fun to entice a girl to stand near the mudhole and then throw a large rock into same, thus splashing mud and water all over her dress and shoes and face and hair.

This usually caused the girl to cry, except in the case of Cordie Mae Poovy, the meanest girl in school. Once, in a moment of insanity, I threw a rock into the mudhole and splashed Cordie Mae.

She ran me down on the ballfield and hit me in the mouth and then dragged me back to the mudhole and washed away my sins and the blood that covered my mouth.

Another time, I spotted my dog, Butch, wallowing in the mudhole in my front yard. I jumped in with Butch, clothes and all. My mother beat me for the remainder of the afternoon and through the early portion of the evening.

Butch, the scoundrel who instigated the entire affair, shook himself off and then curled up under my grandfather's truck and went to sleep.

There is one thing you can't do in a mudhole, however, and that is fish. People who fish in mudholes are a little fuzzy, which brings up the name of the legendary "Gums" Garfield, who hadn't had teeth since Roosevelt's second term.

Gums was more than a little fuzzy, and my boyhood friend and idol, Weyman C. Wannamaker, Jr., a great American, enjoyed playing tricks on him.

One day, Weyman said to Gums, "Hey, Gums, you like to fish?"

"I love to fish," replied Gums.

Weyman then explained to Gums about the big mudhole over behind the Baptist church.

"I caught a seven-pound catfish there last week," Weyman said.

Gums immediately went home and got his cane pole and hurried to the big mudhole behind the Baptist church. The preacher, preparing his Sunday sermon, watched Gums for a time from his study and finally could stand it no longer.

He walked out to the mudhole and said to Gums, "Who put you up to this?"

Gums told him.

"Don't you know he was just kidding you?" said the preacher. "There aren't any fish in a mudhole."

"I know that, preacher," replied Gums, as he pulled a clean hook out of the water. "That's why I wasn't using any bait."

I would like to dedicate this column to Cordie Mae, Butch, Weyman, Gums, and the preacher. Also, to my buddy down in Statesboro who bet me a lunch I couldn't write an entire column based on a country mudhole.

"Buddy"

I get sentimental about dogs. I can't help it. If you have ever looked deep into a dog's eyes and felt he was urgently trying to give you a message, then maybe you will understand what I was feeling when I wrote the following.

On a Back Road

My grandfather would have called the dog a "sooner."

"Just as soon stay in the house as out," he would have laughed.

The day was ending, but a long drive home remained. I had stopped for gasoline in one of those all-purpose country service stations, the kind where there is always a little boy with a dirty face and a dog hanging around.

The little boy was buying milk for his mother. The dog was yawning and scratching.

"That your dog?" I asked the old man pumping the gasoline.

"Took up here," he said.

"Fine-looking dog," I went on.

"Smart, too," said the man. "Watch this."

He locked the pump to "on" and walked over to the dog. He held out his hand, and the dog responded by lifting a paw. Smart as a whip, that dog.

"How long you had him?" I said.

"'Bout a week," said the man.

"Any bother?"

"Not a bit. I figure somebody put him our of a car. That little boy that was here buying the milk wants him, but his mama won't let him bring the dog home. Says every dog he brings home gets run over, and it upsets the little boy something awful."

That was an instant memory. I had a losing streak with dogs, too.

There was "Snowball." Every child eventually gets a furry white dog named "Snowball." My daddy bought me mine the day after he got back from Korea. "Snowball" got it from a laundry truck.

"Butch" was later. He chased cars. One day, he caught one.

The vet said "Pokey" had pneumonia. He allowed me to pet my dog one last time, and then he took "Pokey" into a back room, and I never saw my dog again.

I had "Plato." Now there was a dog. I lost him in a divorce settlement, believe it or not. I gave up dogs after that. Missing a dog is a worrisome pain.

"This dog got a name?" I said to the man at the station.

"I call him 'Buddy.'"

The old man scratched the dog, and "Buddy" nuzzled close to the source of affection.

I petted the dog myself. He was obviously of a generous mix, a young dog with patches of white and yellow and black. I tried the paw trick, and "Buddy" responded on cue. Impressive.

I like dogs because they forgive easily, know little or nothing about revenge, and will settle for thirty seconds of care and attention if that is all you have to spare.

I have a house and it is empty, and I have considered adding a dog to the premises. But then I decided that is foolish because I often sleep where I fall, and I do not want a lonely dog on my conscience.

I paid the man for the gasoline and started to get back in my car. The dog was staring at me, or maybe it was just my imagination. Regardless, I stared back.

"You like that dog, don't you?" said the man, smiling.

"That's a fine dog," I said.

"Why don't you take him with you? I got another dog at home."

I gave him five or six excellent reasons why I couldn't and drove away.

It's been a week now. It was dark that night and I wasn't familiar with the road. I doubt I could ever find that country service station again, even if I wanted to.

Which, you understand, I don't.

Saturday Night Fever

News Item: The Ku Klux Klan is on the rise again.

Not much exciting ever happened in my hometown after the trains on the Atlanta and West Point line quit stopping for passengers. This was rural Georgia, early fifties.

But then there was that one week of anticipation, of wonderment, of an amount of sheer terror for boys of eight and nine.

I can still see the posters somebody nailed to fence posts:

"KLAN RALLY."

"SATURDAY NIGHT."

"STAND UP AND BE COUNTED."

"SAVE THE WHITE RACE."

I didn't understand, and neither did any of my friends. I asked my grandfather, the wisest person I knew.

"The Ku Klux Klan," he said, and he explained the best be could, with an unmistakable element of praise in his voice. The Ku Klux Klan, he said, was a sort of private police department.

You take a man who isn't making certain his wife and children have enough to eat, or a man who isn't working when there is work available, or a scoundrel who has left his fields unplowed to escape the sun in a beer joint, then the Klan, my grandfather explained, pays him a visit and suddenly he is more aware of his responsibilities as a father, husband, and citizen.

You don't pass off boyish curiosity that easily.

"What do they do to him?" I wanted to know.

"They flog him," said my grandfather.

"With what?"

I think he mentioned buggy whips and maybe leather straps. He said the visitations normally occurred after dark.

I didn't sleep very well that night. Nor the next, nor the next, because each day more information filtered down about what would happen Saturday night.

Those men, that "Klan," they wear hoods, somebody said. White hoods, with holes for their eyes and their mouths.

They burn crosses.

Sometimes, they burn people. The story was all about, unconcealed from the tenders who hung on every word. A black man—only nobody said "black man"—had been accused of something called "raping" a white woman up the road in the county seat some years before.

The Ku Klux Klan took care of him, the story went. They nailed his scrotum—only nobody said "scrotum"—to a stump and gave him a rusty razor blade and then set the stump on fire.

My grandfather said he doubted any such thing actually happened.

"You stay away from there Saturday night," my grandfather said.

Three of us, on bikes, were the first arrivals. We hid behind a clump of trees.

Spectators began piling in from all over, from as far away as LaGrange and even Columbus. They came in cars and on the backs of flat-bed trucks to an open field that was soon packed with humanity, or something that at least resembled it.

The three of us, we trembled when out of the darkened woods came a marching band of hooded men. Their torches lit the night.

They sang "Onward Christian Soldiers" as they marched.

The men aligned themselves shoulder-to-shoulder toward the crowd. One of the men stepped forward and began to speak about things my grandfather had not mentioned in his explanation. Race-mixing. Mongrelization, whatever that was. Nigger-this. Nigger-that.

An old man sat down front and said a lot of "Amens." Some older boys in the back were drinking something from a fruit jar.

When the speaker finished, the other hooded men set a torch to the ground, and a cross of flame errupted. The rally was closed with a prayer.

My grandfather was waiting for me when I returned home.

"You go to the Klan rally?" he asked.

I admitted my disobedience. It wasn't necessary. I was still shaking.

My grandfather took me into his arms. There was a long quiet. And then he said softly, but firmly, "Don't be afraid. Yellow cowards can't hurt you."

My grandfather, holding a frightened little boy and changing a long-held attitude, needed to hear himself say that, I think now, just as much as I did.

Ode to a Church Fan

After this column appeared in the newspaper, I received nearly a hundred church fans in the mail. This sort of work does have its benefits.

Somebody took a poll the other day concerning how Americans feel about going to church during these trying times, and the published results said the takers and the leavers were split something like 50-50.

I polled myself and decided I still enjoy going to church because it's OK to sing out on the choruses, but there are some things about the modern church that bother me.

In some churches, for instance, sermons are shortened during the football season so nobody will miss a one o'clock kickoff, and let us all stand and sing the first and third verses of "Drop Kick Me, Jesus, Through the Goalposts of Life," which, in case there are any doubters, is a real song.

You can also tithe with a credit card nowadays, and that seems almost too convenient and impersonal, and most churches—even the little white frame country churches where you can still hear an occasional "Amen!" from the back row—have adopted progressive attitudes toward air-conditioning.

So it's more comfortable in church today, but air-conditioning giveth, and air-conditioning taketh away. Gone for good are those paper fans with the wooden handles that were always available in the hymnal racks on the backs of pews.

It never bothered me to be hot in church because I thought being hot in church was a part of God's Great Plan. Sweat it out, brother, because that's just a sample of what awaits the backslider.

Down home on August Sunday morning, the church is packed, and the message from the pulpit is fire and brimstone, and the congregation squirms as one.

You can *feel* the fire. You can *smell* the brimstone, and the closer the preacher gets to the everlasting flames, the faster the fat ladies in their print dresses fan themselves.

But there were other uses for church fans besides fanning away the Devil and the dog-day heat. You could swat noisy children and flies with church fans.

"Goat" Rainwater used to chew on the wooden handles, but "Goat" was always chewing on something like pencils or crayons. My mother said he probably had a vitamin deficiency.

A person could also learn a lot from a church fan. I learned what heaven looks like. The fans in our church were provided by the local funeral parlor, and at election time, a politician or two would bring in a batch.

On one side of a church fan would always be a picture of Jesus sitting with children and a lamb or two and a pony in a soft meadow near a brook.

That was obviously heaven to an eight-year-old, and I would stare at that picture during the sermon and wonder if pony rides were free when you crossed over Jordan. Certainly, I finally decided. That's why they call it "heaven."

On the other side would be the commercial message of the funeral parlor or the politician who had placed the fans.

"Hillside Funeral Home. All Insurance Policies Honored. Twenty-four Hour Ambulance Service. Ask About Our Chapel Rates."

Or, "Elect Buster Knowles State Senator. Veteran. Family man. Deacon. Honest."

Buster Knowles wasted a lot of money providing church fans, because he was never elected. He always included his smiling countenance on his fans, and he looked too much like the crooked Indian agent on "Tales of Wells Fargo."

Fortunately, I have what is probably one of the last church fans. A person who knows of my concern for their demise gave me one, and I am forever in his debt.

One Sunday soon, I may even take my fan to church, and in case the sermon runs a little long, I can stare peacefully at the picture of heaven while the rest of the congregation sweats through a hell of a thought:

God and Jimmy the Greek forbid, but if the preacher doesn't stop in five minutes, there goes the opening segment of "The NFL Today."

The Last of the North Georgia Trout Hounds

Another dog story, mostly true.

Suches, Ga.

Never take a dog trout fishing. I know that; all experienced trout fishpersons like myself know that.

But the dog, who lived up on the hill from where I was hiding from civilization, had followed me around all day and we had become fast friends.

The dog had a number of pleasing characteristics, one of which was he didn't beg or whine when I opened a can of Vienna sausages and a package of soda crackers for lunch.

I despise begging, whining dogs. Plus, I despise sharing my Vienna sausages and soda crackers with any living thing.

Ah! The North Georgia mountains in the springtime. I am in a peaceful valley with a trout stream running through it. In the morning, a mist hangs over the valley, but soon the sun will burn the mist away and the brilliant surroundings will look as if they belong on an artist's canvas.

The afternoons are for rocking on a porch and for dozing off and for wondering why, if such settings are so gorgeous and peaceful, so many of us insist upon living in cities.

Maybe the answer had come from a young member of the family up the hill who owns the dog. She had mentioned that she will be graduating soon from the little high school down the mountain. I asked her what her plans would be afterwards.

"Leaving," she answered. "The only thing to do around here is raise collards."

I said raising collards was an honorable and worthwhile endeavor, but I don't think she heard me. We all go off to cities when we are young, because we don't know any better.

Then, we never quite summon the courage to get back out, because we can't get used to the idea of living more than four blocks from a convenience store.

Back to the dog. As sundown approached, it was time I tried to remove some of the trout from the stream. The dog followed me.

The reason you don't take a dog trout fishing is because dogs bark and scare off all the fish. I didn't read that anywhere. It is just a fact of nature that makes perfect sense to me.

"Go back," I shouted at the dog, but the dog ignored me.

I waded into the stream and made my first cast. The dog waded into the stream, too. One of two things was happening.

Either the dog had become so fond of me, he had to be at my side every moment, or I had stumbled upon one of the rarest of all breeds of dogs, the long-eared, North Georgia trout hound.

I'll keep this short. I waded on up the stream, and the dog waded with me, and, sure enough, the dog had a barking attack and so much for catching any fish.

I gave up after an hour and walked back to my porch and started rocking again, the dog still at my side. Soon, however, I heard the people up the hill call the dog to his dinner.

The dog forgot about our comradeship in the stream and his infatuation with me and left me alone with another can of Vienna sausages and another package of soda crackers, which the dog obviously didn't care for in the first place. Neither did I at the moment. I had planned on trout.

Later, as deep night fell over the valley, I wished for just a moment I was back home in the city. The city does have its advantages, you know. One is that I live only four blocks from a Del Taco.

I hope they fed that damned dog collards.

Gobbledygook

A warm Thanksgiving message about how to get even with a turkey of a neighbor.

I have no idea what finally became of the old coot, but I always think of him around Thanksgiving because he was the first turkey I ever met.

I'm not certain of the exact characteristics of a person who qualifies as a turkey, but I can spot a turkey person when I see or hear one.

Jerry Brown, governor of California, is a turkey, for instance. So are Anita Bryant and Reggie Jackson, the ballplayer, and anybody who would go on television to advertise his used car lot.

The aforementioned old coot was really a turkey, however, because besides being utterly obnoxious and full of any number of unmentionable stuffings, he also raised turkeys.

Turkey turkeys, the kind that have feathers and make dumb, gobbling sounds.

He was our neighbor when I was a kid, if you can call somebody who constantly complains and constantly makes a nuisance of himself a neighbor.

He lived in a large, white house. His backyard was where he kept his turkeys, maybe 300 of them. His pen bordered my grandfather's bean patch.

Let me tell you some things about turkeys:
• Turkeys don't have very much to do, so they gobble a lot.
• One turkey gobbling isn't a problem. Three hundred turkeys gobbling at once, twenty-four hours a day, is enough to wake the dead and drive the living slap crazy.
• Turkeys smell.
• Turkeys are easily spooked.
• A nervous turkey is a skinny turkey. That costs the turkey farmer money and makes him nervous.
• There is nothing more impossible to deal with than a nervous turkey farmer.

One of the local churches saved its money and bought a new bell. Our turkey farmer neighbor complained every time the church rang its new bell.

It spooked his precious turkeys.

My grandfather had a tractor. He used it in his bean patch, which bordered the turkey pen. Whenever my grandfather would plow in his bean patch, out would come the featherbrain, ranting and raving.

The sound of the tractor bothered his stupid turkeys.

I used to play a game in my front yard. I would throw rocks into the air and hit them with a broomstick and make believe I was a member of the 1959 Dodgers lining a shot off the wall at Comisky Park against the White Sox in the World Series.

One afternoon, Duke Snider ripped an Early Wynn hanging curveball over the bean patch and over the fence into the turkey pen.

The rock caught an unsuspecting turkey flush. Now, there was one less turkey to gobble all night, but I had to pay for the damage by handing over my allowance to gobblebrain for six months.

There was, however, one subsequent moment of revenge. In the stillness of the midnight, a child who shall remain nameless crept across my grandfather's bean patch to the turkey pen.

He lit an entire pack of Black Cat firecrackers and threw them in amongst the turkeys.

Gobblegobblegobblegobblegobble!" went the turkeys.

"Arrrrrrrrrgh!" screamed the angry turkey farmer running out of his house still in his pajamas.

You, of course, will be eating turkey Thursday. I'll just have a ham sandwich and laugh at the satisfying memory of once having watched 299 turkeys and one old buzzard have a group nervous breakdown. Feathers may still be flying.

10

WOMENFOLK

One Rear End to Another

I received a very nice letter from Ann Landers after this article appeared. She thanked me for mentioning her name and then gave me some of her famous advice: "Find yourself another line of work."

I never miss Ann Landers in the newspaper because she always has an answer for any questions you can imagine:

"Dear Ann Landers,

"My husband came home last night with lipstick on his collar. When I asked him about it, he said he didn't know how it got there. I knew he was lying, so I broke his arm.

"Did I react too strongly, or should I have broken his other arm, too?—Big Hilda, Syracuse."

"Dear Big Hilda,

"It depends. If this was the first time your husband came home with lipstick on his collar, I would have to say you may have overreacted. A good punch in the belly would probably have sufficed.

"But if he makes a habit of coming home with such 'evidence' showing, I think you may have let the little worm off lightly."

The other day I was reading Ann Landers' column, and there was a letter from a woman in White Plains who asked:

"What is happening to our culture with so much emphasis on female rear ends? A person can't turn on the TV without seeing a close-up of a woman's derriere."

To which Ann Landers answered, astoundingly: "I don't have the slightest idea."

Imagine Ann Landers being stumped!

Frankly, it wasn't that tough a question. The woman from White Plains told Ann Landers she had seen an ad for jeans on television that had "popped my eyeballs."

She also said she had seen other ads for things like fanny smoothers, fanny shapers, and fanny padders.

"What," the woman went on, "is the explanation for this intense preoccupation with the fanny?"

I'll take it from here, Ann.

This "intense preoccupation" with the fanny is really nothing new. Men have always ogled women's most movable part, and with the new assertive attitude of the modern-day woman, we have learned the male hindpart is quite interesting to the female.

As far as more female rears on television these days, the answer there is simple:

Women buy a lot of things that have to do with their rears—jeans, pantyhose, girdles, diet foods, disco records—and men don't care what is being sold as long as they get a good look at a nice pair of hips occasionally.

There is one commercial that immediately comes to mind. Two women are discussing a particular undergarment that leaves no tell-tale rings or bulges when they walk around in their tight-fitting slacks.

But you never see the two women. All you see is their rear ends.

FIRST REAR END: You don't look like you are wearing anything underneath your tight-fitting slacks.

SECOND REAR END: Of course I am, silly. I'm wearing new Underwonders. No tell-tale rings, no bulges, and the freedom they give me is just fantastic!

A lot of people, like the woman in White Plains, might think a commercial with two walking rear ends is dumb and tasteless, but I'll take it any day over the one where you see the inside of a pipe being unclogged by a glob of Drano.

There is nothing dirty about the human tushy, and unless it reaches double-wide, mobile home proportions, it can be a thing of beauty.

I would advise the woman from White Plains to go water her petunias and stop sweating the small stuff. And I find it rather refreshing, incidentally, that the world's biggest know-it-all, Ann Landers, sometimes falls flat on her can just like the rest of us.

When You Gotta Go

It is my understanding that the female employees at Cagle Poultry Company and their management finally came to an agreement on who could go to the restroom when and for how long. Behold, another victory for human understanding.

I am having a difficult time deciding which side to take in the great debate at a Macon poultry processing plant over employees' restroom privileges.

Nearly two hundred workers have walked off their jobs at the Cagle Poultry Company after the plant manager, a man, sent around a memorandum advising the workers, mostly women-persons, that terrible things could happen to them if they didn't cool it on trips to the company restrooms.

Length of visits also get a mention. One company official was quoted as saying time wasted by employees in the restroom had cost his firm "thousands of dollars."

I don't doubt that. Over the years, I have noticed women tend to spend a great portion of their lives inside restrooms.

You take ball games and concerts. Rarely are there lines to the men's rooms at ball games and concerts. But there are always lines to the women's.

I have no idea what a woman does once inside a restroom at a ball game or concert, but it takes forever if you are waiting for one to come out.

Previously, I have been squarely behind the idea of installing a thirty-second clock inside women's restrooms.

On the other hand, there are some areas where I believe the less rules and regulations, the better for all concerned. Restrooms are one of those areas.

Through one of my reliable sources in Macon, I have obtained a copy of the Cagle Poultry Company memorandum involving "abuse of emergency restroom privileges." Those privileges, notes the memorandum, are spelled out precisely in Plant Rule No. 39.

The memorandum was signed by Malcolm Clark, plant manager, who issued the following new guidelines:

"Any employee will be allowed to visit the bathroom eight times in any four-week period, with a five-trip limit in any two-week period of the four weeks.

"Maximum time away from job is five minutes."

Mr. Clark also stated what would happen to those radicals who didn't follow his new guidelines:

"First offense: Verbal warning.

"Second offense: Written warning.

"Third offense: Three days off without pay.

"Fourth offense: Discharge."

That's not all. The crafty plant manager has also devised a way to insure that workers do not abuse their five-minute restroom time limit.

Each employee is to be issued a "bathroom card"—or "B-card"—to be kept in a rack next to a time clock outside the restrooms. It is to be the responsibility of all employees to clock in upon entering the restroom and to clock out once their business has been conducted.

"Special guards" are to make sure nobody tries anything tricky.

"First offense: Disciplinary layoff.

"Second offense: Discharge."

There is, of course, the sticky situation of employees who have to visit the restrooms in order to take medicine. Mr. Clark thought of that.

The memorandum states that if an employee needs additional visits to take medicine, the employee must have a note from a doctor. If after three weeks the problem is not corrected, the employee gets a leave of absence to correct it.

Company officials weren't talking to reporters Friday. Workers said the rules were "unjust and demeaning." Both sides were meeting—along with Labor Department representatives—to work out a possible solution.

Don't compromise, girls. I think I have decided whom to back here. Work me like a dog. Cut my pay. Steal my pension. But tell me I can't go to the restroom when I'm damn good and ready, and you can take Plant Rule No. 39 and flush it.

Will You Still Respect Me in the Morning?

Quite frankly, I never saw anything wrong with a woman calling me for a date. In fact, I encouraged it. I wonder why nobody ever called?

One of the papers last week ran a series of articles for its women readers entitled "How to Meet Men . . . Now That You Are Liberated."

One part of the series caught my eye because it was about how a liberated, single woman should go about asking a man for a date and what she should suggest they do if he accepts.

"Why should a woman sit passively by the telephone waiting for a man to call her for a date?" the author—apparently a liberated, single woman—asked.

"No reason," she answered herself, "when a woman can make the first move."

I agree. And as a single male, I would more than welcome women calling me to ask for dates. I have spent a great portion of my life calling to ask them.

I want revenge.

I want *them* to hear what mocking, hysterical laughter sounds like on the other end of the telephone.

I want *them* to feel the pangs of regret and embarrassment when a voice says, "You must be outta your mind, Horseface."

I want *them* to experience the intense rejection when the object of their affection suggests further efforts would be fruitless, as in "Bug me one more time, creep, and I'm calling the cops."

It's no picnic asking people for dates, you know, and I simply do not understand why so many of the women I have honored with an offer of my company have thought it necessary to respond abruptly and often downright crudely.

But forget the revenge. I hold no grudges. I will even make it as easy for you as I possibly can.

Don't sit around pondering over what to suggest for our rendez-vous if I see fit to accept your invitation. Over the years, I have suggested a number of fun and clever things I like to do on dates.

As you will see, the dimwitted women who have turned down these opportunities don't know a good time when they are handed one on a silver platter.

When calling, order by number, please:

1. COOKING MY SUPPER: My favorite meal is country fried steak smothered in sawmill gravy, creamed potatoes, butterbeans, squash, spring onions, thinly sliced tomatoes, and unsweetened ice tea.

After supper, do not worry about thinking of something else for us to do. After a meal like that, I would prefer to lie down on the couch and take a little siesta.

2. RUB MY BACK.

3. WATCHING BALL GAMES ON TV: One of my favorite things to do on a date. Make sure the beer is cold and plenty of snacks are within reaching distance of my seat in front of the television.

If you would prefer to do something else while I watch the ball game, that is fine. Just be sure you're back in time to start the fire in the grill.

4. DOING MY LAUNDRY: When you have a break between cycles, maybe I could tell you some of my favorite jokes.

5. HANGING OUT WITH SOME OF MY FRIENDS: We'd treat you just like one of the guys, unless we decided to go to a beer joint, of course. You could wait in the car and read one of those women's magazines that tell you how to avoid getting stretch marks.

6. FISHING: I like to fish, but I do not like to bait my hook, because sometimes when you stick a hook into a Louisiana Pink, they squirt at you. If you will bait my hook for me, I'll let you borrow my new scaler when you clean the fish.

7. WASHING MY TRUCK: Real fun on an afternoon date. Afterwards, we'll go for a spin. I would let you ride up front with me, but that's where my dog sits.

8. LISTENING TO MY ALBUMS: Soft lights and the Statler Brothers. This is what I do when I feel really romantic. Another glass of Ripple, my pet?

9. GOING BOWLING: Lots of laughs and it won't cost you much, except for the beer I drink and shoe rentals.

10. FOOLING AROUND: But promise you'll still respect me in the morning.

Mayor Hot Lips

This was one of my favorite political stories of the year. Incidentally, it had a happy ending. Teddy Kennedy rode Jane Byrne's endorsement to a bellyflop in the Illinois Democratic primary.

Chicago Mayor Jane Byrne's leap from the Carter camp to the Ted Kennedy fold obviously has major political implications for the 1980 presidential election. But it also says something else scary.

It says that men, even the president of the United States, are still stupid when it comes to reading the intentions of women.

To get the full impact of the situation, let us review exactly what happened in the Byrne-to-Carter-and-then-to-Kennedy escapade:

A few weeks ago, President Carter got all dressed up in his tuxedo and flew to Chicago to appear at a fund-raising dinner for Mayor Byrne.

Mayor Byrne got all dressed up too. She wore her white party dress. And a good time was had by all.

Mayor Byrne said she thought the president was a swell guy and knocked everybody on his tomato aspic by saying—so the Carter people thought—she would support her dinner guest for the 1980 Democratic nomination.

President Carter then strode to the podium and talked about what a terrific job Mayor Byrne is doing in Chicago and promised her some big federal grants for her city.

The back-scratching out of the way, Mayor Byrne then kissed the president. I saw her do it on television. She put one smack on the old boy, and he grinned from the Loop to downtown Gary, Indiana.

"Do you think she really meant it when she said she would support you?" an aide asked the president on the flight back to Washington.

"How can you ask such a question?" the president shot back. "She kissed me, didn't she?"

It was only a matter of days before Mayor Byrne had announced she had changed her mind and would now lend her support and that of the Chicago Democratic "machine" to Ted Kennedy.

President Carter should have known better, of course, but then he is just a man, and men are always naive when it comes to being kissed by women.

Men have always thought if a woman kisses you, it means something special. It means she is your girl, she will go with you to the prom, she will give you something nice for your birthday, she will hold your hand in the moonlight.

She won't go around kissing everybody else.

Baloney. I still remember my first kiss. It was from Kathy Sue Loudermilk, the school sex symbol. I felt the earth move.

What I really felt was a half-dozen other guys lining up to be next.

What women have always known about men is that if you kiss one of the big oafs, he'll be eating out of the palm of your hand.

I had hoped that when a woman reached the high position of mayor of a major city, she would no longer resort to such tactics, but Mayor Byrne's plot is evidence I was only dreaming.

The president came courting, and Mayor Byrne played him for the fool. She cooed and smiled and lured him into her web and then "sealed" their new partnership with a kiss.

My Chicago sources tell me Mayor Byrne has used this technique all along. Since she has been mayor, they say, she has kissed practically everybody in town, including a number of city officials who thought getting kissed by the mayor was a sign of job security, only to find their desks cleaned out and the doors to their offices locked while the mayor's lip prints were still fresh on their cheeks.

Whether Ted Kennedy can keep Her Two-Facedness on his side remains to be seen, but at least the Kennedy people are trying to learn from the Carter mistake and the mistake men have been making since the Garden of Eden.

A memorandum has been circulated from Kennedy campaign headquarters to all male Kennedy workers and to the senator himself, detailing rules to follow in case of any contact with Mayor Byrne of Chicago.

"If she puckers," goes Rule No. 1, "run for your life."

Plowing Up the Cornrows

I wonder if women really appreciate it when men take the time to give them guidance and counseling like this:

Normally, I try to refrain from any comment concerning the latest in women's fashions and style. There are a couple of reasons for that.

One, my taste in that area tends to be a bit tacky. For example, I miss the hot-pants-and-white-boots look, and there is nothing like a dame in short shorts and high heels.

Two, it doesn't do any good to tell women what they should wear and how they should look. Women simply won't listen to such constructive criticism.

If women would listen, we would never have had to endure the sack dress and that awful period when all coeds were wearing baggy blue jeans, sweatshirts, and combat boots in an apparent effort to look like female versions of "Skag" on the way to the blast furnace.

Despite all this, however, I no longer can remain a silent observer, because now women are doing something really stupid. I don't care how many letters and calls I get from fire-breathing feminists, I'm going to say this anyway:

The Bo Derek braided look, the "cornrow" hairstyle that apparently is about the sweep the nation, is absolutely hideous.

Allow me to bring those who have been sleeping for a couple of months, or who don't read *People* magazine or watch the Phil Donahue TV show, up to date.

This movie called *10* came out, see. It starred a young woman named Bo Derek, who since has become the nation's latest lust-object, replacing Farrah and the blonde cutie on "WKRP" and other assorted, curvaceous airheads.

The movie's plot would bore you, so all that is really necessary to know is that this "Bo" (silly name for a girl) wore her hair in "tightly woven plaits, laced with beads," as *People* magazine described it.

I can describe it better. As appealing as the child most certainly is from the forehead down, her hair looked like somebody had made a terrible mistake.

Frankly, her hair looked like something the Chinese might use to count on, or the result of shampooing with Drano.

But this ridiculous Medusa-like hairstyle called the "cornrow"—a fairly appropriate name, I might add—is spreading like a bad case of dandruff, and it must be stopped. Otherwise, we might soon be up to our eyeballs in once-attractive women who have all become rope-heads.

There are plenty of reasons, my sisters, not to give in to what is nothing more than a Hollywood-bred fad. Please pay attention while I list them:

1. If you want to make yourself appear to have just hit town from another planet, there is a method much less drastic than having your hair cornrowed. Have one of your eyes moved to the middle of your head, for instance.

2. A cornrow at most Hollywood beauty salons can cost as much as $400, says *People*, and can take up to ten hours to complete. For four hundred smackers, you can have your entire chassis rebuilt with money left over for four new pairs of pantyhose.

3. Cicely Tyson, the brilliant actress, also is a gorgeous woman. There was a picture of Cicely Tyson in *People* magazine with her hair in cornrows. She looked a lot like Stevie Wonder.

4. Cordie Mae Poovy, a girl in my school, was the first female in this country to wear her hair in cornrows. That's because her father ran a dairy farm and one afternoon she got her head caught in one of the milking machines. We used to spend recess throwing rocks at Cordie Mae Poovy.

5. Experts are saying if you wear your hair in a cornrow for too long, all your hair might fall out.

6. I hope it does.

My Angel

I gave Billy Bob Bailey the honor of announcing my third marriage, which occurred on February 10, 1980. At this writing, some six months later, we are still blissfully happy. And they said it wouldn't last . . .

Fort Deposit, Ala.

Billy Bob Bailey is my name and plumbing is my game. People around here like to say, "If it'll stop up, ol' Billy Bob can unclog it."

They got that right. You take Mrs. Arlene Watts' kitchen sink. Mrs. Watts, a lovely child who was once named Miss Fort Deposit Seed and Feed Show Princess, has had all sorts of problems with her kitchen sink lately.

As a matter of fact, that sucker has backed up every afternoon for two weeks, and Billy Bob has been out to her house every day for hours at the time, and I've just about wore my new auger slap out.

I think I finally got the job completed, though, and I'd bet my dog Rooster against a one-eyed mule that sink don't back up again for at least six months, which is just about the time Arlene's—I mean, Mrs. Watts'—husband, Harvey, will have to go out of town again.

But my problem ain't what you're interested in readin' about today, so sit back and get ready for some of Billy Bob's best writin'.

As many of you know, plumbing ain't my only talent. I also write a column for the local weekly called, "The Straight Flush with Billy Bob," and people down here think I hung the journalism moon.

I get to write occasionally in your big Atlanta paper, too, because that scoundrel Lewis Grizzard is always needin' me to bail him out, like the time he said he had come down with some mysterious illness.

He comes down with a lot of mysterious illnesses, just about every time he goes out and tries to drink all the see-through whiskey north of Bainbridge. If it flows downhill, that fool will put ice in it and try to drink it.

But this is a special occasion, indeed. Y'all have heard the rumors.

The boy did it, folks. Got married. It happened right here in Fort Deposit, Aladamnbama, last Sunday afternoon.

Grizzard couldn't get a license in Georgia because up there you have to list all your previous marriages. Georgia doesn't give you enough lines for Grizzard to put all his down.

In Alabama, you just have to list your latest foul-up and the reason for it. By "reason," Grizzard put down, "She kept burnin' the cornbread."

It was a nice ceremony. The bride wore red. I was the best man, of course, and Rooster helped get everybody seated and then bit the bride's daddy when he made a complete fool of himself as soon as the preacher got to that part about, "If anybody here has any objections to this marriage . . ."

After the wedding, there was a reception over at the diner, and everybody in Fort Deposit must have come, because it took six pairs of jumper cables to get that crowd cranked and out of there when it was over.

Rooster said he thought the best thing they served was the individually wrapped Slim-Jims and the fried chicken necks, but don't pay much attention to him because that dog will eat anything he can outrun.

There was also a beautiful ice-carving of a possum, and the cold duck they brought over from the Moose Club was dee-vine.

Of course, everybody wants to know why Grizzard decided to do it again. That boy gets married like most folks eat popcorn.

Well, I can tell you why he did it. I knew the answer when I saw him watchin' his new bride pour quarters in the jukebox with one hand and hold a longneck Blue in the other.

"Listen to what she plays," he said, all moon-eyed.

The girl may not have any taste in men, but she knows her music. She played a little Conway, followed that with Willie, and then she played that new song that goes, "We used to kiss on the mouth, but it's all over now."

"Can she cook, too?" I asked the groom.

"Can George Corley Wallace sing 'Dixie'?" Grizzard asked me back.

That's all I needed to know. Number Three likes country music and her beer in a bottle, she won't burn the cornbread, and I didn't get a close look, but it appeared to me she's still got all her teeth, too.

I thought ol' Lewis put it as good as it could be put when he looked up at me, still sober at the time, and said, "I didn't have no choice. An angel don't come by every day."

You Can Call Me "Papa," or You Can Call Me . . .

Father's Day doesn't have anything to do with "Womenfolk," which is the name of this chapter. On second thought, if it weren't for womenfolk, Father's Day would be just another Sunday.

Sunday was my first Father's Day. What I mean is, Sunday was my first time to be a father on Father's Day.

That's not exactly right, either. What I am is a stepfather, but my stepchildren are young—seven and four—so they didn't know any better than to give me a gift anyway.

I was hoping for a case of imported beer. I got socks. I always get socks when I wish for beer.

Let me tell you about my stepchildren.

The seven-year-old is a girl. The four-year-old isn't. Their average age is 5.5, which means there is a great deal of yelling and screaming and whining and crying at my house. My wife, their mother, is constantly yelling and screaming and whining and crying.

I think that comes with being the mother of two children at the age where they are trying to give everybody around them a nervous breakdown.

I came home from work and found my wife in tears. I asked her what was wrong. She said the four-year-old had run away.

"Don't cry," I said. "He'll come back."

"He already did," she replied. "Why do you think I'm crying?"

Actually, my stepchildren don't bother me that much. Whenever they get out of control, I go down to the bus station and buy a ticket for someplace like Butte, Montana. I never get on the bus, but it is comforting to know I could in case something drastic happened, like the four-year-old finding out where I hid his Big Wheel.

Those of you who do not live around children may not know what a Big Wheel is. It is a tricycle-like vehicle made of plastic. When it is pedaled across pavement by a four-year-old, it makes a sound unbearable to the adult ear.

Gestapo agents used small children riding Big Wheels to force information from captives during World War II.

I've been a stepfather for four months. The first big decision a family has to make when a stepfather moves in is what the children should call him.

We discussed "Papa," but "Papa" sound about sixty and German. I am neither.

"Big Daddy" was one of my suggestions, but my wife pointed out I have nothing in common with Burl Ives in Cat on a Hot Tin Roof, including his money, so we threw out that one.

Finally, we decided the children should call me by my real name, "Lewis." My wife, who doesn't have to be that respectful, gets to call me by my nickname, which is "Hey, You."

The first order of business a stepfather must handle when he takes responsibility for stepchildren is to bring a new sense of discipline into their lives.

I am a stern disciplinarian. Last week, the seven-year-old wanted to run away and get married. I said, sternly, "You'll have to ask your mother first."

I must admit children have been an adjustment for me after my years of bachelorhood, and I would not be totally truthful if I said there weren't times I ask myself how the devil I wound up a daddy when my fastball is basically intact.

But being a stepfather isn't something a man should take lightly. If you will pardon my sentimentality for a moment, I know a man who became one twenty-five years ago, and he still offers advice and guidance to a stepson about to ride off the backside of his thirties.

For the sake of the two stepchildren who live under my roof, my Father's Day prayer for 1980 is that I can do half for them what my stepfather did for me.

Part III
Don't Sit Under the Grits Tree With Anyone Else But Me

To
Helen Elliott
who believes in angels.

CONTENTS

1

SOCIAL STUDIES

If you hang out around salad bars, work in a bank, have a cute name like "Traci," speak a foreign language, are a professional athlete who says, "Hi, Mom" when you're on television, are overweight, slurp your soup, jog, are a lardbutt, wear padded bras, or don't like old-fashioned soda fountains, maybe you'd better pass up Chapter One and go directly to Chapter Two. . . .

Take This Salad Bar and Shove It

It finally happened to me the other night at dinner in a restaurant. First, the waiter brought water and bread, and then the menu.

After taking my order, he said, "You may help yourself to our salad bar."

It had been some time coming, but the band of restraint inside me finally snapped.

"I DON'T WANT TO HELP MYSELF TO YOUR SALAD BAR!" I screamed.

"SALAD BARS DRIVE ME INSANE!" I continued, my eyes rolling back in my head.

"I think he's speaking in tongues," a woman said to her husband in the booth next to mine.

"Shut up, Gladys," said the man. "He's just high on a jalapeño pepper."

"YOU CAN TAKE YOUR STUPID SALAD BAR AND SHOVE IT!" I went on, now completely out of control.

The waiter, in complete shock, fetched the restaurant manager, who calmed me with buttered saltines.

I have been foursquare against the idea of salad bars since they first reared their ugly lettuced heads in American restaurants.

It is a matter of principle with me.

Whenever I go out to a restaurant, and pay good money, I expect the following:

• Good food.

• No loud music or pinball machines in the area where you actually eat.

• To be waited on hand and foot.

If I want to go to the trouble of preparing my own salad, I will do it in the privacy of my own home, where I can eat it in my underdrawers if I so desire.

"But," salad-bar types are always arguing with me, "with a salad bar, you can put exactly what you want, and how much you want of it, on your salad."

I can get the same thing and never move one inch from my seat.

"Waiter, what do you have available for salads in this establishment?"

"Sir, we have lettuce, tomatoes, cucumbers, mushrooms, radishes, peppers, onions, bacon bits, and Italian, Thousand Island, French, and Groovy Garlic dressings."

"I'll have a heaping serving of everything but the radishes (radishes taste like a ping-pong ball would probably taste if it were solid), heavy on the Groovy Garlic dressing."

I sit there while my waiter, who is a trained professional in this sort of thing, prepares my salad.

Frankly, it is difficult to find my sort of restaurant these days, one that doesn't dispense its salads from a salad bar. Even the fast-food chains have come over:

Welcome to El Flasho's Taco Take-Out: Mi Salad Bar Es Su Salad Bar."

Soon, I expect all sorts of other establishments, even those that aren't normally associated with food, to get involved.

"Bubba's Transmission Shop: If We Can't Fix It, It Ain't Broke, Visit Our Salad Bar."

Or, "Henning, Henning, Henning, Watts and Schmedlap, Attorneys at Law. Featuring the Best Salad Bar in Town."

I simply can't understand the appeal of making your own salad in a restaurant. If you think that's fun, try something really dynamite like grinding up your own hamburger.

Which probably is the next fad in American restaurants. You stop off on the way to the restaurant and pick up a few pounds of hamburger, potatoes, and salad mixings.

At the restaurant they show you into the kitchen, where you cook your own dinner, and then you serve your own table. Afterwards, you get to clean your table, and then wash your dishes and mop. Hot water is extra.

And will the last customer to leave please remember to turn off the lights?

All Quiet in the Bank

I often have wondered why more people don't suffer nervous breakdowns when they go into banks. Each time I go into a bank, I emerge with sweaty palms and a pounding heartbeat.

That is because each time I go into a bank, I become so frustrated that I want to rant and rave and scream, but it always is so quiet in a bank, which is something else that frustrates me.

Why should people be quiet in a bank? I can understand being quiet in a library or in a funeral home, or even in a doctor's office because there are sick people around, but what's the big deal about keeping your voice down in a stupid bank?

What could they do to you if you suddenly started making a lot of noise while standing in line waiting for a teller?

Is an officer of the bank going to come out from behind one of those wooden doors with the brass nameplates and say, "I'm sorry, sir, but you will have to deposit your money in another financial institution if you can't learn to be quiet while you are in the bank"?

Of course not. Banks just have conned us into thinking they are some kind of big deal where you have to whisper and wear deodorant like when you're in a fancy-smancy restaurant.

Standing in line in a bank is just like standing in line at the grocery store waiting to buy tomatoes. You can chat and sing and even make sucking noises through your teeth and they're still going to sell you those tomatoes because they want their greedy hands on your money.

Next time you're in a bank, break into "The Star Spangled Banner" and I promise nobody will do a thing, except that maybe a few people in your line will think you're nuts and leave the bank, and then you will be able to get to the teller more quickly.

That's something else that drives me crazy about banks. When they build banks, they always build a lot of teller windows. I bank at a small bank. There are maybe ten teller windows at my bank.

Never in the history of my bank have there been more than five tellers behind windows at one time, and three of them always have "Next Window Please" signs keeping customers away while the line stretches out the front door.

If there are ten teller windows, why can't there be ten tellers? Where ARE the other tellers? Probably back in the vault being beaten for making an effort to hurry through transactions with less than fifty people waiting in line.

But let me tell you what REALLY cracks me up about banks. Their pens. The ones that are chained to the penholders that are nailed to the desks where you are supposed to fill out your deposit slips.

Every time I go into my bank, it's the same with those pens. I go to the first desk and one of the penholders is empty because somebody has ripped off the pen.

So I pick up a second pen, but it doesn't work. I shake, rub it across the paper a couple of times, and shake it again. Still, it doesn't work.

I go to the second desk. Same problem. Either the pens have been lifted or they don't work.

Why, I have complained, can't a bank maintain a couple of pens that work? And how can I trust a bank to keep my money safe when it can't even keep an eye on a couple of crummy pens?

But nothing ever changes. The next time I go into my bank, the pen situation will be the same, there still will be two tellers for ten windows, the line will be long and you would think somebodyy just had died the way everybody is being so careful to whisper.

If I had the guts, I would start making sucking noises through my teeth and fill out my deposit slip with a pink crayon.

"T" Is for "Traci"

Lisa, who is in the second grade, was sending out Christmas cards to her girlfriends at school the other evening.

"How do you spell 'Shannon'?" she asked me.

I told her.

"And how do you spell 'Tracy'?" she went on.

I told her that, too. Only it turned out I was wrong. Nobody spells "Tracy" like that anymore. Now, they spell "Tracy" like this: T-r-a-c-i.

Names are like anything else. They come and they go. What has happened since I was a kid is we've had a complete turnover in the sort of names people give to their children.

What the present generations of parents is doing is naming their children "cute" names, like "Shannon" and "Traci" and "Debi" and "Marti" and "Pipsie" and "Amy."

For boys, names like "Sean" are big these days, along with "Chad," "Trey," "Geoff," and "Biff," which is what people used to name their dogs.

Don't get me wrong. I think people can name their kids anything they want. The man for whom the Lear Jet is named, for instance, put "Shanda" on his daughter.

But there are some great names that appear to have been all but forgotten.

When was the last time you heard of a kid named Clarence, for instance? Good name, "Clarence."

Or how about a "Thelma"? There was even a song about a Thelma:

> *"T" for Texas,*
> *"T" for Tennessee,*
> *"T" for Thelma,*
> *Woman made a fool out of me.*

Imagine bringing out the same emotion with "'T' for 'Traci.'"

I went to school with a lot of Arnolds. In fact, one of the craziest people I have even known was named Arnold. Arnold Davenport.

It was in the second grade, I think, when Arnold Davenport found a worm on the playground and ate it. You have to be crazy to eat a worm.

And how many children do you know named Marvin these days? Be careful of anybody named Marvin, too. I went to school with Marvin Millingham, who distinguished himself by allowing a cherry bomb to explode in his hand to show his girlfriend, Imogene Norsworthy, how much courage he had.

Marvin's mother wanted him to be a concert pianist, but so much for that. Imogene Norsworthy, meanwhile, wasn't impressed and started going with Arnold Davenport.

Being from the South, I was used to double names. The possibilities were endless:

BOYS: Billy Bob, Billy Joe, Billy Frank, Bob Billy, Joe Billy, Frank Billy, Jim Bob, Joe Bob, Joe Frank, Willie Joe, Joe Willie, Bobby Earl, Henry Lee, Lee Roy, and one of my all-time favorites, Jack Joe Jenkins, who later married Imogene Norsworthy and moved to Johnson City.

GIRLS: Betty Joe, Bobbie Jo, Jo Jo, Jessie Jo, Jessie Jewell, Jo Beth, Sophie Jo, Sophie Mae, Cordie Mae, Hattie Mae, Linda Lou, Lisa Lou, Betty Lou, Betty Lou Ann Sue, and Kathy Sue Loudermilk, who made Imogene Norsworthy look like a sack of sweet potatoes.

As for me, I was named for my father. His name was Lewis, too. Once, I asked my mother what they would have named me if I had been a girl.

"Same thing," said my mother. "Your father would have insisted."

Thank the Lord it never came to that. Imagine a girl going through life with a name like "Lewis." Some things are worse than eating a worm.

Language Snobs

Most Americans have no interest in learning another language. Learning how to speak English good is hard enough.

There was this one kid from my hometown who went off to the big university and took a lot of French courses. When he got home, he went all over town bragging he had become bilingual.

His entire family was shamed, and the Methodist minister prayed for his retrieval from the deviates who had led him into such a depraved state.

In other countries it is nothing for mere schoolchildren to speak several languages. In high school I took two years of Spanish, but they made me do it.

I hated Spanish. Two years of Spanish, and here is my entire Spanish vocabulary:

> *Si.*
>
> *El beisbol es un juego de Mexico y*
> *Norte America, tambien.*
>
> *Ricardo Montalban.*
>
> *Del Taco.*
>
> *Pepe Frias.*

Pepe Frias, incidentally, plays *beisbol* for the Los Angeles Dodgers. He plays like he just had a bad batch of tacos.

What prompted me to think about all this was a report from the U.S. Embassy in Afghanistan. In case you missed it, a Russian soldier fighting in that country recently sought refuge in the U.S. Embassy.

But there was a big problem. None of the Americans at the U.S. Embassy could interrogate the soldier because none of the Americans spoke any Russian, and the Russian didn't speak any English.

Think about that. About a zillion Russian soldiers came marching across the border in Afghanistan months and months ago, and we still don't even have anybody there who would know what the devil they were talking about if he overheard Russian generals discussing whose border they were going to cross next.

I think the big problem is Americans are snooty when it comes to other languages. Why should WE learn their language? Let THEM learn ours.

That attitude is one of the reasons that when you go to France these days, and a waiter finds out you are an American, he deliberately spills hot coffee in your lap, and if there's not already a fly in your soup, he'll find one.

The point is, the State Department is stupid for not having somebody who speaks Russian in our embassy in Afghanistan, and I just remembered another story that happened in my hometown. It involves a French exchange student and Claude (Goat) Rainwater, who worked at the local service station.

Goat Rainwater had never been outside the county. But he did watch a little television, and he made the tenth grade before he quit school.

Once the church sponsored a French student to come to live in various homes for the summer. The idea was that maybe some of her culture—and language—would rub off on the rest of us.

The first day she was in town, we took her—Michelle—to meet Goat Rainwater.

"Goat, this is Michelle," one of the group said. "She's from France."

"Wellll," replied Goat, realizing this wasn't your everyday, garden variety drop-in at the service station, "*Como esta usted, Senyoreetar?*"

Nobody bothered to correct him, and instead of Michelle teaching us any French, we taught her to cuss like an American sailor who has just been rolled in a bar on the dark side of Tijuana.

Hi, Mom

I have watched a lot of football games on television this year. In some ways, football is a lot better on television than it is in person.

The rest rooms are not as far away when you watch the game on television, for instance.

What else is great about watching the game on the tube is you get to see the players close up. Sometimes they will even show taped interviews of the players while the action is slow on the field.

"While the action is slow on the field, let's show you an interview with Dallas linebacker Eldo (Mad Dog) Rado taped before the game."

"Eldo, what are Dallas's chances of getting into the Super Bowl this season?"

"Well, you know, if we, you know, can, you know, win, you know, a, you know, couple of, you know, more, you know, games this, you know, season, then, you know, we, you know, got a, you know, pretty good, you know, uh, chance, you know."

It doesn't say anywhere in the standard NFL contract that a player must be able to play pass defense and handle the English language at the same time.

What has become a silly practice on televised games, however, is focusing a camera on players while they are on the sidelines, drinking Gatorade, spitting, or eating some of the astroturf.

It is human nature to attempt to perform, or say something clever, when you go one-on-one with a television camera.

But all football players say the same thing in that situation. They say, "Hi, Mom."

If I have seen one football player say, "Hi, Mom," to a television camera this season, I have seen a thousand.

What is this, "Hi, Mom?" Football players make tons of money. Why don't they pop for a long distance call occasionally and say, "Hi, Mom," then, instead of using up precious time on network television that costs the average sponsor millions?

I would like for a football player to think of something original occasionally when he is before the camera.

"Hi, Dad" would do for starters.

Or, "I would like to take this opportunity to thank both my parents for making me eat the right foods and get my rest so that I would grow strong and tall and be able to come out here on Sunday afternoons and tear my opponents limb from limb."

And why stick to relatives?

"Hi, Bettyann, I know I said I would call, but, golly, the big game was coming up and we had practice all week, and I got this bad case of jock itch, and then I got drunk and lost my playbook, and that girl who answered the phone at my apartment when you called the other night was my cousin from Shreveport who's a nun."

Or why not try to say something intelligent or meaningful to the audience?

"Remember, my fellow Americans, that the game of life is a lot like football. You have to tackle your problems, block your fears, and score your points when you get the opportunities; otherwise, some bad dude like Mean Joe Coca-Cola is gonna come along and stomp your head right into the ground."

The only player who never says, "Hi, Mom" when he is on camera, as a matter of fact, is Dallas' Eldo (Mad Dog) Rado. That's because he doesn't have a mother. They grew him in a forest in northern California, you know.

Abundant Americans

We have studies for practically everything today—studies to see why frogs leap and why rabbits hop and why birds don't fly upside down.

One of my favorite studies lately was the one about fat people. A group in Maryland studied fat people and concluded they are being discriminated against almost as much as blacks and "other minorities."

I didn't know that. See why we have to grant all those tax funds to have studies?

David Tucker, the consultant who directed the study for the Maryland Human Relations Commission, said fat people are victims of discrimination in nearly every aspect of life.

He said fat people have trouble getting jobs because employers don't want them in contact with the public.

He said employers tend to characterize fat people as "lazy, lacking in self-discipline, not well-motivated, sloppy, unclean, and, in one case, smelly."

He said owners of theaters and sports arenas don't make their seats wide enough for fat people, and he probably should also have mentioned airplane seats, because I know a fat person who has to buy two seats every time he flies. If the arm rests won't go down, he straddles them.

We do discriminate against fat people, don't we?

We poke fun at them. There was a guy I knew in college. He was fat as a pig. That's why we called him "Hog-Body"—Hog-Body Spradlin.

I never did know Hog-Body's real name until years later when I ran into him at a cocktail party and he was wearing a name tag. His real name was Norbert, which explains why he never complained when we called him Hog-Body.

We especially poke fun and discriminate against fat women. You never see fat women doing pantyhose commercials or selling shampoo on television.

The first question out of any man's mouth as soon as a blind date has been arranged for him is, "She isn't a fat girl, is she?"

That comes immediately after he has been told she makes her own clothes and "all the girls like her."

I think it was Alex Karras, former football player, broadcaster, and some-time actor, who said the worst thing I have ever heard said to a fat girl.

It supposedly happened at a dance when Alex Karras was a student at Iowa. He was in the clutches of a rather large young woman, but, being the nice fellow that he is, he wanted to pay her a compliment.

He came up with the classic, "You don't sweat much for a fat girl."

Alex Karras is no nice fellow. He is a cad.

We also bicker at fat people about going on diets.

My friend Ludlow Porch, an Atlanta radio announcer, isn't exactly slender. ("The local Little League team," he is fond of saying, "gets in shape by running a few laps around me.")

He hates to go to the doctor because he doesn't want to be told to go on a diet again.

"I went to see the doctor the other day," he was telling me. "He said, 'Ludlow, you're overweight.'"

"I said, 'I know that, doctor, and you're short. I can lose weight, but what are you going to do about your situation?'"

My idea is that we lay off fat people. No more discrimination, no more cute remarks. We could even cut the word "fat" out of our vocabularies.

Instead of saying "fat people," let's say "abundant Americans." "Roly-poly" and "plump" and "rotund" and "obese" and "porky" are words no member of polite society should dare say from now on.

In fact, the only time "fat" should really be accepted is when it refers to a body of our government handing out a "fat grant" so a group of "fatheads" can fool around for six months getting "fat" doing an idiotic study.

No Place for Soup-Slurpers

The question most often asked in this country today must be, "Smoking or non-smoking?" You hear it every time you step onto an airplane or a train, and some restaurants are beginning to separate customers who smoke from those who don't.

That's nothing. When you call for a taxi in New York, you can even request a non-smoking driver.

So determined are we to keep the two groups apart, I wouldn't be surprised if we eventually have smoking and non-smoking states.

The smokers, for instance, could all go live in industrial states where the air already is so foul they couldn't do any further damage to it.

Non-smokers could have what is left, like Montana, where the only pollution problem is an occasional moose with poor personal hygiene.

I happen to be a smoker, and I also happen to be an advocate of segregating smokers and non-smokers. One, I don't want to make anybody around me uncomfortable when I smoke, and two, who wants to be with an uppity group with clean lungs that probably also is into jogging and health foods and never has a light when you need one?

I also would like to take this whole idea a step further. If we are going to separate smokers from non-smokers in public places, why not make the same separation when it comes to other annoying habits?

Like throat-clearing in theaters and non-throat-clearing in theaters?

"Non-throat-clearing," I could answer, and be removed forevermore from the jerk who apparently inhaled a pigeon and the feathers tickle his tonsils every time there is soft dialogue that needs to be followed closely.

I could go on. I think I will:

• Loud-talking in restaurants and non-loud-talking in restaurants.

Put me in the section where people came to eat, not to deliver the Gettysburg Address and other orations with mouths full of zucchini.

• Soup-slurping and non-soup slurping.

Some people don't know how to eat soup. They fill their spoons too full and then, because the soup is hot, suck it into their mouths a small amount at a time.

That makes a slurping sound that is both annoying and crude. I would rather sit next to somebody who smells like a moose than somebody who slurps his soup.

• Nose-blowing and non-nose blowing.

It should be against the law to blow your nose in public. It's not, so let's separate those who do from those who don't, especially when food is being served, soft music is being played, or there is to be a great deal of praying.

• Cosmetic-applying and non-cosmetic-applying.

I detest seeing a woman applying her paint and/or powder in the company of others. Seat those who would commit such a *faux pas* far from ordinary people who get sick at the smell of nail polish and at the sight of pooched lips awaiting a new coating of gloss, especially if it is that ghoulish lavender color disco queens and other vampires wear.

• Gum-chewing and non-gum-chewing.

Gum-chewers make loud, smacking noises, and they have a habit of throwing their gum on the floor when they are finished with it. Then I always come along and get it stuck on the bottom of my sneakers. That makes me want to kill gum-chewers.

For their own safety, put them off by themselves where, if they all want to sound like Secretariat enjoying an order of oats, nobody will hear them.

• Affection-displaying and non-affection-displaying.

You would be surprised how many couples nowadays wait until they are in a restaurant or a theater or on an airplane to play kissy-mouth and engage in all the squeezing and giggling that goes with it.

You don't think that can be disturbing? Look around you. Times, they are a-changin'—and the distraction is even greater when the two with the smoochies both have mustaches.

Running With Rosie

I admit I never had much interest in running until recently when I found out you can cheat at it. Now that I know you can cheat, I accept running as being a real sport.

Heretofore I thought it was just something bored housewives and guys who were in the drama club in high school did occasionally because they had never known the joy of sweating.

You can put in the fix in practically all our favorite athletic competitions. Baseball had its Black Sox scandal, basketball its point-shavings of the fifties, and somebody is always stealing a playbook in football, or doping a horse, or shooting an East German swimmer full of strange hormones.

But running? I never thought anybody cheated at running. I remember when some of my friends first started running.

"Who plays tennis or softball?" said one, an out-of-work actor. "Running is *pure*, man."

But then we come to the case of female runner Rosie Ruiz, the first woman to come across the finish line at the Boston Marathon, the Super Bowl of running.

Other runners, including the woman who finished second to her and spectators, claimed Rosie had not run the entire 26.2-mile course, but had slipped into the pack two miles from the finish line for a record time and a victory that is reportedly worth a lot of bucks in endorsements. Pure, man.

The stink caused a number of subsequent investigations and news conferences and a great deal of confusion. The problem, of course, is that the sport of running never has had to deal with a cheating scandal before and wasn't equipped to handle it.

What running needs to circumvent any such embarrassments in the future is a set of guidelines to follow in checking out finishing runners to make certain they completed the entire course.

The National Union for Running Development has offered a standby list of methods to be considered.

Following are some of the NURD suggestions:

• FOOT TEST: After twenty-six miles, a runner's feet should emit a certain odor. Each finishing runner will be asked to allow a foot judge to smell his or her feet. If the judge is rendered unconscious, there is a good chance the runner completed the entire course.

• JOGBRA TEST: No qualified female runner would attempt twenty-six miles without an official "jogbra." All the top women runners wear them. Any female finisher without such equipment should be detained for more questioning. Any male runner wearing a "jogbra" should be detained, period.

• SHOE TEST: Runners finishing in sandals, disco boots, moccasins, anything a cowboy might wear while walking the pasture, or barefooted should be considered suspicious. Any runner finishing in flip-flops should be placed in the same holding cage with the guys wearing "jogbras."

• BREATH TEST: Finishers who reek of Gatorade or orange juice probably are legitimate. Finishers who reek of gin or vodka probably are just drunks who wandered out of the nearby bar to see what all the commotion was about.

• BURMA SHAVE TEST: "Burma Shave" signs will be posted every five miles along the course, and each finisher must be able to recite what appeared on each sign in order. For instance:

> *Here Sits Rosie,*
> *Brokenhearted.*
> *She Finished Fine,*
> *But She Never Started.*
> *Burma Shave.*

Lardbutts Need Love, Too

I went out to the baseball game the other night to watch the Braves lose, and I noticed local fans have formed the habit of booing Bob Horner.

For those of you who do not follow the sport, Bob Horner is this blond kid from out West someplace who is supposed to be some kind of whiz-bang ballplayer.

He's being paid three times what the president makes, but so far he hasn't produced returns proportionate to his pay.

For example, there was his performance the night I caught his act. Four times he came to the plate with runners in scoring position in a tight game. Four times he looked like your Aunt Mildred trying to hit the ball.

There was also his defensive play. Your Aunt Mildred may not have Bob Horner's arm, but I'll bet she can cover more ground at third base.

I've heard all sorts of reasons for why Horner's play has been lacking. There was all that commotion over his contract, then Ted Turner wanted to demote him to Richmond at the first of the season, and he has had many injuries.

I always figured his biggest problem was he's a lardbutt. Lard-butts, because of the way they are built (bottom-heavy), have a difficult time in sports. Plus, despite the fact some of my best friends are lardbutts, they tend to be a little on the lazy side.

Roy Amos was a lardbutt, for instance. In the fifth grade, Roy Amos could hit the ball a long ways during recess games, but he would make somebody else run the bases for him. Also, Roy didn't like to bend over.

So that was my theory concerning Bob Horner: He's a lazy lard-butt who doesn't like to exert a lot of effort or bend over, just like Roy Amos.

But I was wrong, and when I am wrong I want to be the first to admit it. It was Horner's teammate, pitcher Al Hrabosky, who finally discovered the exact nature of Horner's problem.

Hrabosky has this radio show. When it was announced Horner would have to sit out a few days' games recently because of a "stomach disorder," Hrabosky said on his radio show it was not a stomach disorder at all, it was the dreaded "Heinekenitis."

I did some further checking and also learned that Horner picked up the "bug" one evening after a game in St. Louis.

How ashamed we all should be for booing him. A man in his condition cannot be expected to perform up to par.

And I should know. I, too, have had "Heinekenitis" and many other forms of it, such as "PBR Syndrome" and "Strohzema," both of which are just as painful, but don't cost as much to contract.

The symptoms normally begin when you awaken in the morning. They are headache, nausea, dizziness, nervousness, and you want to drink a lot of water, but you don't want to move around a lot or hear any loud noises.

Imagine a person being asked to catch a ground ball or run around a bunch of bases or listen to a screaming crowd in that condition.

When I have "Heinekenitis," it is a chore just to brush my teeth, but I do it anyway because another symptom is your mouth feels like the Chinese army spent the night there.

I think we all owe Bob Horner an apology. He is a sick man, doing the very best that he can, fighting a disease that has brought misery and suffering to millions.

Let us also remember the immortal words of Roy Amos, who said, "Lardbutts need love, too."

This is that apology, Bob. Hang in there, kid, and get well soon.

Forgiving the Bra-Padders

It would be easy to allow the case of Deborah Ann Fountain—the "little something extra girl"—to deflate and pass quietly into the void known as old news.

It never has been the nature of this column to turn its back when it senses that only the tip of a mammoth iceberg has been uncovered, however.

To refresh everyone's memory, Deborah Ann Fountain, Miss New York, went to Biloxi, Mississippi, to compete in the Miss U.S.A. beauty contest.

We all know how beauty contests work. A group of lovely young women strut around in nearly nothing for a couple of days and then a winner is picked, based on her talent and poise.

Miss Fountain decided she could improve her talent and poise by making it appear she had large breasts. So she stuck inch-thick padding into her swimsuit.

Competition can be very keen at a beauty contest. Miss Fountain's attempted trickery was discovered when a contest official, tipped by another contestant, went backstage and ripped down Miss Fountain's swimsuit and uncovered much more than just Miss Fountain.

How many other contest officials volunteered to go backstage and rip down Miss Fountain's swimsuit is not known.

Miss Fountain did what any red-blooded American beauty queen would do after such an experience. She filed suit. In her suit, she contended that four other contestants had silicone implants to boost their bust lines and that twenty other contestants had padded their bras too.

What concerns me is not Deborah Ann Fountain—she has padded her bra and now she must wear it—but just how common is this practice?

If twenty other contestants in the Miss U.S.A. pageant did, in fact, pad their bras, and four more had silicone implants, that means that half the field was cloaked in the dark veil of deceit.

What does this do for the credibility of other women who also are tying to cash in on their, well, talent and poise?

Dolly Parton, for instance. Say it ain't so, Dolly. Jane Russell, still doing bra commercials, and she remembers when Ronald Reagan was breaking in. Is that all you, Jane? And, heaven forbid, but was Janet Cooke wearing falsies when she wrote "Jimmy's World"?

There was a girl in my high school who learned a near-tragic lesson from attempting to be more than she was. During a vacation trip to the beach, she met a charming young man who asked her if she would like to take a swim in the surf.

She'd love to, she said, and met him on the beach in a daring swimsuit. In order to impress the young man even more, she had padded the top of her suit to capacity.

As the two strolled into the surf, they suddenly stepped into much deeper water. The young man went all the way under and came to the surface gasping, only to find his companion not even neck-deep in the water.

Before she could offer an explanation, the padding in her swimsuit sprang loose, and she sank quickly. Only the expert swimming abilities of her young man saved her from drowning.

I would suggest we now grant a National Day of Amnesty for all American women who have the courage to come forward and admit that they have in the past, or are presently, falsifying their pretenses.

This is a forgiving time in which we live. We will forgive Deborah Ann Fountain, of course, and we will forgive any other women who are willing to get it off their chests, so to speak.

We even forgave the girl in my high school, ol' what's-her-name with the floating swimsuit.

One Limeade for the Road

The Last Soda Fountain. Put it up there with *The Last Picture Show*, a marvelous motion picture, and with "The Last Cowboy Song," currently a raging country hit where Willie Nelson joins in on the last chorus.

But The Last Soda Fountain is neither a movie nor a song. It is reality.

The place was Springlake Pharmacy, and it was located near my home in Atlanta. There are memories.

Springlake Pharmacy is where I met Barney, my all-time favorite wino. Barney would sit outside Springlake on a slab of concrete and pour out his bottled dreams from a brown paper sack.

There was the day I saw two punks, they were maybe ten and eleven, throwing rocks at Barney. Barney wasn't bothering anybody. Barney was just drifting away for a time, and he was too weak and too drunk to dodge the rocks.

I chased the kids away. Barney thanked me by asking for a dollar. Barney is dead now.

Springlake is where I bought toothpaste and shampoo and cough syrup and newspapers and once, when I forgot a rather special Valentine, one of those gaudy red boxes of chocolates she pretended to appreciate.

Springlake was where a person could belly-up to the counter of an honest-to-god, just-like-back-home-in-a-small-town soda fountain and ask and receive delights the likes of which are rare and precious indeed in the urban eighties.

Milkshakes. Not milkshakes out of some machine you have to eat with a spoon. That's not a milkshake. At Springlake, you got a milkshake constructed by a human hand scooping real ice cream into a cup with real milk, and you could *drink* the darn thing, as the Lord intended.

Limeade. Real limeade, made out of real lime juice, handsqueezed from real limes. Thousands of limes were rendered juiceless over the years in Springlake. As far as I know, there is no other place in the continental United States that serves as good a limeade as did the soda fountain at Springlake.

I could go on. Cherry Cokes. Coca-Cola syrup, carbonated water and a shot of cherry juice. Good hot dogs. Ham sandwiches with thinly sliced tomatoes.

And nobody behind the counter wore stupid uniforms, and they didn't sell cookies in a funky little box, and the chicken noodle soup was called "chicken noodle soup." At some fastfood establishments today, chicken noodle soup would be called "Soup McNoodle."

My old pal, Estin, was numero uno behind the Springlake soda fountain counter. He spoke only when a grunt wouldn't do just as well.

And then there was the lady who worked with him. I never got her name. Somebody said she was Estin's niece. One day I ordered a ham sandwich and some potato chips from her. She delivered the ham sandwich. She forgot the potato chips, which were located on a rack behind the counter.

"You forgot my potato chips," I said.

"You got two legs," she replied. "Get your own potato chips."

It was that sort of friendly service that kept me coming back to Springlake, hallowed be its name.

Springlake, thirty-odd years at the same location, closed recently to the sound of a bulldozer's snort. A new shopping center went up next door, and the Springlake building was sold, and the Springlake owner decided to move his pharmacy and to pass the soda fountain along to the ages.

I walked inside for one last look.

"We're all just about in tears," said a lady helping dismantle the shelves. "It's a sad day."

The Last Soda Fountain. Let us mourn its leave, for nothing similar remains to take its place.

"Soup McNoodle." How utterly disgusting.

2

CORDIE MAE AND THE GANG

It has been my pleasure to have known a lot of great, and near-great people in my time: Cordie Mae Poovey, Hog Phillpot, Kathy Sue Loudermilk, Mavis Boatright, all the Rainwaters—especially "Spot" and "Goat"—the late Curtis "Fruit Jar" Hainey, and my boyhood friend and idol, Weyman C. Wannamaker, Jr., a great American, who first showed me my way around a 1957 Chervolet. . . .

Hog Takes a Bride

What fun it has been keeping up with the big news in Britain: Prince Charles, who is thirty-two, is taking a bride, and she is cute, bubbly, nineteen-year-old Lady Diana Spencer, who giggles a lot.

The couple will marry in July, and some celebration it should be. I was trying to remember other big-deal marriages in the past, and I thought of Julie Nixon and David Eisenhower and Ari Onassis and Jackie Kennedy and Grace Kelly and Prince Rainier of Monaco, of course.

And then I remembered the one we had back home, when Harold "Hog" Phillpot married Cordie Mae Poovey, and everybody in town came. Pound for pound, it was the biggest wedding in the history of the county.

Hog tipped the Toledo at nearly 300. Nobody ever knew exactly how much Cordie Mae weighed, but her daddy used to say, "If I could get $1.25 a pound for that child, I could pay off my truck."

Now that I think about it, Hog and Cordie Mae had a great deal in common with Prince Charles and Lady Diana.

Hog proposed in a garden, too, right in the middle of his daddy's collard patch, where Cordie Mae was picking a mess for her supper. Cordie Mae could eat a wheelbarrow load of collards and still want to fight you for yours. When Cordie Mae was hungry, she had the personality of a water buffalo with a gum boil.

329

Hog also was in his thirties when he married Cordie Mae, who was just nineteen, like Lady Diana. Cordie Mae wasn't one to giggle very much, however. When she laughed she made a sound like a dump truck being cranked on a cold morning.

I don't know the exact plans of Prince Charles and Lady Diana's wedding, but if it is anything like Hog and Cordie Mae's, it will be a dandy. I managed to locate a yellowed clipping from the local newspaper that described the event:

"Mr. and Mrs. Lark Poovey take pride in announcing the marriage of their daughter, Cordie Mae, to Mr. Harold "Hog" Phillpot, son of Mr. and Mrs. Grover Phillpot, at the Mt. Giliad Free Will Baptist Church Saturday, April 11, 1959, at three o'clock in the afternoon.

"The groom is a graduate of the Nuway Recap School and currently is employed by Elroy's Gulf and Tire as Elroy's night manager. The bride, former state high school girls' wrestling champion (heavyweight division), is the popular bouncer at the Gateway Recreation Hall and Beer Joint.

"The wedding service was delivered by the Rev. Vernon 'Jericho' Walls, and the bride was given away by her father, a prominent sheetrocker and dog breeder. Miss Teeter Combs played several selections on the organ, including the traditional 'Wedding March' and her speciality, 'On Wisconsin.'

"The bride's outfit was designed by Arnold's Tent and Awning Co. The happy couple exited the church under crossed lug wrenches, held by employees from Elroy's Gulf and Tire.

"The reception was held in the basement of the church, where the Rev. Walls' wife, Sharinda, served Hawaiian Punch to one and all. Following a wedding trip to the nearest Burger Chef, the couple will reside in the Lonesome Pines Trailer Park, Row Five, Trailer M, a handsome double-wide."

It's hard to believe it's been more than twenty years since Hog and Cordie Mae got married. They're still together, incidentally, but they had to move from Lonesome Pines into a house. Cordie Mae gained so much more weight that she was wider than the trailer.

Mean Mo-Sheen

The Chrysler Corporation has made another big decision. It no longer will produce those big ugly cars nobody will buy—heaps like the Chrysler Newport, the Dodge St. Regis, or the Plymouth Grand Fury, whatever that is.

From now on, Chrysler will produce only intermediate-sized ugly cars nobody will buy. Won't somebody do Chrysler a big favor and pull its plug for good?

I've known for a long time why Chrysler can't sell cars. It has nothing to do with size. It is because Chrysler is trying to sell cars to a generation it never bothered to impress when we were in high school.

Nobody in my school would have been caught dead driving a Chrysler. The principal always drove a Chrysler, or something like it—a DeSoto, for instance, which was worse than one of those fat, black Buicks with the holes in the sides.

The shop teacher, meanwhile, usually was the one with the pale blue Plymouth without chrome or a radio, and the band director drove a brown Dodge.

How can all that possibly affect Chrysler today? Don't you see? It is in high school that a person, especially a boyperson, first gets hooked on cars. It is during that period he forms certain attitudes and makes certain value judgments concerning automobiles that he will carry into manhood.

In the late fifties and early sixties, you couldn't have gotten a date with Cordie Mae Poovey, the ugliest girl in school, driving a Chrysler.

Now we all are grown, but the anti-Chrysler feelings linger, so we're all out buying those little Japanese imports, which we really don't want—but at least there is no chance of being mistaken for a shop teacher in one.

I have a couple of suggestions for Chrysler that could save the farm.

One, forget all the plans for the intermediate-sized cars, or any-sized cars that look like anything you have built in the past two decades. Face it. Those dogs won't hunt.

Two, beg, borrow, or steal the designs to the greatest car ever made. Produce something that at least closely resembles it, and in six months, I promise you will have won over the entire generation of customers you blew twenty years ago.

I am speaking of the 1957 Chevrolet.

There never has been such another car as the '57 Chevy. Its lines were classic, and its back seat was roomy. Its grillwork and fins said, "Here is power, here is speed." And its back seat was roomy.

It was THE car of my youth. A guy driving a 1957 Chevrolet could get a date with ANY girl in school, up to, and including, Kathy Sue Loudermilk, the Collard Festival queen.

I never owned a '57 Chevy, but my boyhood friend and idol, Weyman C. Wannamaker, Jr., a great American, did. A convertible. A red one. Hottamighty, what a car!

He had "Sassy Chassis" written on the hood, and he had flames painted on each door. Weyman called his car his "mean mo-sheen," and occasionally he even would allow me to drive this piece of automotive genius, like when he was busy discussing an upcoming algebra exam in the roomy back seat with Kathy Sue Loudermilk.

I can hear Weyman now, giving me instructions on how to drive his car. "Eyes forward, stupid," he used to say.

So maybe it's a long shot, Chrysler, but nothing else has worked. Give Americans a mo-sheen like the '57 Chevy and maybe they will remember there are some things in a car more important than gas mileage. And maybe they will tell the Japanese to go eat some fish heads.

Besides, their stupid little cars with those cramped back seats have been taking the fun out of American automobiling long enough.

Making Sense of the Census

What I like most about the taking of the census is that it's fair. Once every ten years everybody counts, and everybody counts the same:

One.

Even Bo Derek. Imagine, Bo Derek a "one." Somehow, I can't imagine that.

Something else I like about the census: It's thorough. Most Americans probably mailed in their census reports April 1, but canvassers soon will be going into places like pool halls, dives, and fleabag hotels in big cities to count heads.

That is important because, otherwise, a pool shark or a wino could be missed. The last time there was a census, for instance, my boyhood friend and idol, Weyman C. Wannamaker, Jr., a great American and part-time pool shark and wino, wasn't counted. He was taking a nap (passed out) underneath a load of turnips in the back of his pickup truck when the census-taker came around.

I can't wait for the results of the census to be released. I realize a great deal of the information we gave the government is supposed to be kept confidential, but this census thing is costing the taxpayers a bundle, so why shouldn't we be privy to some of the juicier material?

I just happen to have with me a list of questions I would like answered by the census:

• The 1980 census had the audacity to ask people if they have indoor plumbing. Did any of my neighbors mark "no"? (I have always suspected the Bloomingraths. They spend an awful lot of time going back and forth to Mr. Bloomingrath's "tool shed," and they never have any beer parties.)

• Does anybody really live in North Dakota?

• What is the population of my hometown, Moreland, Georgia? The last time there was a census taken, there were 300-plus but that was before the Rainwater family moved out. (There were so many Rainwaters, they ran out of names for the last four children and had to name then after dogs in the neighborhood. "Spot" Rainwater was one of my closest friends.)

• How many teen-agers are there in America, and when will they all grow up so rock music will finally die out?

• Ten million people live in New York City, where the air is foul, the streets are dirty and the weather is terrible. Hardly anybody lives in Yellville, Arkansas, where the mountain air is refreshing, there are many streams and rivers for fishing and boating and swimming naked, and you don't have to lock your doors at night. Why?

• Who is the oldest person in America, and has he or she ever jogged?

• Under "sex," how many people put down "undecided," and are any of them in my tennis club?

• How many people in America are named "Engelbert Humperdink"?

• Did the name "D.B. Cooper" show up anywhere?

• When is my wife's birthday?

• And, finally, just exactly how many people do live in this country, and with the government doing the counting, how can I be certain that figure is correct?

I can't. If the government knew beans about simple arithmetic, it wouldn't just now be balancing its own checkbook for the first time since it was taking the 1960 census.

Incidentally, they missed Weyman C. Wannamaker, Jr., in 1960, too. He hid in the family "tool shed," which used to be none of the government's damn business.

Pucker Princess of '62

A jeweler friend of mine mentioned recently you can get as much as $150 by digging out your old high school class ring and selling it at what still remains a good price for gold.

I really hate to use this forum for something so personal, but I haven't been able to find my old high school class ring, and I just remembered what happened to it.

What happened to it was Mavis Boatright, a girl in my school, the night at the drive-in movie when I asked her to go steady. Going steady with Mavis Boatright, which really everybody did at one time or the other, meant French kissing her on the mouth if you came across with something of value she could wear to impress her girl-friends.

"How about my letter jacket?" was my first offer, during the intermission between *Gidget Goes Hawaiian* and some Doris Day thing I wanted to French kiss on the mouth through with Mavis Boatright.

"What sport?" she asked.

"Debate," I answered, proudly.

"Pass," said Mavis, who was not exceedingly intellectual, but her parents allowed her to stay out until midnight, thus giving her great bargaining powers.

Plus, the girl could kiss. A Mavis Boatright lip-lock was something to behold.

My next offer was my foam-rubber dice that hung from the rear-view mirror of my car, but Marvin Waterman had made the same offer the night before, and Mavis had told him to go French kiss a bird dog, which is exactly what she told me. Mavis had some kind of quick wit about her.

"How about the ring?" she finally asked.

I was afraid she would ask that. Getting a boy's class ring meant it was something really serious, something that might last as long as a month. I didn't want to spend an eternity with Mavis Boatright. I just wanted to press my lips tenderly against hers and feel the tinge of excitement run down my spine as she bent my head against the movie speaker.

"I can't give you my class ring," I said.

"So we'll sit here and watch Doris Day go on a crying jag for two hours," Mavis responded.

I gave her my class ring, and my lips were numb for a week. It wasn't long after that, however, she ran off with Marvin Waterman and got married, and she never bothered to return my ring.

Now, I want my ring back. I've tried everything to locate her, including calling around in my hometown, but nobody has any idea whatever happened to Mavis and Marvin.

This is simply a shot in the dark, a last-ditch effort. Maybe you will read this, Mavis, and return my ring.

These are difficult times, and, quite frankly, I could use the cash it would bring. I'm planning a small cookout for a few friends, and the 150 big ones would just about cover the buns and pickle relish.

There also is a matter of principle here, Mavis, and you know what I'm talking about. After That Night, you told every girl in school that kissing me was like drinking warm buttermilk.

Do you realize how long it was before I got kissed again after that? Do you realize how many Doris Day movies I had to sit through after that? Do you know I got so sick of Doris Day that every time she started one of her crying jags I wanted Rock Hudson to bash her one?

That's exactly what I would like to do to you, Mavis. Bam! Right in your kisser, legend that it was. Bitter, Mavis, is the man scorned and $150 in the hole for one night of passion with the pucker princess of 1962, wherever you are.

"When It's Refill Time in Heaven"

I stopped for lunch in one of those meat-and-three-vegetables places the other day and, much to my surprise, the waitress brought my iced tea in a quart fruit jar.

You don't see that sort of thing any more, but fruit jars have a significant history, and I even get a little sentimental when I think about them. More about that later.

First, for those who are not familiar with the fruit jar, it is a wide-mouthed, glass container normally associated with the process of canning, as in the canning of vegetables and fruits.

These containers also may be called "Mason" jars for the name of the company that produces state-of-the-art fruit jars. But people who say "Mason jar" instead of "fruit jar" probably are a little snooty and sleep in pajamas.

In the past, in certain parts of rural America, it was quite common for people who couldn't afford regular glassware—and slept in their underwear—to use these fruit jars as part of their table settings.

You take a family in my hometown, the Rainwaters. The Rainwaters were too poor to afford glasses, so Mrs. Rainwater always served beverages in fruit jars.

Claude "Goat" Rainwater was one of my best friends, despite the fact that he rarely bathed. Mrs. Rainwater would serve Goat his food and his fruit jar on the back porch with the dog.

There are certain advantages to drinking from a fruit jar.

The wide mouth allows easy intake of the liquid inside the jar, whether it be iced tea, buttermilk, lemonade, or something more potent.

It is so easy to drink from a fruit jar, as a matter of fact, that it is virtually impossible to keep whatever you are drinking from pouring over your chin, down your neck, and onto the front of your shirt.

There was a man who lived in the woods near my hometown who sold a certain beverage that was so potent you wanted to be careful not to get any on your shirt because it would ruin your shirt. It would eat through sandpaper and cut out engine knock, too.

As I finished my lunch and poured down the last of my iced tea from my fruit jar, my sentimentality got the best of me as I thought of one of my favorite people from my youth.

I am speaking of the late, great Curtis "Fruit Jar" Hainey. Fruit Jar got that name because he was never without one stuck in his coat or in his back pocket.

It usually was filled with the clear liquid—and an occasional bug or leaf the strainer missed—that he purchased from the aforementioned man in the woods.

I can see ol' Fruit Jar now, ambling along.

"Where you headed, Fruit Jar?" we would ask.

"Refill time," he would answer, smiling and holding up his empty jar as he headed for the woods.

Fruit Jar spent so much time drinking there was a notch on his nose from where the top of his jar pressed against it.

"That stuff's gonna kill him someday," the women from the church used to say.

Sure enough, it did. He went one jar over the line one cold night. The blind girl wrote a song for him and sang it at the funeral after the preacher got through. She called it "Lord, Remember Fruit Jar When It's Refill Time in Heaven."

Goat Rainwater even took a bath for the services. A man like Curtis "Fruit Jar" Hainey doesn't die every day.

The Birth of the Jeans Craze

There is an awful lot of conversation these days concerning the case of fifteen year-old actress-model Brooke Shields and her pair of tight-fitting Calvin Klein jeans.

Miss Shields made a commercial in her tight-fitting Calvin Kleins and also made a few, ahem, suggestive remarks.

The public was outraged. The commercials were yanked off television.

This accomplished two things:

• It made Miss Shields, whose talent is not exactly lengendary, into a big star. Her previous accomplishments included playing the role of twelve-year-old hooker and getting stranded on an island with nothing but her ragged loincloth and somebody who was a boy but wasn't her brother. Brooke Shields is fifteen going on thirty-five.

• It sold the diddly out of Calvin Klein jeans.

Frankly, I don't know what the fuss is all about. For years, blossoming young women have been fitting themselves into blue jeans two sizes too small for them. Women just naturally do something to a pair of jeans that a hairy-legged boy can't.

You take Kathy Sue Loudermilk, for instance. It was Kathy Sue Loudermilk who started the blue-jean craze that is now sweeping the world.

She actually wore the first pair of designer jeans ever made to the annual Fourth of July Barbecue and Street Dance in my hometown on July 5, 1954. (July 4 got rained out that year.)

Her jeans were designed by her mother, the former Edna Pearl Simpkins, who fashioned them from a flour sack.

Unfortunately—or fortunately—Edna Pearl didn't quite have enough sack to fit Kathy Sue, and she came up a couple of sizes too small.

When Kathy Sue arrived at the dance, the band stopped playing, people stopped dancing, the Baptist preacher broke into a prodigious sweat, and Goot Niles swallowed a brand-new plug of Brown Mule chewing tobacco.

Of course, there was some outrage expressed concerning Kathy Sue's outfit back then, too. The ladies of the church passed around a petition to ban Kathy Sue's britches from future town gatherings and gave it to the Baptist preacher, who had to drink two quarts of lemonade to cool down every time Kathy Sue's name was mentioned.

"Let's be sensible, ladies," the preacher said. "She's only a child."

"My grandmother's hat," said Goot Niles' wife, Ruby Jean, who also chewed Brown Mule.

Finally the preacher said he would speak to Kathy Sue's mother, Edna Pearl, but by that time she was already working on sack jeans for almost every young woman in town.

Even Cordie Mae Poovey got a pair. Cordie Mae was a big girl who sort of reminded you of a semi hauling hogs. It took five flour sacks and seven yards of elastic for Edna Pearl to make Cordie Mae's jeans.

"The Blob! It lives!" said my boyhood friend and idol, Weyman C. Wannamaker, Jr., a great American, the first time he saw Cordie Mae in her new outfit. She kneed him in the belly and sat on him until it was nearly dark.

When people got too sophisticated to buy their flour in large cloth sacks, Edna Pearl had to get out of the jeans business.

Too bad. Brooke Shields in a pair of Calvin Kleins is kid stuff. Kathy Sue Loudermilk in a pair of Edna Pearls would make a good man leave home, or Cordie Mae Poovey wasn't two sizes bigger than a train wreck.

3

BOY
COLUMNIST

There are many lessons to be learned from the following chapter, such as how to inspect the cap of a wine bottle before your screw it off, where to get a good tattoo, what to do with your polyester leisure suits, how to tell whether or not something that goes bump in the night is about to get you, and where grits come from. This is a very intellectual chapter. . . .

Drinkin' Wine, Spodee-Odee

I have been checking around, and I have unearthed an incredible discovery: Very few newspapers have a wine columnist.

How absurd. Do newspapers not realize more and more Americans are drinking wine these days? Do they not realize there has been a tremendous increase in the number of wine commercials on television? And think how many fat, out-of-work actors that has helped.

Wine. What an intriguing subject. There have been odes written to it, and songs written about it, as the classic Jerry Lee Lewis rendition of:

> *Drinkin' wine, spodee-odee,*
> *Drinkin' wine.*
> *Drinkin' wine, spodee-odee,*
> *Drinkin' wine.*
> *Drinkin' wine, spodee-odee,*
> *Drinkin' wine.*
> *Pass 'at bottle to me.*

Historically, wine-drinking songs rely more on a catchy tune than lyrical quality.

By now you are probably saying to yourself, "Hey, this guy really knows his wine." But, of course.

339

I go way back with wine, back to when I was thirteen and I went off with my boyhood friend and idol, Weyman C. Wannamaker, Jr., a great American, who had swiped a bottle of something called Eleven Cellars, a rather indelicate port, from the storeroom of the local beer joint.

"Shall you taste, or shall I?" asked Weyman as he unscrewed the cap.

"Be my guest," I said.

"It's a good wine, but not a great wine," said Weyman after the first chug. "The bouquet leaves something to be desired, but its mood is rich."

Indeed. I required medical attention before the day was out. I told my mother I had been eating persimmons.

My knowledge and appreciation of wine was enhanced by a close association with one of the nation's leading wine experts, Ralph (High-Lift) Turnipseed.

When I was a kid, the county in which I lived was dry. That is, you had to buy your booze from a bootlegger in order to keep the church people happy.

One week the local bootlegger went on vacation, and Ralph was left without his normal supply of wine. So he drank Vitalis instead. After that, when he walked, he always picked up one of his legs much higher than the other. Thus, "High-Lift."

High-Lift preferred what he called "walking-around wine," a half-pint of just about anything that would flow downhill. Half-pint bottles would fit in his back pocket, and he therefore would not be bothered by having to carry around a large paper sack.

When he was sixty-five, the doctors told High-Life he wouldn't live another six months if he didn't slow down on his drinking. So he started drinking a lot faster after that and, sure enough, he was nearly eighty when he died. In a motorcycle accident.

Anyway, what this country needs is a good wine columnist and, once again, I must step in to fill the void. Here are a few tips to remember about wine from my very first wine column:

• Always check to see if the seal of the cap is intact before you allow the waiter to unscrew the cap off the bottle. If the seal has been broken, chances are the help has been nipping from the bottle back in the kitchen and may have refilled the portion they drank with water or 7-Up.

• Remember, it's white wine for fish or poultry, red wine for meat. For sardines and soda crackers in the alley, a nice, slightly pink MD 20-20 (any month) is certainly acceptable.

• Never order Wild Russian Vanya unless there is a CPR expert in the restaurant.

• If you're ever in Terre Haute, call EV-7-4433 and ask for Gladys. What's that got to do with wine? Take her a bottle of Gallo Thunderbird and you'll see.

Next time I will discuss what kind of paper cups are best when serving Cold Duck.

The Secrets of My Past

My admiration for Dan Rather, heir to CBS anchorman Walter Cronkite, went up a notch when I read he had admitted in an interview with *The Ladies Home Journal* he has used heroin.

"Not socially," says Rather, but "so I could write a story about it" when he worked in Houston.

Rather also said the experience was "a special kind of hell."

It is only right that a newsman of Rather's stature, who is entrusted with the faith and admiration of millions who watch him dole out the evening news, makes public any previously hidden incidents in his past that would be unveiled later and possibly cause him to lose credibility and respect.

We ask our politicians to open their backgrounds and checkbooks to public scrutiny, so why shouldn't we expect the same from our newspersons?

I'm glad I asked that question, because I am here today to make my life an open book, just like Dan Rather.

As a reader, you have every right to know whether I am a sane, normal person or whether I am some kind of dope-headed sicko who probably has been arrested a couple of times and doesn't like football.

We will do this in the form of an interview. First question, please:

Q. Have you ever "experimented" with drugs?

A. Yes. As part of a general science project in the seventh grade, I fed my neighbor's cat six bottles of aspirin to see what effect the six bottles of aspirin would have on a cat.

Q. And your findings?

A. After eating six bottles of aspirin, a cat will lie very still.

Q. You are evading the real question here. Have you, yourself, ever indulged in an illegal drug, such as marijuana?

A. I cannot tell a lie. Once at a party in Chicago I was with some weird people, and the host, who wore a lot of neck chains and didn't button the front of his shirt, passed around a marijuana cigarette to all his guests.

When it came my turn, the cigarette was very short. I attempted to smoke it, but I sucked the fire into my mouth, instead.

Marijuana causes large blisters on your tongue, so I don't smoke it any more.

Q. Have you ever been arrested?

A. No, but once I received a substantial penalty for early withdrawal from my passbook savings account. The bank teller hit me in the mouth.

Q. Have you ever undergone treatment for a psychiatric disorder?

A. That was in the third grade when the county health teacher was called in to question me concerning why I wouldn't go out of the building during recess to play with the rest of the children.

Q. And what did the health teacher find was your problem?

A. I was scared stiff of Cordie Mae Poovey, the meanest girl in school, who used to pound on my head during recess because she didn't like my looks.

Q. Do you ever drink to excess?

A. Only on weeknights. On weekends, I get blitzed.

Q. Are there any abnormal sexual tendencies in your background?

A. No, but I had a cousin who was a thespian.

Q. Is there anything more you would like to add to this investigation?

A. Just one more thing. When I wrote this column I was high on a plate of Uncle Sam's Red-Hot Texas Chili.

What's Preppy and What Ain't?

If you haven't picked up your copy of *The Official Preppy Handbook*, you absolutely must do so. Otherwise you might commit some horrid *faux pas* such as entering the wrong school, thereby being cursed for life as a member of the Great Unwashed.

For those who still are not certain exactly what a preppy is, he or she is a person who was to the manor born, so to speak, who is aware of all the social graces—and disgraces—and who always wears just the right clothing, goes to just the right vacation spots, and, of course, belongs to just the right clubs.

A snob, in other words.

It is important to know who and what is preppy today, since the ruling class has taken over the country again.

The *Official Preppy Handbook*, currently a runaway best seller, goes for the modest price of $3.95. But even at that, a lot of people probably will never get around to purchasing a copy of *TOPH*, and that concerns me greatly.

Who will lead the masses out of their ignorance? Who will tell the working class to turn up the collars on their pink Izods, to always keep a reserve pair of deck shoes and to name their children Muffy, Corkie, and Topsy (girls) and Chip, Kip, and Trip (boys)?

Many citizens, especially those whose club affiliations are with organizations bearing the names of large, hairy animals found in Canada, don't have the slightest idea that they should always wear gray flannels when having lunch at the Palm Court with Grandmother.

I am here to help these people. "Grizzard's Guide to What's Preppy and What Ain't" is available right here in this very column for free. So save your $3.95 and go buy a couple of six-packs of *brewskis*, an official preppy term for beer. Drinking beer is certainly preppy, as long as you don't do it between bouts at the wrestling matches.

CLOTHING: Throw away anything that resembles polyester, even relatives with stretch marks. A preppy wouldn't wear polyester to a ditch dig. Men, khaki is always safe, and women should stick to shirtdresses, wrap skirts and Calvin Klein jeans.

Women should never wear tank tops, especially if they have tattoos that would be exposed.

SCHOOLING: If you currently are enrolled in the Columbia School of Broadcasting, Harold's College of Transmission Repair, any public school, any barber school, or the University of Arkansas, you probably should commit suicide, or at least stay home nights.

CLUBS: When you hear the term "Junior League," do you think of (a) a spiffy women's service organization or (b) what the Kansas City Royals play in? If you answered "b," the Kiwanis wouldn't have you.

HOBBIES: The favorite hobbies of preppies are things like bird watching and collecting Chinese porcelain and Franklin Mint coins. Sorry, no preppy ever square-danced.

MONEY: You need a lot of this to be a preppy.

Take the following test to see if you qualify:

1. Is L.L. Bean (a) the senior senator from Idaho now that Frank Church is gone, (b) a vegetable, (c) a promising middleweight contender, or (d) a famous place in Maine where preppies like to shop?

2. Is Dom Perignon (a) a baseball player from someplace like Cuba, (b) a disease of the esophagus, (c) the CBS correspondent from Ankara, or (d) a very expensive champagne?

3. Is Perrier (a) Ronald Reagan, Jr.'s, best pal at dancing school, (b) the capital of South Dakota, (c) a nasal decongestant, or (d) bottled water preppies drink when they have a hangover?

If you answered anything but "d" on any question, go wait in the truck, Ripple-breath.

Dr. Feelbad

I was browsing through the papers when I ran across an interesting, but alarming, statistic: twenty percent of the medical costs in the country are being paid out by hypochondriacs—people who are convinced they are sick, but nobody will listen to them, especially doctors.

I have been a practicing hypochondriac for years, and I can't begin to tell you of the suffering. I have had symptoms of every known disease, but never have I been able to find a doctor who agrees with my diagnosis.

Like the time I had toe cancer. Toe cancer is when your little toe becomes swollen and sort of bent out of shape and hurts when you walk.

I went to my doctor, convinced my toe would have to be removed that afternoon, but hoping the leg, at least, could be saved.

My doctor took one look at my toe and said my shoes were too tight. So I changed to a half-size larger shoe, and my toe got better, proving loose shoes to be a definite cure for toe cancer.

This twenty percent thing bothers me because that is a bundle of money for hypochondriacs to be paying out to doctors to be told nothing is wrong with us. Hypochondriacs don't go to doctors to be told nothing is wrong; they go to be assured something most certainly is.

I think I have a solution to the problem. Rather than a doctor, what hypochondriacs need is another hypochondriac—like me, for instance—to tell them they are just as sick as they think they are, which would make them very happy. And think of the money they would save in doctor bills.

Maybe I could write the first newspaper advice column for hypochondriacs. They send in their symptoms, and I use my many years' experience diagnosing my own health problems to diagnose theirs.

Let's give it a practice run. I'll be "Dr. Feelbad, the hypochondriac's best friend," and the column would work something like this:

Dear Dr. Feelbad: After playing tennis, I get a terrible pain in my elbow. My doctor says all I have is common "tennis elbow." But I think it is something much worse. Which of us is correct?

—D.A., Pittsburgh, Pa.

Dear D.A.: You are. What does your doctor know about tennis? You don't have tennis "elbow." You have tennis "arm," and it probably will have to be amputated eventually, and you won't be able to play tennis. You will become a recluse and have to sit around staring out the window all the time. Have a nice day.

Dear Dr. Feelbad: I have a terrible headache. My wife says it is because I got smashed last night, but I know better. I know it probably is a brain tumor and I won't live until morning. How do I break the news to my wife?

—Checking Out, Mobile, Ala.

Dear Checking Out: Your diagnosis is absolutely correct. But wait until you and your wife are in bed and then break the bad news to her gently. But don't keep her up too late. Remember, she has to get up in the morning. You don't.

Dear Dr. Feelbad: I know the seven danger signals of cancer, and I worry about them all the time. But are there any others I could be worrying about, too? I'm getting bored with the first seven.

—Betty, Laredo, Texas

Dear Betty: You bet your boots there are. Here are some of my other favorite danger signals to worry about: Drowsiness toward midnight, increase in bellybutton lint, and sudden loss of memory after a half-dozen tequila shooters.

Dear Dr. Feelbad: Last evening I experienced chest pains and difficulty breathing. Incidentally, my girlfriend, Bearnice, who weighs 300 pounds, was sitting on me at the time. Could I have heart trouble?

—Slim, Terre Haute, Ind.

Dear Slim: Probably not. Bearnice's last boyfriend wrote in about the same thing, but all his problem turned out to be was four broken ribs, bruised kidneys, and a squashed liver. Sorry, better luck next time.

Mr. Cool

A couple of dashing young fellows named Gregory Smith White and Steve Woodward Naifeh have written a book on what men should do to be cool.

The book is titled *Moving Up in Style*, and it teaches men how to dress, what to order in a fancy restaurant, and why scratching your privates in public isn't such a good idea.

The only problem with the book is it is too expensive. It costs $10.95. For $10.95, you could by a case of beer or take a date to the wrestling match.

Who's got $10.95 to blow on some dumb book that gets all involved in what wines are from where and which ones you should drink with what? Just remember not to order a bottle with a screw-off top, and you can't go wrong.

What I am getting around to is this: I know a great deal about being cool myself, having been to three state fairs and to Daytona Beach when I was in high school.

I also know why this distasteful ethnic joke is supposed to be funny:

What are they drinking these days in Poland? Perrier and water.

So there is absolutely no reason to go out and blow $10.95 on Gregory Whozits and Steve Whatshisface's book when, for the price of this newspaper, you can read my occasional "Mr. Cool" column where male readers write in and ask questions concerning style and good taste.

Are you a male? Do you have a question concerning style and good taste? Is so, write "Mr. Cool," in care of me, and if you're lucky, I'll pick your question to answer, and all your friends will get to see your name in print.

Incidentally, a couple of bucks in the envelope and Mr. Cool will personally see to it that you get lucky, which still saves you nearly nine dollars.

Here is the Mr. Cool column for today; jut to give you an idea of how the deal works:

Dear Mr. Cool: I am thirty-two and have been dating my current girlfriend, who is twenty-five, for six months. So far, we have not kissed because I am afraid of where it could lead. Has it been long enough that I should go ahead and give in? Mom says "no."
—**Skippy Winthrop III, Spartanburg, S.C.**

Dear Skippy: If you're as dippy as you sounded in your letter, I doubt if kissing could lead anywhere but to total revulsion for your girlfriend, who obviously is after you for your bucks.

So tell your Mom to take a hike. Just remember, while you're kissing, it's not cool to peep to see if she has her eyes closed.

Dear Mr. Cool: Me and my woman, Betty Louann Sue, went out drinking the other night. I ordered us two cans of beer, and the waitress brought us two glasses. I know one of the glasses was for Betty Louann Sue to drink her PBR out of, but what was the other one for?—**Ronnie Ray Tucker, Vidalia, Ga.**

Dear Ronnie Ray: The answer to that question would only confuse you. Go put another quarter in the juke box and punch E-4, "We Used to Kiss on the Lips, But It's All Over Now."

Dear Mr. Cool: Is it ever permissible to wear white socks? —**Harley Fingers, Birmingham, Ala.**

Dear Harley: Certainly. While hanging out at the Moose Lodge or attending your bowling team's annual banquet, for instance. Also, white socks may be worn with anything made of polyester, or anybody named Betty Louann Sue.

Dear Mr. Cool: What is the proper wine to serve with Boston Scrod?—**Telly Cervantes, Malibu, Calif.**

Dear Telly: Anybody who would eat something called "scrod" wouldn't know the difference. Start with Ripple and work your way down.

Dear Mr. Cool: I want to get a tattoo. All my friends—Butch, Leroy, and Killer—have them. Butch and Leroy have theirs on their forearms. Killer has his on his chest. Where is the best place to get a tattoo?—**Bevo Scrump, Palatka, Fla.**

Dear Bevo: Pete's Transmission Shop and Tattoo Parlor, West Memphis, Ark.

Wrong Shade of Red

Since I have been writing a column, I have been called a lot of names.

"Redneck" is a favorite among many of my loyal readers.

"You redneck, why don't you ride off into the sunset in your pickup?" they write when they particularly enjoy one of my columns.

"Buzzard" is another favorite, because it sort of sounds like my name. Actually, "buzzard" and "Griz-ZARD," which is the way my father taught me to pronounce my name, don't sound alike at all, but they sort of look alike, which is enough for me to get ten or twenty letters a week that begin:

"Dear Buzzard, I will never read your column again."

What is interesting about that is two weeks later, I receive another batch of hate mail from the same creeps, uh, fans.

Anyway, this is all leading up to something, I think, and that is to inform you that for the first time in my career, I have been called a "communist."

Actually, I have been called even more than that. I have been called a "liberal, socialistic communist," which is really calling somebody something, like when you say a person is a "dumb, hillbilly redneck" or a "lizard, gizzard buzzard."

Robert E. Crout of Greenville, South Carolina, an important textile town located somewhere near Interstate 85, is the one who called me that name.

He wrote a letter to my editor that said, "It is my firm opinion that the majority of readers with common sense are tired of the liberal, socialistic, communist view of Lewis Grizzard."

My editor, who is a close friend of mine, couldn't wait to publish that letter.

What had Mr. Crout so upset, apparently, was the fact that I recently published a copy of the official senility test they are going to give Ronald Reagan, who is nearly as old as baseball, when he starts forgetting things like where he sent Alexander Haig and why.

"It is about time," continued Mr. Crout's letter, "all of us begin to remember a few of the 'Communist Rules for Revolution'. . . .

"Get control of all means of publicity and thereby divide the people into hostile groups by constantly harping on controversial matters of no importance and destroy people's faith in their natural leaders by holding (them) up to contempt, ridicule and obloquy."

My mother read that letter. So did my wife, and my minister, and maybe even both of my ex-mothers-in-law, who probably made copies and passed them around.

I demand equal time:

Mr. Crout, I am a lot of things. A Methodist, for instance. But I am not now, nor have I ever been, a commie. I have never read the

"Communist Rules for Revolution," as you quite obviously have. I don't even know who wrote them.

Furthermore, how could I be a good commie if I don't even know what "obloquy" is? It probably is some swill of a soup they serve to poor suckers who get sent to Siberia.

Mr. Crout, I was a Boy Scout and a Little Leaguer. The only political parties in which I involve myself are election-night bashes with free food and booze. I own two "America: Love It or Leave It" bumper stickers, and I know all the words to Merle Haggard's patriotic ditty, "Walkin' on the Fightin' Side of Me."

I love the memory of John Wayne, the Dodgers, hot dogs with mustard, apple pie a la mode (even when you can't get any ice cream to put on it), my mother, college football, fuzzy puppies, cold beer, and courthouse squares. Walter Cronkite gives me goose pimples.

I don't drink vodka, and I once observed that Russian women give the plain-toed work boots they wear a bad name.

Me, a rotten, pinko commie? That's a hoot. Whoever heard of a commie in a pickup? They ride around in those foreign-made vans with slogans printed all over the side. Everybody knows that.

So go take a brain scan to see if anything shows up, Mr. Kraut, or Mr. Croop, or whatever your name was. Better yet, go stick your head in a bucket of obloquy.

Cooter Brown Award

The time has come to announce the winner of the First Annual Drunk-As-Cooter Brown Award. The award is named for the immortal Cooter Brown, who could get drunker than anybody.

Once Cooter got so drunk he wandered into the middle of a church service and began babbling incoherently.

"Praise the Lord!" somebody screamed out. "That man is speaking in tongues!"

"No, he's not," said somebody else. "It's just Cooter Brown trying to sing, 'There Stands the Glass.'"

"There Stands the Glass," I might explain, is a Webb Pierce classic, a favorite of many a drinking man.

This award, conceived by me, neither encourages nor condones drinking, but I do feel if someone distinguishes himself in that area, he should not go unrecognized.

The winner of the First Annual Drunk-As-Cooter Brown Award goes to a fellow I know, Rigsby, who got so drunk on a recent business trip that he checked into his hotel twice.

"Nobody gets that drunk," I said.

"Yes, they do," said Rigsby. "I got off the airplane, went straight to my hotel and checked in. But I didn't go to my room. I met some business associates in the bar, and we proceeded to drink for several hours.

"We got pretty much oiled and decided to go somewhere for dinner. I drove my rental car. I parked it in front of this brick wall.

"When we came out of the restaurant, after dinner and some more drinks, I cranked the car, the accelerator stuck, and I went smashing into the brick wall."

"Anybody hurt?" I asked.

"No," Rigsby replied, "but the car was totaled."

"What did you do then?"

"Well, my associates suggested I push the car away from the wall, call the police, and tell them that while I was in the restaurant, my car was smashed and whoever did it drove away."

"Did the scheme work?" I inquired.

"I think the police were really going for my story," said Rigsby, "until they found the brick in the grillwork of the car."

"Did they book you?" I went on.

"For being drunk, of course," Rigsby explained, "and also for carrying a concealed weapon."

"A concealed weapon?"

"You're not going to believe this: I had ordered a steak for dinner, but I couldn't eat it all. So I asked for a doggie bag. I also thought of the fact that if I were going to eat the rest of my steak later in my room, I would need a knife.

"When nobody was looking, I slipped my knife into my inside coat pocket. I tried to explain that to the officers, but they didn't believe me, especially since I had been so intent on taking the knife, I had forgotten the doggie bag with the rest of my steak in it."

His associates, Rigsby said, finally were able to obtain his release in the wee hours of the morning. He took a taxi back to his hotel.

"I was still drunk," he said, "so I checked in again. It was the next morning before I discovered I had two keys and two rooms. I should never have drunk those last six tequila shooters."

The selection committee (me) already is looking for candidates for next year's award. If you think you or somebody you know qualifies, enter soon. Remember, the bigger the fool you made of yourself, the better chance you have to win.

"I'll drink to that," said Rigsby, whose latest escapade was getting soused and losing his rental car.

"I parked it somewhere in the Midwest," he explained. "I just can't remember which state."

Cooter Brown, rest his soul, would have been proud.

Journalism Lesson

The $1.6 million libel judgment handed down against the *National Enquirer* in favor of entertainer Carol Burnett may not have sounded like earth-shaking news to most of the nation, but to those of us in the rumor and innuendo business, it was a landmark decision.

Such a thing could lead to the unspeakable: columnists, like yours truly, might have to start dealing in facts.Most of us became columnists because gathering facts is hard work and facts will ruin a good story quicker than anything.

Most readers, I have found, know little about how a newspaper works. In order to show you just how much trouble this Carol Burnett thing could cause, let me give you a little short course in print journalism that you won't get on "Lou Grant."

First, there is the "legitimate" press. Newspapers in big towns like Atlanta, Washington and Boston and New York and Chicago, and newspapers in little towns like Paducah and Moline and Valdosta are "legitimate" newspapers.

That means they actually pay "reporters" to go out and gather "facts." Their columnists are the only ones who can just make stuff up.

(There is an exception to every rule, of course, as in the case this week of the *Washington Post* reporter who won a Pulitzer for a figment of her imagination. Too bad the *Post* editors never noticed her potential as a columnist.)

On the other hand, there is the "illegitimate" press, like the *National Enquirer* and other such newspapers one usually can purchase in supermarkets. Reporters, columnists, the publisher— EVERYBODY—on these newspapers writes gossip, trash, and totally unfounded rumors like Secretary of State Alexander Haig is really a robot and Richard Nixon has the controls.

So they stick it to the *National Enquirer* today. Tomorrow, it could be the "legitimate" press they come after, and who they will come after first are stiffs like me who have to test our imaginations day after day. Anybody can report the "facts."

Prominent local businessman Ernest T. Broomthistle, of Broomthistle and Farkle, was fined $10 in City Traffic Court today for an illegal lane change on Oak Street.

Who wants to read dull garbage like that? Any columnist worth his salt could do a lot more with ol' Broomthistle. Stand back and watch me work:

"So the cops have finally nabbed ol' Ernie 'Big E' Broomthistle, the big-biz bigwig of Broomthistle and Farkle, local manufacturer of women's hosiery, and, according to certain sources, a few other unmentionable garments that are listed only in a 'special' catalog, not readily available to the general public.

"The charge against Broomthistle, who always wears sunglasses and drives a big black car, was 'illegal lane change.' Don't make me laugh. He was stopped on Oak Street, only five blocks from the Three Moons Lounge. What does that tell you?

"A little checking also indicated Broomthistle's partner, Milburn Farkle, lives on Oak Street with his wife, Mona (alias Boom-Boom), former Miss Oklahoma City Rodeo, 1959. Mr. Farkle, it seems was out of town on business the day his partner and alleged best friend, Broomthistle, was caught weaving all over the road just a few blocks up from where his wife was home all alone, probably wearing some of those unmentionable garments from the 'special catalog.'

"The judge who handed down the paltry $10 fine against Broomthistle was Judge Garvin Pendergrass, incidentally. Some interesting connections between Broomthistle and Pendergrass also have been uncovered.

"Pendergrass, for instance, is originally from Virginia. Broomthistle is from Delaware. Both states were included in the thirteen original colonies.

"One other thing. Both men are bilingual."

If they ever do come after me like they went after the *National Enquirer*, I hope the jury will remember just one thing: It ain't easy being a genius.

A Word for Insomniacs

Because of my vast knowledge of many subjects, readers write to me and ask all sorts of questions.

Some of the questions aren't very nice. Like when are you going to leave town? And, how did a creep like you get a job with the newspaper?

However, I do get intelligent, interesting questions, and one that came recently was quite intriguing. The question had to do with insomnia, which millions of Americans, including myself, suffer in varying degrees.

The question was: "Dear Mr. Grizzard, I have insomnia. I lie awake all night long in my bed and hear strange noises which make me very nervous and, of course, unable to sleep. What are these noises and are they really nothing to worry about?"

The letter was signed. "Scared Silly, Tupelo, Mississippi."

I am glad you wrote to me, Scared Silly, and I hope I can help. From childhood, we all are frightened of "things that go bump in the night." Some of us grow out of this fear, others do not.

You obviously haven't grown out of this fear, and neither have I. For years I have suffered from insomnia because I know "something" is out there in the dark. I can hear "it" creaking and crawling and coming to get me.

I especially hear these noises when I have watched the Friday Night Horror Double Feature or when I had lots of garlic for dinner.

I am sorry I can't allay your fears, Scared Silly, but I still may be able to offer some assistance by identifying the noises you may be hearing and explaining what they mean.

Incidentally, do not read this while you are alone or where something can sneak up behind you.

• CREEEEEAK! This is a sound commonly heard in the night by insomniacs and other chickens. It probably is nothing. Then, again, it could be the sound of one of your doors slowly being pushed open by an escapee from a local mental institution who inspired the movie *The Texas Chainsaw Massacre*.

• BLIP! BLIP! BLIP! Probably nothing more than a dripping faucet. But what if it were something else? What if it were the sound of blood slowly dripping onto the floor? Your floor. The floor in the next room. A wounded, mad-dog killer has escaped from the authorities and is looking for another victim. Either that, or Dracula has come to suck the blood from your neck. I'll take my chances with the mad-dog killer.

• BLAM! I hear that sound all the time. It's nothing, I tell myself. A book fell off a table. It's the ice maker in the refrigerator. The wind blew one of the shutters against the side of the house. Burglars are working their way to the bedroom to finish off any possible witnesses. Demons, like the kind that got Linda Blair, are throwing my den furniture around. Killer bees are building their hive in the attic.

• WHOOOOOSH! That's nothing. That just somebody flushing a toilet. But you are alone in the house.

• THUUUUMP! Anybody who has ever been awake at night knows this one. You always hear it as you are just about to doze off. You awaken and you lie there, listening for another sound. You are afraid to move. If you move, "it" will know where you are and "it" will find you. If you should hear a second THUUUUMP, don't even bother to scream.

I hope this helps, Scared Silly, and be sure to write me again if there is anything else I can do. Incidentally, before you go to bed tonight, there is one other thing I should mention.

"It" was last seen near Tupelo, Mississippi. Sweet dreams.

True Grits

I was hoping that four years of Georgian Jimmy Carter in the White House would finally clear up the matter of grits. Grits have been so terribly misunderstood by people who are from parts of the country other than the South.

But, alas, Georgia's Jimmy is only a few weeks from departing Washington in favor of Californian Ronald Reagan, who wouldn't know grits from granola, and I fear grits will never cross the gap that has left so many yet unaware of the history and many uses of one of America's most interesting foods.

As one of the nation's leading experts on grits (my mother served them every morning for breakfast), all I can do is try to light the way for those still blinded by prejudice and fear.

Grits won't bite you. Grits taste good and they're good for you. Just sit back and relax and put yourself in my hands and let's go. "DISCOVERING GRITS: GRIZZARD'S GUIDE TO A SOUTHERN DELICACY FOR FOLKS FROM NEW JERSEY AND PLACES LIKE THAT":

• The origin of grits:

Cherokee Indians, native to the Southern region of the United States, first discovered grits trees growing wild during the thirteenth century. Chief Big Bear's squaw, Jemima Big Bear, is said to have been out of oatmeal one day, so she gathered the tiny grits growing from the grits trees and cooked them in water for Chief Big Bear.

After eating the grits, Chief Big Bear ordered his squaw, Jemima, burned at the stake.

Later, however, Southern planter Jim Dandy found grits taste a lot better if you put salt and pepper and butter on them. Grits really took off in the South after that. Today, grits orchards may be seen from the Carolinas to Florida and west to Louisiana.

At some orchards, tourists may "pick their own grits." If you decide to give it a try, make cetain each grit you pick is ripe and firm. Raw grits tend to stick to the roof of your mouth and have been known to choke even large goats.

- How grits got their name:

From the Cherokee word, *greyette*, which means "corn pebbles." The Cherokee thought grits were tiny versions of corn. They even tried to make bread from grits, which brought about another big run on squaw-burning.

- What does the word "hominy" mean?

It is Southern for "blended voices," as in, "That quartet sure has nice hominy, don't it?"

- How to prepare grits:

First, go out to your grits tree and pick a peck of grits. Wash, then allow to soak in warm buttermilk for an hour. Add two tablespoons Jack Daniel (Black Label) Tennessee sippin' whiskey and one cup branch water.

Stir, bake at 450 for approximately one hour. Cover with sawmill gravy, add butter, then salt and pepper to taste. Cheese (Kraft American) optional.

Must be served hot. Cold grits tend to get gummy. You wouldn't serve cold, gummy grits to communist sympathizers from New York.

- What are some other uses for grits?

Patching blow-outs. Snake bite. Bathroom calking. In some parts of the South it is even believed grits will grow hair. This is doubtful. Grits do make a delightful party punch, however. Just add more Jack Daniel.

- How can I order my grits tree?

By sending $38.95 for each tree desired to "Grits-a-Grow-Grow," in care of me. Add $15 if you want to take advantage of our special offer for our handy "Grit-Picker," which will save time and wear and tear on your hands when you go out to gather your grits off your new grits tree.

- What else may I order from "Grits-a-Grow-Grow"?

A special brochure outlining how you can purchase valuable vacation property at our new Alligator Point resort in Florida and about six zillion copies of Amy Carter's Washington Coloring Book. Order now while they last.

4

ORDINARY PEOPLE

The best stories are true stories, the real stories about real people. . . .

Team Man

The little boy who lives at my house is about to embark upon his first season of organized baseball. He is barely housebroken, but they have something called Tee-ball for youngsters still only a short pop fly from the cradle.

In Tee-ball, there is no pitcher. The ball sits on a tee, perfectly still, to make it easier for the child to swat it.

A golfer probably invented Tee-ball.

Regardless of how easy they made it for kids in Tee-ball, the little boy who lives at my house is going to have some problems.

First, he doesn't understand the basics of the game of baseball. I thought boy-children were born with the knowledge of how to run the bases, as in you run to first first.

Not so. When he tried out for his team, his coach asked him to run the bases.

He ran to second first, to third second, to home third, and then slid into first last.

Actually, it wasn't a slide, it was more of a *crawl*.

Later, I asked the little boy why he crawled on his stomach into first base.

He said, "That's the way baseball players do it because they don't want anybody to see them sneaking into the base."

Oh.

The biggest problem he is going to have, however, is with his thumb-sucking.

Now, let's go over thumb-sucking for a moment.

There is nothing wrong with it. Sucking one's thumb does not make one a bad person.

It is just a habit, a way children relax and relieve tension. Adults have double martinis, kids have thumb-sucking.

If double martinis were suddenly taken away from them, a lot of adults probably would suck their thumbs.

I am certain the little boy eventually will dispense with sucking his thumb, but likely not before his first game of Tee-ball and that's the big trouble here.

I had never thought of this before, but after going out into the yard and tossing a few balls around with the little boy to get him ready for the season, I realized how hard it is to play baseball and suck your thumb at the same time.

Consider: The child is a lefty. He bats, throws, and sucks left.

So, he's playing the outfield and a long fly ball is hit in his direction. The winning run is at third, one out. The runner will try to tag and come home.

The little boy runs for the ball, which is no easy task with a thumb in your mouth. He catches it, but before he can make his throw to the plate, he must remove his thumb from his mouth, hoping the rest of his throwing hand will follow.

The split second he loses with all that wasted motion allows the winning run to score. He is the goat of the game.

I tried to make that point to him.

"You don't want to let the rest of the Cardinals down, do you?" I asked him, appealing to his conscience.

"No," he replied. "I'll try to remember not to suck my thumb when there is anybody on base."

At least the kid's a team man, thumb in or thumb out.

Learning a Lesson

WASHINGTON, D.C.—The kid was twelve, maybe thirteen, and he had sad eyes and a look about him that said he wanted to cry.

But he wouldn't cry, because streetwise kids from the tough neighborhoods are cried out by his age.

He was standing at the entrance to Washington's bustling Union Station, hiding, sort of, behind one of the giant pillars.

All about him were travelers, coming and going, and why he picked me, I don't know. This taxi had dropped me off with my bags. My train would leave in fifteen minutes.

"Can I carry your bags to the train, mister?" the kid asked.

I travel a great deal by train. The way you get your bags down to the train is you find a dying breed called a "redcap," and he puts your bags on the train, and then you pay him maybe two dollars for the service.

Sometimes you can find a redcap. Sometimes you can't. I looked around. I didn't see a redcap. I had more bags than I could handle. Time was running out on me.

I looked at the kid again. Maybe this is some kind of new sting, I thought. The kid takes my bags and when I turn my head for a moment, he is gone, and so are my bags.

But not this kid. Don't ask me how I knew that, I just knew that. Listen, I said to myself, at least he's trying to *work*. He could be out trying to break into a house or into somebody's car.

So just as I was about to turn over my bags to the kid, up walks a redcap.

"Get out of here, kid!" he shouts, and the kid recoils at first, and then makes a stand of it.

"I ain't doin' nothing wrong," the kid says to the redcap, and then they go one-on-one.

"You got no business out here!"

"I'm just tryin' to make a coupla dollars. What's wrong with that, man?"

"Ain't nothin' wrong with that, except it's my two dollars you tryin' to make."

"I got a right to work out here, too."

"You ain't got no kind of rights to work out here. You too young, for one thing."

"I ain't too young."

"The hell you ain't. And you ain't paid no union dues, either, man."

At this point, the kid is stymied. Also, imagine my predicament. Now, my train is leaving in ten minutes, and I'm still standing outside the station.

A station security guard appears out of the air.

"What's the problem?" he asks the redcap.

"Stupid kid's out here hustling my bags, that's the problem," the redcap answers.

Eight minutes to go until train time.

"Don't you know you have to be hired before you can go to work out here?" the security guard asks the kid.

"I just wanted to make a coupla dollars. What's wrong with that, man?" repeats the kid.

"It just don't work that way, son," says the security guard, and by now the redcap has my bags on his cart and he is wheeling them to my train, which I barely will make.

I left the kid with the security guard.

As I handed the two dollars to the redcap for putting my bags onto the train, he said to me, "Don't worry about that kid. He'll learn soon enough. It's every man for himself out here."

Kids. It just takes them a while to catch on, that's all.

Good News

Earl Sheriff, sixty-eight, is custodian at the little high school in the village of Fredericktown, Ohio, which is near Columbus.

You ought to hear them talk about "Mr. Sheriff" around the school.

"He's the sweetest, kindest, most helpful man I've ever known," one of the teachers was saying. "We couldn't get along without him."

Still, nobody knew much about Earl Sheriff's background until one day when some of the students, who were in the midst of a course called U.S. Wars, casually asked the custodian if he knew anything about WW II, the Big One.

Earl Sheriff knew quite a bit. He had lived through it, as a matter of fact, and the students asked him to come and lecture the class.

So here is the school custodian lecturing in the classroom, and Sgt. Earl Sheriff talked about how he had served as a light machine-gun section leader and how he had hit Utah Beach with the 121st Infantry as part of the first replacement unit in after D-Day.

He also mentioned fighting through the hedgerow country of France and into the Hurtgen Forest. And he brought along his Purple Heart—he was wounded three times—and his Silver Star and his Medal of Luxembourg.

"The light machine guns went ahead of the infantry," Earl Sheriff told the students. "We were up there where we could look the Germans in the eyes. It was hell, but we had a job to do, and we did it— and a lot of good boys got killed."

An old soldier remembers, and today's high school students, ages fifteen through seventeen, listen to stories of a fabled time when Americans went to war wearing white hats, and "technical problems" didn't scrub missions. Somebody fixed the machine and the fight went on.

Ancient history, in other words.

When Earl Sheriff finished his lecture, one of the students asked him if he ever saw any of the men he had fought beside.

The custodian said there was an annual reunion of the 121st, but he had never been able to attend.

"Never could get time off from work," he said. Another problem is that his wife is an invalid.

I wondered about those students. Did they really care today how we gave Hitler hell, and what the cost of it was? Have we been on a losing streak so long they could not look at the old man in front of them and sense his pride for having a job to do, and for having done it?

Get the picture here. As the students' teacher put it, "This is still middle America. This is mostly a farm community. These are good kids. They care."

They do. I'll keep this short. What the students did was canvass the school and ask for donations. They raised $250, and they gave it to Earl Sheriff for a round-trip airplane ticket to Macon, Georgia, this week.

There he will attend the reunion of the 121st Infantry Regiment for the first time.

"Seeing all those fellows again," he said, "was always a dream of mine. Now it is coming true."

A group of high school students in 1980 have dug deep into their pockets for an old soldier who fought with our last winner.

You're always clamoring for "good" news out there. This should be a gracious dose.

Forgotten Hero

I heard him tell the story so many times.

He and his men were camped in some godforsaken place in Korea. The Chinese had just entered the war in November. The year was 1950.

"They caught us completely by surprise," he said. "I looked up at this hill and every gook on earth was coming over it."

War was nothing new to him. He had fought his way through France, leading nineteen-year-olds, six years earlier.

"Fighting Germans," he would explain, "was one thing, but fighting these crazy people was something else. German soldiers were intelligent, they thought like Americans. You could figure out their next move.

"These people, the Chinese, were nuts. They didn't value human life. You'd kill one and ten more would come over that hill to take his place." His company was being annihilated. He was sure he would die. He had a wife and a kid back home.

"About thirty of us, the last ones left, dug a pit and held them off for hours," he would go on. "But they finally pitched a mortar right in the middle of the pit. It took off the head of this kid. I'll never forget seeing that. The chaplain got it, too.

"There was so much smoke and noise, I didn't know if anybody else around me was alive. I pulled some bodies over me and prayed they wouldn't notice me."

Maybe it was the prayers. The enemy didn't notice him. He waited under the bodies for hours, afraid to bat an eye, afraid to move for fear of being discovered.

Finally, he stood up. There was total silence around him, a sea of dead. He looked around in the pit. He found a young soldier still breathing. He poured water out of his canteen onto the young soldier's face. He came around.

"I knew he was hurt, but I had to move him," he explained. He carried the soldier as he wandered into the night. When he became so tired he couldn't go another inch, he sat down under a tree and propped the soldier against the tree next to him.

He slept. Sometime in the night, his only companion died.

He continued to wander, now alone, through the next morning. It was a friendly North Korean soldier, who had been forced into duty and was hiding himself, who saw him and befriended him and saved the man's life.

He took the American back to where his family was living in a lean-to at the base of a mountain. He put the American in a hole and covered the hole with boards and straw. Each day for six weeks, he would emerge from his own hiding place to bring the American rice in the hole. The American could hear enemy troop movement around him.

Water seeped into the hole, but the American didn't dare come out for fear of being discovered. His feet froze. When it was finally safe to travel, he said his steps were like "walking on two basketballs."

The friendly soldier eventually led him back to the American lines. The Army notified the man's family that he was no longer missing in action. After a hospital stay in Pearl Harbor, he was allowed to come home.

He had distinguished himself. He had fought two wars for his country. He had a head full of shrapnel, two bullet holes in his hip, and he wouldn't be able to sleep without first emptying a bottle of amber medicine.

His wife and his son and his mother-in-law met him at the train when he arrived home. A local newspaper reporter showed up, too.

But there was no band, no parade, no well wishes, nor a message from his commander-in-chief. He never complained, of course, but later there was little, if any, rehabilitation, either. He never really made it back from that pit in Korea from under the bodies of those dead friends.

His feet bled every day. He died a drunk and a pauper.

We didn't do anything wrong welcoming home the former hostages from Iran. They deserved every yellow ribbon, every hand held out toward them.

But a lot of heroes who preceded them went virtually unnoticed, and for one in particular, I've felt a twinge of bitterness lately. I demand at least that.

Townsend

Jim Townsend died soon after I wrote the following piece. I'm convinced he is presently in heaven, trying to con Hemingway and Voltaire into doing something for the new magazine he's starting.

This will probably read like a book review, but it's not. It's a story about a friend of mine who recently had a book published, a special friend more people genuinely love than just about anybody else I know.

His name is Townsend.

Yeah, he's got a first name, "James," and a middle initial, "L.," but you don't need any of those. He is "Townsend," always "Townsend," forever "Townsend."

His book is *Dear Heart* (Peachtree Publishers), and in his book Townsend takes you from Lanett, Alabama, his hometown, to any number of magic places, with numerous stops in Atlanta, a city he describes as the best city in America for "rearing a family, living in safety, and moving around without unreasonable delay."

One of the reasons so many people love Townsend so much is because he would be optimistic with all four engines out and the tail section on fire, flying through a hurricane.

Townsend, among other things, founded *Atlanta Magazine*. He edited it and nursed it, and he did the same in Cincinnati and in New

Orleans and you name the town, chances are Townsend put his genius to work there at some point.

But Atlanta, how the man loves Atlanta.

In the introduction to *Dear Heart*, fellow author and friend Pat Conroy says of Townsend and what he's meant to this city:

"Atlanta, forgetful city, feisty and brawling and on the go, has not yet honored Jim Townsend, has not paused to thank the man, has not slowed down for one single act of gratitude and appreciation to the man who helped to invent the image of Atlanta.

"But when the history of Atlanta is written, and when they talk about who created the soul of this city, they will have to deal with the brilliant, mercurial, contradictory, and infinitely complex figure of Jim Townsend."

I first met Townsend in a bar. When you met Townsend a few years back, you always met him in a bar.

"Grizzard," he said to me. "I've got a story only you can do." Townsend said that to all the writers.

You didn't always get paid. Lee Walburn, now editor-in-chief of *Atlanta Weekly*, explains on the back of Townsend's new book why that never really bothered you as much as it probably should have:

"Townsend is a lovable old basset hound of an editor whose eloquent cajolery has charmed a million words from hundreds of writers—sometimes for pay, sometimes for promises. The sharing of this collection from his own jewel bag of words pays all debts."

Townsend finally whipped his boozing problem. Now he's got another bear to fight. Cancer.

Still, he's down almost every day on the seventh floor at 72 Marietta Street where *Atlanta Weekly* comes together. He edits. He writes notes. Townsend is the most eloquent note-writer who ever doodled across a scratch pad.

His book sings. There are tent revivals, twenty-fifth anniversary parties at ice cream parlors, and he explains what a "gradualist" is, and you meet H. L. Hunt and Count Alexis de Sakhnoffsky, and there is a piece about Townsend's daddy who was sharecropping cotton in West Georgia when McKinley was shot down in Buffalo.

I just want to say one more thing, and I want to say it directly to Townsend:

I read your book in one easy sitting, and I won't be satisfied until I've read more. You're beautiful, dear heart. Just beautiful.

No Easy Way Out

We aren't, well, close, but we've had a few high times together, enough to keep us reminiscing for a couple of hours at least before we have to start telling the same stories over again.

So I was shocked when I heard the news. This man, a young man, put a .38-caliber pistol to his head. And pulled the trigger.

Say you are just trying to get somebody's attention or sympathy. You take a few pills and wind up getting your stomach pumped out in the hospital.

I'm no shrink, but I know that if you put a pistol to your head and pull the trigger, you are serious about leaving us.

It's like the man's attorney said later: "Imagine his surprise when he woke up and found out he wasn't in the Promised Land after all. He was right back here with the rest of us."

Yeah, he lived. Barely. They were already talking about where to send the remains.

I went to see him in the hospital the other night. I'm not going to mention his name. He's had enough bad publicity in his life already, and there are two children who carry his name.

"You look awful," I said to him.

"Can you believe this?" he laughed. His spirits were surprisingly high. "The last thing in the world I try to do, and I louse it up."

He spared no details.

I already knew about his divorce. Then he ran afoul of the law. Nothing big-time, but enough to bring the heat close enough to feel it.

Then, there was the lady. Stop me if you've heard this one before.

"I thought she was really special," he said.

"They've got that way of fooling us sometimes," I said.

"I just fell apart," he said. "All I could think of was I wanted out. I wanted my ticket punched."

"So what did you do, uh, wrong?" I asked. He held a finger of his right hand to his head and explained to me what the doctors had explained to him.

"They said I held the gun at an angle, so the bullet went through my right eye and out above my left eye. They said most people who shoot themselves in the head hold the gun straight, and it blows their brains out."

Above his left eye was the hole where the bullet left his head. He has lost his right eye. I made some crack about women thinking eye-patches are sexy. He is lucky he isn't blind.

I had to ask. I had to ask what it felt like to nearly die. You've read all those stories of what people saw and felt before they miraculously escaped death's clutches.

"I don't remember anything," he said. "There was a thud in my head after I pulled the trigger, and then, two days later, I woke up and I didn't know if I was in heaven or hell. I just knew I had an awful headache and there were tubes all over me."

There was something else I had to ask. I wanted to know if he was happy he had missed the obit page after all his efforts to make it there.

"I tried to get out, and I didn't make it," he answered.

He is no manner of a poet, and I had never seen sensitivity in him before. But he had something he wanted me to read. On a yellow sheet he had scribbled out the following words:

I am an incurable romantic. I believe in hopes, dreams, and decency. I believe in love, tenderness, kindness, and family. I believe in mankind.

But I must never let my happiness depend entirely on another person's thoughts, whims, or demands. Nor can I forget the value of honesty, the harshness at times of reality, and warmth of life itself, nor the need for love.

Nice thoughts. I got up to leave.

"If you write something in the paper about this," said the man, "will you do me one favor?"

"Sure. What?"

"Tell anybody who's thinking of doing what I did not to do it. It's not the easy way out after all."

Dark Eyes

It's an old story. She was seventeen at the time. She's more than twice that now, but still dark-eyed and beautiful. The first time I saw her, half of my life ago, she nearly took my breath.

It was a small town in the hills, and her mother taught in the little high school. Her father split when she was a baby. Her mother never remarried. There were no more children.

Her mother raised her on grace and good manners.

"Mama," she would say, laughing, "Mama always told me to act like she was looking over my shoulder. I always knew that, somehow, she was."

The child grew to be a beauty, and also a scholar. Besides that, she sang in church and visited the old people.

The boys flocked around her and vied for even her slightest attention. Those were simpler times.

She conquered high school in a matter of days. Cheerleader, clubs, a dozen handsome fellows already left in her wake by her junior year.

She was perfect. Life was perfect. Nothing could go wrong.

Something went wrong. Forget about a drug, booze, or sex angle here, however. This was the early sixties, small town, and Homecoming Night at the high school stadium.

She was one of the finalists, and she would win, of course, because she was the most popular girl in school. The homecoming queen would be chosen by ballot of the student body, the results to be announced at half time.

She was dazzling that night, a girl-child on the fine edge of womanhood.

The results were announced. She won. Her mother beamed; she had done her best under some tough circumstances.

There was another family in the town that was THE family in town. If you worked in town, normally you worked for THE family. They lived in the big house with shade trees framing the drive up to the front door.

And there was a daughter in the family, too, the same age as dark-eyes, and she was a member of the Homecoming Court that night, too.

When the name of the queen was announced, the mother of the loser stormed school officials and demanded that the ballots be recounted. Don't forget, THE family gave money for the new gymnasium and bought uniforms for the band.

The ballots were recounted. At the end of the game, there was a simple announcement. There had been a mistake. There was a new homecoming queen.

They made dark-eyes give back her crown and her roses.

"I thought I would die," she said. "And I think I would have if it hadn't been for Mama. The embarrassment was incredible. Mama said, 'Go back to school, face whatever comes. If you run from this, it could change your entire life.'"

She didn't run. She went back to school. And when it was her time, she caught a bus out of town and never looked back.

We met again by chance the other day. I didn't mention the story, and neither did she. She's been a resounding success. The lady has guts.

I do wish I knew whatever happened to Miss Homecoming, though. I hope she got fat.

5

EATING LIVER AND OTHER SINS

One thing that has always puzzled me: everytime I write a column in which I mention God, at least five people write me a letter and threaten to kill me. . . .

Preacher Jokes

We had the minister over for dinner the other evening, and I think this all is a part of my wife's grand plan to civilize me. Next, she probably will want me to start sleeping in pajamas. Cowboys don't sleep in pajamas, but how could a woman know that?

Anyway, back to the minister coming to dinner. I had all sorts of rules I was to follow:

• You can have a beer or two, she said, but don't get out of your mind and start wanting to sing Maurice Williams and the Zodiacs songs like you do when it's just a regular party with your weirdo friends.

• And above all, don't tell any of your preacher jokes.

My wife was very emphatic about that last rule because she knows I enjoy telling jokes about preachers.

I don't know how I got started collecting jokes about ministers, but I have what must be hundreds in my repertoire, most of which are entirely within the bounds of good taste. You even can tell them at a Rotary Club luncheon.

I have short preacher jokes:

How do you tell the difference between a Northern Baptist preacher and a Southern Baptist preacher?

A Northern Baptist preacher will tell you there ain't no hell. A Southern Baptist preacher will tell you, The hell there ain't!

(For what they pay you to tell jokes at a Rotary Club luncheon, it does just fine.)

I also have long preacher jokes:

Once there was this small town where the Methodist preacher and the Baptist preacher, both of whom were quite young, rode bicycles. One Sunday morning the Methodist preacher was riding his bicycle to church and he spotted the Baptist preacher who was on foot.

"Where is your bicycle, brother?" the Methodist preacher asked.

"My heart is heavy," replied the Baptist preacher, "I think a member of my congregation has stolen it."

The Methodist preacher was appalled. "I think I can help you," he said. "When you're in the pulpit this morning, preach on the Ten Commandments. And when you come to 'Thou Shalt Not Steal,' you bear down on it, and maybe the person who stole your bicycle will get the message and be moved to return it to you."

The Baptist preacher said he would try his colleague's suggestion. Two weeks later they met again. Sure enough, the Baptist preacher had his bicycle back.

"I see my plan worked," the Methodist preacher said.

"Not exactly," said the Baptist preacher. "I did preach on the Ten Commandments, but when I got to 'Thou Shalt Not Commit Adultery,' I remembered where I left my bicycle."

That was the specific joke my wife had in mind when she told me not to tell our minister any of my preacher stories.

It was a marvelous dinner party. Just before we called it a night, the minister turned to me and said, "Hey, did you hear about the preacher who ran off with the church's money and went to Las Vegas?"

I hadn't heard.

"Part of the money he gambled away. Part of it he spent on booze. Part of it he spent on wild women. The rest of it, he just squandered."

Amen, brother.

The Lord's Collection Agent

Rose Emmett, who loved the Lord and didn't mind sharing her meager fixed income with him, received a certified letter a couple of weeks ago in Atlanta from none other than Oral and Evelyn Roberts.

Oral Roberts, of course, is the famous evangelist and faith healer. Evelyn is his wife.

"Dear Sister Emmett," the letter began. "Evelyn and I have knelt and prayed over every word in this letter before dropping it to you."

I probably don't have to tell you what the letter was about, but, for the record, let's go over it again.

Out in Tulsa, Oral Roberts is busy trying to raise money for something called the "City of Faith." What Oral Roberts wants to do is build a sixty-floor hospital complex, which would be the tallest building in Tulsa, as a "testimony to the glory of God."

Oral Roberts' "City of Faith" project has run into problems lately. First, his "partners," donors offering funds for the building, have been a little slow with their contributions. Also, a Tulsa group headed by a local physician has openly opposed Roberts' project as unneeded in the area.

In another fund-raising letter recently, Roberts came up with a real zinger. He says that May 25, he spoke to Jesus and Jesus said he would speak to Oral Roberts' "partners" to assure that the project will be completed.

In his vision, incidentally, Roberts said Jesus appeared as 900 feet tall.

Rose Emmett was one of Oral Roberts' "partners" who had been a little slow in contributing lately. That apparently is what prompted Oral and Evelyn to send her the certified letter.

Mrs. Emmett's daughter sent me the letter. I will quote from parts of it:

"The (City of Faith) construction is standing right outside my window. . . . The enemy is on an all-out attack, and we are facing one of the largest emergencies we have ever faced. Can you imagine what the enemies of this ministry would say if Oral Roberts failed?

"This letter you are now holding can be the greatest letter you have ever held. It can be a door to not only the answer to this emergency we are facing, but also the miracle that you need.

". . . God spoke to my heart to present this emergency to you like this: If you saw a beautiful home or an automobile for sale for $100, you would be foolish not to buy it (even if you had to borrow the $100 and pay it back in small monthly payments.)

"This emergency we are facing is more than just a house, or automobile. It is a crisis for God. If we do not meet it, this ministry will suffer as never before. . . .

"Remember," the letter closed, "if you do not have the $100, we will be praying here in Tulsa that God will lead you, as He did Evelyn and me, to where you can get it."

There was also a P.S., one last plea from Oral Roberts:

"I am going to cancel my plans and wait right here on this (enclosed) envelope from you. . . . Oral Roberts is here praying . . .

waiting . . . watching the mail for the answer from you concerning this emergency for God's work!!!"

You can stop "praying . . . waiting . . . watching" now, Oral. You can also stop counting on Rose Emmett to stroll down to her friendly finance company to pick up the hundred she could have so easily paid back in small monthly payments.

Your letter arrived three months too late. Back in July, Mrs. Rose Emmett, eighty-five, died of a brain tumor in the nursing home where your certified letter was mailed.

"Mrs. Emmett had sent him money before," said her son-in-law. "That's how they knew where to find her. The letter made me boil. Imagine asking an elderly lady like that on a fixed income to go out and borrow the money to give him if she didn't have it."

Just imagine.

The Lord works in mysterious ways, but when it comes to downright chicanery, some of his self-appointed "crusaders"—not mentioning any names—wrote the book.

Interviewing Reverend Falwell

For weeks, this column attempted through legitimate means to reach the Rev. Jerry Falwell, head of the Moral Majority, to discuss his recent "interview" with *Penthouse* magazine.

As most everyone knows, Reverend Falwell claims he was tricked and was not aware that the interview he gave would appear in *Penthouse*, a publication that involves itself with frontal nudity and bad words, and even allows advertisements of liquor.

My attempts to reach Reverend Falwell went for naught, however.

"Does your newspaper print advertisements for moving pictures?" I was asked by one of Reverend Falwell's press aides.

"Of course," I said.

"Even those rated R and X?" the aide asked.

"Those are especially popular with our readers," I answered.

"Then you may NOT interview Reverend Falwell," said the aide, hanging up the phone.

I refuse to be put off that easily. The public has a right to know. Behind these glasses and this frail, unassuming exterior beats the heart of a lion in pursuit of his prey.

I am proud to announce I have just returned from Falwell's Lynchburg, Virginia, headquarters and I got my interview, despite the odds against me.

I disguised myself as a duck.

"Your name?" I was asked at the reception desk.

"A Mr. Chuck Duck to see Reverend Falwell," the receptionist called to Falwell's secretary.

"Go right in, Mr. Duck," said the receptionist.

"What is the purpose of your visit?" the secretary asked.

"I would like to interview Reverend Falwell," I said.

"And whom do you represent?" she continued.

"Duck Daily," I said.

"Does your publication involve itself with any sort of lewdity, such as photographs of naked bodies?"

"An occasional graceful swan in a wading pool," I answered, "but nothing graphic. Mostly, it's just news of interest to ducks."

"Such as?" the secretary persisted.

"Oh, what to do when you get a cold in your quacker, or how to react if your son or daughter starts dating a duckbill platypus."

"I thought you said there was no lewdity in your publication," the secretary said.

"We keep it clean," I said. "We don't even spell out the word 'sex' in our articles. We use the phrase 'you know what.' Last week, for instance, we carried an article titled, 'After Hours Down by the Old Millstream: The You-Know-What Life of a Wild Goose.'"

I could tell I had won the secretary over. She buzzed her boss.

"Reverend Falwell will see you now," she said. I was ushered into the reverend's office. Plush, but not extravagant.

"Chuck Duck of Duck Daily, Reverend Falwell," I said. He was pleasant and open and held steadfastly to his contention that *Penthouse* had hornswoggled him.

"But it won't happen again," he insisted.

As I emerged from his office, a large rabbit sat waiting.

"And whom do you represent, Mr. Rabbit?" asked the secretary.

"*Popular Mechanics*," said the rabbit, winking to me as I waddled out the door.

Out With Sin

Now that the Moral Majority is exercising a great deal of influence upon our government and our society, it should be obvious that sin is out.

During the sixties and seventies, sin definitely was in. Avarice certainly had its moments, but Lust probably was the big sin of that period.

Even women, heretofore believed totally pure, got involved, and women's magazines suddenly were carrying more than recipes for apple strudel.

Lust among women hit an all-time high when a magazine published a centerfold of famous actor Burt Reynolds in the nude.

Maggie Smeltingham, a seventy-seven-year-old spinster from Grove City, Alabama, lusted with such fervor upon seeing Mr. Reynolds' photograph that she swallowed her snuff and had to have her stomach pumped.

"If I met such a man face to face," a local minister said of Mr. Reynolds, "I don't know what word I could use to describe him."

"After I caught my breath," said Maggie Smeltingham, "I would call him, 'Sugar Pie.'"

Now that sin is out, many citizens may have questions concerning exactly what is a sin and what isn't. To help make such distinctions, I contacted my local Moral Majority precinct captain, the Rev. LeRoy "Lucky" Fandango.

The Reverend Fandango is a former professional wrestler who was converted while his head was being rammed into a ring post by his opponent, the Masked Onion No. 2.

"Sin," said Fandango, "is very simple to identify. Just ask these three simple questions:

"1. Is it fun?

"2. Does it feel good?

"3. Is it fattening?

"If you answered 'yes' to any of those questions, you can just bet your boots it's a sin."

"Bet your boots?" I asked.

"Poor choice of words," said Fandango. "Betting, or gambling, offers a certain amount of thrill and excitement, so you can forget it."

I asked Fandango for some more specific examples of sin.

"Gum-chewing, for one," he answered.

"Gum-chewing is a sin?"

"Not in itself," said the Reverend, "but for where it can lead.

"A person starts chewing gum, and the next thing you know, he will go to Lifesavers. After Lifesavers come soft drinks, then booze, and then shooting pool and smoking and cursing and reading filthy magazines."

Moral Majority, of course, has its lists of "no-no" magazines. I asked Fandango to mention a few.

"*Playboy*," he said. I expected that. "And *Hustler* and *Penthouse* and the swimsuit issue of *Sports Illustrated* and *National Geographic*."

National Geographic is a sinful magazine?

"Sections on thatch huts in Ireland are fine," said the Reverend Fandango, "but be sure to stay away from anything having to do with tribal rites or lion hunts."

No drinking, no smoking, no lusting at pictures in magazines. So what does the Moral Majority recommend we do for leisure activities?

"There are lots of possibilities," Fandango explained. "Quiet meditation can be a real hoot once you get into it, and prayer-group softball games are okay, as long as nobody wears short pants. The Rev. Jerry Falwell Coloring Book is available on order, and have you ever just sat and watched milk curdle?"

"Might as well," I answered. "Can't dance."

"Dance?" The Reverend Fandango recoiled in horror. "Don't even say the word!"

Saying Grace

The five-year-old boy who lives in my house is learning to say the blessing.

"LET ME SAY THE BLESSING!" he bellows as we sit down to the table.

"*GOD IS GOOD!*

"*GOD IS NEAT!*

"*LET US ALL THANK HIM!*

"*FOR ALL WE CAN EAT!*

"*YEA, GOD!*"

My stepson is the only person I know who prays in a primal scream. Not only does God get the message, but so does everybody else within six blocks of our kitchen.

The "Yea, God" blessing is his favorite because it is more a cheer than a blessing, and the child is a human megaphone.

But tolerance is very important here because it is a big deal for a child to learn to say the blessing before the family meal. And it's not that easy, either.

First, you have to think of something to say. I remember when my parents first asked me to say the blessing.

MY FATHER: "Say the blessing, son."

MY MOTHER: "And don't mumble."

ME: "ThankyouGodforthemashedpo—"

MY MOTHER: "You're mumbling."

ME: "—tatoesandthegreenbeansandtheporkchopsandthe—"

MY FATHER: "Amen. That was very good, son, but you don't have to thank God for EVERYTHING on the table."

I wasn't going to mention the rutabagas.

After mastering a nice little blessing your mother thinks is "cute," and doesn't hold your old man away from the grub too long, you move into the "clever" blessings stage.

Everybody knew this one:

"Son would you please say grace?" your mother would ask, bowing her head.

"Grace," you would reply, howling at your genius.

"Whaack!" would be the sound of the back of your father's hand across your face.

Then there was the old favorite:

> Good bread,
> Good meat,
> Good Lord,
> Let's eat!

That was good for the backhand across the face AND getting sent to your room without any dinner.

If you really got brave, you could use this one:

> Bless the meat,
> Damn the skins,
> Back your ears,
> And cram it in!

That could get you reform school.

When it came to smart-aleck blessings, my boyhood friend and idol, Weyman C. Wannamaker, Jr., a great American, had no peer.

His all-time classic was the following:

> Thank you, Lord, for this meal,
> We know you are the giver.
> But thank you, Lord, most of all,
> That we ain't havin' liver.

Weyman's father tried to send him to reform school, but the warden was afraid he would be a bad influence on the other "students."

Soon, my stepson will be in the stage of saying "clever" blessings, but I am not going to whack him across the face.

I am going to make him eat liver, smothered in rutabagas.

6

A THIRD LOOK
AT LOVE
AND MARRIAGE

I get letters from people who say, "What have you got against women?" What could I possibly have against women? I've married three of them. . . .

The "Love Boat"

Atlanta is blessed with a number of nearby lakes where people go to fish and swim and sail and ski. It is at a marina on one of these lakes where sits what locals have come to call the "love boat" after all these years.

It is a dreadful little houseboat. Somebody painted it white a long time ago, but now the paint is peeling off.

It has a couple of tiny windows that are always closed. A giant padlock keeps would-be intruders out.

Picture this disaster tied amongst expensive, plush houseboats with three and four bedrooms and air conditioning—floating suites.

"You take somebody for a walk along the marina," one of the lake dwellers was telling me, "and they see beautiful boat after beautiful boat, and then they come to the love boat. They all ask. 'What in the world is this thing?"

For fifteen years, she has appeared at the marina. For fifteen years, every Tuesday and every Thursday, she has arrived in the marina parking lot in an expensive, late-model car.

For fifteen years, every Tuesday and every Thursday, she has gotten out of her car and walked down to the dock, clicking her high heels as she has stridden hurriedly to the love boat.

The locals describe her with awe.

"Beautiful," said one. "An absolutely beautiful woman."

377

"Stunning," said another.

But she never speaks. For fifteen years, she has never spoken to the others tending to their boats along the dock.

She arrives at the love boat, takes out a key and unlocks the door. She goes inside. In a few minutes, she emerges and sweeps the small deck.

Rumor has it she occasionally will sweep the deck of the boat in the scantiest of pajamas. This is only a rumor.

Soon after she has finished sweeping and has returned inside the love boat, he arrives. He arrives in a sleek cabin cruiser. He is as handsome as she is beautiful.

He docks his boat, ties up and goes to the love boat. He doesn't speak to the others, either.

He has his own key. He unlocks the door and goes inside.

Sometimes, it is an hour before the couple emerges. Sometimes, an hour and a half. But always, they emerge together. She walks with him back up the dock to where his cruiser is tied. They do not speak.

They both step onto the cruiser. He pulls away from the dock and then drops her off at the bank, thus saving her the walk back up the dock.

She goes to her car and drives away. He pulls his cruiser away from the marina and speeds to a nearby bridge that crosses the lake. There, he waits until she drives over the bridge.

As she passes, he stands out on his boat. They wave a final goodbye.

For fifteen years every Tuesday and Thursday, the pattern never changed.

Recently, there has been a change. She is still beautiful, they say. She still drives the nice, expensive car. He still comes dashing up in the cruiser, and they still spend the hour or so in the love boat, and then he waits for one last wave goodby at the bridge.

"It's sorta sad now, though," said a man who docks near the love boat. "After fifteen years, they've cut out Tuesdays."

It Runs in the Family

The big joke around the office lately goes something like this:

"What did you get in the Grizzard pool?"

"The Grizzard what?"

"The Grizzard office pool—how long he'll stay married this time."

That's not very funny, especially when you consider that my secretary, Miss Wanda Fribish, paid a buck to enter and got "eight days."

So I've been married a few times before. Big deal. My Uncle Gaylord, the traveling salesman, recently married his fifth wife, Aunt Mildred, and they are blissfully happy.

Aunt Mildred, incidentally, performs at the Bump 'n' Grind Lounge and Truck Stop near Tulsa, which is where she met Uncle Gaylord one night while she was dancing on his table.

As for me, things are going swimmingly at home. It's been six beautiful weeks, and I had forgotten the difference marriage can make in a person's life.

Hot meals on the table. Back rubs. Clean underwear. And the little woman really seems to enjoy it all.

There will be those detractors, of course, who will continue to insist this heavenly wedlock will never last, no matter what.

But they do not realize how serious I am about making this marriage work. Besides, one more bomb and I'm getting precariously close to double figures.

To prove my rightful intentions, I am about to do something drastic. I am about to reveal publicly the contents of my little black book, the one with all the names of all those delightful lovelies with whom I became acquainted during my single days.

That is a big step for any man, but I am more than willing to take it—and perhaps also provide an opportunity for those lonesome, deprived bachelors in the audience to find the right companion.

Any woman whose name appears on the following list is fair game. My wings, once flapping in the single breeze, have been clipped.

Here goes:

• Marcia Glimstein: waitress. Gets off work at midnight and loves to boogie until dawn. Blonde. Also brunette and redhead, depending on which party ring she's wearing. Shriners welcome.

• Sylvia Mudd: automotive maintenance coordinator. (Works in car wash.) Shining disposition. (Personality of a jar of Turtle Wax.) Bugs on her bumper. (Severe acne problem.) Off Thursdays. (And all rainy days.)

• Shanda Ripplemeyer: stewardess. Sort of. Works air-freight runs in the middle of the night. Wears "Marry Me—Ship Free" T-shirts and sweats a lot. Perfect afternoon date, especially if you need to unload a truck.

• Rhonda de Haven: poet, artist, and checkout girl at Kroger store. Latest works include still life of a cucumber and poem entitled, "Ode to a Frozen Pork Chop." Weird, but cute.

• Mary Jane "Pumpkin" Palmer: cheerleader for professional hockey team. The puck has a higher I.Q., but you ought to see her Zambonis.

• Pauline Gooch: elementary-school teacher. Looking for husband. Wants big family. Could stand to lose a few pounds. Could play linebacker for the Steelers. Fun date if you've never been out with the Goodyear Blimp.

• Natalie Foyt: used car salesperson. Divorcee. Gets dates by running classified ads in personals section. Look under "Clean, 1-owner."

• Tina Marina: crack television news investigative reporter. Won Emmy for in-depth series entitled, "Turning Right on Red: Friend or Foe?" Smart. Witty. Raises chinchillas.

• Alexandria "Bulldog" Mankiewitz: terrorist for local militant women's lib group. Shaves three times a week and then eats the razor blades. Tattoo on left forearm reads, "Born to Raise Hell." Former roller derby star. Idea of a good time is rolling truck drivers.

• Candy Cain: Model, Dancer. Call Sly Fox Escort Agency. Furnishes own film. Uncle Gaylord's fourth wife.

Stand by Your Man

There simply is no way to consider a juicy scandal like the one involving former Rep. John Jenrette of South Carolina and his pretty blonde wife without taking sides.

I'll take his. Rita Jenrette has a big mouth.

Years ago, women who told their husbands' secrets in public would be stripped of their bridge club memberships and, in cruder societies, flogged. Today, they get 10,000 words in *Playboy* magazine and an hour on Donahue.

As if John Jenrette didn't have enough troubles. First, he gets caught in the Abscam web. Then, he loses his bid for re-election and has to resign from the House in disgrace and tears. Then, his loving, trusting wife, who insists she will "stand by his side," turns stool pigeon.

In one magazine article, she calls her husband a "flamboyant womanizer" and spares no details. He's a boozer, she tells the world.

The FBI wants to put the poor guy in shackles, and his wife is calling press conferences to tell about the holes in his underwear.

So John Jenrette decides to split for a few days. Who wouldn't want to get away from darling Rita at this point? And while he's gone, the roof really caves in.

He leaves her a bogus number in Miami, so she calls up reporters and announces she's filing for divorce. Then, she's packing her husband's clothes in their Washington townhouse and she comes across a shoe box filled with large bills that amount to $25,000.

Where do you think the money came from, Mrs. Jenrette?

"Probably my husband's take from Abscam," she answers. Whatever happened to "love, honor, and keep your trap shut while the heat's still on?"

Why didn't she say her husband follows little old ladies to the bank and then robs them of their Social Security payments to get all that money? She couldn't have made it any worse on the poor fellow.

Rita Jenrette has been on my bad side ever since she wagged her tongue at Moose Clubs and said she didn't want to go back to another one because the men all walk around with antlers on their heads.

What does Rita Jenrette know? Think of the good that Moose Clubs do simply by never turning away a thirsty wanderer traveling through an otherwise dry province.

I think Rita Jenrette is trying to attract attention to herself, and I wish she would go away. She is a very dangerous woman, as a matter of fact. What if all wives decided to blow the whistle on their husbands when they caught them in a little hanky-panky?

My wife could tell the world I don't pick up after myself, and that I snore, and that I am afraid to take shots, and that I won't watch horror movies alone, and that sometimes I forget to change socks for days, and that one of my little toes is bigger than the other one.

One of my little toes IS bigger than the other one. That is because one night I was walking through the house barefoot with no lights on and rammed one of my little toes into a sofa leg. And it still is swollen and roughly twice the size of my other little toe and it is shaped sort of like Idaho.

What I was doing walking through the house barefoot with no lights on is, I was headed to the kitchen for a cold pork chop.

There is something comforting about a cold pork chop. Unless, I would imagine, you're married to one like Rita Jenrette.

The Orange Sherbet Room

I promised myself that after I got married, again, I wouldn't write those boring domestic sort of columns nobody really wants to read.

But the other day I came home from work and found my wife with two men who were doing something very strange in the living room of our new house.

They were painting the walls orange sherbet.

"What do you think?" asked my wife, beaming.

"You're doing our living room in early banana split?" I asked.

"You don't love me," said my wife.

I do love my wife, but I never have seen the walls of a living room painted the color of orange sherbet.

You know what orange sherbet looks like. Deer hunters wear vests that color so that other deer hunters can spot them in the underbrush a half-mile away and won't think they are deer and blow holes in them. Nobody will ever shoot a deer hunter in my living room.

Decorating a new house has been a completely unique experience for me. When I was a bachelor, which I have been on a number of occasions, it never took me very long to decorate my living quarters.

I had a black Naugahyde couch I always put in the living room, despite the fact that some liberal got up a drive to do away with Naugahyde couches because of the number of little Naugas they had to hit in the head with lead pipes to make even one Naugahyde ottoman.

I usually mounted a velvet portrait of a bullfighter somewhere, a picture of me shooting a basketball in the tenth grade, a Willie Nelson poster, and the plaque they gave me when I covered the Liberty Bowl football game in 1967 that says I am an honorary citizen of Memphis, even though I never have forgiven that city for not disappearing with the Mississippi riverboats.

Most apartments don't have dens, so I didn't have to worry about decorating my den.

If I had had a den, I probably would have put my collection of twenty-four beer bottles from all over the world there, and I also would have spread some *Playboy* and *Time* magazines around, to say that I not only was with it sexually and socially, but I also knew Hodding Carter was not the name of a new plant food.

My bedroom, you ask? Va-va-voom, my bedroom, they ask! Double mattress with a sag on one side and the Roy Rogers spread my mom bought me when I was ten.

Decorating our new house, I have learned I needed a lot of things I never knew I needed.

Ten zillion houseplants, for instance. *Plants?* In the hallways, my wife has planted a couple of *trees*. They're called *foyerus interruptus* or some such, and the kids want me to build them a house in the top of one.

We have new light fixtures, ceiling fans, French doors that separate this room from that room, more new bookshelves than your local public library, and lots of new trinkets.

I mean, we have *lots* of new trinkets. Little glass doodads that look sort of like the glass blower was on glue or something. In order to get ready for Christmas early, we even have a five-decked, glass-enclosed set of figurines that depict the first fifteen years of the life of Christ.

We have a wood-carved pig, four brass ducks and fifteen paintings of flowers and little girls in bonnets. And nothing made out of Naugahyde.

"What effect," I asked my wife, "are you trying to create with a room the color of orange sherbet?"

"You have no taste whatsoever," she replied. "It's not orange sherbet, it's 'coral,' and I want an outside-indoors effect, Bahamian, sort of Humphrey Bogart in *Casablanca*, Rick's Bar with the ceiling fan and all of that."

I went down to the basement where all my old furniture is stored, dusted off my black Naugahyde couch and took a nap.

Tips for No. 3

When actor Ryan O'Neal gets married to actress Farrah Fawcett, Ryan O'Neal and I will have something in common. We both will be into our third marriage.

Mr. O'Neal and Miss Fawcett plan to tie the knot as soon as possible, the couple announced recently from Venice, which is something Mr. O'Neal and I don't have in common.

I made the announcement of my engagement to No. 3 while standing on the bar in a beer joint located just on the outskirts of Fort Deposit, Alabama.

You would be surprised how many people get married for the third time. A close friend of mine also just got married for the third time.

"Couple more of these," he said to me at the reception after the wedding, "and we'll have enough (ex's) between us for a girls' field hockey team with two cheerleaders."

I didn't think that was very funny, and neither did my friend's new bride, who elbowed him in the belly when he said it.

I wish Mr. O'Neal and Miss Fawcett the very best. They deserve each other, say Hollywood insiders.

I just hope Mr. O'Neal realizes it's different the third time around. The first time you have no earthly idea what you are getting into, and you normally botch it.

The second time, you are a veteran, but still prone to many rookie mistakes. If you go back a third time, you have entered the big leagues, and there can be no more excuses.

Around poker tables, they have a saying: "Put up or shut up, cowboy." The same applies to a man entering his third marriage.

I have nearly eight months of being married for the third time under my belt. It has been a learning experience, from which I now offer the following advice to Mr. O'Neal and to any other man about to go for a three-bagger, an awful choice of words. How to make it work the third time around:

• Go shopping in antique stores with her once in a while, even if it absolutely kills you. It beats shopping for antiques in a bar at midnight, which, you must realize by now, is no fun at all.

• Don't complain if she puts a black sock with a navy blue sock. Life is too short to spend one second worrying about socks.

• Don't come home a-drinkin' with lovin' on your mind. (Loretta Lynn said that before I did, but it's still strong advice.)

• Don't fool around.

• If you are going to fool around anyway, when you get caught (notice I said, "when" instead of "if"), lie like a dog.

• Speaking of lying, tell her she's pretty even when she isn't wearing make-up and her hair is in curlers and she's wearing flip-flops and your old football jersey.

• Don't give her a new blade for her hacksaw on your anniversary.

• Shop for her underwear.

• Pick yours up off the lousy bedroom floor once in a while.

• When you are in a restaurant alone with just her, the champagne, and the candlelight, never say, "You know, this place has really gone downhill since I and (a) my first wife, (b) my second wife, were here."

• Keep a bottle of mouthwash on your bedside table.

• Have some laughing children around.

• Refuse all telephone numbers.

• When there is obviously something wrong with her, and you ask, "What's wrong with you?" and she replies, "Nothing," leave the house immediately. There is something wrong with her.

• Forget candy and flowers. By now you must have figured out what they really like are airplane tickets to places where the sun shines, and Volvos.

• Her back itches, too, dummy. You scratch occasionally.

• Above all, being married the third time means always having to say you're sorry. If you had done that the first two times instead of pouting, there wouldn't have been the need for a third time.

White Bread or Bust

My wife has insisted I give up white bread.

"There is absolutely no food value in white bread," she informed me.

"But it tastes good," I replied.

"Hedonist," said my wife.

I've given up so much already. I'm not supposed to eat a lot of eggs or drink a lot of milk because of cholesterol. Cake and pie and candy do something strange to my blood-sugar level.

Cokes. I used to drink a lot of Cokes, but the doctor said switch to diet drinks. On diet drink cans, there is a warning about saccharin causing cancer in laboratory animals. I assume those animals are rats.

I don't worry about rats getting cancer that much. Rats are little and they just sort of look unhealthy in the first place. When they find out a couple of Diet Pepsis will give an elephant cancer. I'll become much more concerned.

What else? I don't smoke anymore, I gave up vodka tonics out of respect for my head and liver. Now that I'm married again, I'm on the streets a lot less.

White bread was sort of my last holdout. Let me tell you what I like about white bread:

It's soft. I hate hard bread. When I lived in Chicago, all they ever served in restaurants was hard, dark bread.

"What will you have sir?" the waitress would ask.

"Tuna salad, hold the hockey pucks," I would reply.

"Tuna salad, no bread!" the waitress would scream to the cook.

How I longed for some of those marvelous, delicious "brown 'n' serve" rolls, the kind they used to serve in truck stop restaurants of my youth with the $1.25 hamburger steak (which is now the "chopped sirloin" that goes for seven bucks).

White bread makes better sandwiches, too. Take, for example, a banana sandwich, a rare delicacy I used to carry to school for lunch. Cover the inside of two pieces of white bread with mayonnaise, then put the bread around several slices of barely ripe banana, and the result is divine.

Imagine a banana sandwich on dark, hard bread. The mere thought of such a hideous concoction turns my stomach.

"Go ahead and eat white bread and ruin your digestive system and see if I care," my wife says.

"Toast me a loaf of that dark bread and I'll go replace the shingles on the roof," I reply, and the white bread/dark bread debate is off and running again.

She will win in the end, of course. I will give up white bread, just like I did all the other pleasures I miss.

But I have made one promise to myself that I hope I am allowed to keep. It is a dream that is constant:

On my sixty-fifth birthday, I am going to a nice, cool place like the grassy bank of a river. I am going to take with me a carton of Marlboro cigarettes, a quart of vodka, several bottles of tonic, lime, and crushed ice, a loaf of thinly sliced white bread, mayonnaise, a banana, and a nineteen-year-old girl.

I am going to smoke all the Marlboro cigarettes, drink all the vodka tonics I please, and top it all off with a banana sandwich on white.

The nineteen-year-old girl?

After I've finished with all the other stuff and if I'm still alive, I will sing her a love song.

"Love" Versus "Lust"

I always try to listen closely when the pope makes one of his official statements. As I understand it, His Holyship has one of the better pipelines to the Big Rulemaker, and I don't want to miss anything I might be tested on later.

But I, along with millions of others, was caught completely off guard with the recent papal pronouncement that it is a sin to lust after your own wife.

Now there's a real kick in the libido if I ever heard one.

We went all through this lust business four years ago when soon-to-be-elected President Carter admitted he had "lusted in his heart" after women other than the voluptuous Rosalynn.

What is it about the presidential election? Four years later, soon-to-be-unelected President Carter hasn't got time to lust after anybody with Ronald Reagan on his back, but it's the pope, of all people, who brings the subject up again.

I like the pope. He's got a nice smile. He appears to have a sense of humor, and he is a warm, sensitive man of peace.

But he doesn't know beans when it come to love and lust. Otherwise, he couldn't have become pope, if you know what I mean.

But a worldly person like myself, well, I know my share about love, and I have personally lusted on a number of occasions, most recently during the movie *Dressed to Kill*, starring Angie Dickinson.

A man who can watch Angie Dickinson in certain scenes in *Dressed to Kill* and think about needing more salt for his popcorn is badly in need of an oil change.

And as far as lusting after one's wife is concerned, that's been the problem for a long time now. Instead of lusting after their wives, men have been lusting after their secretaries and their neighbors' wives, and the 8.5 at the end of the bar. And if more men would, in fact, lust after what's in their own ballpark, watch the bottom fall out of the divorce rate.

I've read a number of explanations of "what the pope was trying to say." The best one said what the pope meant was a man should "love" his wife and not merely "lust" after her as a "sex object."

Okay, I think most men can certainly live within those boundaries.

But before we put this matter to bed, or rest, maybe we should make some clear distinctions between "love" and "lust."

"Love" is when you bring her home a present and it is not a special occasion.

"Lust" is when you bought it at Frederick's of Hollywood, and Candy Barr wouldn't be caught dead wearing it.

"Love" is when you take a romantic cruise together aboard a sailboat.

"Lust" is when the boat belongs to her husband, who is in Cleveland on business.

"Love" is when you met at a church social.

"Lust" is when she answered your ad in *Hustler.*

"Love" is when she watches "The NFL Today" to learn all of football's positions.

"Lust" is when you have memorized every diagram in *More of the Joy of Sex.*

"Love" is when he invites you to a movie.

"Lust" is when it is playing in his bedroom, the one with the mirrors and burning incense.

Got the picture? What a fun column to write, and I would like to point out just one more thing before I go:

Is it just my imagination that the people who usually are the most vocal about sex also are the people who engage in it the least?

Nineteen Was a Long Time Ago

She was ten the first time I saw her. So was I. She was tall and gangly and put together sort of funny.

"Is that girl going to be in our class?" asked one of my pals as we looked her over the first day of the new school year.

"I hope not," I said. The last thing we needed in the sixth grade, I reasoned, was another girl. What we needed was a good second baseman. Funny how childish priorities go.

But we both grew, she out of her gangliness. Suddenly her proportions were nearly perfect. Me, I was out of my preoccupation with baseball and into a keen interest in the opposite sex.

It was in the ninth grade that the whole blasted thing began. We went on a Sunday school hayride together, and I had never been kissed until I was kissed by her, and so, six years later, I married her.

You don't know a damn thing when you are nineteen. It should be against the law to get married when you are nineteen.

But I was spending every week missing her, and I was absolutely terrible and out of place with anybody else. I knew when I was thirteen that I would marry her, so why wait any longer?

The little church was packed. My best man, as we stood in the anteroom awaiting her arrival down the aisle, said to me:

"Look, stupid. I can have us both 500 miles away from here by morning. Just say the word."

The next morning I was in our honeymoon bed.

We lasted—I forget exactly—four years, maybe. What went wrong? I'll tell you what went wrong. We were kids, children.

I went one way in my head. She went another. It broke our mothers' hearts.

So there I am in this huge department store and people are running all around doing their Christmas shopping, and the last person I figured I would run into, I ran into.

She looked great. Still blonde and thin. Still with the fashion. We talked for fifteen minutes.

She lives in another city. She has a husband and two kids. She was home just for a visit.

"Tell me about your wife," she said.

I raved.

"And how is it with you?" I asked.

"He's great," she replied. "I would have never made it without him.

"You always wanted to be a writer," she went on. "Are you satisfied now?"

"What's satisfied?" I asked back. "The more you get, the more you want. It's human."

We went back and forth like that. In these situations, there is another sense that takes over. You *sense* what to say, and what not to say, and what to ask about, and what not to ask about.

And you *sense*—simultaneously—when it is time to end it. The present reality hovers.

"We were so young, weren't we?" she asked, adjusting her coat to leave.

"We didn't know a damn thing," I answered.

"I'm such a different person now. All that back then is like a dream. God, how did you put up with me? Remember the time I cried when it was my birthday and you went to a ball game? How stupid."

"That wasn't stupid. I shouldn't have gone to the ball game."

"Do you still complain about your socks not being mated exactly right?"

"Yeah. My wife goes nuts when I do that."

"There is one good thing, though," she said.

"What's that?"

"Neither one of us got fat, did we?"

"No, neither one of us got fat."

I took her hand and shook it. She went one way. I went another.

7

CATS AND DOGS

The more I think about it, I really don't dislike cats. It's cat-lovers who are dangerous, and that is explained in detail here. As for dogs, I've never had one to ask, "Where have you been for so long?" "Why didn't you call if you knew you were going to be late?" and "Why do we never talk?" If for no other reason, I appreciate dogs for never having asked me questions I prefer not to answer. . . .

"Butterbean" Goes to Camp

I first thought our dog, who is large and shaggy, was mentally retarded. That is because our dog was doing some strange things. I will list some of the strange things our dog was doing.

• Eating plants. House plants, out-of-the-house plants, also trees and flowers. Imagine this big, shaggy dog walking up to a blooming hybeiwhatzit and eating the sucker, petal by petal. If there were any bugs or bees in the plants or flowers that fell victim to my dog, she would eat them too.

• Wrestling with our youngest child. He is four and about a third the size of our dog. Our dog was making the child's life miserable. Whenever the child made any sort of quick move, the dog would think he wanted to wrestle her, and she would pounce upon the poor little snipper and flip him around like he was no more than a stuffed toy. The child would cry, quite obviously, which would make the dog bark. None of this sort of thing ever happened to me when I was single.

• Running away from home. I spent a great deal of money on a fence for my dog. She would have been out of Alcatraz in eight seconds. My dog would dig her way under the fence and then disappear and I would have to go look for her. Once she escaped and I found her talking to sailors in a bar in Norfolk.

On top of all that, our dog was quite disobedient. "Butterbean" (not her real name) would not come when you called her, nor would she do any tricks, nor would she eat anywhere but seated at the table. (She would wrestle the four-year-old for his chair, then

391

tease and tantalize him with scraps and bites from her plate, poor kid.)

As head of the family, I decided to do something about our dog. I took her to the vet.

"There is nothing wrong with your dog mentally,' said my vet. "She's just a high-strung animal with a dominating personality. You should send her to obedience camp."

Dogs go to camp? Certainly, said my vet, and when they return they don't eat plants, terrorize four-year-olds or hustle drinks off sailors, and actually will eat Alpo off a dish on the back porch.

This I had to see, so I enrolled our dog in an obedience camp. The first week was murder. She short-sheeted two counselors, mugged poodles for their canteen money and called me at two o'clock in the morning, collect, howling to come home.

At the end of the week I had to pay for the damages she had caused (she chewed up all the volleyballs and flushed cherry bombs down the commodes) and then pleaded with the camp director, who once trained killer dogs for combat, to allow her to stay.

"Dogs will be dogs," I laughed.

"Your mutt's a menace to society," he said.

The second week, things began to get a little better. She made a friend—a Doberman. They chased alligators together in a nearby swamp, then shared a large tree for lunch.

Counselors reported her to be less aggressive and even taking part in the crafts classes. She made a leather belt and a wallet with "Dad" etched across the front. I must say I was touched.

The third week, she wasn't the same dog at all. She was elected council representative from her kennel and even had begun helping some of the younger, less experienced campers learn the ropes.

"Dear Mr. Grizzard," the camp director wrote me after the third week. "I am happy to say 'Butterbean' (not her real name) is progressing wonderfully, and she will be able to come home very soon."

Well, that day finally has arrived. This afternoon I will drive out to the obedience camp to pick up our dog. Despite all the problems in the past, we've missed the old girl, and it will be nice to have her home.

The thing with the Doberman never worked out, incidentally. One afternoon he tried to get fresh with our dog and she broke three of his paws, tied a knot in his tail and put him in the camp infirmary for six weeks.

The Comeback Cat

I have a very real problem at my house involving a cat. I don't like cats. I never have liked cats. I never will like cats, and that is the problem.

A cat has moved into my house. I went out of town for a couple of days. When I returned, I opened the front door, and there stood a cat—a brown cat with a speck of white on its tail.

I say "its" tail because I don't know if the cat is a boy or a girl, and I don't know how to tell the difference without resorting to some unthinkable snooping.

First, I asked the cat a question, which was an idiotic thing to do, but have you ever noticed how people are always asking their pets, especially cats, questions?

"Mommie's little darling want some din-din?" Etc.

I asked the cat, "How did you get inside my house?"

The doors had been locked. The windows were secure. Maybe the cat came down the chimney?

"Did you come down the chimney?" I asked the cat.

I did it again. I asked a dumb animal a question. What do you do next, stupid, suggest a couple of games of backgammon?

I shooed the cat out of my house, and so much for my cat problem.

Hardly. The next morning, I awakened to something furry crawling around on my head. The cat was back, and the cat was in my bed. That's impossible. I had put the cat out myself, and I had locked the doors and pulled the damper down in the chimney.

"Who put you up to this?" I asked the cat, obviously no longer in control of my faculties.

I put the cat out again.

But the cat came back. Don't ask me how the cat gets in my house, but it does. I finally reached such a point of frustration that I enlisted the help of one of my neighbors, Mrs. Framingham, a worrisome old biddy who keeps a lot of cats around. I told her how the cat was driving me up a wall.

"You wouldn't hurt the little darling, would you?" Mrs. Framingham asked me.

"I wouldn't consider any permanent injuries," I responded.

"You lay one hand on that cat, and I'll break both your arms," said Mrs. Framingham, who had a typical cat-lover's attitude: Be kind to animals, or I'll break your nose.

"Why not give the poor little creature a chance?" she went on.

"It obviously likes you, and it needs a home. Why not just accept it?"

No way. Cats are sneaky—and try to get a cat to roll over and play dead or chase a stick or do all the neat things a dog will do.

Cats think they are above that. Plus, I don't want a pet that bathes more often than I do.

"Shush," said Mrs. Framingham. "Give the poor dear two weeks. In two weeks you will love it. The two of you will be inseparable. That's the beauty of cats. They grow on you."

I gave the cat two weeks. I still don't want a cat. Besides, while I was typing this, I thought of an obvious solution to the problem.

All I have to do is make the cat feel unwanted. No rough stuff, just a few subtle hints that no purring, meowing little pest is going to get the best of me, no matter what the old bat down the street says.

You don't think I mean it? From now on, daddy's little precious is going to have to sleep in its own room. And our trip to the basketball game next week is definitely off.

Scooter

Kathy Williams is an attorney. She lives in Avondale, a suburb of Atlanta. Until five months ago, she lived alone. Then, Scooter came to live with her.

Scooter was a fuzzy brown puppy. If he had any papers, he didn't have them on him.

"He just walked up out of nowhere," said Kathy Williams. "He was wearing a collar, but he had no license. I fed him. He just stayed. He would hang around in my back yard, except when he walked across the street to play with the children over there. He loved children. And they loved him."

One day she came home from work and Scooter was gone. Dogs often wander away. He would be back.

He never came back.

"What was so funny about this was I had never really cared about dogs before," Kathy Williams explained. "But there was something about this little dog. I called him 'Scooter' because he sort of scooted along on his tummy when he ran. He was just a mixed breed, but after he was gone, I really missed him.

For five weeks, Scooter was missing. Kathy Williams put an ad in the paper, under "Lost Dogs." She watched the papers to see if anybody might have found her dog.

There is a lake in Avondale. Every night she would walk around the lake and call for her dog, hoping he might return.

What else she did was visit DeKalb County Animal Control once a week to see if Scooter had been picked up.

"I was so afraid they would find him and kill him before I could claim him," she said. "I told everybody down there what he looked like, and I had them on alert for my dog."

Last Tuesday, Kathy Williams made her weekly visit to the De-Kalb pound. She found Scooter.

"I've never been so excited in my life," she said. "I couldn't wait to get him out of there."

Here is where the plot thickens.

A woman at the desk told Kathy Williams not to reclaim her dog. When a dog is picked up in DeKalb County, she explained, an officer writes out a citation for whoever reclaims the dog. That person then has to go to court and pay a fine for violating the DeKalb leash law.

"She told me to wait until Thursday, when Scooter had been in the pound for seven days, and then I could just adopt him. That would cost me $41, but he got shots and everything, and I wouldn't have to go to court or pay a fine," Kathy Williams explained.

"I walked back into the cage area, and there was this guy named Jeff, and he told me to do the same thing. I mentioned I really didn't own the dog, that he had just taken up at my house, but he said it didn't matter. If I reclaimed the dog, then I would have to get the ticket."

Kathy Williams took the advice. Before she left, however, she made certain everybody involved knew to make certain nothing happened to Scooter.

"They laughed at me because I went on about it for so long," she said. "But I just couldn't have anything happen to my dog."

Kathy Williams left Scooter at the pound. Thursday morning, she returned to pick him up. On her way, she stopped to buy him a new collar, some flea and tick powder, and a Slim-Jim as a reward.

"When I walked into the place, I could sense something was wrong," she said. "I went back to the cage were Scooter had been, and he wasn't in there." Kathy Williams started asking about her dog. Nobody would give her a straight answer. Finally, somebody gave her a straight answer. There had been a mistake. Scooter had been killed.

"They tried to give me another dog," said Kathy Williams. "I didn't want another dog. I wanted Scooter."

"We made a terrible mistake," said Major Harold Davis, who is in charge of the DeKalb facility. "A note was written and attached to a dog, saying to hold the dog for the lady. But the note was placed on the wrong dog.

"But people ought to think about these things. If your dog got picked up, don't take a chance. Get that rascal out of here. Take the ticket. Pay the fine."

Kathy Williams isn't sleeping so well these nights because she didn't do exactly that. But why was she given advice to the contrary by personnel at the pound?

And how could somebody be careless enough to kill the wrong dog?

"I told that lady," said Major Davis, "when she gets ready for another pet, to call us. We'll help her in any way we can."

A nice gesture. But somehow I get the feeling she won't be calling.

Pet Killer

You have to know basset hounds to love them. I have known and loved two. I lost one in a custody battle. The other, who is three months old, lives in my house now. The dog's name is Barney. Soon he will be the size, and shape, of a canoe.

Somebody else who owns a basset hound was telling me, "They're awful dogs, really. They bark too much, they get their ears in their food and then they get their ears on everything in the house, they won't mind, and they shed all over your furniture.

"But you take one look at those big, sad eyes and you're hooked."

I know the feeling. So do Tom and Diana Thorington of Atlanta. They have a basset hound. His name is Lance. He's two years old and he has national champions on both sides of his family. (If you really love a dog, it doesn't matter if his pedigree is more impressive than your own.)

A couple of weeks ago the Thoringtons took Lance when they went to an afternoon party at a friend's house. The friend has a large lot, so they let Lance out to play with the friend's dog, a mutt. Basset hounds are not snooty.

Sometime later the people at the party heard shots being fired across the way at a neighbor's house. The host of the party and the neighbor were not close friends. Soon you will see why.

The host and Tom Thorington left the party to see what the shooting was about. They saw the neighbor firing away at Lance and the mutt.

When they reached the man, the mutt was already dead. They didn't see Lance.

"Did you shoot my dog?" Tom Thorington screamed at the man.

"Shot two of 'em," the man replied, laughing.

"You are a rotten, no-good son of a bitch," said Tom Thorington, who was being nice.

The man put his rifle, a .22, to Tom Thorington's chest.

"I think I'll shoot you next," he said.

Tom and his friend started to walk away.

"I'll shoot you in the back," said the man.

Tom and his friend kept walking. They got lucky. Crazy with the rifle didn't shoot.

Tom began calling to Lance. A couple of minutes later he heard a muffled sound from the weeds. It was Lance, with four bullets in his throat. And more, all over his body. There were even bullet holes in Lance's long, floppy ears.

"He was shot at least ten times," Diana Thorington told me later.

"Can you imagine somebody sighting down on a basset hound TEN times?"

I've never heard of a blacker heart.

The Thoringtons rushed Lance to the local vet.

"The vet told us to forget it," said Diana. "He said there was no way Lance would make it. But we begged him to try. We love that dog so much."

Another dog, named Rip, gave some blood, and a miracle happened. Lance lived.

Okay, some nut shoots your dog and then threatens to shoot you. What do you do about it?

"We went to the police," said Diana Thorington, "but they said there was nothing much they could do. The laws about shooting dogs are pretty weak. The police said if we filed charges it would just mean a big hassle, and probably nothing much would come of it. The man was on his own property."

It is not written that life must necessarily be fair. So the Thoringtons' friend's dog is dead, and the Thoringtons' basset hound, with a little help from his friend, barely made it, and el sicko with the gun is still off his leash.

It is written, however, that a creep who would kill one family pet and then pull a trigger ten times on what is one of God's most loving creatures will, sooner or later, get his.

Every dog has his day, so to speak. Knowing that, I rest a little easier. Not much, but a little.

8

SPECIAL
OCCASIONS

The holidays. They bring out the best and the worst in people.
April 15 is not a holiday, of course, but it should be. It brings out the
most in people. . . .

The Morning After

News item: Another New Year's Eve is just around the corner.
"Harvey, wake up, Harvey."
"Whatsmattah?"
"Nothing's the matter, Harvey. I just want you to wake up."
"Whatimeisit?"
"Past 10, Harvey."
"Gladys, why do I have to wake up, Gladys? It's New Year's Day. I wannna sleep until the football games."
"I can't sleep, Harvey. Not after your performance last night."
"What did I do last night?"
"You don't remember?"
"I don't remember, Gladys. I was drunk."
"Drunk? 'Drunk' isn't the word for it, Harvey. You were 'blitzed.' You were 'stoned.' You were sickening."
"What could I have possibly done that was so bad, Gladys?"
"I'll tell you what you did. You made an absolute fool out of yourself at 'the Blantons' party. I can never show my face in this neighborhood again."
"So I got a little drunk. It was New Year's Eve, Gladys. I always get drunk on New Year's Eve."
"Harvey, you danced with Harriet Blanton's dog all night long."
"So?"
"So you thought you were dancing with Harriet Blanton. You told the dog how much you were enjoying the hors d'oeuvres and you tried to get Harriet to roll over for a sausage ball."

"I did that?"

"That's not all, Harvey."

"Omigod. What else?"

"You got into a fight with Ralph Beetleman."

"The skinny guy with the fat wife?"

"Gloria."

"Gloria who?"

"Gloria Beetleman, Ralph Beetleman's wife. She's the reason for the fight. You asked Ralph what he fed his land whale."

"I said that?"

"You said it, Harvey. Then, Ralph Beetleman took a punch at you. He missed, but Gloria kneed you in the belly and you were out for half an hour."

"So I danced with a dog and insulted a beer truck. Big deal, Gladys."

"There's more, Harvey. Your poured a drink on Mildred Pillingham."

"Where?"

"In the living room."

"No, I mean . . ."

"Down the front of her dress, Harvey. Mildred Pillingham is in my car pool."

"I don't want to hear any more, Gladys."

"You're going to hear it, Harvey. I am ruined in this town, and you are going to hear it all. Your burned a hole in the Blantons' new couch with a cigarette. You ate the floral arrangement in the dining room. You put your head in the punch bowl, and when the party was over, we found you in the backyard howling at the moon."

"With Harriet Blanton's dog?"

"With Harriet Blanton. She got just as wasted as you did."

Artie's Tax Service

Some people, believe it or not, actually file their income tax returns weeks and months ahead of the dreaded April 15 deadline. These people are normally well off, and they have their own accountants and use their refund checks to go to resorts in Mexico or the Caribbean.

(You may be asking, "What is a refund check?" Don't bother. It would only confuse you.)

I feel sorry for these people. They don't realize what fun and excitement they are missing by not waiting until the last minute to have their income taxes prepared.

It is the same thrill you get from waiting until the last minute to do your Christmas shopping or to rent a tuxedo for the annual Moose Lodge Dance and Fish Fry.

Procrastinators, like myself, enjoy the adventure and danger of living on the brink of disaster. Only a few days remain before the fifteenth, but I haven't even bothered to look for my W-2 forms yet.

That's because I can do what I always do—wait until a couple of hours before the deadline and pay a visit to Artie (Three Fingers) McGuirk's Friendly Tax Service and Pool and Recreation Hall.

You would love Artie's place. Get your taxes done, shoot a little pool or maybe talk to Artie about important sports questions like point spreads.

This is a special year at Artie's incidentally. Artie is back after a brief absence. Ask where Artie has been, and one of his friendly goons, er, associates, will answer simply, "On a long trip. What's it to ya?"

Of course, there are other places I could go to get my taxes done at the eleventh hour. You hear about them on television about this time every year.

There is Mr. Loophole Tax Service, for instance. What bothers me about Mr. Loophole, however, is all the offices are in trailers sitting in shopping center parking lots. What if I am audited and come back to Mr. Loophole looking for help and there is a shopping center carnival where the trailer used to be parked?

Then, there's H&R Schlock. The man in the three-piece suit, seated in a comfortable chair, comes on the screen and tells you all the reasons you should use his tax service.

"Reason No. 11 for using H&R Schlock Tax Service: If the IRS calls you in for an audit, we'll give you a new tie for your appointment."

Artie and his trained staff of professionals offer even more:

• All preparations and consultations are strictly confidential. As Artie says, "One peep about who fixed this return, and you'll sleep with the fishes."

• All possible deductions are taken. Artie is very careful here. One year he missed some deductions for one of his best clients, Crazy Carlo (The Shark) DeRogatis, and Crazy Carlo deducted two of Artie's fingers as a penalty.

• Each member of Artie's staff has spent years learning about taxes. One spent ten to twenty in Joliet learning you can't hide the fifty Gs you picked up in a land fraud deal.

• If you are indicted and thrown into the slammer, Artie will send you cigarettes and reading material once a month until your release.

• If you do happen to get a refund check, Artie insists you bring it to him to be cashed. You pay only a small service charge of ninety-five percent.

• If you try to cash your refund check elsewhere and take a little trip to Mexico or the Caribbean, Artie will have a member of his staff consult with you further when you return—and your tax problems will be over.

Permanently.

Mayhem and Marshmallow Chickens

Millions of Americans will take part in the annual ritual of the Easter egg hunt today. The adults will hide candy eggs and other sugary surprises, and the children, dressed in their Easter finery, will vie to see who can fill his or her basket first.

Among other bad things that will happen, there will be a lot of arguments.

Larry, eight, and Debbi, five, will happen upon the chocolate bunny prize, hidden in the tall weeds near the swing set, at precisely the same moment.

"It's mine!" Larry will scream.

"I saw it first!" Debbi will counter.

Both children will being to cry and pull at the choclate bunny.

"Now, children," Larry's mom will interrupt. "Let's settle this fairly. Which of you is the oldest?"

"I am, Mom," Larry will say.

"Then you get the chocolate bunny prize," his mother will conclude. Mothers always take care of their own at an Easter egg hunt.

"Waaaaaaaa!" Debbi will scream, running to her mother. "Larry's mother took my chocolate bunny prize and gave it to Larry because he is older than me!"

"Don't worry, darling," Debbi's mom will say. "I'll fix that pushy broad."

A lot of hair-pulling and scratching and screaming later, the two adults will be pulled apart by the cops. Meanwhile, Larry has dropped the chocolate bunny prize onto the ground and the dog is eating it, and Debbi has brained a four-year-old for his marshmallow chicken.

That's another thing about Easter egg hunts. The younger the child, the more hazardous egg hunts can be to both the kid's mental and physical well-being.

Let's say you are two. You barely know how to locate your mouth. And they expect you to be able to run around in an open field and find Easter eggs?

The older kids will find eggs, of course. They'll find 'em by the dozens, but you won't have a blasted thing in your stupid basket, so you will get frustrated and you will start to cry because you feel inadequate. Later, when you flunk out of college and join a religious cult, it will all be because you couldn't find an egg when you were two.

There also is the chance you won't live through the egg hunt in order to grow up to be a total failure. Kids are vicious when it comes to eggs. They will trample other children, hit other children with sticks, kick other children—whatever it takes to wrest an egg from the possession of an opponent in the hunt.

We used to have egg hunts at my school. I hated them because of Frankie Garfield, the school bully. At first, Frankie would go to the trouble of actually making an effort to find his own eggs.

But bending over to pick up eggs was a lot of work for Frankie, so he eventually took to waiting until after school and then searching through every kid's basket and taking his pick of the loot.

Once he caught Alvin Bates hiding a creme-filled duck in his back pocket. Frankie decorated Alvin's face with the creme-filled duck and then hit him in the belly. Alvin always stayed home sick after that on egg hunt day.

The cruelest Easter egg hunt story I know, however, occurred in Philadelphia, where they put on an egg hunt for children in the outfield grass before a Phillies baseball game. The fans booed the kids who couldn't find eggs.

There is something about an Easter egg hunt that brings out the worst in all of us.

A Mother's Side of the Story

Lillian Pye had a son. His name was James Scroggins, and he was an Atlanta policeman, like his daddy before him. He was also a husband and the father of three children.

James Scroggins was thirty when he died last October. Lillian Pye remembers every detail of what happened to her son.

"He had worked his regular day shift at the police department," she began as we talked last week. As we talked, I could hear the hurt in her voice. It still runs deep.

"He went home, and then he got in his car, a Volkswagen, and

started for night classes at DeKalb South. He wasn't drinking or
anything. He was just going to class.

"There was this other car, and an eighteen-year-old was driving it.
A boy. He lost control of his car. He hit a bridge, and then he ran into
my son. The boy's car skidded 500 feet.

"It took them two and one half hours to cut my son out of the car.
They would never even let me see the car. All he ever said after the
wreck was, 'I'm an Atlanta policeman. Take me to Grady.' He knew
Grady had the best when it came to emergencies."

When they finally got Lillian Pye's son out of his car, it was too
late to do anything more for him.

The other driver wasn't seriously injured. It happens that way
sometimes.

"He was drunk," Lillian Pye said. "That boy was drunk." There is
bitterness to go with her hurt.

"They told me when they took him out of the car, he was filthy and
nasty and he was drunk."

DeKalb County charged the other driver with vehicular homicide.
He went to trial. I'll let Lillian Pye tell the rest of it.

"At the trial, you should have seen that boy. His lawyer had told
him exactly what to do. He had gotten a shave and a close haircut. He had on a new suit of clothes. He pleaded for mercy from the
court.

"And you know what the judge gave him? He gave that boy five
years probation and a $1,000 fine. That's it. Five years probation and
a $1,000 fine. My son was killed, and that boy got off free. They
didn't even take his license away.

"And you know something else? We never heard from him, and we
never heard from his family. Not one word. They didn't even want to
know if my son's wife and children could keep a roof over their
heads, and they had a rough time of it until all the insurance was
settled.

"I wrote the judge a letter and I said, 'I know you have a job to do,
but you didn't do it very well.' I don't want that boy to get away with
this. I don't want him driving around so he can do the same thing
again."

I talked to DeKalb traffic investigators about the accident that
killed James Scroggins. They agree with Lillian Pye that justice
wasn't done.

But there is nothing they can do now. There is nothing anybody
can do.

On second thought, yes there is. Lillian Pye admits she's called
"everybody in town," television commentators, newspaper people.

All she wanted, I think, was the opportunity to tell her side of the story.

Now, she's had that opportunity, and what we can do for her is listen.

A mother misses her dead son on Mother's Day. What we can do for her is listen and, if just for a moment, share her hurt and her frustration.

It's the least, the very least, we can do.

The Last Hunt

Thanksgiving reminds different people of different things. It always reminds me of the first and last time I went hunting. That is because the first and last time I went hunting was on Thanksgiving Day when I was twelve.

Going hunting after the big Thanksgiving feast was sort of a tradition among the menfolk in my family, and when you were a boy child and reached the age of twelve, you finally were able to go along.

Imagine my glee when my grandfather and uncles and cousins explained what we would be doing on the annual Thanksgiving Day hunt:

First, we would carry these heavy guns and hike over half the county, through briars and under barbed-wire fences and down in gullies, if that was where the dogs took us.

Then, if anybody happened to spot a rabbit, he would promptly blow it to bits.

After the Thanksgiving Day feast the year I was twelve, I hid in the pump house and hoped they would leave on the hunt without me.

"What's the matter, son?" asked my uncle when the dogs flushed me out. "You don't want to go hunting with the rest of the men?" He put a lot of emphasis on the "men."

I'd rather spend the afternoon with my foot caught under Grandma's rocking chair is what I wanted to say, but I didn't say that at all.

"I was just in here checking the pump," is what I did say, and then it was off to the woods on the hunt.

Let me tell you what I think about going hunting:

If you want to take a gun and go out and shoot down defenseless animals in the forest, that's your business.

I just happen to think hunting is unfair. Maybe if they changed the rules of hunting, I would feel better about it.

What I would do is issue guns to all the deer and rabbits and ducks and whatever else people hunt.

If you think hunting is an exciting sport now, wait until your prey can shoot back.

I don't like to hunt, but I do like to fish. "Same thing as hunting," you might be saying.

Not at all. First, there are not guns involved in fishing. Second, the fish has a choice of whether or not to bite the hook.

Hunters will also argue that they go out in the woods and kill for food. I don't believe that, not with a Del Taco on practically every corner in town.

Anyway, back to my first and last hunting trip on Thanksgiving Day when I was twelve:

It was cold and wet, and we must have walked thirty miles.

"Your best bet to kill a rabbit," explained my uncle, "is to find one sitting on its bed. That way, you don't have to shoot a moving target."

I prayed not to find a rabbit sitting on its bed, or on anybody else's bed.

My prayer was answered. As a matter of fact, nobody in the group even fired a shot, and there was a lot of cursing the dratted luck at the end of the day. I think the dogs had a good time, but it doesn't take much to make a dog happy.

When it came time to go hunting the next Thanksgiving, I feigned a strange seizure that affected my ability to keep from screaming at the top of my voice, so nobody wanted to take me on the hunt because I would scare off the rabbits. Every year, I managed a new excuse. When I was eighteen I left home, and the question of going hunting has never come up in my life since.

In summary, what I think about hunting may be likened unto the perspective on the matter of one Ralph "High-Lift" Turnipseed, a man in my hometown who walked funny—he lifted one leg much higher than the other when he walked because of something strong he once drank because the local bootlegger was on vacation.

"Goin' rabbit-huntin' today, High-Lift?" somebody asked him on the street one day.

"Hell, no," High-Lift responded. "I ain't lost no rabbits."

Double-Dose of Hard Times

The response to this plea for help for Betty Hubbard was incredible. She and her son got their kitchen table and much more.

There is bad in the world and, sometimes, it seems to scream out to be noticed. But there is much good, too, and Christmas brings it forth in gushes.

Betty Hubbard sat on what was a piece of lawn furniture before somebody bent the frame. Betty's son, Joey, who is fifteen, sat on the floor. I took one of Betty's two chairs. A second visitor sat in the other chair.

Betty Hubbard talked about her life. I caught myself looking away to avoid her eyes when she cried.

"I never thought I would come to anything like this," she said. "We ain't got a thing."

She is fifty. She looks older. She's been a "widow woman" for ten years. She has an older son who she says is a "bad influence" on young Joey.

She moved to Atlanta from neighboring Rockdale County to look for a fresh start for her and the boy.

She has asthma. She is unemployed. She and Joey live in a hole of an apartment near Grant Park.

"I apologize for the way this place looks," Betty said. "Me and Joey got out a bucket of water and scrubbed these floors, but it didn't do no good."

We are seated in the living room. There is a small table near the door. On the table are pictures of Betty's sons. Between the two chairs is a locker. There is a small lamp on the locker. It is the only light in the house.

There is no table in the kitchen. There are two bedrooms in the apartment, but only one bed.

"Joey has to sleep with me," said Betty Hubbard. "A lot of folks might have something to say about that, but if he don't sleep with me, then he has to sleep on the floor. I ain't lettin' my baby sleep on no floor. He's all I got."

The sky is gray, the weather is cold. For the first two weeks Betty and Joey were in the apartment, they did not have the money to have the gas and power turned on. They huddled under blankets and burned candles.

Betty gets $400 a month in welfare payments. She hands over $220 for the apartment. She's being robbed. She borrowed from her landlord to put down the deposits for the gas and power.

"We had a home once," Bettty goes on, breaking into tears, "but it got away from me. It's hard for a widow woman and two boys."

There was a silence in the room.

"I don't lie to my doctor, so I won't lie to you," Betty Hubbard continued. "We've all done some drinking. Me, and both the boys. All it done was cause fighting and misunderstanding. But there were times we didn't have nothing to eat. Where there ain't nothing to eat and somebody comes around with a drink, you just can't help but take it."

Betty Hubbard's apartment is a curse. Crumpled magazines and newspapers on the floor. Towels over the windows. Something caught my eye hanging on the wall, a baby's Christmas stocking marked "Joey," and a Christmas scene torn from a calendar. Christmas finds the darndest places.

Hard times come in different degrees. Betty and her boy Joey have caught a double-dose. They're flat busted and it's Christmas Eve. They don't ask much:

• Some pants for Joey. He has only one pair. He is thirty in the waist and thirty length.

• Some shoes for Betty. Her only pair are worn moccasins.

• A small bed for Joey. And something where the two of them could sit down for a meal.

• Food. They ate sardines and soda crackers for Thanksgiving.

• An old television. "A boy naturally wants a television," said Betty Hubbard. "When I get back on my feet, that's the first thing I'm going to do, get my boy a television."

• Employment. Betty, with her asthma, is limited. She says she is good with children and once worked in a nursery. Joey is strong.

You hear these stories every Christmas. And you can't help everybody. And there are probably people even more deserving than Betty and Joey Hubbard, and, besides, we've got our own families to take care of.

But when the party is over and the wrappings are off the gifts, and Friday brings back reality, Betty and Joey still won't have a kitchen table.

Christmas Moose Smooch

I was driving along and listening to Christmas carols on the radio, and I started thinking back to those wonderful days when I was a kid and we used to draw names for the annual class Christmas party.

What a blast that was. What fun to share Christmas gifts with your classmates.

A bunch of cheap, ungrateful toads, all of them.

In the third grade Alvin Bates got my name. Alvin Bates was the kind of kid who would bring a candy bar for afternoon recess and lick it all over before taking a bite so nobody would ask him to share it.

In the third grade Alvin Bates gave me one of those stupid wooden paddles with the balls and the rubber strings attached. You hit the stupid ball with the stupid paddle and the stupid ball, attached to the rubber string, comes back and you hit it again.

Terrific. Fun for any awkward child under six. For fifty-nine cents, which is exactly what Alvin Bates shelled out for the paddle and the ball, he could have bought me something useful and educational, like a copy of *Stag* magazine they kept on the back shelf at the drugstore.

Stag was nothing compared to the magazines they have today, but in 1954, seeing a picture of a lady in a girdle could make your month.

Later I reaped revenge. I drew Alvin's name in the fourth grade, and I gave him a subscription to *Boy's Life*. Anybody caught reading *Boy's Life* was obviously a complete (a) mama's boy, (b) nurd, (c) sissy, (d) wimp, (e) fruit, (f) several other things I can't mention here.

"Hey, Four-Eyes," we used to taunt Alvin on the playground, "what's the centerfold this month in *Boy's Life*? Picture of a pup tent?"

Alvin spent most of his fourth-grade year crying.

In the fifth grade, Frankie Garfield, the school bully, drew my name.

Having your name drawn by Frankie Garfield was both bad and good. The bad part was Frankie's usual gift wouldn't exactly fit under the class tree.

The good part was Frankie's gift was a promise he wouldn't beat you up for at least a week.

"I let you live, Duck-Face," Frankie would say.

The worst thing that ever happened to me, though, was in the sixth grade when Cordie Mae Poovey, the ugliest and meanest girl in school, drew my name.

Cordie Mae was from a poor family, and she never had much money to spend on a gift. A pair of socks, I figured. Or a box of peanut brittle.

Worse. I opened my gift from Cordie Mae, and all I found was an envelope with a note inside that read, "Merry Christmas. I give you the gift of love. One (1) kiss and one (1) hug. Meet me after school. Cordie Mae."

I'd kiss a pig first. And Cordie Mae was as strong as she smelled. She could break a couple of ribs.

After school I ran as fast as I could, but she finally chased me down, hammerlocked me, and then planted one right on my mouth. Smmmmmmmack!

"How'd you like that, big boy?" asked Cordie Mae.

"Ever smooched with a moose?" I answered.

"Ever been run over by a herd of reindeer?" replied Cordie Mae, who had no sense of humor whatsoever.

The swelling in my nose went down in a couple of days, but it was a week before my eyes opened again.

9

ELECTION YEAR

I covered the 1980 presidential election from New Hampshire in January to the Republican Convention in Detroit in July to the Democratic Convention in New York in August, and I was standing there with the rain falling on Plains when Jimmy Carter came home on Inauguration Day, beaten and tired. I am convinced anybody crazy enough to go through what a person has to go through to get elected president is very likely about halfway to being completely bananas by the time he spends the first night in the White House. . . .

Too Late for the Duke

The more I think about it, the less I can find wrong with the fact that a movie actor is running for president of the United States.

Look who else has run for that position in the past—surveyors, architects, several generals, a couple of newspaper editors, a bankrupt haberdasher, even a peanut farmer, lest we forget.

But did it have to be THAT movie actor? When this country finally got around to picking somebody off the silver screen to make the mad dash for the White House, did it have to be, as he has been described, "the Errol Flynn of the B-movies"?

Ronald Reagan, for crying out loud? *Love Is On The Air* Ronald Reagan? *That Hagen Girl* (with Shirley Temple) Ronald Reagan? Supporting actor to a chimpanzee in *Bedtime for Bonzo* Ronald Reagan?

Do you realize Ronald Reagan originally was cast for the lead in *Casablanca*? Can you imagine that? Reagan in the role Bogie made a classic?

Let's face it. Ronald Reagan may have been lousy in *Hellcats of the Navy*, but he was terrible in another clunker, as Grover Cleveland Alexander, the baseball player.

Of all the actors we had to choose from to run for president, we took the man who once sold 20-Mule Team Borax on "Death Valley Days"?

411

You're looking for a movie-actor president? Just consider who else was available that we passed up:

• HENRY FONDA: Looks like a president, talks like a president, acts like a president. Did anybody see Henry Fonda in *Fail Safe*? He played the president and wound up ordering the bomb dropped on New York City. I told you he would have made us a good president.

• JIMMY STEWART: Well, ah, it might, ah, take him a long, ah, time, to make, ah, a state of the, ah, union address, but at least, ah, everybody in the, ah, country could do, ah, an impression of the, ah, president, don't you, ah, see?

• WALTER PIDGEON: Tall, distinguished. Plays a lot of senators and other big shots. My mother always thought a lot of Walter Pidgeon.

• CHARLTON HESTON: Normally thought of as an airline pilot or a chariot racer, but be honest with yourself.

You want somebody in the Oval Office who can handle a crisis, right? So would you pick squatty Ronald Reagan with that funky hairdo of his, or tall, handsome Charlton Heston, last seen, incidentally, drowning heroically in a sewer following an earthquake?

• GREGORY PECK: I always have been a big Gregory Peck fan since I saw him in *The Man in the Gray Flannel Suit* and later in *To Kill a Mockingbird*.

Gregory Peck would not waffle on the issues. We elected Eisenhower, didn't we? Then give MacArthur his chance.

• ROBERT STACK: Law and order candidate. Congress starts acting up and Ness and the boys come around to straighten them out.

• CHARLES BRONSON: Want somebody to get tough with the Russians? Here is somebody to get tough with the Russians. "One more word out of you, Leonid, and I'll bust your face in." That kind of get-tough-with-the-Russians.

But what am I saying here? Fonda, Stewart, Heston, etc. Lightweights, all of them, when you consider the man who should be in Ronald Reagan's shoes right now.

Tall in the saddle, he was. A soldier. Tough, but fair. A patriot. What this country needs is a good dose of true grit. He had it.

Ronald Reagan, Ronald Smeagan. This country decides it wants to elevate a movie actor to the threshold of the White House and we pussyfoot around until the Duke is unavailable.

Sort of makes you sick to your stomach, doesn't it, pilgrim?

"What He Meant to Say Was . . ."

To follow the presidential campaigns, one can all but ignore the statements and charges of the candidates and other influential individuals and wait for the clarifications that always follow from aides.

Some notable examples to clip and save:

• Ronald Reagan implies President Carter supports the Ku Klux Klan by making a snide remark about the president opening his campaign in Tuscumbia, Alabama, which, according to Mr. Reagan, is "the birthplace of the Klan."

WHAT AIDES SAID MR. REAGAN REALLY MEANT TO SAY: "Governor Reagan really meant to say he wishes Coach Bear Bryant and the University of Alabama football team another great season.

"He would also like to add he wants to visit Tuscumbia, himself, very soon to see his dearest and oldest friend, Helen Keller, who he remembers so well as such a talented dancer in all those old Hollywood musicals."

• President Carter implies that Mr. Reagan is a racist.

WHAT AIDES SAID MR. CARTER REALLY MEANT TO SAY: "The President really meant to say Mr. Reagan is spending too much time 'racing' round the country making unwarranted attacks on his record. Also he wanted to mention that Mr. Reagan has solicited the campaign help of stock car 'racing' king Richard Petty.

"And just because the President's statements were misinterpreted while he was standing in the late Dr. Martin Luther King, Jr., hometown church, surrounded by every black leader from here to Satchel Paige, it must be considered only a mere coincidence.

• Mr. Reagan says the United States' efforts in the Vietnam War were for a "noble cause."

WHAT AIDES SAID MR. REAGAN REALLY MEANT TO SAY: "'Spanish-American' instead of 'Vietnam.' Just a mere slip of the tongue. It could happen to anybody."

• Mr. Reagan gets his Chinas mixed up.

HOW AIDES EXPLAINED THAT: "The governor didn't have his hand pocket world Atlas with him at the time, and even if he did, 'little' China appears as such a tiny speck, anybody could overlook it, like Rhode Island in our own country.

"Incidentally, the governor will be campaigning in that great state soon, and we hope everybody who can will be out to greet him when his plane lands at the airport in Hartford."

• President Carter charges that Mr. Reagan, if elected, would lead the country into war.

WHAT AIDES SAID MR. CARTER REALLY MEANT TO SAY: "What he really meant to say was if this nation ever has to go to war, then Mr. Reagan would be a terrific person to lead us into it. As a second lieutenant, for instance, up ahead of all the troops, trying to knock out an enemy machine gun nest."

• *Time Magazine* quotes Miss Lillian Carter as saying, "Sometimes when I take a look at my children, I wish I had remained a virgin."

WHAT MISS LILLIAN'S FRIENDS IN PLAINS SAID SHE REALLY MEANT TO SAY: "She really meant to say that sometimes when she takes a look at her children, she wishes she had remained a virgin."

• Dr. Bailey Smith, president of the Southern Baptist Convention, makes the statement that "God almighty does not hear the prayers of a Jew."

WHAT THE DEACONS SAID DR. SMITH REALLY MEANT TO SAY: "He really meant to say God doesn't listen to the prayers of Jews, or of hardly anybody else, on WEDNESDAYS. That's the day he takes off to listen to blow-hard politicians ask forgiveness for all the lies they've told the previous week."

Debates and Rat-Killings

The headline in Wednesday's paper said it all about Tuesday night's debate between Jimmy Carter and Ronald Reagan: "Carter, Reagan Both Feel Goals Achieved in Debate."

Of course Carter and Reagan both felt their goals were achieved in the debate. That's the problem with presidential debates. They are not like wrestling matches where one guy runs another guy's head into one of the ring posts and you can pick a clear winner.

A presidential debate is more like a rat-killing.

I don't know how many of you have ever been to a big league rat-killing before, but they work like this:

The rat-killers, armed with .22 rifles, hide behind some bales of hay in the barn. Some corn has been spread about to entice the rats to enter the arena. The lights are turned out.

As soon as it sounds like there are a number of rats gnawing on the corn, the lights are turned on and the rats are momentarily blinded. The rat-killers then cut down on the rats from behind the hay bales with their .22s.

This sounds a little one-sided in favor of the rat-killers, and it is, but the rats do get a nice meal before being blown away, and because rats are such pests, they don't deserve a fair shake anyway.

And after the rat-killing is over, both sides can always rationalize a victory.

Let's say some of the rats get away:

"A clear victory for our side," says the spokesrat. "Those clowns couldn't hit a bull in the bohunkus with a bass fiddle."

"Another win for us," counters the head rat-killer. "We didn't want to shoot them all so we could have another rat-killing."

Rat-killings and presidential debates. Just alike. Also, throw arguments with your wife into the same category.

I did the only sane thing for the debate Tuesday night. I watched it in a bar. After the debate was over, I polled the joint.

Three drunks were for Carter. Three drunks were for Reagan. The bartender was a Libertarian, and the waitress likes Anderson because he reminds her of her uncle in Tupelo who has the local pocket-fisherman franchise.

I kept my own scorecard. I tried to be as fair as possible. Here is how I rated each man's performance:

• HAIR—Carter's was neatly parted on the side-of-the-week and appeared to have been blow-dried. Reagan, meanwhile, had apparently slicked it down with Royal Crown. Wetheadsville with enough Grecian formula Nine to turn chalk black. HAIR TO CARTER.

• SMILE—Carter, for a smiler, didn't smile much. Perhaps he was having another flare-up of what George Brett had. Reagan smiles like used car dealers smile. SMILE TO REAGAN.

• SUIT—Robert Hall Ronnie looked like he just stepped off the cover of *GQ*. Unfortunately, a 1953 issue. SUIT TO CARTER.

• FACIAL COLOR—Carter looked like he had just seen Lester Maddox seated on the panel of inquisitors. Reagan had been pancaked a golden brown. FACIAL COLOR TO REAGAN.

• GRASP OF THE FACTS—Neither candidate appeared to know as much as Barbara Walters. GRASP OF FACTS TO BARBARA WALTERS.

What I am going to do is declare the 1980 Great Presidential Debate a deadlock and make only one other observation:

I wouldn't take Barbara Walters to a rat-killing. She'd scare off all the rats.

The Spirit of '76

Four years ago Wednesday morning, I awakened where I had fallen the night before, in an apartment on the thirtieth-some-odd floor of a high-rise apartment building in Chicago. The view was of Lincoln Park and Lake Michigan. The monthly rent was astounding.

I splashed some water on my then-bearded face and opened the front door. At my feet were two of Chicago's daily newspapers.

The message screamed across the front of both:

"IT'S CARTER!"

Thank the Lord I didn't dream it, I remember saying to myself.

Carter. Jimmy Carter. Former governor of that backward outhouse of a state, Georgia. Peanut farmer. Imagine that. Peanut farmer from Georgia running for president of the United States.

They used to ask me about him, Carter, and about Georgia. Chicagoans used to ask. "What's it really like *out there* in the South?"

"Out there" in the South. The West is "out there." The East is "over there." The North is "up here." The South is "down there." We spend millions each year to educate the heathen. And we have such vast ignorance right here in our own country.

A girl in Chicago once asked me. "Do you have any nice restaurants 'out there' in the South?"

"Surely," I answered her. "Mention my name, and maybe you'll get a good seat at the counter."

I took it all. I answered their questions. I assured them cotton wasn't growing in downtown Atlanta.

I explained we do not say, you all," we say, "y'all," and we never use it in the singular.

I explained about grits. Unless you put some butter or cheese in them, they taste awful.

And I hurt a lot. The South was, in fact, rising again. I could read about it every day, I could hear about it on the seven o'clock news.

So why was I, a true son of the red clay whose granddaddy once owned the egg-suckingest dog in Coweta County (dog's name was Edna), stuck in Chicago?

Grizzard Buzzard luck, I supposed. Can't kill nothing. Can't find nothing dead.

I pulled as hard for him as I ever have pulled for anything, anybody. I prayed over it. ". . . And, Lord, if you can't help me, then at least please help Jimmy."

The night he was nominated, I couldn't hold back the tears. I ran up a hundred dollars' worth of phone calls with 404 area codes.

I got Dorsey Hill on the phone. Dorsey grew up in Rome, Georgia. "Sumbitch," he said, "don't it make you proud?"

But that was only half the battle. There was still Ford. This girl with the high-rise apartment gave an election party, and I told her I wouldn't come if any Ford people were going to be there, so we had just a small gathering (Carter lost Illinois in '76, too), but that made the victory just that much sweeter.

Four years ago Wednesday morning, I read both Chicago papers from front to back, but filled with triumph as I was, I was also never so homesick in all my life.

I think you would have had to have been away from the South to see what Jimmy Carter getting elected president in 1976 really meant to the South, and to Southerners.

I caught a cab to my office. Usually, I took a bus. I was celebrating. There was a pink memorandum slip awaiting me in my typewriter. It was from a colleague, local boy, who thought Indianapolis was the Deep South. But the man had some degree of class.

"Congratulations," began the note, "y'all ain't trash no more."

I don't know if Jimmy Carter was a good president or not, and I wish Ronald Reagan all the best.

But four years ago on a cold Chicago morning, Jimmy Carter made me as proud as if I had won the damn election myself. For that, I will always be indebted to him.

Always.

Jimmy Earl Comes Home

PLAINS—Standing here in the pouring rain Tuesday, my feet freezing, I wondered what the Ronald Reagans were doing.

Here in Plains, several thousand of us were waiting for a helicopter to drop out of the gray sky and bring Jimmy Earl home. That's what they call the former president of the United States in his hometown. They call him "Jimmy Earl."

I figured the Reagans were probably finished with their spiffy luncheon that had followed the inauguration. They were to have boneless breast of chicken and California wines.

I suppose they were probably getting ready for Tuesday evening's inaugural ball, or maybe they were having a few pops with somebody like Frank Sinatra or Jimmy Stewart or Liz Taylor. They're all such famous friends, you know.

And while I was thinking about the Reagans, I thought about what Bill Godfrey once said. Bill Godfrey played football for the University of Georgia before Herschel Walker was born. He said, "Ain't folks nice to you when you win?"

To the winner Tuesday went the spoils. Ronald Wilson Reagan became the fortieth president. Jimmy Earl Carter Jr., the thirty-ninth, came home to Plains.

He looked awful. He looked tired and he looked drained. They said he hadn't slept in two days, as he battled to the last minute of his administration to see the hostages freed from Iran.

I think the Iranians waited, on purpose, until Reagan had been sworn in before they released the hostages. I also think the Iranians are lower than camel dung.

The crowd at Jimmy Carter's homecoming day Tuesday was vintage Georgian, vintage Deep Southern. A lady said to her husband, "Hep me, Johnny, I don't think I can get my parasol open." The last person I heard refer to an umbrella as a "parasol" was my grandmother.

A woman from Macon told me, "My boss didn't want me to come over here today, but I came anyway. Jimmy Carter's the only man in the world I'd stand in the rain to see."

A little girl, sniffling, stood on the hood of a truck awaiting the former president's arrival. She held a sign that read, "We love you, Jimmy." The rain had drenched her. ABC nearly ran over CBS to get her on camera.

A sign in front of a store on the outskirts of town read, "New Rooster. Too Many Eggs. Sale. 75 Cents a Dozen. Welcome Back, Jimmy and Rosalynn."

The good ladies of Plains had wanted to turn out the world's largest covered-dish supper, and I think they did it. One table stretched an entire block, and it was filled with Southern delights, including fried chicken, and I saw bowls of collards and cakes and pies that were enough to start a riot.

They almost did. The idea was to form a line across the railroad tracks and to proceed orderly down the table, serving yourself buffet style. But several sweet-tooth vultures would not follow those directins and were pilfering from the table despite the efforts of a lady carrying a butcher knife to keep them away.

Jimmy C. Newman sang Cajun music. Tom T. Hall sang "Old Dogs and Children and Watermelon Wine." Despite the rain, the street dance and the fireworks show were still scheduled for later in the evening. I saw two old boys passing a bottle in a sack back and forth. I didn't see Billy.

When he had finally landed and had made his way to the plastic-covered platform in the middle of town, Jimmy Earl made a nice speech.

He didn't brag on himself too much. He talked about the pride he felt in having been president for four years. He said a wife of one of the hostages had said to him earlier in the day, "Mister President, I hope you can meet my husband someday." And the president replied, "I will be with him in Germany this week, and I will tell him you love him."

He asked us all to support the new president, and he talked about how much the Algerian government had helped getting the hostages released.

That started me thinking again. Here stood Jimmy Earl Carter in the middle of Plains, Sumter County, Georgia, talking about Algeria when most of us in the crowd couldn't find it on a map with directions and a head start. Nobody had come to hear about Algeria.

I got the distinct feeling that the reason that crowd showed up in that awful weather Tuesday was to help soften a hometown boy's abrupt fall from the most powerful office in the world back to private citizen. Let the Reagans dance the night away; Georgians took care of their own Tuesday afternoon.

I mentioned dancing. I will forevermore consider it appropriate that after the new president had been inaugurated, after the hostages had been freed, after dog-tired Jimmy Carter had come back to Plains and had made his speech, the last thing he did before the public eye was stand tall on the platform in front of the cheering crowd and take his wife in his arms and dance with her.

The tune was "Dixie."

Senility Test

Now that Ronald Reagan actually is going to be president, let us remind ourselves of a promise he made during the campaign.

Reagan, who will be seventy by the time he is sworn into office, promised to take a senility test if ever the situation arose where there were murmurings about the "crazy old coot over at the White House."

I think it is important that we hold Mr. Reagan to this promise. Being president is a strain on any man. Look at Jimmy Carter. He was nearly twenty years younger than Mr. Reagan when he took office. But by the time he was blown out, he was so confused, he was discussing nuclear proliferation with his daughter, Amy.

You may be asking yourself what sort of senility test Mr. Reagan would take. I'm glad you asked that. Through various sources in Washington, this column has obtained a secret copy of the Official Presidential Senility Test (Republican Version).

Given after, say, two years in office, could Mr. Reagan then pass the following rigorous examination?

1. Place your hand over your heart. Would you say it is:
(a) purring like a kitten? (10 points). (b) Humming like a Model-T Ford? (8 points). (c) Going "flap-flong-blip-bong"? (2 points). (If you are unable to answer this question because you can't locate your heart, subtract five points and do not attempt to operate an automobile.)

2. How would you describe your ability to hear?
(a) Excellent (10 points). (b) Good (6 points). (c) Fair (2 points).

3. YOU WANT THE QUESTION REPEATED A LITTLE LOUDER?
(Subtract five points and try not to doze off during the remainder of this test.)

4. How would you describe your ability to see?
(a) Excellent (10 points). (b) Good (6 points). (c) Fair (2 points). (d) Last week at a meeting with Leonid Brezhnev you shook hands with your chair and sat down in the premier's lap. (Subtract 5 points and forget about SALT III.)

5. True (subtract 5 points) or False (add 5):
Earl Scheib does your hair.

6. Your lovely wife Nancy comes into the presidential bedroom wearing a slinky nightgown. Your first move is to:
(a) Call the kitchen and order a bottle of champagne (10 points). (b) Look for your old Benny Goodman records (5 points). (c) Phone George Bush to see if he wants to come over and watch one of your old movies on the late show. (Subtract 6 points and say you have a sick headache.)

7. The following question has to do with your memory: Back in 1980 you won a resounding victory over your opponent in the presidential election. Your opponent's name was:
(a) Jimmy Carter. (b) Bonzo.
(If you selected (a), add 5 points to your score. If you selected (b), add 4 points. At least you were close.)

8. Another memory question: You were born in:
(a) 1492. (b) 1776. (c) 1812. (d) 1911.
(If you marked (a), (b), (c), subtract 10 points. If you marked (d), an old fellow like you should probably rest a while before we finish this test.)

9. Your youngest son, Ronnie, Jr.:
(a) Plays football for Notre Dame, like you did. (b) Is a professional wrestler. (c) Drives a truck. (d) Hops around on his toes with pale-looking girls and wears leotards.
(If you marked (a), (b), (c), subtract 5 points for wishful thinking. If you marked (d), subtract 10 points for asking your own son to never visit you in the White House until after dark.)

10. As president, your most outstanding contribution to the country has been:

(a) Getting us into war with Canada. (c) Making Woody Hayes secretary of defense. (d) Pardoning former President Carter.

(No matter what you answered, subtract 10 points and have a glass of warm milk.)

HOW YOU SCORED

70-100: The country survived Millard Fillmore; it probably can survive you.

50-69: Get plenty of rest, avoid press conferences, and drink all your prune juice.

30-49: Move around occasionally with your eyes open. Somebody may get the wrong idea.

Less than 30: We have one chance for survival: If you do decide to push the button, maybe you won't be able to remember where they keep it.

Queen Nancy

A number of women I know never did care for Rosalynn Carter, the outgoing first lady.

"She's cold," one described Mrs. Carter.

"She wore that same horrid green dress for four years," said another.

Needless to say, these ladies are very excited now that former actress Nancy Reagan is taking over at the White House.

"She has dignity and charm," said one.

"She wears nothing but Adolfo originals," added another.

I think Nancy Reagan is a very pretty, well-dressed lady, too. But she's pushy. She reminds me of a woman who used to live in my neighborhood, Mrs. Pratt. Mrs. Pratt was pushy.

She was always offering everybody advice on how to wear their hair, what color drapes to hang in the living room, and where to hang the new picture of the bullfighter.

When you were around Mrs. Pratt, you always got the feeling she was looking down her nose at you. One day Mrs. Pratt told Mildred Elrod she was putting on a little weight. Mildred Elrod was offended and fixed it so Mrs. Pratt couldn't look down her nose at anybody again. It was too crooked after that.

I get the feeling Nancy Reagan is looking down her nose at a lot of us. She was educated at the best schools, of course, and she has spent a lot of her time lunching at expensive Hollywood restaurants, and she is great friends with a lot of rich people like Betty Bloomingdale who go around saying, "dahling."

I first got the idea that maybe Nancy Reagan and some of her aides were snooty when one of her California cronies said, "She will bring more to the White House than Amy."

That is downright catty.

There was another remark about Nancy Reagan's style of entertaining.

"She knows how to entertain, and she'll do it with dignity, the way it should be done. There won't be anymore lemonade, cookies, bare feet, hot dogs, and Willie Nelson."

Willie Nelson, as a matter of fact, has starred in two hit movies, two more than the next president, and he rolled around in the hay with Dyan Cannon, not a monkey.

The clincher came when Nancy Reagan was reported to have said she didn't understand why the Carters didn't go ahead and move out of the White House before the January 20 inauguration so she could begin redecoration.

Jimmy Carter remains president and gets to live in the White House until the inauguration. That's according to some silly document like the Constitution, which is always getting in the way when something important like redecorating comes up.

I don't know a thing about Rosalynn Carter except what I read about her in the newspapers and what I see about her on television, but she seems a nice enough person.

She always came across as sincere. Since I wouldn't know an Adolfo from something off the bargain rack at K Mart, her dressing habits never bothered me.

She doesn't know any movie stars, I don't suppose, and she probably has never lunched on Rodeo Drive in Hollywood, and I doubt she even knows Betty Bloomingdale, much less is friends with her, and Rosalynn talks a little funny, like folks do in South Georgia.

But she appeared to do a good job of being a wife to the president, and a mother to their children, and I would hate to see her kicked out of her house before the lease runs out.

Maybe Nancy Reagan simply needs to be reminded of something before she starts her reign.

Just concentrate on being a good first lady, Mrs. Reagan. A queen we don't need.

A Letter to the President

Dear President Reagan,

I purposely waited a couple of weeks before writing you because I wanted some time to think after the attempt that was made on your life. Also, I knew you were up to your ears trying to run our country from a hospital bed.

I am not pretending this will be unique, by any means, but I happen to be one American citizen who is lucky enough to have a public forum, and I see no harm in occasionally using it for expression that is purely personal.

I've got to admit up front I didn't support you in 1980. As a matter of fact, as I stood a few rows behind you as you made your nomination acceptance speech at the Republican Convention in Detroit, I said to a friend standing with me, "He sounds like he's still trying to sell a box of 20-Mule Team Borax."

My friend and I had a good laugh over that. Somehow you seemed unreal to me, too much Hollywood, not enough substance. A man nearly seventy shouldn't look as fit as you do, shouldn't bounce around like you do.

Where was your gray hair? How could you still stand so erect, speak so strongly and keep the demanding schedule those seeking public office must keep?

When you announced you would be glad to take a senility test during your term as president, I said, "Sure he will. If only he can remember where he put it."

I had some problems with your platform, too. I saw you on television night after night, smoothie that you are, telling the American people how you were going to cure inflation, bring down the unemployment rate and give the Russians hell. You *sounded* great, but I listened to a huckster at a carnival once, too, and it cost me two bucks to learn that what silver tongues preach isn't always golden.

I worried about your feelings toward the poor. I worried about what you would do the first time the Russians tried your hand. Would you react too strongly, foolishly, and get us all blown away?

I've got to admit something else, too, Mr. President. I still haven't been able to warm up toward your wife. When she suggested that the Carters move out of the White House early so she could get to the business of redecorating, I secretly hoped her slip would show on Inauguration Day.

Your son, the one that dances, didn't impress me that much, either, especially when he called President Carter a "snake." I respected and supported President Carter, for a number of reasons:

One, I considered him to be completely honest; two, he talks a lot like I do; three, he is the only president in American history to invite me to drink beer in the back yard of the White House while listening to Willie Nelson sing. A man must have his own priorities, Mr. President.

Anyway, I've said all that to say this: I still don't know if you can pull off any of those miracles you promised, and I probably would vote for Jimmy Carter again, given the chance, but I will tell my grandchildren about the time that creep tried to gun you down in front of the Washington Hilton.

You took a slug in the lung and then walked into the hospital under your own power, cracked jokes with the doctors, went through a two-hour operation, and were signing legislation the next morning. And you're a year older than Arizona.

For right now, at least, I don't care what your politics are, I admire your vigor, your strength, and the way you handled yourself in a crisis of the utmost severity: Your own life was threatened.

Your actions said more than all the words you have uttered as president. The citizens of this country and the rest of the world have no more doubt: At the helm of this ship of state stands the toughest old bird in the valley.

> Your fan,
> Lewis Grizzard

10

NUMBER ONE

I attended the University of Georgia in Athens, Georgia, from 1964 until 1968. When I arrived on campus in the fall of '64, the school's football fortunes were at an all-time low.

But the same year I arrived on campus, so did a thirty-two-year-old rookie coach named Vince Dooley. It took him seventeen years to do it, but on January 1, 1981, in New Orleans, Louisiana, Vince Dooley put a Georgia team on the carpeted floor of the Superdome that was good enough to whip Notre Dame, a team made up mostly of people from north of Greenville, South Carolina, and good enough to win the national collegiate championship.

This made me very happy. In the first piece in this chapter, I will attempt to say why. The pieces that follow will attempt to describe some of the people and places that were a part of what one quite loyal to the Red and Black described as "the second greatest story ever told. . . ."

Georgia on My Mind

I was there that first night when Vincent Joseph Dooley, who was younger then (thirty-two) than I am now (thirty-five), coached his first game from the Georgia sidelines. It was a warm September night, 1964, in Denny Stadium, Tuscaloosa. The opposition was Joe Namath and Bear Bryant's fearsome Alabama.

How I happened to be in Tuscaloosa that night is a fairly long story that can be held in check by explaining I was seventeen at the time, about to enter my freshman year at the University of Georgia. The preceding summer, I had gone to see Ed Thelenius, the Bulldogs' "golden voice," who broadcast the Georgia games on radio.

Ed Thelenius, who died in March of 1981, was nice to me and offered me a job on his football crew. Ten a game and my travel and my room and my food. I would "spot" the opposition, point to the name of who had the ball for the other team. Ed Thelenius had a lot to do with getting my career started. They said he suffered a lot in the end. I hate that.

Early in the game that night in Tuscaloosa, a young defensive lineman from Georgia named George Patton stormed through the Alabama line and made a savage hit on Namath for a loss.

In the Georgia radio booth, I was sitting next to the late Bill Monday, the pioneer sportscaster who did color for Thelenius.

"They're ready!" screamed Monday. "Gawga's ready!"

Gawga wasn't ready. Namath passed them silly. The final score was 31-3. The traffic in Tuscaloosa was so bad it took three hours just to get back to Birmingham. Jim Koger, who did statistics for Thelenius, got out of the car and bought some beer. Jim Koger would teach me about a lot of things that season, including how to enjoy warm beer when there is no cold beer around. Incidentally, Jim Koger later found Jesus. There is hope for all of us.

I started classes at Georgia the next week. A lot of people, including some girls, were very impressed when I told them I worked for Ed Thelenius, who mentioned my name at the end of every broadcast.

The following Saturday, the Georgia team, Thelenius, and I checked into the Holiday Inn in Nashville where Georgia would play Vanderbilt in the evening. Thelenius and I ate a steak. We hung around in the lobby. I remember Dooley and Georgia athletic director Joel Eaves talking together. Both seemed very nervous.

Barry Wilson, a Georgia defensive end, intercepted a Vanderbilt pass that night in Nashville, and it led to the first touchdown ever for a Vince Dooley team. The seven points was enough. Vince Dooley, head coach, and Lewis Grizzard, journalism freshman, had their first victory at Georgia, 7-0, over Vanderbilt. We would go on to be 6-3-1. We would ship Georgia Tech and we would ship Texas Tech in the Sun Bowl. Barry Wilson would later become an assistant coach at Georgia Tech.

I left Georgia in 1968. Each game the Bulldogs played while I was on campus had a special memory. I'll list a few:

—Georgia 7, Georgia Tech 0, in Athens, 1964: Driving to the game from my hometown of Moreland—I had been out of school on Thanksgiving break—a woman plowed into the back of my red 1958 Chevrolet when I stopped for gas near Watkinsville. It was her fault, but my driver's license had expired. The Oconee County policeman said he would have to take me to the courthouse, but I told him I had to be at the game to work for Ed Thelenius. He let me go.

—Georgia 18, Alabama 17, in Athens, 1965: Thelenius pounded his fist on the table in front of him after the flea-flicker game that upset the eventual national champions. It was the only time I ever saw him lose control.

—Kentucky 28, Georgia 10, in Lexington, 1965: The coldest I have ever been in my life. I knocked over coffee onto the spotter boards and all over Thelenius. He never missed a beat.

—Miami 6, Georgia 3, in Miami, 1966: I was married by now and no longer working for the football network. My wife—the first Mrs. Grizzard—and I were parked outside the Dairy Queen in Athens, listening to the game on the radio. My wife wanted to talk about something else.

"Shut up!" I suggested to her.

She dumped a strawberry milkshake on my head. We divorced the year Tech beat Dooley for the first time.

—Georgia 21, Auburn 13, in Auburn, 1966: The first Georgia game I had seen from the stands. I had worked in the press box for all the others. One of my fraternity brothers was sitting next to me in the end zone. He brought along a bottle of Jack Daniels, black. We mixed it with Coke and drank all of it. I found out Georgia had come back in the second half to win, after trailing 13-0, by reading the paper the next day.

In the summer of 1968 I went to work as a sportswriter for the *Atlanta Journal*. Those were great years. I covered a lot of Georgia games. The best one was the '71 game against Georgia Tech in Atlanta when Andy Johnson brought Georgia back in the last minute-and-a-half to win, 28-24.

It looked bleak for Georgia that night. The Bulldogs had arrived at Grant Field with a 9-1 record, heavily favored over the Yellow Jackets. When it appeared there was no hope for Georgia, Tech sports information director Ned West walked over to Dan Magill, his counterpart at Georgia, and said, "Well, Dan, y'all have had a great season. I'm so sorry it had to end this way."

When Jimmy Poulos dived for the winning touchdown for Georgia with fourteen seconds to play, Magill walked over to West and said, "Well, Ned, y'all have had a great season. I'm so sorry it had to end this way."

In the fall of 1975, I did a stupid thing. I took the second Mrs. Grizzard and moved to Chicago to become sports editor of the *Chicago Sun-Times*. The Saturday before I began work, I drove over to South Bend, Indiana, to watch Georgia Tech play Notre Dame. Notre Dame won. I had mixed emotions about the outcome of that game.

It was very difficult for me in Chicago because I didn't care who won the Minnesota-Iowa game, or the annual battle between Northwestern and Illinois. I wouldn't walk across the street to see Michigan play Ohio State, either—two mules fighting over a turnip.

Three weeks after I had moved to Chicago, it was Thanksgiving
and Georgia, with another good team, was to play Georgia Tech
Thanksgiving night on national television. The second Mrs. Grizzard had gone home to South Carolina to see her parents. I was
alone.

Fine, I thought. I will purchase several cold beers, and sit back and
watch Georgia play Georgia Tech. The game was to be held on Grant
Field in Atlanta.

There was a problem. My neighbor across the hall in the high-rise,
Near North apartment building in which I lived, had decided to be
my friend. That was fine, except he was from Colombia, and I could
barely understand a word he was saying. He thought I was from
Zanzibar or someplace with my accent.

He invited me over for Thanksgiving dinner.

"No thanks," I said, "I want to watch Georgia and Georgia Tech on
television."

"Who eeze thees Goorgea and Goorgea Tick?" he asked.

I tried to explain. His cat understood more than he did.

"You eeet, jes?" he asked again.

"No," I persisted. "I watch the game."

I cracked a beer and Georgia was scoring like mad. I think the
score was 42-0 at the half. I felt wonderful. Maybe I should go have
some dinner with my new Colombian friend, I said to myself.

The meal was marvelous. We switched the game on in his apartment. Tech was making a comeback.

I was feeling a bit queezy. Tech cut the final gap to 42-26. I asked if
I could lie down.

"Si," said my Colombian friend. "You feel bad, jes?"

"Jes," I said.

"Probably the pot," he said.

"The what?" I asked back.

"The pot. I put eet in the dressing. You like?"

I am 800 miles away from the closest person who loves me, watching Georgia play Georgia Tech with a Colombian who has put marijuana in my Thanksgiving dressing.

I began to make immediate plans to return to Georgia.

I kept up with Georgia football while I was away, thanks to
Dorsey Hill, the world's biggest Bulldog fan. Each week I would
place a call to his house during the Georgia game. He would make
arrangements for someone to be there who would place the receiver
next to the radio.

I would sit in Chicago and listen to the Georgia games. I would do
this in the privacy of my office at the Sun-Times. I would charge the

phone call to the company. I kept watching for somebody to come and get me for doing that, but nobody ever did.

I was in Knoxville the night the 1980 season began. I was sitting next to Dorsey Hill, as a matter of fact. Dorsey never gives up. When Tennessee led, 15-0, I said, "Damn, this is a long way to come to see Georgia get beat like this."

"They're going to come back," Dorsey said, I wrote it off as the heat and the many beers working on Dorsey's head. Georgia came back to win 16-15. I would doubt him only one more time.

It was hot in Jacksonville, seven wins later, too. And Georgia had squandered so many chances to put Florida to sleep, I could feel it slipping away.

Florida scored to lead 21-20 with just minutes to play. Georgia's dream of an unbeaten season, a possible national title, were vanishing before my eyes.

"Let's get out of here," I said to the third Mrs. Grizzard.

Dorsey wouldn't budge. "I've come this far with 'em, I ain't leaving," he said.

We were in the parking lot when the third Mrs. Grizzard looked at the people on the top row of the Gator Bowl stadium and said, "Look, the Georgia fans are jumping up and down."

"Probably just a first down," I said.

"But they're still jumping up and down," my wife continued.

I noticed the Gator Bowl was shaking. I finally learned Georgia had scored on a 93-yard play to win, 26-21.

A number of people were very put out with me for leaving the stadium and giving up on Georgia that day.

"You are a disgrace," said Dorsey Hill.

Maybe I can explain. I am a terribly unlucky person. In several million hands of poker, I have never filled an inside straight nor drawn the third king.

With Georgia behind 20-21 to Florida, I reasoned the only chance Georgia had was for me to leave the stadium. With my luck, if I left the stadium, something incredible, something unforgettable, something I could tell my grandchildren about had I remained to watch, would probably happen. I left the stadium, and something did.

Georgia has me to thank for its comeback against Florida.

After Florida, Auburn fell, and then Georgia Tech, and then we all went down to New Orleans to the Sugar Bowl to play Notre Dame.

I don't know what is is about Notre Dame, but I don't like Notre Dame. I pulled hard for Jimmy Carter to win in 1976, because I was living in Chicago, and here was a man who talked like I did running for president. I pulled hard for him again in 1980 because he invited

me to the back yard of the White House to drink beer and listen to
Willie Nelson sing. But I pulled harder for Georgia to win against
Notre Dame in the 1981 Sugar Bowl.

It meant everything to Georgia. The Bulldogs' first national championship was at stake. It meant nothing to Notre Dame save playing
the role of the spoiler.

Nobody really enjoyed the 1981 Sugar Bowl game. Georgia people
didn't enjoy it because it turned out to be so close, and Georgia had
everything to lose. Notre Dame couldn't have enjoyed it because the
Irish kept fumbling the ball all over the Superdome carpet and
throwing interceptions.

I was frustrated through the entire affair. With six minutes to go
in the game, when it was apparent Georgia would never get another
first down if we stayed in New Orleans until Easter, I began to use
abusive language.

"I can't stand you any longer," said my wife, who promptly left
and went back to the hotel.

When it was finally over, tears welled in my eyes. Let me see if I
can express what it meant to me and so many others.

Alabama has won national championships. So have Auburn and
Tennessee and LSU. And Ohio State or Southern Cal or Texas or
Notre Dame is always winning one. But never Georgia.

Georgia. It's where I was born and where my mother and father
were born. We've had it rough from the start in Georgia. First we get
settled by a bunch of prisoners from England. Then Sherman
marches through and burns everything he can see. People call us
"redneck." We finally get somebody from Georgia elected president,
and nobody likes him.

But on January 1, 1981, the football team representing the University of Georgia, where I went to school, whipped Notre Dame, which
gets movies made about its football teams, and won the national
championship.

Grown men cried.

A friend of mine was sitting next to his fiancee in the Superdome
that day. They were to be married later in the year. The wedding is
off now. My friend explained:

"When I finally knew it was over, when I finally realized they
couldn't beat us, when after all these years of pulling for Georgia
and living with them and dying with them, I realized we had done
won the by-god national title, I started crying like a baby. I couldn't
stop. I looked over and there was my best friend who was at the
game with me. We went to Georgia together in the sixties. We've
been all over to see them play. He was crying, too. It was the most

emotional moment of my life. I reached over and hugged him and kissed him square in the mouth.

"My fiancee wouldn't speak to me the rest of the day. She was mad because I hadn't kissed her first. We broke up soon after that. I just never could figure out why she thought I would have kissed her first. Hell, she went to Clemson."

Herschel Walker of Clyde's Gulf

This piece was written when Herschel Walker was driving everybody crazy by taking his sweet time about deciding which school would get his enormous talents. He did eventually sign with Georgia, of course, and he led the Bulldogs to their perfect 12-0 season, and the national championship.

Herschel Walker is a wonderful young man, incredibly talented athletically, an excellent student, a polite individual who would turn down $2 million from the Canadian Football League after the 1980 season because he didn't think it was the American sort of thing to do.

Perhaps Herschel Walker isn't from Wrightsville, Georgia, at all. Maybe he's from another planet.

WRIGHTSVILLE—Football star Herschel Walker, one of the nation's most sought-after high school athletes, has ended months of speculation by announcing he is no longer planning to attend college but will remain in his hometown to work for Clyde's Friendly Gulf service station instead.

"I simply couldn't make up my mind where to go," said Walker, "so I decided the heck with all of them."

Walker had received hundreds of offers of athletic scholarships but had reportedly narrowed his choices to three schools before making his shocking announcement.

Those three schools were the University of Georgia, Georgia Tech, and Clemson, none of which were able to win him over completely.

"You ever spent any time at Clemson?" Walker asked reporters at his hastily called press conference around the self-service pumps at Clyde's. "The only excitement there is when one of the fraternities holds a tractor wash or the red light in town goes on the blink."

What about the University of Georgia? Walker was asked.

"Four years of hearing. 'How 'bout them Dawgs!' and they would have had to mail my diploma to the funny farm," he said.

And Georgia Tech?

"Good school," Walker responded, "but I checked out who they have playing in the offensive line. Unfortunately, you can't block anybody with a slide rule. I'm afraid I'd get killed."

Walker had earlier indicated some interest in both UCLA and Southern California, but he explained they were out of the running, too.

"All they had to offer was a place to get a good suntan," Walker explained. "Now, I ask you. . . ."

The youngster's surprise announcement was met with disbelief and amazement from coaches and supporters of the three schools Walker had reportedly been considering for his final choice.

Georgia's Vince Dooley said previous plans to rename Sanford Stadium "Walker Field" would have to be scrapped, but the Bulldog head coach said the jersey Walker would have worn at Georgia will be retired anyway.

"We spent a lot of time and effort and most of our recruiting budget on Herschel," said Dooley. "We've got to have something to show for it."

Georgia Tech's Bill Curry fainted upon hearing the news, and three hairs on his head fell out of place for the first time since he was eleven.

"Why didn't he say he was interested in mechanics?" Curry asked, upon being revived. "Some of our top graduates own their own transmission shops or Brake-O franchises. We could have set him up for life."

Clemson's Danny Ford was also stunned.

"Work in a service station? I thought the kid wanted to be with the FBI. We were flying in Efrem Zimbalist, Jr., for his first game. If he had asked, we would have even let him change the tires on the school president's pickup."

Walker bristled at questions that asked what, if any, illegal recruiting tactics had been used to attract him.

"I didn't ask for, nor did I receive, any under-the-table offers," Walker said. "One school did offer me my own private dorm and a summer job as a bank president, but that is quite legitimate.

"I simply looked at what was available to me, and the decision to stay home and work for Clyde seemed the best. Besides, he's giving me Wednesday afternoons off and an employee discount on tires and tune-ups."

"He starts to work Monday morning," said a beaming Clyde. "I don't expect him to learn everything overnight, but the kid's gonna be a great one."

Big Night in ObKnoxville

Dorsey Hill, the world's biggest Bulldog fan, still hasn't gone back to work.

"I declared Monday 'Herschel Walker Day' in the state of Georgia," said Dorsey, "and, of course, nobody with red and black in his heart would work on 'Herschel Walker Day.'

"Tuesday, I was too hung over from 'Herschel Walker Day' to work. I'm going back Wednesday to open my mail, and then I have to take Thursday and Friday off to get ready for Texas A&M."

I've mentioned Dorsey in this space many times before. He graduated from the University of Georgia in 1966. He drove a 1957 Chevrolet convertible and was one of the first inductees into Bubber's Hall of Fame.

For those who received their higher educations elsewhere, Bubber's is a package store in downtown Athens which is steeped in tradition.

Dorsey would walk into Bubber's on a Thursday night, buy eight bottles of Red Hurricane wine (ninety-seven cents a bottle) and disappear for days.

Enough background. Dorsey's excitement this week is appropriate, of course, after Georgia opened its 1980 season with a 16-15 victory over Tennessee Saturday night in Knoxville.

"It ain't 'Knoxville,'" Dorsey always reminds me. "It's 'ObKnoxville.'"

Dorsey has no love for those of the Volunteer persuasion.

I attended the game myself and can now boast of having been a part of the largest crowd ever to gather for a sporting event this side of Ann Arbor, Michigan.

At last count there were 95,228 of us, bunched together in the sweltering heat. Several hundred were reportedly still sober when the game kicked off.

Quite frankly, I got sick and tired of the Herschel Walker recruiting story. I heard to much about where Herschel Walker, an eighteen-year-old, would attend college I secretly hoped he would stay home in Wrightsville and work for Clyde's Gulf.

But I must admit that after watching his performance in ObKnoxville Saturday night, he is apparently worth all the trouble, and whatever else, that it took for Georgia to ink him to a pact, one of my favorite sports cliches.

Have you ever watched a kids' game of football where one kid was so much better than all the other kids you felt sort of sorry for all the other kids?

Herschel Walker looked like that Saturday night. Clearly, he was the best athlete on the field, and my favorite part of the game was where he ran over the safety from Tennessee and the poor youngster didn't move for several moments.

"He won't be able to run over people in the Southeastern Conference like he did in high school," the smart money was saying only a few weeks back. Give him the ball and he could run over the Russian infantry.

Anyway, it was a marvelous experience, and since I was able to get a seat on a chartered bus, I didn't have to endure any of the traffic problems which are the rule around Neyland Stadium and the infamous local highway system affectionately known as "Malfunction Junction."

I also picked up one other Dorsey Hill gem I must share:

When Dorsey Hill goes to a football game, he makes a full-scale tour of it. Dorsey left Atlanta four days before kickoff and drove around the entire state of Tennessee to, as he put it, "get a feel for the game."

"Did you learn anything from your tour?" I asked Dorsey.

"Sure did," he replied. "I learned the three most overrated things in this world are extramarital sex, home cooking, and Rock City."

God Is a Bulldog

JACKSONVILLE, FLA.—Dorsey Hill, the world's biggest Bulldog fan, left here Sunday afternoon, bound for Auburn, Alabama, where Georgia's undefeated football team next appears.

"I don't think you can get from Jacksonville to Auburn," I had said to him.

"You change buses in Waycross and Columbus," Dorsey answered.

"You aren't going home first?"

"Home?" He screamed back. "I haven't worked since Texas A&M, and I haven't slept since Clemson. You expect me to go back home when we play Auburn in only six more days?"

I lost my head, I suppose.

A lot of people lost their heads here Saturday afternoon. Georgia played Florida. Georgia won the game, 26-21. It's a lot more complicated than that, however.

Georgia came into the game ranked second in the nation. To continue to compete for its first Big Banana ever, the national championship, Georgia had to continue its winning streak.

Florida ("bunch of swamp lizards and beach bums," according to Dorsey Hill) wanted to step on the Georgia dream.

Dorsey arrived here Thursday afternoon with thousands of others who made the early departure south from various points in Georgia. Many of those individuals were drunk as five-eyed owls by the time they reached the Florida line.

As local wit Rex Edmondson says, the Georgia-Florida game is the "annual celebration of the repeal of prohibition."

Dorsey waited until Friday to get into his serious pre-game drinking, however.

"I stopped at the New Perry Hotel Thursday for lunch and filled up on collards," he said. "It's hard to drink on a belly full of collards."

Agreed.

Now that I have had time to digest all that did eventually happen in college football Saturday, I think I can say without fear of charges of blasphemy that the whole thing was a religious experience.

"Deacon Dan" Magill, the "Baptist Bulldog," read a prayer Saturday morning to the Georgia faithful in which he beseeched the Almighty to help the Bulldogs "smite the Florida Philistines."

Then, there was the game itself. Georgia behind 21-20, ninety-three yards away, time running out.

"We need a miracle!" screamed Dorsey Hill, now fortified with more than collards.

Georgia got its miracle. Buck Belue to Lindsay Scott, for ninety-three yards and the winning touchdown with only seconds remaining.

If that wasn't enough, there was the astounding news from Atlanta. Georgia Tech had tied No. 1 Notre Dame. Surely, Georgia will be ranked first in America when the ratings are released.

"A tie was a gift from heaven," said Dorsey. "Notre Dame gets knocked out of number one, but Tech doesn't get a win. God is a Bulldog."

Verily.

I must make one confession here. I did it, and I must suffer the consequences.

I gave up at Jacksonville Saturday afternoon. Florida had the ball. Florida had the lead. There was only three minutes to play. I left the stadium. I was in the street when the miracle came.

"You are a gutless disgrace," Dorsey Hill said to me later.

He detailed my punishment:

"We're going to a tattoo parlor in this very town tonight," he began. "And you're going to have '26' tattooed on one of your cheeks in red. And you're going to have '21' tattooed in black on the other cheek. I don't want you to forget what you did."

I won't, but which cheeks is between me and the tattooist.

Charlie Harris

We're talking about thirty years ago. Sanford Stadium on the University of Georgia campus didn't have those double decks and seated maybe half of what it does today.

The players wore those funny-looking helmets, with no face guards, and they wore those awful high-top shoes Johnny Unitas would never give up.

Herschel Walker hadn't been born. Vince Dooley, the Georgia coach, was just a kid player himself.

Korea was happening.

That wonderful year, 1950. That was the year Charlie Harris arrived in Athens to play football for Georgia. Wally Butts was the head coach. Hard times—compared to the '40s and to the present Georgia season—had set in.

But halfback Charlie Harris would help Butts and the Bulldogs pull themselves together again, so the theory went.

He was fast. He was quick. He was, in the day before the term was used, a "franchise," a 1950s version of Herschel Walker, if you will.

He came in from a place called Goodwater, Alabama. Before he would leave, Dan Magill would nickname him, for his fleet moves, "The Gliding Ghost of Goodwater."

Charlie Harris had an excellent career at Georgia. He never reached the heights of a Trippi, a Sinkwich, a Tarkenton, nor, of course, a Walker, but he had his moments. He even captained the track team.

His four Georgia seasons were to be spread out in seven, however. After the '50 season he went into the Marine Corps and put in three years on the Camp Pendleton team.

"We had a lot of people trying awful hard to make that team," he remembered.

Get cut, get sent to Korea. That's pressure.

Charlie Harris came back to Athens after the Marines, played on the 1954-55-56 teams, had a cup of coffee with the Cleveland Browns, and later gave it a brief shot with the New York Titans, forefathers of the Jets, in the first season of the American Football League.

After that, Charlie Harris became a high school football coach, and that is where I met him. He turned up at Newnan High School at the same time I was John Q. Student. He taught my health class, where you learn not to brush your teeth the way everybody brushes their teeth.

But enough of history. I thought about Charlie Harris all day Saturday. Herschel Walker of Georgia was breaking all-time NCAA freshman rushing records. Mike Kelley of Georgia Tech was drilling passes.

Thousands were cheering. And Charlie Harris lay in his bed fighting a dog called leukemia.

It happened last April. Look at Charlie Harris. He's what they call a physical specimen. Still a long-distance runner at forty-nine.

"I was a runner before it became popular to run," he says. "Twenty miles was nothing for me."

The original marathon man. Never drank. Never smoked. Shamrock High principal. Husband. Father. Church man.

"I hadn't been to a doctor in twenty-three years," Charlie Harris said.

But in April, his endurance went. The ten-mile runs became six-mile runs, and then four-mile runs, and then, "I really didn't know what to do. I played under Wally Butts, and I guess I learned it there. You run everything out. Suddenly, I couldn't run it out anymore."

Leukemia was diagnosed. It got worse, then better. Lately, it has gotten worse again.

Charlie Harris and I talked the other day. I owed him at least a telephone call. Besides trying to save my teeth, he did me another favor seventeen years ago.

We talked about the chemotherapy, and the possibility of a bone marrow transplant, and I said the usual stupid things, like "Get well soon" and "If there's anything I can do . . ."

And Charlie Harris said, "What you learn from all this is nobody is indestructible."

Nobody, the man said. Not even the Gliding Ghost of Goodwater.

The lesson is there for the taking.

Charlie Harris died in the spring of 1981.

Mrs. Walker

WRIGHTSVILLE—The way you get to Herschel Walker's house from "downtown" Wrightsville, county seat of Johnson, is you take a right

on Idylwild Street and then you drive halfway back to Dublin looking for a white house on a hill across the railroad tracks.

You miss the house three or four times. When you finally sight it,
you cross the tracks and drive up a dirt road to the small frame
house where Herschel lived until he departed for Athens and the
University of Georgia and fame and what will likely amount to a
fortune before he quits carrying footballs.

Outside the house, dogs appear from nowhere. Two little dogs,
and one big dog who is a dead ringer for the dog that hung around
Spanky and his gang.

"That's Herschel's dog," says one of Herschel's brothers, who has
emerged from within the house. "That car (a red '55 Chevy) is
Herschel's car, too." That car turns out to be Herschel's "second" car.
His main wheels roll under a Pontiac Trans-Am.

Inside the house is the Herschel Walker Trophy Room. Plaques
cover the walls, trophies stand on every available surface. In the
middle of it all, strangely, hangs a frame that surrounds the faces of
Robert and John Kennedy and Dr. Martin Luther King, Jr.

The house is ten degrees past being warm. It is neat and warm. It
is filled this evening with children and grandchildren, and I notice
that Herschel Walker's family's television is black and white.

In a few years, when Herschel turns professional, he can buy his
family color televisions. Wall-to-wall.

I am here to see Herschel Walker's mother because nobody knows
Herschel Walker any better than she does. It has occurred to me
there could be somebody from another planet reading this who
doesn't know who Herschel Walker is.

Briefly, he's the best college football player alive. He plays for the
University of Georgia. He's just a freshman, and you can watch him
Thursday when he and his team meet Notre Dame in the Sugar Bowl.

Christine Walker, the good wife of Willis Walker, works all day in
a local clothing factory. She is a small, pretty woman with a soft,
reassuring voice. God gives mothers voices like that for a reason.

We talked in her living room. She sat on one end of the couch, me
on the other.

I asked her how much Herschel weighed when he was born. He is
the fifth of seven children.

"Eight pounds and three ounces," she answered. I noticed her face
break into a momentary beam. Mothers do that when they remember
when their children were babies.

I wanted to know what he ate when he was growing up.

"Peas," said Christine Walker.

"Peas?"

"That boy loved peas," she went on.

I asked what kind of peas.

"Red-hull peas," she said. "That's all he wanted to eat until he got a little older. Then he started eating hamburgers. I worry about him getting a balanced diet because all he wants is hamburgers."

Herschel Walker doesn't eat a balanced diet.

And he weighs 230 pounds and he runs like the wind. Put that in your blender and drink it.

I asked Herschel's mother if she ever spanked him.

"When he didn't mind," she answered.

I asked her what advice she gave Herschel when he left for college.

"I told him to make sure he leaves some time for his academics. I always stressed academics to him, and he paid attention to that. He always wanted to learn."

I asked her if she were proud of her son.

"Lord, yes," she answered, and there was that beam on her face again.

One other thing I asked her. I asked her if there was ever a time she was against her baby boy playing football.

"I tried to talk him out of it in the eighth grade," she said.

"Why?" I asked.

"I was afraid he might hurt somebody."

Magill

In the university town of Athens, Georgia, there was a pub called Harry's. Not really a pub. Outside of Atlanta, pubs are beer joints. And they served the beer cold and in cans at Harry's, with pickled eggs and a meaty tasty called a "Slim-Jim."

Later on autumn evenings in a simpler time that was the early sixties, the Slim-Jims were a nickel and there would be an inevitable gathering inside and around one of Harry's wooden booths. The crowd—five, six, sometimes seven or eight—would include an assortment of individuals who had as bonds a daily thirst for the canned brew, at least a fringe involvement with University of Georgia sports, and, perhaps most of all, a love for the spun yarn. Some of the stories told there over the years were true.

The floor was open for the first couple of rounds. The silver-haired English professor would recite his dirty limericks again: "There was a coed from Fitzgerald . . ." began everybody's favorite. A sportswriter from Atlanta had a rumor: Dodd at rival Georgia Tech would soon retire. An ex-Georgia football player who never left town or

graduated would insist again that the coaches of the time cussed less
on the practice field than they had in his day. "Three years after I
played out my eligibility," he would begin again, "I still thought my
name was 'Pissant.'"

Soon, however, the chirping of the sparrows would cease. And, as
it always seemed the good Lord had intended, the man of every
evening hour at Harry's, one Daniel Hamilton Magill, would assume
verbal command to speak at great length and with never-ending
embellishment of tales that rivaled those of the deaths of kings.

I was a nineteenish sports editor of the local morning journal at
the time, no more than tolerated by Harry's regulars. Nearly two
decades later there has still been no manner of man to compare with,
the Lord-bless-him, Magill.

Magill is a genuine, living legend, although that may not be apparent at first glance. He is balding. He laughs at his own jokes, and he
turns red in the face. He is married to a Phi Beta Kappa and could
have been one himself. He did as well in school as he did, he says,
because he sat next to "A-plus Mason" and "Straight-A Milligan."
He has three children. Two are girls, both former beauty queens. His
son was a top tennis player at Princeton and is now a heart special-
ist.

Magill, and it is always simply "Magill," may be further introduced in a number of ways. He was Georgia's director of sports
information for thirty years before being named assistant athletic
director, as well as director of athletic department public relations.
Magill is fifty-eight. He is the University of Georgia tennis coach,
and has been since 1955. Magill is also a long-play album on Georgia
sporting history, and he has worked seven days a week, week in and
week out, at it. All of this may be more commendable than epic, but I
have entertained a two-decade-old notion that this man's life was
destined for cinematic exposure.

But consider if one were casting a movie of his life and times. One
would need, say, a Charlton Heston for Magill's own tennis prowess
that continues full-throttle on a senior level. One would need an
Ozzie Nelson for Magill's campus stereotype, and a taller George
Gobel, in his comedic prime, for the Magill wit. And then go out and
find somebody like Will Rogers for tale-bearing qualities.

And remember, too, that here you are dealing with one of the
greatest Deep south accents since man drawled the first "y'all." Tex
Ritter had a fair-to-middling Southern accent. Charles Laughton, of
all people, as Senator Seab Cooley of South Carolina in *Advise and
Consent*, was Hollywood's best attempt. But in Magill, you have
South-in-the-mouth that is matchless.

Such are the problems that arise when the task is to capture Magill in the limits of the printed word. The beauty of one of his stories, one of his lines, can be mocked by a chosen few. But arriving at a suitable re-creation armed only with a typewriter makes coming close all that is achievable.

Suffice it to say, Magill's "great" is not "grate," but "greyette." His "coach" is more "co-atch."

It is only with the preceding rambling characterization and the subsequent apologetic ground-ruling that Magill may be tackled further. What follows knows no order, either. To pull order to Magill would be nearly disrespectful. Offered next is simply Magillobilia that goes in a thousand different directions, trying to keep up:

Magill grew up in Athens and has been a nonresident only twice: once as a Marine officer in World War II and another time as editor of high school sports at the *Atlanta Journal* in the late forties. His father was editor of the *Athens Banner-Herald*, and, at fourteen, the son became sports editor. He was paid two movie passes a week.

It was during these formative years that Magill took his first step toward a lifetime as a matchless promoter. He had taken a dual interest in snakes and tennis and he saw no reason why the two could not be combined for fun and profit.

Magill had served his snake apprenticeship under Ross Allen, who went on to become snake-handler supreme in Florida. Allen had worked at the Athens YMCA camp and young Magill was one of his students.

Soon afterwards, it fell upon Magill to become caretaker of the University of Georgia tennis courts, honest-to-goodness red clay that they were in those days. Magill chose the courts as the logical site for his first great promotion, a Depression-days snake fight between his own Casper Kingsnake and Rastus Rattler, who had been captured in the north Georgia hills and transported to Athens via bicycle by one of Magill's friends.

A capacity crowd was on hand at a dime a head. "The crowd," Magill can still remember and recount with his special flair, "became so large and noisy it frightened the combatants. Neither Casper nor Rastus would move from their appointed corners. It was touch-and-go for several moments."

The promoter saved the farm, however. Magill's stick-prodding of Rastus brought a strike from the prodee, and Magill's leap in retreat satisfied the customers.

"I don't really know what happened," he was to say years later. "But we finally put my Casper and Rastus in the same cage together after it became apparent they were not inclined to fight. I returned to check on them several days later, and only Casper remained in the cage. There was a rather satisfied look upon his face, and he seemed to have gained a few pounds.

Magill later promoted successful high school all-star games in Atlanta while working for the *Atlanta Journal*. He put together a Jack Kramer–Bobby Riggs tennis match in Atlanta in the forties and drew more than 3,000, the largest tennis crowd ever in the South at the time. His Georgia tennis matches have often drawn larger audiences than Georgia basketball games in the massive, 10,000-seat Coliseum. Incidentally, attendance figures at Georgia athletic contests are official: Magill, with a quick glance to the stands, estimates them.

As sports information director, Magill had the responsibility of handing out press box tickets, compiling miles of statistics, and publicizing Georgia athletics. What wasn't a duty, but is now a tradition, is Magill's conjuring of alliterative nicknames for Georgia Bulldogs athletes. There have been some classics:

Bobby Walden, who went on to punt for the Pittsburgh Steelers, was Magill's "Big Toe from Cairo." (Keep in mind that the south Georgia city of Cairo is pronounced "Kay-ro.")

Kicker Spike Jones was "Sputnik Spike."

Savannah running back Julian Smiley was the "Chatham Cheetah."

Halfback Charlie Harris was known as the "Gliding Ghost of Goodwater, Alabama."

Fullback Ronnie Jenkins, a south Georgian, had a couple of Magill nicknames. Magill called him "The Wild Bull of the Flatlands" for his running ability.

"He was a great blocker, too, on the Georgia championship team of 1966," Magill remembered. "He used to literally knock people out with his blocks. I called him the 'Ebullient Embalmer' because he always smiled at his opponent before cracking him. He really enjoyed his work."

Quarterback Andy Johnson, now with the New England Patriots, was Andy "The Unimpeachable" Johnson to Magill. Perhaps Magill's greatest accomplishment, however, was the nickname for German-born placekicker Peter Rajecki, known as the "Bootin' Teuton."

The 1980 season brought Georgia its brilliant freshman running back, Herschel Walker, and Magill reportedly went into seclusion in his back yard vineyard for hours before coming out with "the best I can do right now," that being "Herschel the Unmerciful."

Magill gives credit to one of his understudies in Bulldoggerel, Dewey Benefield of Sea Island, for what he considers an even better nickname for Walker. It was a Benefield poem that followed Walker's debut against Tennessee that referred to the Wrightsville Wonder (my feeble attempt) as "That Goal-Line Stalker, Herschel Walker."

(It's even bettah when you heah Magill pronounce it. "That Goal-Line *Stawlkah*, Herschel *Wawlkah*.")

It was in tennis that Magill's rhyming nirvana may have been reached. It was during the NCAA finals in Athens that the Flouri brothers of Missouri showed up as a doubles act. Long after they had been ousted from the tournament, Magill still delighted in calling them from the press box's public address system: "Will 'Flooorey' and 'Flooorey' from 'Mizoooorey' please report. . . ."

Magill has frequently even been called on by the university to perform duties of great importance. It was Magill who took upon himself the burden of finding a new tennis coach for the university in 1955.

Several turned me down," he recalls. "So finally, I decided I would take the job myself." Later, so the story goes, it was suggested to Magill that Georgia had been lucky he had appointed himself to the tennis position. "Indeed," was his reply.

Indeed, indeed. Magill has built a tennis dynasty at Georgia. His teams have won the Southeastern Conference tennis championship nine of the last eleven years. His 1981 team finished third nationally. Magill was honored in 1980 at the U.S. Open Championships in New York for having recorded his 500th victory as a collegiate tennis coach.

Magill was himself a tennis player and varsity swimmer at Georgia. He has a string of state and Southern singles and doubles tennis titles and still plays every day. It is table tennis at which he may be most adept, however.

He won the state singles championships ten of the twelve times he competed from 1933 to 1958. He also played what legend records as the longest single point in the history of the game, a point he eventually lost. Magill and his opponent were hooked up in a match at the Athens YMCA. In walked an innocent bystander who inquired as to the score: "Three-two, Magill," was the reply. That information in hand, off went the bystander uptown to a movie. He returned to the YMCA some hours later, following a double feature, and was surprised to see the match still in progress. Again he inquired as to the score. Again came the reply. "Three-two, Magill."

There are those who insist that there should be a special Magill Practical Joke Hall of Fame. Two of the incidents that belong there are as follows:

Once Magill was returning with his tennis team from a match in Tallahassee, Florida. The team, traveling in two cars, stopped for gas in Thomasville.

"How do we pay for this, Coach Magill?" asked the player who was driving the car that pulled to the pump first.

"Just tell the man I'll take care of it, and you go on ahead after you have filled up," Magill, in the rear car, answered.

The player did what Magill told him and drove off. After filling Magill's car, the attendant asked Magill to pay for the gasoline he had pumped into the first car.

"Pay for what?" Magill asked. "I've never seen those people in that car before in my life."

Legend has it that it was in Dublin where the authorities finally caught up with the victims of Magill's joke. (They were released in time to win the next match.)

Magill once had a secretary who was the perfect subject for one of his famous telephone tricks. The secretary had arranged a party—complete with champagne—for a Georgia basketball coach who had just completed the school's first winning season since the Roosevelt administration—Teddy's. In the Georgia governor's house at the time was Lester Maddox, a teetotaller who wanted everybody else to be.

Magill answered a rigged call, ostensibly from Atlanta and the state capitol.

"Well, Governor, I don't think the girls have meant any harm with having a little champagne at the party even though this is a state-supported institution," he began. The secretary was aghast. The argument got hotter. Magill ended it with, "Well, to hell with you, too, you little ballheaded bigot!" The secretary, swear those who were there, fainted.

Magill has other accomplishments touching lightly on the near-athletic.

He has, for a long time, claimed the title of world's fastest two-finger typist. He was once challenged by a journalism professor, who typed full fingered. Could Magill's two outdo the professor's ten? Final score: Magill, fourteen lines; journalism professor, twelve.

Magill also claimed the world's two-fingers-only chinup title as well. He would perform on any available half-in door facing. Tragically, he was challenged one day at lunch after a tuna sandwich.

"My hands were greasy, and I slipped off," Magill contends. A broken collarbone was the result.

Magill refers to himself as a "chain soft drink-drinker." He has his own soft-drink machine, which was presented to him by the Athens Coca-Cola Company and is decked with a plaque that bears his name. His addiction to soft drinks is such that there are those who say that in the days he scored Georgia baseball games, he connected a garden hose from the press box to the men's room directly below for nature's calls at mid-inning.

There is no Georgia fan as dedicated to the cause as Magill. There is no Georgia fan who is any more foursquare against the "enemy," rival Georgia Tech, than Magill.

He contends that Georgia Tech's Grant Field has a slightly higher seating capacity than Georgia's Sanford Stadium because the Grant Field seats are smaller. One must thus be a "squint-ass" to enjoy a Yellow Jacket game. Georgia victories and Tech losses on same Saturdays are praised as "doubleheaded sweeps."

Perhaps no voice in history has ever spoken with more bias or with more pure love than when Dan Magill speaks of his University of Georgia. Breathes there a Bulldog with soul so dead that he doesn't respond emotionally to the standard beginning line of every Magill speech:

"My fellow Georgia Bulldogs, chosen people of the Western world."

Doug Barfield

Auburn University, Vince Dooley's alma mater, attempted to hire him away from Georgia after the 1980 regular season. In all the shouting and anxious moments concerning Dooley's decision—which was eventually to remain at Georgia—the forgotten man was the man Auburn fired in order to make room for Dooley, Doug Barfield. Major college football is a cruel, unforgiving sport that can cast you aside on the whims of fools.

Before the Vince Dooley-Auburn thing is put to rest completely, I wanted to bring up one more name.

Doug Barfield.

I've never met Doug Barfield. Frankly, I wouldn't know him if he walked into my office and asked me to dance. But I have this thing about underdogs, and Doug Barfield qualifies as one. In spades.

He was Auburn's football coach until Monday. He spent a total of nine years at Auburn University, five as an assistant coach and the last four as the head coach.

He never had a chance. Seldom, if you follow a legend, do you have a chance, especially in the fickle arena of sports.

Doug Barfield followed the beloved Shug Jordan as Auburn's football coach and it was just a matter of time before the alumni ax fell upon him.

The same thing happened to Bud Carson, who followed Bobby Dodd at Georgia Tech, and to countless others. The man who follows Vince Dooley at the University of Georgia will probably just be marking time until he is canned.

I don't know if Doug Barfield was a good football coach or not, but the only measure these days seems to be: Did you win all your games? A negative answer to that question can have you in the insurance business overnight.

Pepper Rodgers, who got fired as Georgia Tech's head football coach because the alumni didn't like his hair, said to me once: "Coaching is the craziest business in the world. If you're a brain surgeon and your patient dies, you can walk out to the family, look sincere, and say, 'I'm sorry, but I did all I could do.' And you still get paid.

"In coaching, some nineteen-year-old drops the football and you lose the game, and they'll run you out of town."

They were talking big bucks in the will-Dooley-go-to-Auburn crisis. I read $1.8 million. Imagine that. And here was Dooley struggling with the decision:

Do I stay in my beautiful home in Athens and make all this money here, or do I move into a beautiful home in Auburn and make all that money there?

The human side of this story is, what in the devil was Doug Barfield doing all that time?

Auburn has been his home for nine years. He has two children enrolled at Auburn.

"He was torn asunder by all this," an Auburn man told me Thursday.

I remember back several weeks ago when the rumors started flying that Barfield would be fired. A man named Charles Smith, a member of the Auburn Board of Trustees, made all sorts of noise about finding a coach who would be tougher on the players than Barfield.

Charles Smith runs a laundry in Montgomery. Can you imagine having some guy who runs a laundry deciding how well you were performing in your chosen profession?

More on Doug Barfield from my friend in Auburn:

"He's warm. He has more class than he's ever been given credit for. He's kind. And under all this pressure and criticism, he was a man of steel."

While Auburn officials offered Dooley the farm this week, Doug Barfield quietly resigned. He said, "I don't want to be anyplace I'm not wanted." He also said, "But I don't feel like I have to hide my face."

I wouldn't be a football coach if you gave me the pick of the cheerleaders.

Monday, when all the hoopla about Dooley was at its height, Doug Barfield was in Montgomery. He had been summoned for federal court jury duty.

Each prospective juror was asked to stand before the court and give his name, place of residence, and occupation.

Doug Barfield stood and said:

"Doug Barfield.

"Auburn, Alabama.

"Unemployed."

War Eagle.

This One Is Forever

NEW ORLEANS—I am writing this from the sixteenth floor of the Howard Johnson Motor Hotel in downtown New Orleans. I can see the top of the Louisiana Superdome from this perch. It looks more like one of those ominous nuclear power plants than a sports stadium. The truth is, the place exploded, what is now four hours ago.

I am no stranger to madness. I have attended an Indianapolis 500 automobile race, the annual salute to mental illness. That was nothing compared to this.

This was wild. This was crazy. This was downright scary at times.

A cop on the floor of the Dome said, "Thank God they ain't armed."

A security man screamed to no one in particular, "I've got the damn president of the United States in here and I can't get him out!"

A female member of the Notre Dame band, holding onto her flute as she surveyed the incredible scene before her, said, "If it meant that much, I'm glad Georgia won."

It meant that much. Grown men cried. A man kissed Georgia defensive coach Erskine Russell squarely on the top of his bald head. Erk just smiled.

I saw a man get down on his fours and bark like a wild dog (dawg) and try to bite passersby. A woman I had never seen before lifted her skirt to show me her underpants. "Georgia" was stitched hip to hip.

Let me take you back to when the playing of the 1981 Sugar Bowl Football game between Georgia and Notre Dame first began to show signs of the subsequent emotional explosion that it became.

New Year's Eve on Bourbon Street. It's the Red Sea. If there are Notre Dame people in town, where are they?

The 1 Bourbon Street Inn, in the very heart of the French Quarter, is packed with Georgians. The third floor balcony is Bulldog Central. The bathtubs in the adjoining rooms are filled with ice and champagne.

The people in the street, thousands of them, scream, "HERSCHEL!"

The people on the balcony respond, "WALKER!"

A chant aimed at what brave or stupid Notre Damers might be in earshot begins:

"YOU GOT THE HUNCHBACK! WE GOT THE TAILBACK!"

"The Pope's a dope" came out a couple of times, too—there's one in every madhouse.

At midnight there was much kissing and hugging and how-'bout-them-dawging and speaking of dogs (dawgs), the Georgia mascot, "Uga," showed up at the party on the third floor Bourbon Street Inn balcony, and I heard one man say to another:

"Hey, how'd your lip get cut?"

To which the second man replied. "I was kissing 'Uga' on the mouth at midnight and he bit me."

When the sun rose on 1981, there were those still partying from the night before. Three hours before kickoff, the city was covered in red. Red hats, red pants, red shirts—red, I was to discover later, underwear as well.

The Game. So close. God bless Mrs. Walker. Thirty seconds are left, Georgia leading, 17-10. Notre Dame can't stop the clock. At :14 showing, the game ends because every Bulldog from Rabun Gap to Tybee Light and Hartwell to Bainbridge has charged onto the floor of the Louisiana Superdome.

They trampled each other. They trampled the players, the coaches, the press, they ripped down a goal post.

The public-address announcer pleaded and pleaded and pleaded: "Please clear the field! PLEASE clear the field!" They turned off the lights, but the Georgia band kept playing, and the people, that delirious mass of people, kept on celebrating.

It got ugly a couple of times. Secret Service men trying to get Jimmy Carter out of the building shoved a few citizens around.

And then there was this group of little girls, the "High Steppers" from Shreveport or someplace, who had competed for the right to perform at the Sugar Bowl. They were cute little girls wearing cowboy hats. They were left out of the pregame show because the teams stayed on the field too long. They were promised they could perform after the game. They lined up, all neat and nice, but there was no way.

One little girl said. "I don't want to go out there. We might get hurt." They finally gave it up and went back to Shreveport. Sad.

But it was also bright and beautiful and boisterous and an All-American sort of thing that other schools have enjoyed, so now it is Georgia's turn to point the finger to the sky. It may be days before the last Bulldog leaves New Orleans. The streets would not be safe Thursday night.

Number One, by God. Number Ever-Lovin'-One. The sign in the Georgia locker room had said it all:

"This one is forever."

11

PEACH OF A STATE

I was born in Fort Benning, Georgia, in the wee, morning hours of October 20, 1946. As an adult, I have left Georgia to live in another place only once. For nearly two years, I was a prisoner of war in Chicago, Illinois, a cold place where it often gets dark at half past four in the afternoon.

Georgia is a diverse state, with spectacular mountains and a sun-splashed seacoast and piney woods and rolling fields and Atlanta, a city in a park. I love the state like I would a good woman. I revel in her beauty and charm, and I forgive her every fault.

I love the way her people act and think and talk. I love her Macons, her Savannahs, and especially her tiny Snellvilles. I love her good ol' girls who will still cook a man a homemade bisuit in the morning, and I love her good ol' boys who weren't bothering anybody, and then Billy Carter's brother went and got himself elected president.

There was that country song, "If I Ever Get Back to Georgia, I'm Gonna Nail My Feet to the Ground." I did. And I have. . . .

Shove It Up My What?

I received an angry note the other day from a Ms. Gloria Schmaltz, who used to live in Atlanta. Now she lives in Portland, Maine.

Believe it or not, I have been to Portland, Maine. It is a seacoast town, a little dingy as I recall, but lobster was cheap.

Ms. Schmaltz's note was brief, but there could be little question as to what had raised her ire.

Me.

It seems some of Ms. Schmaltz's former friends in Atlanta had sent her one of my old columns that concerned what I consider to be a major issue—homemade biscuits.

Ms. Schmaltz read the column and then wrote me the note.

"Reading it," began her message, "helped me remember why, at age thirty, I retired to the North. It is good old boys like you that bring out my hairy-legged worst."

Then, Ms. Schmaltz really got nasty.

"You can take your South," she wrote, "and shove your biscuits up your Confederarse."

Pretty talk, Ms. Schmaltz.

I really feel terrible about all this. Here a woman has moved all the way from Atlanta to the dingy little seacoast town of Portland, Maine, just to get away from the strain of Southern male we know as the "good ol' boy."

Shucks, Ms. Schmaltz, was it something we might have said? Was your mother frightened by a pickup truck while she was carrying you?

Perhaps you were offended by our music, Willie and Waylon and Merle and Conway. Sorry, we just like to pat our foot occasionally and hear a song or two about cheatin' and hurtin' and old dogs and children and watermelon wine.

I've got it. You think we drink too much. I guess we do, but a good ol' boy's longneck beer is sort of his security blanket, like if somebody insults the good name of Richard Petty, you are secure in the knowledge you are holding onto something you can break over his head.

We're loud, maybe? I guess we are, but we're colorful. Know how many good ol' boys it takes to screw in a lightbulb, Ms. Schmaltz?

Four. One to screw in the lightbulb, one to write a song about it, and two more to start a fistfight in the parking lot.

And then there's football. You probably don't care a thing about football, do you, Ms. Schmaltz? Good ol' boys do, of course, and that probably bothers you.

But give us that, Ms. Schmaltz. A fellow has to have something to hold his interest when he's not fishing or playing with his dog.

And that column I wrote about biscuits really bothered you, didn't it? You have to understand I wrote it as a public service.

Do you realize the divorce rate in this country? All I did was quote the great philosopher Jerry Clower, who is of the opinion that if more women would cook homemade biscuits for their husbands in the mornings—instead of serving those horrible impostors that come from cans—the divorce rate would go down.

I also wrote that women who wouldn't cook homemade bisuits occasionally probably wouldn't shave their legs, either.

That was just a little joke, Ms. Schmaltz, but I noticed in your note you mentioned something about being "hairy-legged" yourself. That certainly doesn't make you a bad person, but in the words of my boyhood friend and idol, Weyman C. Wannamaker, Jr., a great American, "I wouldn't take a hairy-legged woman to a rat-killin'."

All I am saying, Ms. Schmaltz, is don't judge us too harshly, and please try to understand that good ol' boys need love and understanding, too.

Incidentally, since your heart obviously wasn't in the South you left, I, for one, am glad you got YOUR Confederarse out.

Of Giggling Yankee Girls

I made a 300-mile automobile trip recently, and I noticed the summer's wanderlust has brought out the hitchhikers in great numbers.

I still offer an occasional lift to a hitchhiker, despite the fact that next to "Always wear clean underwear, you might be in a wreck," my mother's favorite piece of advice was, "Never pick up a hitchhiker."

But how can I resist? In my youth I rode my thumb to all sorts of wondrous places, like once all the way from my hometown in Moreland, Georgia, to Daytona Beach, Florida, and back.

I never spent more than two hours at any one stretch without a ride, and a carload of Yankee girls picked me up just outside Palatka and took me the rest of the way into Daytona.

To a Georgia country boy of sixteen, getting to ride in the same car with a group of Yankee girls is a rare and, as I was to discover later, valuable experience.

"Talk for us," they would plead, and I would say things like "yawl" and "dawg" and "grey-its," and they would giggle and talk about how cute I was.

Many years later, standing uncomfortably alone at a bar on the east side of New York City, I recalled that experience, and in a loud voice, began to say "yawl" and "dawg" and "grey-its." Soon I was surrounded by a gaggle of giggling Yankee girls talking about how cute I was.

It doesn't take much to impress Yankee girls, bless their hearts.

The surprising thing about the hitchhikers I saw on my trip was they all looked rather unkempt.

I even saw a young man hitchhiking with no shirt. He obviously was a rookie. There are certain rules every hitchhiker should know, and the first one is: Never try to catch a ride looking like you've just escaped from reform school.

When I was hitchhiking, I always tried to portray the right-young-man-probably-trying-to-get-to-his-grandparents'-house-for-a-visit image.

You don't need a coat and tie for that, but neat clothing and a recent haircut are important, not to mention a look of sincerity about you that will assure the driver trying to decide whether to pick you up that you likely remain after Sunday School for the worship hour and you don't make a habit of cutting throats.

Also, it is important to remember: Once you have gotten a ride, to keep your mouth shut. Let me explain why:

A friend and I were hitchhiking together. My friend was from a very religious family. We caught a ride with a man and his wife.

A few minutes after we had been picked up, the man lit a cigarette. My friend said to him from the back seat, "Please put out that cigarette."

The man said, "Why, kid?"

And my friend said, "Because if the Lord had intended you to smoke, he would have given you a smokestack, that's why."

The man pulled over and put us out of his car. It was the middle of the night somewhere near Eastaboga, Alabama.

"If the Lord had intended you to roll," the man said, "he'd have put wheels on your butts."

We spent the remainder of the night in a cornfield. Big-mouth stayed awake and prayed for a ride that never came. I slept. And dreamt of giggling Yankee girls.

How to Spell "N-e-k-k-i-d"

A picky reader wrote recently to protest the way I often choose to spell the word that means not having any clothes on.

The dictionary way that word should be spelled in "n-a-k-e-d." Sometimes it is okay to spell it that way. Most of the time, however, I prefer to spell that word "n-e-k-k-i-d."

There most certainly is a difference. "Naked" does, in fact, mean having no clothes on. "Nekkid," on the other hand, means not having any clothes on and you're up to something.

For example:

"We all come into this world naked."

But, "Let's get nekkid and run through the woods."

My point here is that a writer, especially one from Georgia, should not have to be chained to the formal spelling of a word when another spelling and pronunciation conjures a better image of what the writer is trying to portray.

Take the word "police." That does just dandy when you type something like, "Police in Toledo today announced the arrest of. . . ."

But that doesn't work when you want to type, "Why are all the police in Bogalusa so fat?"

In that case, the word must be changed to "poh-lice," as in "Joe Billy hit Marvin on the head with a beer bottle and then Darlene called the *poh-lice*."

I hope this is making sense. Regardless, let's go onward, and, as long as we're in the area of law enforcement, consider the words "motorcycle" and "siren."

I prefer "motor-sickle" and "sireen," as in, "The *poh-lice* were chasing Joe Billy on their *motor-sickles* and their dang-blasted *si-reens* were loud enough to wake the dead."

A colleague and I were dicussing this very same matter recently, and he brought up the problem of "threw" and "through."

"If you say, 'He *threw* something *through* something,' it sounds sort of weird," my colleague explained.

And how do you get around such a problem? Simple. By the use of one of my favorite words, "thowed," as in "He *thowed* something *through* something."

I could go on all day:

• "Business": That is fine unless you are describing a Southern male involved in the selling and trading of previously owned automobiles. Then, he is in the used car *bidness*.

• "Ask": There is no such word south of Louisville, Kentucky. The word is *ast*.

• "Sucker": Sometimes that works. Most of the time, *suckah* seems to say it so much better.

Let's end this with a simple exercise: Using the new spellings you have learned for the words mentioned above, make up a cute little story. Okay:

"Joe Billy and Darlene of Bogalusa had a thing going on, but one day Joe Billy caught Darlene and Marvin running *nekkid* through the woods. Joe Billy chased down Marvin and *thowed* him through the bushes and then hit him up side the head with a beer bottle.

"Darlene called the *poh-lice*, and here they come on their *motor-sickles* with their *si-reens* turned up loud enough to wake the dead.

"The *poh-lice* caught Joe Billy and hauled him off to jail. Marvin had fourteen stiches and missed two weeks off from his used car *bidness*.

"Darlene, meanwhile, ran off with Harvey, another poor *suckah* who's *astin'* for trouble."

Snellville: Part I

My father was born in Snellville, Georgia, in a house on a hill that now stands above the Thriftown store off highway 78. When he was a young man, he was in the retail hot dog business here. "I ran a wienie joint," is how he described it.

"One day these two old girls in a '36 Essex coup lost control of their car and ran all up in my little wienie joint," he'd laugh.

Was there any damage?

"Was there any damage? There wasn't an onion left, son. Not an onion."

I went out to my father's grave Saturday afternoon. We brought him home when he died and buried him next to Adolphus and Eugenia, his parents. The cemetery sits in a corner of a pastureland across the road from Zoar Methodist Church, out a ways from town.

I don't really know why people go and stand over graves. It's been seven years. But it was peaceful out there Saturday. Black Angus cattle were grazing to the right, and I hadn't seen that in a while.

Zoar church was established in 1811. It's frame and painted white and probably hasn't changed that much in all this time. They've added on to the back, it looked like, and there may be air conditioning now. That spoiled the memory of a favorite scene—the women fanning themselves on hot Sunday mornings with those fans Zack Cravey used to hand out when he was running for Georgia fire commissioner again.

Snellville is maybe twenty miles from downtown Atlanta. It used to be no more than one of those proverbial bumps in the road to Athens.

You take the Stone Mountain freeway and then two-lane 78 east to get there. Traffic can be tough. Snellville has graduated into a full-fledged bedroom community of Atlanta. Population is 7,000 and growing.

There is a housing development called Lake Lucerne in the area. Lake Lucerne is formerly Possum Pond. Snellville cometh of age. But its pace is more sensible. I was assured the drugstore still serves Coke as God intended: Two squirts of syrup and a dash of carbonated water.

Snellville gave itself a "day" Saturday. There was a parade, of course. Senator Sam Nunn was the grand marshal. It's not an election year, so there were no long speeches.

There was a Jaycee barbecue. Six hundred-fifty chickens went to heaven, and you could have all the iced tea you could drink. The Monroe Girls Drum and Bugle Corps hasn't missed a parade since

Moby Dick was a minnow. They were there. Gordon Tanner and the
Junior Skillet Lickers danced, the Matthews Family Gospel Group
sang about Jesus, and a Marine band played "God Bless America"
while the old men stood at attention.

That evening they had a baseball game. I went with Ludlow Porch
of WRNG radio, Snellville's most celebrated citizen. We sat in the
Bermuda grass along the rightfield line and fought off the mosquitoes. "Only one thing worse than mosquitoes," Ludlow said, "and
that's running barefooted through the pasture and stubbing your toe
on a stob."

Snellville's South Gwinnett High played Gainesville. The game
was tight. Both managers chewed Red Man and spat a lot. I caught
the Gainesville signs. Right hand across the letters and two spits for
steal.

The score stood 1-1 in the middle innings when a South Gwinnett
batter fouled a couple off behind the screen into a corn patch and
then lined a pitch over the centerfield fence into what we used to call
a pine thicket; 2-1. In the same inning, another South Gwinnett
batter homered to right. The South Gwinnett pitcher, a youth called
"Bonut," as in "donut," held off a Gainesville rally in the last inning,
and the Snellville team won the game, 3-1.

They build all those big stadiums and pay out all that money. It
was here I saw a sixteen-year-old shortstop go deep into the hole,
stab the ball, turn completely around and throw the runner out by a
half step.

Both teams met in the middle of the field when the game ended and
congratulated each other. Admission was free.

Afterwards, there was a street dance up at the Thriftown parking
lot.

"I've been everywhere there is to go, and I've done everything
there is to do," the old man used to say. "I probably should have
never left Snellville."

I used to wonder what he meant by that.

Snellville: Part II

The startling success of "Dallas," CBS' prime-time soap opera, has
the other two networks searching feverishly for something to rival
the giant hit.

"We don't want a carbon copy of 'Dallas,'" a source at NBC said,
"but we do want a program that would offer the same week-to-week
suspense."

"Exactly," echoed a high-ranking executive at ABC. "Networks have copied each other for too long. We want our own 'Dallas,' but not really a 'Dallas,' if you know what I mean."

I love that big-time television talk.

I was going to hold back on this for a few more months, but with all the hoopla "Dallas" got over the weekend for finally revealing who plugged J.R., I suppose I should go ahead and release the news:

Yours truly is busy at work on a script for a new television prime-time soap opera that he will sell to the highest bidder, who may then blow "Dallas" halfway to El Paso.

Get the picture. The camera pans the horizon, and then the triumphant name is spread across the screen:

"SNELLVILLE"!

Yes, television fans, "Snellville," the dramatic new series that follows the lives and loves and trials and tribulations of the Gooch family of Snellville, Georgia, bedroom community to the booming metropolis of Atlanta.

You want strong characters, I'll give you strong characters.

Meet Billy Oscar (B.O.) Gooch, the tyrannical eldest son of Grover (Big Tuna) Gooch, who founded the powerful Gooch Fish Market, "Your Channel Catfish and Mullet Headquarters in Snellville and Gwinnett County since 1913."

Then, there is B.O.'s mama, Big Tuna's wife, Pigella (Miss Piggie) Gooch, who can scale and clean a mess of bream in two shakes of a cow's tail.

Which brings up Sophie Jo Gooch, B.O.'s wife, who wasn't bad looking until she got hooked on Twinkies, and now she's the size of the county dump truck.

One day a man was passing through Snellville and saw Sophie Joe standing in front of the fish market.

He walked inside, and B.O. asked if he would like to order a mess of channel cat, fresh from nearby Possum Pond.

"No," said the man, looking out the window at Sophie Jo, "but what'll you take for your whale?"

Also in the script is Wanda Joe, Sophie Jo's dynamite little sister who comes to visit the Gooches for the summer. And then there is B.O.'s younger brother, Norbert (Oyster Face) Gooch, and his wife, Carmelita, whom he met when she came through town doing a motorcycle act for the carnival.

The immediate family also includes Darlene Gooch, precious granddaughter, whose parents deserted her for the nightlife and bright lights of Loganville.

Here's the plot: You put all these people in the same double-wide mobile home at the Bid-A-Wee Trailer Park, and the possibilities are endless.

B.O. is fooling around with Sophie Jo's sister, Wanda Jo. Sophie Jo, meanwhile, is just sitting there feeding her face another batch of Twinkies.

B.O. is also trying to run his brother, Oyster Face, out of the family fish business at the same time Oyster Face's wife, Carmelita, is laid up with three broken ribs and a cracked head from trying to drive her motorcycle up the steep side of Stone Mountain.

B.O. is a no-good creep whose clothes always smell like fish. The only friends he has are local cats who always follow him when he walks down the street.

The plot thickens when, in the last episode of the season, B.O. is beaten senseless with a frozen bass by an unnamed assailant.

Who shot J.R.? Who cares? Who belted B.O. with a frozen bass? "SNELLVILLE"! It even smells like a hit.

The Sweetwater Inn Open

It was something out of a dream urbanites with rural roots probably still have occasionally if they haven't forgotten what home was like.

Saturday afternoon in a small town. It is hotter than the law should allow. Fat folks, old folks, and dogs seek the shade. Nothing is moving with any semblance of speed save the Southern Railway freights that roll through town on their way to the yards in Atlanta.

A number of wise men had gathered at the Sweetwater Inn in Austell—maybe twenty miles from downtown Atlanta out I-20. I can't describe the Sweetwater Inn in any other fashion. It is a beer joint, classic in both appearance and clientele. I mean no disrespect. I hold beer joints dearer than most. I did my undergraduate sin in one.

The juke box is mostly Conway and Loretta and Waylon and Willie. They got a dime for a Tampa Nugget but only eight cents for a King Edward Imperial. A chopped barbecue sandwich is seventy. Sliced is eighty. A longneck Bud is fifty-five. The beer is moving ten-to-one better than anything else on this day.

Inside the conversation ranges from politics to sports to inevitable fishing lies. A man swore he caught 508 catfish out of Sweetwater Creek. Another man cast doubt. It was too hot to take the disagreement any further.

Outside they were pitching horseshoes. A couple of times every
year, Don Mitchell—who owns the Sweetwater Inn—gives a tournament. This was doubles only. The Sweetwater Inn Open Horseshoe
Tournament. Open because they came not only from Austell, but
also from Powder Springs, Mableton, and even Conley. Trophies are
the prizes.

From what I could gather, the horseshoe pits in the pine grove out
behind the Inn used to be the Forest Hills of horseshoe pitching in
Georgia. Once, state tournaments were even held there. But a few
years back, pitching on a state level sort of galloped away and now
Don Mitchell just gives his own tournaments and the boys get together for the frolic they provide.

A relic of a grander day is still in evidence, however. Underneath
the vines and brush that border one side of the pit area, a sign,
bearing the names of former state horseshoe champions, has fallen
in rust and apparent neglect.

During the tournament Saturday, one of the contestants—several
longnecks into the afternoon—relieved himself upon the sign. Other
sports send their grand masters to halls of fame and cast statues in
their likenesses. Old horseshoe pitchers, it would seem, are not as
fortunate.

The game is to fifty. The tournament is double elimination.
Ringers count three. Leaners, one. Any deviation from that scoring
system is immediately put down. "Barnyard horseshoes," they call
it. Some pitchers throw a flop. There are also three-quarter and one-
and-a-quarter throws, depending upon the number of revolutions
the shoe makes en route to the stob. A competition horseshoe weighs
two-and-a-quarter pounds. Don Mitchell gave another tournament a
few weeks ago on Austell Day and calculated that three tons of
horseshoes went back and forth between the stobs.

The action had been underway a couple of hours by the time I got
there. Only three teams were left. Wayne and his partner Mack
already had a loss. Gene and Paul had not been beaten and neither
had Don and Bud. They were to meet head-on.

There were fifteen in the audience. Fourteen watched from
wooden benches. One stationed himself under a pine tree to the rear
of the pitchers. It was there he eventually gave in to the beer and the
sun, and it was there he missed the Sweetwater Inn Open Horseshoe
Tournament as he slept the sleep of the innocent.

Gene wore Bermuda shorts in the showdown match and went to
his truck before the first pitch for something to help in the heat. Paul
stuck to the beer. By a prior commitment to each other, Bud and Don
weren't drinking. Don, said Bud, had been saved recently.

Paul was off from the very start, and Bud and Don jumped to an early lead. Two sets of double ringers off Bud's low, accurate flop throw put his team over the top. Paul and Gene then met Wayne and Mack in the losers' bracket. Wayne is the Frank Tanana of Austell horseshoe pitchers. He and Mack moved into the finals and took Bud and Don twice—50-42 in the final game—for the championship. Wayne threw twenty-eight ringers and three sets of doubles in that final.

I asked him his secret. I think he was serious. "Don't get too drunk," he said. Don't let them put your name on that sign, either, Wayne.

You forget things like this can still happen, that places like this still exist. I had a good time. So did another spectator who had just moved into Austell from Miami. He sat there with a chew in one side of his mouth and a cigar in the other. He drank his beer in long gulps.

At one point he walked over to me and said, "All I need now is a scarlet woman."

"How's that?" I responded.

"I've got everything else," he said. "I'm chewin', I'm smokin', I'm drinkin', and, dammit, I'm cussin'."

We drank a toast to the good times.

Billy

I guess we should have known the Billy Carter story was not going to have a particularly happy ending when we saw him posing for a picture wearing a hat made out of pop-top rings from beer cans.

You may or may not remember that picture, but I do, and I remember thinking at the time I saw it that a man in full control of himself and his destiny likely would not pose for such a picture.

America needed Billy Carter back when he burst through the screen door of the nation's consciousness, grinning that boyish grin of his and pulling on a can of PBR, back in 1975.

We were just getting over stuffy old Nixon and all sorts of other disasters, and here was some redneck galoot who said what he thought, got drunk when he pleased, and would wear no man's necktie, no matter that his high-hatted brother was trying to be the president.

So, the nation took to Billy Carter for a time, like a child takes to a new bauble, and Billy Carter responded to the call by going around doing weird things like posing for the picture with the pop-top hat.

Everybody wanted to drink a beer with Billy Carter in those days. Including me. I found my way to Billy's service station in Plains one afternoon with this good ol' boy from Chicago who was down for a visit, and we must have drunk half a case each, and finally I had enough to ask Billy if he'd pose for a picture with me and my friend.

Billy would have posed for a picture with a snake in those days if somebody would have held its head still. My friend took the picture back to Chicago and showed it around and was a mild celebrity himself for having mixed in such company.

I don't think Billy Carter ever intended to do anything wrong. He simply got caught playing a game in which he didn't understand the rules. Good ol' boys from Plains and other rural outposts know they've done wrong when they spend a night in jail, get fired from their jobs, cuss in front of the preacher's wife, or run their trucks in a ditch.

Making insensitive remarks about this group of people or that group of people or taking silver saddles from this nation or that nation, or relieving yourself under the sky when nature calls, isn't anything to give a second thought about.

But Billy Carter's brother happened to be president, so when the booze got to Billy, and the business deals started to get heavy, and the Libyans started to court him, and instead of being "cute" he was now "tacky," the nation reacted in the typical American way. It dropped Billy Carter like a hot potato.

I was reading the latest about him the other day. The IRS is on his tail for $100,000 in taxes owed.

"They're out to get me," Billy said.

And they'll get him. The IRS always gets its man.

Rosalynn Carter said the other day that Jimmy is doing just fine in his role as ex-president. He'll write a book, of course, and make a lot of speeches, and, in his spare time, there's always his woodworking.

I suppose Miss Lillian will continue to get along, and sister Ruth has her career and sister Gloria still is playing harmonica, I suppose.

Meanwhile, Billy is still trying to make a living and keep the IRS wolves away from his door, and he's not even supposed to have a drink anymore. I wonder if he's still able to muster that boyish grin.

Historians will identify further the legacy of the Carter administration, but already I can name at least one of its unsuspecting victims: brother Billy, who would have been better off if he'd just waited outside in the truck while Jimmy went in to be president.

Moon Over Moreland

MORELAND—This was home for a long time. The lady responsible for me has been sick, but there was still enough left from gardens past to put a gracious plenty on the supper table. We sat up until well past ten. The main topic of conversation was the standard warning from the lady that too many cocktail parties can clear a path to destruction. She's right, you know.

Moreland is in Coweta County, forty miles southwest of Atlanta. The last census said 300 people live here. There are no traffic lights. There are two churches. One is white frame. The other is red brick. They sink you in one. They sprinkle you in the other.

Some of the better memories relate to sport. The Baptist Church sponsored a baseball team. I was a Methodist nine months of the year. Summers, I sang a different ecclesiastical tune for obvious reasons.

We played the games on the field behind the grammar school. It doubled as a rock pile. Anything hit on the ground was an automatic lethal object. Somebody had to stand deep behind the batter's box to save foul balls from being lost in a sea of kudzu and milkweed. An even greater danger was a foul ball landing in a bird dog pen past the weed patch. Bird dogs won't normally bite, but they will chew a baseball beyond recognition and further use in a New York minute.

I won't mention his name because he might still be in reading distance, but the funniest thing that ever happened was an over-weight teammate swinging mightily at a pitch, missing it, and split-ting his tight-fitting uniform pants in the rear.

In his haste to make the game on time, he had neglected to wear underdrawers. Moon over Moreland. The game was halted a half-hour while he streaked home to have his mother repair the damage. He never lived it down, of course, but the child also never left home again without one snug pair covering his boobango and a spare in his pocket in the event of another such emergency.

We never heard of tennis or golf. Never *heard tell* of tennis or golf, as went the native tongue. Basketball was an outdoor game. Football was choosing-sides touch in the lot across from the Methodist Church.

The street was one goal line. A sapling was the other. My cousin, a great receiver, went long toward the sapling end of the field. As he turned to take in the pass, he caught the tree flush at full stroke. A brilliant career ended at the same moment. So did prayer meeting, just beginning inside the church, when they heard what my cousin called that sapling after he came to.

I drove around for nostalgia's sake after the lady's breakfast the other day. Even Moreland has changed here and there.

Where we played touch football stands an edifice the county has erected. "That sonufabitchin' saplin'" was gone. I smiled at what might have been my cousin's avowed revenge against it. There are even a couple of tennis courts where I remember a cornfield. Wonders never cease. The old baseball field has lights now and a screen to stop foul balls. I suppose those bird dogs went to their last hunt and chewed the stitches out of their last Reach Official a long time ago, anyway.

I walked out into the dew that covered centerfield. Little Eddie played centerfield. There was the day I was pitching. We led 3-2, or maybe 5-4. It was late in the game, and the other team had runners on. I grooved one and the batter hit a shot to deep center. How can I still recall that sinking feeling? How can I still recall Little Eddie, without a prayer, running a full gait, chasing after what would surely fall to the red clay earth and roll halfway to Luthersville?

A few months after that Little Eddie was dead. The car went out of control, and he was thrown from his seat. He couldn't have been more than fourteen. His folks took it hard. It tore the town apart.

He caught the ball. Little Eddie ran and he dived and, by some grace, he caught the ball.

A Little Piece of Heaven

Except for the time my mother and I were following around the man who gave me this name and the couple of years I was held prisoner of war in Chicago, the splendid state of Georgia has been home.

I love the South. I have few good memories that did not come from within its bounds. I especially love Georgia.

I am a product of its public schools. I attended its state university, just like Herschel Walker, the football player, does now.

I love the incredible diversity of this state, the largest state east of the Mississippi River. (That will win you some bar bets.)

Georgia has miles of beautiful coastline, but the mountains of North Georgia have an even stronger hold upon me. I can lose myself for weeks among them. And Georgia has the massive, piney flatlands of its broad southern bottom, and it has spectacular, cosmopolitan Atlanta, and it has hundreds of crossroad towns like Hahira and Split Silk and Roosterville and Primrose, where they talk and move slowly, praise the Lord on Sunday mornings, and generally are made of the good, strong stuff that holds a society together.

It hasn't been easy for Georgia. I moved to Chicago in 1975. In 1975, people in Chicago would ask me, "Are there any nice restaurants 'out there' in Georgia?"

I did my best.

"Georgia," I pointed out, "is 'down there.' Omaha is 'out there.' And there are a couple of nice places to eat. Mention my name and maybe you'll get a good stool at the counter."

We've been called "rednecks" and worse. We've been terribly misunderstood. Chicago remains a hotbed of racial contempt, but I was chided during my sentence there for the unfair, stereotype vision of hooded Klansmen walking every street from Rabun Gap to Tybee Light.

H. L. Mencken once described Georgia, and the South, as an "intellectual Gobi." H. L. Mencken made that observation from the lovely city of Baltimore.

But we had our moment in the sun, Georgia and Georgians did. Tucked away in a little corner of the country, the rest of the nation discovered us four years ago, and we enjoyed a brief flirtation with celebrity status.

Suddenly, in Chicago's Division Street bars, my drawl was an object of great interest.

"Say something Southern," they would demand.

"Sumbitch," I would answer. They would howl.

A Chicago friend wanted to try grits. I invited him to my apartment for a Deep South breakfast. Along with the grits, the menu included country ham, red-eye gravy, and biscuits.

As the breakfast was being prepared, the friend walked into my kitchen, took one look at the biscuit dough and said, "So, that's grits?"

How we lost the war remains a mystery to me.

Jimmy Carter brought us out of our relative obscurity. He was our governor, and then he ran for president in 1976 and got himself elected.

I was just sitting here thinking: It all comes to an end Tuesday. Ronald Reagan will become the new president. Jimmy Carter will return home. Georgia will be out. California will be in.

I received a Christmas card with "Jimmy and Rosalynn" stamped on the bottom a few weeks ago. I framed it. A man is lucky to make one presidential Christmas card mailing list in his lifetime. I don't look to do it again.

There probably will be a period of adjustment for us. No more network commentators broadcasting from downtown Plains, no more "Georgia mafia," and Billy Carter gives way to a smart-mouth son who wears very tight pants.

But we will adjust. We always do. And what will be left in the place of all that attention of the four previous years will be what was here all along.

A little piece of heaven, just south of Chattanooga.

Y'all come see us. You heah?